Ngā Ti.

Ngā Tini Whetū

Navigating Māori Futures

Mason Durie

First published in 2011 by Huia Publishers
39 Pipitea Street, PO Box 17–335
Wellington, Aotearoa New Zealand
www.huia.co.nz

ISBN 978-1-86969-452-4

National Library of New Zealand Cataloguing-in-Publication Data
Durie, Mason.
Ngā tini whetū : navigating Māori futures / Mason Durie.
Includes bibliographical references and index.
ISBN 978-1-86969-452-4
1. Maori (New Zealand people)—Economic conditions—Maori
(New Zealand people)—Social conditions. 3. Maori (New Zealand
people)—Politics and government. [1. Tāngata whenua. reo.
2. Hauora tinana. reo. 3. Tikanga rua. reo. 4. Ohaoha. reo.]
I. Title.
330.08999442—dc 22

Contents

List of Tables

List of Figures

Acknowledgements

Tēnā koutou katoa.

This book owes much to the many people and organisations that kindly invited me to present papers at conferences between 2003 and 2010. Convening a conference, whether at the World Bank in Washington or on a marae in Aotearoa New Zealand, demands considerable time and effort as well as a deep appreciation of the context within which development is occurring. Without exception, the convenors of those conferences designed programmes that were not only pertinent to current debates and interests but were relevant to the future and to advances at local and global levels.

In comparison to the number of other speakers and participants, my contributions were relatively small; it was always enriching to hear other themes and perspectives and to listen to viewpoints that spanned a wide diversity of peoples, countries, subjects and challenges. Over the seven years that encompass the timeframe of *Ngā Tini Whetū*, I have been privileged to learn much from others, to witness thoughtful exchanges between experts, and to hear inspirational messages built around the hopes of scholars and communities for a better world in the years to come. Although different, insofar as the messages were variously focused on indigenous development, Māori development, gains in health, and futures planning, the twin themes of human advancement and the resolution of problems that hinder advancement were never far from the surface. This book is one way of adding to their efforts and endorsing the themes they promoted.

An academic environment lends itself well to the articulation of ideas and an analysis of the determinants of progress, and I am grateful to Massey University for the opportunities for research and for enabling me to participate in the several conferences and symposia both in New Zealand and overseas.

As with the earlier volume, *Ngā Kāhui Pou: Launching Māori Futures*, Huia Publishers have again provided invaluable help and advice, and I am grateful for their willing assistance and expert opinion.

Finally, without the longstanding support and encouragement of my wife, Arohia, and her perceptive comments on texts as they were drafted, this collection of papers would not have been possible.

Kia ora.

Mason Durie

Introduction

'Ko tini whetū ki te rangi
Ko Rangitāne nui ki te whenua.'[1]

For centuries the heavens have provided navigational markers for ocean voyagers. Because the appearance of stars can be predicted according to the season, and the positions of stars are consistently aligned to magnetic compass points, constellations of stars such as Te Pae Māhutonga,[2] act as sentinels in unchartered waters. Without recourse to the stars it is unlikely that Māori would have reached Aotearoa or that settlers from the northern hemisphere would have found land in the south. Further, quite apart from their navigational qualities, stars have fired the imagination of generations, acting as sources of wonderment and inspiration and challenging adventurers to seek new fields and remote domains.

The combined themes of navigation on the one hand and discovery on the other are germane to *Ngā Tini Whetū: Navigating Māori Futures*. This book is about the future and Māori journeys towards the future. It does not discount the past nor disregard the many expeditions made in bygone years but it recognises a changing seascape and the need for voyages that will go in search of new destinations. Importantly, those voyages will be more likely to reach preferred landings if their passages are illuminated; not necessarily by celestial lights but by pointers that can bring lucidity to murky waters. Moving ahead, towards new levels of achievement, new technologies, new alliances and new economies, will require more than simply a message of hope or good intention. It will be necessary to read the signs of change and to know how change can be managed and manipulated to deliver the best results for the most people. Taking charge of the future rather than charging into the future will be an increasingly relevant challenge for tomorrow's leaders. They will need to identify stars that can point the way.

Ngā Tini Whetū: Navigating Māori Futures is a sequel to *Ngā Kāhui Pou: Launching Māori Futures.*[3] Both books discuss perspectives relevant to Māori in the years ahead and highlight Māori aspirations, experiences, and excursions in contemporary times, often in novel situations. The papers in *Ngā Kāhui Pou* had been presented at conferences and seminars between 1999 and 2002 and represented views that were pertinent to those years. *Ngā Tini Whetū* follows a similar pattern but contains a set of twenty-five papers presented at various conferences in New Zealand, Australia, Canada, Malaysia, and the USA between 2004 and 2010. Though less than a decade separates the two books, the gap between them is sufficiently long to have seen the emergence of trends and challenges that were barely visible in 2002.

Papers in this book cover a wide range of topics and are primarily about Māori journeys and indigenous aspirations in a rapidly changing society and in a world that has become increasingly complex yet, ironically, more accessible. Global climate change, global mobility, global technological advancement now rival national policies and programmes as factors that can accelerate or undermine Māori advancement.

Although each paper in *Ngā Tini Whetū* has been broadly shaped around the topics selected for particular conferences and by the associated academic disciplines, they share similar and often overlapping messages. Inevitably, in order to preserve the integrity of each chapter, this has resulted in some repetition. But apart from minor editing to maintain a consistent style, each chapter is essentially the same as the original presentation. The 'Māori dimension' traverses a range of subject areas and can be seen as a cross-cutting theme that is relevant to many disciplines and a number of policy areas. The holistic thrust highlights the shortcomings of a sectoral approach and also points to the limitations of inquiries that act in isolation from other fields of inquiry. In that respect the breadth of Māori development is challenging conventional approaches to the acquisition of knowledge and understanding. While specialist knowledge in any particular area will open up new territories and add depth to understanding, the complexities of a future world will also demand a capacity to integrate multiple threads so that a coherent fabric can be woven.

Global transitions and trajectories form part of the rubric within which change is discussed; indeed it would be futile to speculate on Māori futures without considering the impacts of worldwide trends. New Zealand, like other countries, is not immune from global influence. However, although the Māori and indigenous focus is contextualised by global challenges and discoveries, the book contains an equally strong focus on Māori distinctiveness, a cultural reality that provides a unifying link and a starting point for discussions about the future. Maintaining Māori distinctiveness in the face of competing international forces will be a major challenge in the years to come as it was in the nineteenth and twentieth centuries. It is unlikely that Māori distinctiveness will be unchanging or inflexible; people will change and cultural markers will shift. Earlier experiences suggest that culture changes as society changes. But there is also evidence that even in the face of threatened assimilation an underlying ethos remains; and within that ethos lies Māori distinctiveness.

Many, though not all, of the papers in *Ngā Tini Whetū*, are built around the twin themes of past accomplishments and future directions. For convenience they have been grouped into four sections.

The first section, Indigenous Development, contains papers from six conferences attended by international scholars and practitioners. In this book, indigenous populations refers to those peoples who have long and close relationships with defined territories that have endured over centuries, and who have distinctive cultural, social and linguistic characteristics as well as their own systems of knowledge. Two papers deserve special attention. The most recent, 'Mental Health Promotion in a Global Village' (2010) draws on concepts related to indigenous resilience in order to construct a framework for mental health promotion. Integrated solutions (a holistic approach), distinctive pathways (retention of cultural integrity) and goals that empower (indigenous wellbeing) were identified as key principles for mental health promotion at global, national, and local levels.

In 2006, 'Indigenous Resilience: From Disease and Disadvantage to the Realisation of Potential', was the title of a keynote address at PRIDoC,[4] a conference for indigenous medical practitioners from the

Pacific. Indigenous resilience, as distinct from indigenous illness, was explored as an alternative way of understanding indigenous health, and conference participants were encouraged to look beyond disease so that human potential could be visualised. Demographic transitions, human capability, cultural affirmation, attitudinal biases, the economy, lifestyle environments, policies of the state, indigenous mobility, and indigenous leadership were discussed. As determinants of resilience they mediate between successful outcomes and outcomes where disease, disadvantage and deficit prevail.

Other papers in the Indigenous Development section draw attention to the progressive incorporation of indigenous values, customs and methodologies into mainstream systems. In the Narrm Oration at the Melbourne Institute for Indigenous Partnerships, for example, indigenous partnerships with universities were discussed (chapter six). The interface between the two knowledge systems was seen as a rich source of discovery and innovation with mutual gains and flow-on benefits to wider society. At the same time, the relationships between academic departments and wider indigenous communities were seen as pivotal to mutual benefits and shared understandings. A similar conclusion was reached in 'Towards Social Cohesion: The Indigenisation of Higher Education in New Zealand' (Malaysia 2009): 'Universities have the potential to demonstrate social cohesion and also to prepare graduates for leadership roles in promoting a society that can model inclusiveness without demanding assimilation.'

The second section in *Ngā Tini Whetū: Navigating Māori Futures*, is more sharply focused on Māori development. It contains eight papers that explore the major trends in Māori education, whānau wellbeing, economics and politics. Two of the papers, delivered in 2008 and 2010, were part of the annual Te Papa Tongarewa Treaty of Waitangi Debates. Together they paint a picture of a changing environment. By 2005 there was increased Māori confidence in the Treaty as a means of redress but, by 2010, with the emergence of iwi as major economic players in New Zealand, there were signs of a reduced reliance on the Treaty as the sole or even main vehicle for advancement. Both papers consider the constitutional positions of Māori in a future New Zealand. So does 'Race and Ethnicity in Public Policy: Does it Work?' presented at a conference where the impacts of social policies and programmes were under the spotlight. The paper sought to provide a response to a political address at Ōrewa that had advocated the removal of 'special' provisions for Māori. But the 2004 paper concluded that policies, programmes and practices purporting to be 'blind' to race and ethnicity were often premised on cultural norms of the majority and in that sense were themselves biased. Acknowledging ethnicity in an explicit manner was seen as preferable to covert policies that 'mask diversity, compromise best outcomes, and foster an assimilatory approach.'

Another paper in the Māori Development section, 'Te Tai Tini: Transformations 2025', reviewed Māori progress over the preceding quarter century and then identified specific areas where new developments might occur. While acknowledging the substantial gains since the first Hui Taumata in 1984, a futures strategy for 2025 that incorporated strategies for increased capability in the Māori workforce, high achievement, governance and leadership, and whānau capacities, was suggested.

The following year, at the fifth Hui Taumata Mātauranga, the role of whānau in education was discussed ('Whānau, Education and Māori Potential') with a conclusion that success for Māori students will be more likely where whānau and school can share positive attitudes, aspirations, and expectations. 'From Indigenous Exclusion towards Full Participation: The Māori Experience' was presented at the Human Resource Development Forum in the World Bank, Washington, DC. It outlined progress made in early childhood education for Māori, tertiary education and health workforce development and identified four key goals for the future including a participatory goal, an indigeneity goal, a goal of balanced outcomes, and an anticipatory goal – a capacity for long term planning.

The third section in *Ngā Tini Whetū* is primarily about Māori health. Several aspects of health development are examined including health promotion, the ageing population, quality care and understanding health ethics relevant to Māori. The impacts of recent health programmes are also considered and Māori responses to health and disease are discussed particularly as they relate to mental disorders, respiratory diseases and diabetes. 'Indigenous Participation in Mental Health: Māori Experience', was the subject of a paper presented to the Australian and New Zealand College of Psychiatrists in Melbourne, in memory of

Dr Mark Sheldon. It identified a number of catalysts that had facilitated the development of a strong Māori mental health workforce and the progressive indigenisation of mental health services. Māori cultural perspectives had provided a philosophical basis; improved dissemination of information and new knowledge had led to greater levels of awareness among Māori families and communities; government health policies had explicitly identified Māori health as a priority area; innovations in the delivery of health services had increased accessibility as well as effectiveness; independent Māori mental health providers had created choice for service-users; and active Māori mental health workforce development had led to a greatly expanded workforce in the mental health system.

Innovation was the focus of 'Indigenous Health: Catalysts for Innovation'. An analysis of factors contributing to innovation, based on a century or more of Māori health development, showed that three preconditions were associated with successful breakthroughs: first, a need for change could be demonstrated; second, transformative leadership was available; and third, there was shared enthusiasm for change. Innovation could be represented as a process involving communities, government and the health sector, all committed to programmes that would lead to gains in health. Although focused on the future, discussions about Māori health also took into account the efforts of earlier generations, building on past gains rather than promoting radical shifts in approaches to Māori health.

The fourth section of *Ngā Tini Whetū* includes three lectures that collectively made up the Paerangi Lecture Series, 2009. The suite of lectures encompassed economic development and sustainability ('Pae Matatū: Sustaining the Māori Estate'), health and wellbeing ('Pae Ora: Māori Health Horizons'), and Māori relationships with the Crown ('Pae Mana: Waitangi and the Evolving State'). All three lectures considered the position of Māori in the year 2020 and used futures methodologies to create a series of scenarios.

Arising from the 'Paerangi lectures' four major conclusions were evident. First, the Māori estate will continue to grow both in diversity as well as volume. An expanding land base will be augmented by fisheries, radio-frequencies, real estate and commercial shares. Second, Māori health and wellbeing will increasingly be a product of empowered whānau and whānau will be the most sustainable and effective agents for change. Third, rather than maintaining an adversarial relationship, the full impact of the Treaty relationship between Māori and the Crown will be the way in which both parties can work together to shape an agenda for the future. Fourth, the standing of Māori in Aotearoa New Zealand will not be defined solely or even mainly by notions of legal sovereignty but by the range, strength and impact of national, global and iwi alliances. The intense focus on the Crown will diminish in favour of relationships with the private sector, other indigenous peoples, and overseas commercial interests.

The future

Predicting the future is complicated by a rapidly changing environment. The pace of technological innovation, for example, will defy predictions about communication, biological engineering, and modes of learning. But despite the advancements, some trends are already apparent, at least to the extent that they provide pointers to future possibilities. A trend towards an ageing population for example is already obvious; greater inter-ethnic marriage is evident across the world; and the increasing occurrence of natural disasters point to escalating climate change. Moreover there is some truth in the Māori expression: 'Ki te titiro whakamuri, e kitea ai ā mua.' ('We can see our future behind us.') History has a habit of reinventing itself, if not by the exact repetition of events and situations, then at least by recurring themes such as warfare, discovery, competition, regard for future generations, and a desire for autonomy.

Ngā Tini Whetū attempts to scope the future by examining past trends, reading the early signs of change, scanning the horizon, and, on the basis of what might be possible, constructing alternate scenarios. But future visioning also depends on an ability to look beyond the immediate realities in order to engage in vigorous imagining.

People who spend each day addressing crises and problems such as diabetes, domestic violence, alcohol and drug misuse, school failure, poverty, unemployment and inadequate housing, can be easily convinced that there is little hope for the future. But, just as twenty-five years ago it would have been hard to imagine a generation of young

Māori who were fluent Māori speakers, or to think that thousands of Māori learners would be as comfortable online as offline, so too imagining the future on the basis of today's problems is not a good predictor of tomorrow. The point is that the vicissitudes of today should not be allowed to obscure the prospect of a bright tomorrow; too often expectations of Māori failure dictate a future premised on the inevitability of failure.

In the second decade of the twenty-first century, and despite adversity and inequity, there are strong signals that Māori futures will be both rewarding and productive. A distinction between future makers and future takers is reiterated in *Ngā Tini Whetū*. Future takers feel powerless to change their world; their main challenge is to make the best of a bad deal. Future makers, on the other hand, do not accept a fatalistic philosophy. Instead they are keen to identify the trends, grasp the tools available to them, and then create the type of future they prefer.

If there is a single message to this book, it is that Māori have the knowledge, skills and foresight to create a future where younger generations, and generations yet to come can prosper in the world, and at the same time live as Māori.

Indigenous Development

1. Mental Health Promotion in a Global Village (2010)
2. Indigenous Resilience: From Disease and Disadvantage to the Realisation of Potential (2006)
3. Indigenous Transformations in Contemporary Aotearoa (2007)
4. Global Transitions: Implications for a Regional Social Work Agenda (2009)
5. Towards Social Cohesion: The Indigenisation of Higher Education in New Zealand (2009)
6. Indigenous Partnerships: The Academy as a Site for Enduring Relationships and the Transmission of Old and New Knowledge (2009)

CHAPTER 1

Mental Health Promotion in a Global Village

Key note address to the Sixth World Conference on the Promotion of Mental Health and the Prevention of Mental and Behavioral Disorders: 'Addressing Imbalances: Promoting Equity in Mental Health', Washington DC, 17–9 November, 2010.

Introduction

The Sixth World Conference on the Promotion of Mental Health and the Prevention of Mental and Behavioral Disorders presents another opportunity for nations, communities, health professionals, policy-makers, and citizens of the world to consult with each other and to consider how gains in mental health might be achieved. The often overwhelming demands of mental health crises and the growing need for effective treatments for mental disorders leave relatively little time to explore pathways to positive health and the prevention of ill health. Nonetheless, mental health promotion and the prevention of mental and behavioural disorders have emerged as important disciplines and have justifiably secured recognition on mental health agendas across the world. The extensive range of papers and large number of participants at the Sixth World Conference are evidence of the substantial body of knowledge and the equally large body of practice that now characterise the disciplines of promotion and prevention.

The two dimensions – promotion and prevention – are related though not necessarily in a direct manner. Mental health promotion is only peripherally concerned with the prevention of mental disorders; it is aimed at whole populations and includes people who would be unlikely to develop a mental illness, as well as those who are at risk for mental illness. But by raising the level of wellness in communities, there will inevitably be a reduction in the severity and prevalence of debilitating conditions such as anxiety or depression. Similarly, efforts to prevent major psychiatric disorders such as schizophrenia and dementia do not necessarily focus on improving the mental health of all people, but by expanding the knowledge bank about mind and body they inevitably generate pointers for wellness and the maintenance of good mental health. There is therefore, a close relationship between promotion and prevention, the more so because very often the same people are involved in both endeavours.

It is now universally accepted that the determinants of mental illness include socio-economic factors such as inadequate housing, economic disadvantage, limited access to health and education, family dysfunction, as well as intrinsic factors such as atypical neurological pathways and maladaptive psychological patterns. Most modern mental health services recognise these three sets of determinants – socio-economic, biological, psychological – and offer treatments that span these domains, though often without the benefit of an integrated plan. Health promotion also focuses on those three areas though it is more cognisant of the impacts of wider societal trends on human health and has a broader lens that accommodates whole populations.

The Melbourne Declaration, developed at the Fifth World Conference on the Promotion of Mental Health and the Prevention of Mental and Behavioral Disorders, challenged governments to adopt policies that supported good mental health and called on all people working to improve mental health and wellbeing to advocate for human rights and the protection of indigenous peoples and their cultures, eliminating stigma, building alliances across governments and across communities, and empowering individuals and communities to take their own actions to improve mental health. The Declaration also drew attention to protective factors (such as cultural identity, education, sport and recreation), and risk factors (such as alcohol and drugs, discrimination, physical illness, and violence).[1]

Global challenges

While mental health and wellbeing are largely discussed in connection with national priorities and local communities, the mental health impacts of global trends have become increasingly more apparent. In contrast to earlier times when nations were separated by vast distances or by walls of silence that prevented sharing of information, no longer is any nation immune from events occurring in other parts of the world. Information technologies, greater international mobility, and world forums such as the Conference on the Promotion of Mental Health and the Prevention of Mental and Behavioral Disorders, have created a stronger sense of common purpose among nations and a readiness to learn from each other. While distinctive cultural, ethnic, and religious influences remain important in local communities, there is a growing realisation that the problems associated with mental health and wellbeing also have a significant universal component that transcends many of the differences between populations and between states. Global health has added a new dimension to the disciplines of health promotion and disease prevention.[2]

Apart from the commonalities that characterise people everywhere, the universal component is increasingly the result of significant developments occurring simultaneously in many countries. Positive developments such as trade agreements between nations, or commitments to limiting nuclear weapons can reasonably be expected to bring health benefits, at least to participant countries. Other developments, however, are giving less cause for optimism. Far from generating gains in health or wellbeing, many global trends are posing major threats to health and wellbeing in both developed and developing countries. Moreover, though the worldwide impacts of social, cultural, economic, technological and environmental changes have consequences for all nations, they do not necessarily impact equally on all countries or on all sub-populations within countries. Not surprisingly, those most at risk live in countries that are already suffering the most and include groups already excluded from dominant societies.

Because major global determinants of health seem remote from the day-to-day lives of individuals and families, and in any case may be regarded as beyond the skills and resources of local communities, they may be afforded secondary attention. Improving understandings of the nature of addictive behaviours or increasing people's awareness of maintaining mental health, could well be identified as more beneficial to particular communities.[3] Local efforts to improve mental health and wellness are crucial to mental health promotion and need to be strongly endorsed by states. But the increasingly relevant global dimension should not be dismissed on the grounds that it is too difficult to fix or too remote to warrant concern. The facts suggest the opposite: global mental health promotion will be a necessary complement to global development and a necessary extension to the discipline of mental health promotion.

This paper identifies five major global trends that are likely to have significant consequences for human health and equally significant implications for mental health promotion (especially for indigenous peoples): cataclysmic disasters, demographic transitions, resource attrition, cultural diffusion, and electronic knowledge transmission. Although none of the trends is entirely new, their rate of escalation has become a source of increasing concern.

Cataclysmic disasters

In July 2010, a heat wave in Europe resulted in the deaths of many older people and led to the hospitalisation of infants, the chronically sick and infirm. The punishing heat, with temperatures as high as forty degrees centigrade, sparked a series of health warnings across the northern region. In Germany dozens of passengers on three trains had to be removed and some were hospitalised after temperatures reached fifty degrees when the air conditioning broke down. Violent thunderstorms were triggered over France, Germany and the Low Countries with large hailstones, squally winds and risk of flash flooding in places.

The 2010 Pakistan floods, also in July 2010, followed heavy monsoon rains in the Khyber Pakhtunkhwa, Sindh, Punjab and Balochistan regions of Pakistan. Over 2000 people died and the United Nations estimated that more than twenty million people were injured or homeless as a result of the flooding[4], exceeding the combined total of individuals affected by the 2004 Indian Ocean tsunami, the 2005 Kashmir earthquake and the 2010 Haiti earthquake. At one point, approximately one-fifth of Pakistan's total land area was underwater due to the flooding.

A month later more than 440,000 people were evacuated in Hainan after the heaviest rains for decades inundated 90 percent of the Chinese island in the South China Sea. The floods affected 2.7 million people in sixteen cities and more than 3000 houses were destroyed by flooding along with nearly 170,000 hectares of crops. Then in October 2010 a tsunami and a volcanic eruption killed over 200 people and injured hundreds more in Indonesia.

To aggravate the situation, in September 2009 a tsunami in the South Pacific, generated by two earthquakes, wreaked havoc in Samoa and Tonga leading to the deaths of 200 people and widespread destruction of homes, schools and hospitals. Already facing hardship and already threatened by rising sea levels, the incident was a major threat to the economy and the survival of the two nations.

The impact of similar events on two countries with quite different standards of living and wellbeing was apparent in 2010. First, an earthquake measuring 7.1 on the Richter scale led to the loss of an estimated 300,000 lives in Haiti in January 2010. Then in September 2010 an earthquake of a similar magnitude and similar depth led to the destruction of large parts of Christchurch in New Zealand; thousands of homes were declared unsafe and many iconic buildings dominating the inner city had to be demolished but there was no loss of life. In February 2011 another devastating earthquake hit Christchurch and lives were lost, but there was much less loss of life than in Haiti.

Climatic extremes are now commonplace across the world and the link to global climate change is indisputable. Inevitably the poorest countries in the world will suffer the most. Across developing countries, millions of the world's poorest people are already being forced to cope with the impacts of climate change. Increased exposure to drought, to more intense storms, to floods and environmental stress is holding back the efforts of the world's poor to build better lives for themselves and their children. Climate change will undermine international efforts to combat poverty.[5]

The changing climate will inevitably affect the basic requirements for maintaining health: clean air and water, sufficient food and adequate shelter. Even before the Pakistan disaster, each year, about 800,000 people die from causes attributable to urban air pollution, 1.8 million from diarrhoea largely resulting from lack of access to clean water supply and sanitation, and from poor hygiene, 3.5 million from malnutrition and approximately 60,000 in natural disasters.

In the long run, however, the greatest health impacts may not be from acute shocks such as natural disasters or epidemics, but from the gradual build-up of pressure on the natural, economic and social systems that sustain health, and which are already under stress in much of the developing world. These gradual stresses include reductions and seasonal changes in the availability of fresh water, regional drops in food production, and rising sea levels. Each of these changes has the potential to force population displacement and increase the risks of civil and international conflict.[6]

Demographic transitions

A further global threat to mental health and wellbeing stems from changes to the world's population. The changes are occurring along two related axes. First the world's total population is increasing at unprecedented rates. The current population is around 6.6 billion, over half of whom live in urban environments, but if the present rate of increase continues it will result in a total world population of over 10 billion, high enough to trigger population controls such as war, disease, and famine as postulated by Thomas Malthus. The increase is largely due to high fertility rates, mostly in developing countries. By 2050, even if fertility rates reduce to medium forecasts, the global population will have expanded to 9.1 billion; but if they reduce to low fertility rates, the world's population will reach 7.8 billion.[7]

While high fertility rates in developing countries are contributing to a global population explosion, the second most significant demographic transition has been an increase in life expectancy in developed countries. In New Zealand for example, the median age in 2031 will be forty-one years compared to thirty-six years in 2006 and the average life expectancy for women will be eighty-five years (seventy-eight years for men).[8] Within the total population, however, the Māori (indigenous) sub-population has a lower median age and a life expectancy shortened by around four years for both men and women. Although the difference is diminishing, the pattern is not dissimilar to that in other developed countries where the standards of indigenous health and wellbeing are lower than national averages. Other ethnic minority groups also have lower reported life expectancies. In Canada for example the life expectancy for the 'Registered Indian' population is 6.5 years less than for the non-indigenous population and more than twelve years less for the Inuit-inhabited regions of Canada.[9]

Resource attrition

A direct consequence of climatic extremes and a high global population will be the per capita depletion of vital resources such as water and food.

Droughts, floods, cyclones, and rising tides will inevitably reduce the amount of land available for pastoral farming while the loss of livestock coupled with the devastation of crops following natural disasters will apply further pressure on food sources. So while an increasing population will lead to a demand for greater food supplies, the reverse is likely to happen – food supplies will be less at a time when more will be required. Almost certainly food shortages will not be felt uniformly across the world. The developed countries will continue to battle the health impacts of too much food while developing countries will experience higher levels of malnutrition – and the attending health risks. By 2009 the overall number of hungry people had surpassed one billion people, the highest regional Global Hunger Index scores being in South Asia and Sub-Saharan Africa. Malnutrition among children under two years of age is one of the particular challenges to reducing global hunger; it can cause lifelong harm to health, productivity, and earning potential.[10]

Climate warming will add other complications to the food chain. Warmer ocean temperatures will not only generate unseasonal currents and landward winds but will also create problems for fish that live within a narrow temperature range. Already the depletion of fishing stock through overfishing has required the introduction of quota management systems; further reductions caused by higher oceanic temperatures and the possibility of viral diseases will simply add to the diminishing availability of fish for world markets.

Reduced food resources will also occur as a result of environmental pollution. The consequences of toxic run-off, chemical despoliation, unmanaged waste disposal and inadequate sewage systems threaten the integrity of land and its suitability for growing food or feeding livestock. Perhaps most important, environmental degradation will lead to contaminated water supplies, rendering clean water a highly prized commodity that will be inaccessible to much of the world's population.

Indigenous peoples have had particular concerns about the impacts of development on indigenous lands and waterways. Climate change and global warming have posed significant challenges for indigenous communities worldwide, threatening traditional lifestyles, biodiversity and sustainable development. Without land and natural resources, indigenous peoples will be unable to preserve their unique cultures. The identities, histories, and aspirations of indigenous peoples are inseparable from their lands, resources and territories, which hold special significance for them. When their rights are violated, they lose their livelihoods. Threats to the usage of traditional lands raise the possibility that language, culture, religion and identity will be threatened.[11]

Cultural diffusion

A further potential threat to the health and wellbeing of many communities within nation states, and especially to indigenous health and wellbeing, is related to global mobility and global colonisation. Cultural and ethnic diversity is a reality of modern living. High levels of mobility between countries for education, business or permanent emigration, have led to multicultural societies where the world's dominant languages and cultures prevail, at least in commerce and education. The global dimension has been further accentuated by multinational brands that have westernised eastern countries and easternised some western countries. Participation in worldwide markets has advantaged many populations by improving job prospects, economic opportunities, and access to the world's art, music, literature, and scientific knowledge. There is also some evidence that the economic aspects of globalisation have had positive global responses in addressing the social determinants of health. Efforts have been made to cut across existing national, international and institutional boundaries to address issues of transnational reach, whether articulated as goals (for example the Millennium Development Goals), broadly stated themes (for example alleviating poverty and social exclusion, and gender empowerment) or control of such health-damaging products as tobacco (for example the Framework Convention on Tobacco Control). Even disease-specific global initiatives are increasing their responses to the challenge of contemporary globalisation.[12] But notwithstanding the benefits, the globalising experience has also generated a hybrid type of culture that has the potential to undermine local cultures including languages, traditional foods, and family customs.

Perhaps the most crucial negative impact of a global culture has been the breakdown in traditional social structures of culture and of language. While outsiders seek ways of reducing inequalities in the provision of services and changing behaviour to promote healthy lifestyles, indigenous peoples are looking at ways in which culture, language and tradition can be strengthened and passed onto future generations.[13] Community knowledge is the essence of the social capital of the poor and the source of their survival strategies. It is rooted in tradition, contemporary in nature and is constantly evolving as individual and community responses to the challenges posed by their environment.[14]

The substitution of a hybrid culture for local cultures that have nurtured populations for centuries carries with it threats to individual and group identity, alienation from learned ways of coping, and reduced social cohesion in supportive networks.

Electronic knowledge transmission

Across the world revolutionary information and communication technologies have transformed access to knowledge and participation in social networks. Digital technologies have shrunk the globe to the extent that instant communication is as possible between islands, continents, and hemispheres as it is between individuals living in the same village. Moreover, the accelerating pace of change shows no signs of slowing down. At the beginning of last century the idea of a satellite network in space, covering every part of the globe and feeding back information in real time, was pure science fiction. Looking forward from today, the idea that every part of the natural and built environment will be part of a sensor network, constantly 'talking' to itself, other networks and humans, seems hard to imagine, but the beginnings of these networks are already being built.[15]

Information highways will contain so much information that much of it will remain dormant; human capacities to integrate, utilise, and understand multiple data sets will not be able to keep pace with technology.[16] Unlike earlier forms of communication, the new technologies will find their way to all parts of the globe and will be potentially available to populations that are currently disadvantaged by lack of access to education, health knowledge, and career options. *E*-learning, *e*-health and *e*-work will bring the prospect of new ways of knowing, greater relevance, more efficient time management, and overcoming the barriers of remote isolation.

Between developed countries and developing countries, however, the educational gap is enormous. While access to primary education has improved, increases in the share of the population achieving secondary education has been slow. In most developing countries low levels of secondary education have been the major barrier to educational achievement and participation in the knowledge society.[17] Developing countries will need to face more complex situations than developed countries; they will have to be able to respond to scientific discoveries and technological innovations and to do so under serious financial constraints. Rather than replicating educational systems relevant to more developed countries, education ought to reflect local needs, local educational goals, and delivery modes such as distance education, that are available and make sense to learners. Relevance is a critical ingredient. Education that has cultural relevance, and can be applied in local as well as global contexts, is especially important for indigenous learners who live in two worlds – the indigenous world and a world shaped by global values.[18]

The relationship of education to health is well established. Educational achievement and higher health status are directly linked. Electronic transmission of knowledge will also be increasingly important as health literacy increases and people become more active in the management of their own health. Online health advice is already a reality for many consumers and a task for both education and health professionals in the future will be to act as online guides for learners and patients.

Three principles for mental health promotion

The mental health impacts of all five global challenges have been extensively researched. Cataclysmic disasters for example will inevitably be followed by prolonged and often irresolvable grief, post-traumatic syndrome, depression, anxiety, resort to alcohol and drug use, and a wide range of physical comorbidities.[19] An ageing population will not only be associated with increased prevalence of the disorders of old age, but will also impose strains on the working age population and on children who are themselves nearing retiring age. A global population explosion will increase competitiveness, add to the levels of personal stress, increase tension between different groups, and create a larger cohort of marginalised urban dwellers. Similarly a diminishing resource base will predictably result in malnutrition with the attending mental health problems and a greater risk of local and national acts of aggression aimed at securing control of valuable land or water.

Global mobility will pose particular threats to indigenous peoples. Having already experienced loss of language and culture after earlier colonisation, new waves of global brands, values, and corporate missions will compete with the growing revitalisation of indigenous insights and traditions. Identity diffusion, reduced self-esteem, and higher levels of family dysfunction will pose significant threats to mental health. Meanwhile the dissemination of information and knowledge through electronic communication technology will open new horizons but it will also lead to the exclusion of those who are not part of the knowledge society. Socio-economic exclusion is a major determinant of poor mental health.

Integrated solutions

The complexities of the challenges ahead are such that complex solutions will also be required to address them or at least to reduce their negative impacts. The Commission on Social Determinants of Health identified three principles to underlie action for health equity: improved living conditions of daily life, equitable distribution of power, money and resources, and measures to understand the problem and assess the impact of action.[20] Taking into account the wide frame adopted by the Commission, it is clear that mental health promotion cannot be considered as an independent course of action. Instead integrated solutions will be increasingly necessary to meet old and new risks to mental health and wellbeing. The principle of integrated solutions recognises that no single sector, discipline or service has all the answers.[21] Mental health promotion must become part of a comprehensive set of actions that include economists, environmentalists, biologists, statisticians, technologists, advertising agencies, social entrepreneurs, politicians, and for profit organisations.

Sectoral divisions and professional interests create artificial boundaries that do not fit with the real worlds where people live their actual lives. Improving the mental health of all people needs to take into account a range of economic, environmental, social, cultural and biological perspectives. Structural, political, and methodological barriers between social and economic factors are especially unhelpful. The economic single bottom line is a flawed measure of human wellbeing that fails to consider environmental, social, and cultural contributions to health.

Social transfers go some way to addressing the socio-economic divide but do not necessarily lead to secure economic positions or human empowerment. There is in fact some evidence that prolonged dependence on social transfers actually undermines wellness. The point nonetheless is that mental health and wellbeing cannot be achieved unless economic security is paired with social advancement.

In addition to the integration of social and economic factors, a similar case can be made for the closer integration of physical and mental agendas. Distinctions between mental health and physical health are also becoming less and less tenable. Comorbidities are more frequent than previously recognised.[22] To a greater or lesser extent, a physical illness is always accompanied by symptoms of mental distress. Similarly, people with mental disorders are just as likely, if not more likely, to also have a physical disorder. Greater emphasis on primary health care as a site for mental health interventions would lead to an increasing shift away from practices dominated by the treatment of severely ill patients to practices that focus on holistic health. In that respect they would tend to mirror indigenous health perspectives where spiritual, intellectual, physical, and family dimensions are afforded equal attention.[23]

The principle of integrated solutions also has implications for the relationship between individuals and collectives such as families. Type 2 diabetes for example is advancing across the globe in epidemic fashion. Typically it affects individuals in their fourth decade but is now increasingly evident in teenage years. Though treatment is based around individual patients, there is general agreement that the diabetic pandemic is a reflection of changing family patterns of diet and community nutritional norms. Family therapists have made similar connections between patients with mental health problems and the dynamics within families; treating individuals without reference to influential environments is as limited as promoting mental health while ignoring the economic, social and cultural environments where people live their day-to-day lives.

Distinctive pathways

Bringing together multiple sets of expertise, resources, and information, the integrated solutions approach fosters cooperative approaches to mental health promotion. In contrast, a second principle for mental health promotion identifies pathways that are distinctive to some populations but not necessarily to others. Distinctive pathways arise from population diversity; they build on the link between positive mental health on the one hand, and the varied ways in which people understand wellness on the other.

Culturally based systems of knowledge, for example, explain health and wellness from perspectives that are different from scientific knowledge. Those systems may be based on religious beliefs, ethnic customs, or indigenous world views; faith, rather than empirical studies underlies knowledge, and longstanding experience with the natural environment provides a framework for understanding the world.

For indigenous populations, the relationship between people and the environment forms an important foundation for the organisation of indigenous knowledge. Mātauranga Māori, Māori knowledge, is based on those understandings; it draws on observations from the natural environment, and imbues land and people with a life force (mauri) and a spirituality (tapu).[24] In psychological terms, the landscape is part of human identity and becomes a basis for the categorisation of life experiences, and the shaping of attitudes and patterns of thinking. Because human identity is regarded as an extension of the environment, there is an element of inseparability between people and the natural world. The individual is a part of all creation and the idea that the world or creation exists for the purpose of human domination and exploitation is absent from indigenous world-views.[25]

According to the celebrated North American indigenous scholar, Vine Deloria, 'Most tribes were very reluctant to surrender their homelands to the whites because they knew that their ancestors were still spiritually alive on the land.'[26] His comments underline the link between the physical and social environments but also emphasise the significance of resources as collective and intergenerational, and the importance of land for health and wellbeing. The significance of land as a distinctive pathway towards health and wellbeing is becoming increasingly relevant as the impacts of climate change are felt and indigenous world views may well contain part of the formula for achieving carbon neutrality.

While distinctive landscapes are important contributors to indigenous mental health and wellness, estrangement from culture has become increasingly frequent in communities where global colonisation has displaced local cultures. Given the importance of a secure cultural identity as a marker of good mental health, many indigenous peoples who are minorities in their own countries have initiated programmes to retain culture and custom, including language. On the 2008 International Day of the World's Indigenous People, the Secretary-General of the United Nations, Ban Ki-moon, noted the silent crisis confronting many of the world's languages, the overwhelming majority of which were indigenous peoples' languages. In his message he warned that the loss of indigenous languages would not only weaken the world's cultural diversity, but also the collective knowledge of the human race.[27]

While indigenous peoples are embarking on programmes that will revitalise their native languages, governments also have some responsibility to promote and maintain languages that are not spoken as a first language elsewhere in the world. The argument that an indigenous language is of little value because it is not used for international commerce, overlooks the significance of language as a core component of culture, and thus is a determinant of health and wellbeing. Mental health promotion is about creating domains where the language of choice can be spoken, heard, and written.

Goals that empower

The goals of mental health promotion are essentially about empowering people to take control of their own lives in ways that are adaptive, responsible, satisfying and rewarding. A sense of mastery refers to the extent to which people see themselves as in charge of their own lives.[28] An empowering continuum recognises a series of goals relevant to different stages and different circumstances. Following a natural disaster, for example, providing food and shelter must be the immediate goals, followed by assisting victims to come to grips with multiple losses, injury, and financial distress, and then rebuilding relationships, confidence and the skills needed for post-disaster lives. Goals that focus only on surviving a crisis are incomplete insofar as they do little to deal with the mental health impacts of adversity or to generate the skills necessary to manage crises in the future.

Similarly reducing socio-economic disparities between populations, by, for example, providing adequate housing and food vouchers, lifts levels of wellbeing but does not necessarily lead to optimal wellbeing. Although providing the essentials for life are important goals for populations who experience poverty and destitution, mental health promotion recognises another level of wellbeing characterised by positive self-esteem and regard for others, self-management, and self-determination. Unless the provision of basic needs is accompanied by education, training, the prospect of meaningful employment and political voice, the risk of lifelong dependency will count against optimal mental health and wellbeing. A 'lack of control of destiny' has been identified as a significant factor in wellbeing and self-management. It recognises that a feeling of futility arises from a perceived inability to assume control over day-to-day life and decision-making.[29]

Full participation in society is an important proxy measure of empowerment. Social exclusion leads to economic marginalisation which in turn creates inequality of opportunity and greater risk to health.[30] Full participation includes access to community goods and services, participation in education at all levels, participation in the economy, and political participation.

Recognising the marginalised position of indigenous people, and their exclusion from key societal institutions, four key factors have been recommended for indigenous participation in society and the economy in Latin America. First, since it is the most significant driver of income, more and better quality education is critical. Second, improving health status, especially malnutrition in children, can lead to better education outcomes. Third, social services should be more accountable to indigenous peoples and better attuned to indigenous worldviews and aspirations; and fourth, consistent data collection that enables indigenous peoples to be identified is a prerequisite for planning and action.[31]

The role of education as a vehicle for full participation has been recognised as an essential step towards empowerment and indigenous populations are generally underrepresented in tertiary education. Reducing indigenous barriers to education can be approached from two directions. First, efforts can be made to reduce socio-economic inequalities so that hardship is alleviated and students are able to contemplate deferring the need for an immediate income in favour of higher education and longer term benefits. Second, barriers can be reduced by ensuring that tertiary education institutions are able to embrace indigenous worldviews so that pedagogies, research methodologies, campus facilities, and the academic staff can endorse cultural identity and inspire students.[32] Māori experience in New Zealand has shown that both approaches are necessary; reducing inequalities is a critical determinant of full participation in higher education while expanding the context for higher education institutions is an essential prerequisite for students whose world views are not entirely shaped by western academic conventions. Moreover, the outcomes of participation go beyond indigenous students; there are benefits for the nation as a whole and for the broad goals of creating and transferring knowledge.[33]

Whānau Ora

In addressing the global trends that impact on health and wellbeing, the principles of integrated solutions, distinctive pathways, and goals that empower have the potential to make substantial contributions to human lives. They have national and international application but can also be applied at local levels. A programme that has elements of all three principles is currently being implemented in New Zealand. Known as Whānau Ora – well families – the programme aims to improve the health and wellbeing of Māori families, many of whom have significant levels of social and economic disadvantage. The programme is built around an integrated approach to service delivery, distinctive cultural paradigms, and family capabilities that lead to self-management.

Whānau Ora was a response to evidence that a sector-based approach to disadvantaged families was failing to generate sustainable solutions. Instead it tended to create a level of dependency that in turn reduced mastery and increased fragmentation of effort.[34] In the Whānau Ora approach services usually delivered by separate health, education, housing, employment, social welfare and financial agencies are combined into a single service that places families at the centre. The challenge has been to create a system that enables separate government agencies to unbundle resources and budgets in favour of a dedicated Whānau Ora fund. Providers who participate in the scheme must be able to demonstrate competence in social, economic, cultural and environmental interventions as they might apply to families.[35]

Two-dimensional integration forms the basis of Whānau Ora practice: the integration of social, cultural and economic dimensions, and the integration of individual interests with family capabilities. A distinctive pathway also underpins the programme. Quite apart from generating social and economic inclusion, active participation in Māori language, culture and networks is fostered. Families that may have been alienated from culture and other indigenous resources are provided with the tools and information to access indigenous institutions and cultural pathways. In addition, rather than focusing only on the resolution of crises within families, practitioners are concerned with the development of family capabilities so that self-management and family aspirations can be realised.[36] The aim is to empower families so that they can have a sense of mastery and control over their own destiny.

A health promotion matrix

Building on the three principles: integrated solutions, distinctive pathways, and goals that empower, it is possible to construct a matrix that has application at global, national, community, and family levels (see Table 1.1 following). The matrix has implications for mental health promotion insofar as it highlights the need for inter-sectoral and interdisciplinary collaboration, the application of cultural distinctiveness to mental health promotion, and the delivery of interventions that lead to empowerment of populations, communities and families.

TABLE **1.1** A mental health promotion matrix

	Integrated solutions	Distinctive pathways	Goals that empower
Global action			
National action			
Community action			
Family action			

CHAPTER 2

Indigenous Resilience: From Disease and Disadvantage to the Realisation of Potential

Key note address to Rapu Oranga: the Pacific Region Indigenous
Doctors' Congress, Rotorua, 7 December, 2006.

Pūkawa 1856

The Pacific Region Indigenous Doctors' Congress (PRIDoC) 2006 occurs
150 years after an historic event in New Zealand. In November 1856,
1600 tribal leaders gathered at Pūkawa, Lake Taupo, to discuss strategies
that would enable them to better cope with mounting risks associated
with migration from England, Scotland, Australia and other parts of the
globe. Loss of autonomy, alienation of resources, especially land, and lack
of voice in governance were major concerns for the participants.[1]

Hosted by Iwikau te Heuheu, a chief from Ngāti Tuwharetoa, the
ostensible purpose of the meeting was to select a Māori king who could
provide a focus for united action and a unified approach to slow down the
sale of tribal lands. Even though kingship might impose excessive demands
on tribes and was not entirely compatible with the customary style of
leadership based around tribal structures, tribal authority, and tribal
independence, the meeting agreed that the selection of a king was one step
towards refocusing Māori energies to meet changing circumstances.[2]
Eventually, although he was not at Pūkawa, Potatau te Wherowhero became
the unanimous choice for king and finally agreed to be anointed in 1858.[3]

There are two reasons why the Pūkawa meeting has relevance for
indigenous doctors from the Pacific region. First the participants at
Pūkawa recognised that the imposition of new political, economic and
social agendas demanded an innovative response to ensure survival.

PRIDoC is also concerned with new solutions to deal with contemporary situations. Second, however, although survival was indeed a real threat in 1856, mere survival was not regarded as a sufficient endpoint; the more significant goal was to establish an environment where the indigenous people of Aotearoa could flourish and prosper, with a sense of equality and a capacity for self-management. Pūkawa provided a platform for nurturing resilience. The PRIDoC focus on excellence captures some of those same aspirations.

Characteristics of resilience among indigenous peoples

There is now worldwide concern for the health of indigenous peoples.[4] At the fifth session of the United Nations Permanent Forum on Indigenous Issues in 2006 a programme of action dedicated to the world's indigenous peoples was launched. Indigenous people make up 6 percent of the world's population, accounting for some 370 million people spread across seventy countries. Most have high mortality rates for specific disease and injury with substantially lower life expectancy than non-indigenous peoples.[5]

While efforts to redress the problems have largely focused on managing disease and injury, other approaches have explored reasons why some groups exposed to similar stresses and risks have remained well and even flourished. For example, despite threats of genocide and ethnocide, indigenous peoples in the Pacific have endured and prospered to the extent that they are now in significantly stronger positions than they were 150 years ago.

Superimposed on adversity and historic marginalisation, indigenous resilience is a reflection of an innate determination by indigenous peoples to succeed. Resilience is the polar opposite of rigidity. It provides an alternate perspective to the more usual scenarios that emphasise indigenous disadvantage, and allows the indigenous challenge to be reconfigured as a search for success rather than an explanation of failure.

Indigenous success, often the product of resilience, has several dimensions but essentially encompasses individuals and groups, a capacity for positive engagement, and a level of autonomy. Much of the literature on resilience centres on the potential of individuals to overcome personal trauma and succeed. However, resilience is also about the achievements of collectives: families, whānau, communities, tribes, mobs, and whole populations. Success in that sense is a shared experience which reflects an ability to adapt and a propensity for turning adversity into accomplishment.

Two broad capacities underpin indigenous success. The first one is the dual capacity to engage with indigenous culture, networks and resources, and to engage with global societies and communities. The duality recognises the two worlds within which indigenous peoples live and the skills needed to negotiate both. Successful engagement with the indigenous world is facilitated by spiritual and cultural competence and acceptance by communities, while engagement with global societies is eased by the acquisition of technical skills, educational qualifications, and a capacity to deal with bias and prejudice.

A second aspect of indigenous success is built around autonomy and self-management. It applies equally to families, communities and whole indigenous populations. Resilience is less likely if indigenous futures are premised on the aspirations of others. Instead indigenous success requires a capacity for indigenous approaches to governance and management that are compatible with the world views of families, tribes, and indigenous communities while at the same time being attuned to wider societal values and economies. Autonomy does not necessarily mean an independent pathway but seeks opportunities for collaboration and cooperation on the basis of equality and shared goals.

The determinants of indigenous resilience

Resilience is shaped by many forces acting alone or together. They can be grouped into broad determinants: demographic transitions, human capability, cultural affirmation, attitudinal biases, the economy, lifestyle environments, policies of the state, indigenous mobility, and leadership.

Demographic transitions

In 1856 the Māori population was in a state of decline. Even by 1836 there were reports that the population had been reduced by more than a quarter and by 1906 it was estimated at 45,000 – a reduction of more than 75 percent from 1806. Although extinction was widely predicted in 1906, not only did Māori survive, but within a century they had become more numerous than at any other time in history. Even though changes to statistical definitions of Māori make it difficult to draw exact comparisons, there is strong evidence of a substantial and sustained increase in the Māori population. In the 2001 Census 526,281 New Zealanders identified as Māori with a median age of twenty-one years.[6]

Further, although accounting for some 15 percent of the total New Zealand population in 2006, by 2051 the Māori ethnic population will almost double in size to close to a million, or 22 percent of the total New Zealand population. Even more dramatic, by 2051 of all children in the country 33 percent will be Māori, and the percentage of the population over the age of sixty-five will steadily rise from 3 percent (1996) to 13 percent (2051) as life expectancy increases.[7]

While the figures vary from country to country, and stages of development are either accelerated or delayed, many of the demographic trends observed for Māori are common to indigenous peoples in the wider Pacific: fast-growing populations, a lower than average median age, and a large cohort of young people. Of the Australian indigenous population for example, 40 percent are below the age of fifteen years compared with just 21 percent of the non-indigenous population.[8] In addition there are early signs of an ageing population; gradually the median age will increase as life expectancy rises.

In addition to the overall growth in indigenous populations, two particular trends have special relevance for resilience: youthfulness and increases in the numbers of older people. Youthfulness can be associated with high levels of risk taking and in that sense represents a threat to good health, but it is also a sign of vitality, potential and a greater likelihood of innovation. And an increase in the proportion of older people not only reflects greater life expectancy but also an increased capacity for the intergenerational transmission of culture, wisdom and leadership.

Human capability

Insofar as resilience is about overcoming adversity and reconciling tensions within complex and often contradictory societies, much depends on human capabilities to manage new environments and wield together indigenous world views with views derived from western perspectives of science, business, law and environmental management. Two indicators of capability of particular relevance to PRIDoC are indigenous participation in tertiary education and indigenous representations in the health workforce.

There are signs that on both counts indigenous participation is increasing. For Māori learners for example there have been significant gains. Retention rates for sixteen year olds at secondary school increased from 47 percent (in 1987) to 63 percent (in 2003). Between 1983 and 2000 the percentage of Māori students who left school with no qualifications decreased from 62 percent to 35 percent, while at the tertiary level, between 1993 and 2004 Māori participation increased by 148 percent. By 2002 Māori had the highest rates of participation in tertiary education of any group aged at twenty-five years and over. Although the significant improvement masked the fact that Māori were still five times more likely to enrol in government remedial training programmes and three times less likely to enrol at a university,[9] around 7 percent of the total university population in 2005 is Māori. Most of the recent tertiary education growth has occurred through accredited tribal learning centres, wānanga, which increased enrolments from 26,000 students in 2001 to 45,500 in 2002.[10]

Similar growth has been seen in the composition of the health workforce. As one way of addressing the disproportionate representation of Māori in most illnesses and injuries, workforce development has become a high priority for improving Māori standards of health. In 2000, Māori made up around 14 percent of the total population but only 5 percent of the national health workforce.[11] In order to increase the size of the workforce, there have been deliberate efforts to attract Māori into the health professions through affirmative action programmes – or programmes that have similar aims. In 1998, for example, the University of Auckland launched Vision 2020, a programme designed to significantly increase Māori entry into the medical school. By 1984 there had been around five new Māori medical students each year but by 2004, the number of new Māori entrants had increased to twenty-four.[12] Similar trends have been seen in the qualified medical workforce. From an estimated workforce of around sixty in 1984, there are now over 200 Māori medical practitioners across a range of specialties, accounting for 3 percent of the total active medical workforce. In addition scholarships have been offered from a number of sources as incentives to encourage enrolment in other disciplines such as nursing, social work, clinical psychology and addiction treatments. The number of Māori dentists, for example, has increased from four or five in 1984 to forty-four in 2005.

Indigenous education in Australia has seen similar developments. There have been significant increases in the number of indigenous Australians enrolled in higher degrees – over 25 percent between 2001 and 2003 – and a discernable shift towards 'indigenising the curriculum' has been evident.[13] Further, a best practice framework for the recruitment and retention of indigenous Australians into the medical workforce was launched in 2005 by the Australian Indigenous Doctors' Association (AIDA). This framework, set out in the AIDA report, *Healthy Futures*, has been endorsed by the government and accepted by Australian medical schools as a template for action.[14]

An important aspect of human capability building – and especially germane to indigenous resilience – has been the incorporation of indigenous world views into education and training. It is no longer acceptable that education and training should lead to the abandonment of an indigenous identity. As an agent of resilience, capability building requires that professional, technical and interpersonal skills are learned in a way that strengthens identity so that students and trainees can bring indigenous inventiveness to the workplace and ultimately provide services that will be relevant to indigenous peoples.

Cultural affirmation

A third determinant of indigenous resilience is linked to the ways in which indigenous language and culture are expressed in modern times. Language resilience is shown by the proportion of people who speak an indigenous language and the number of domains where that language can be heard. Where indigenous people are a minority population, and even occasionally where they are a majority such as in Ireland, indigenous language domains are generally limited and there is debate about the appropriateness of applying them to all fields rather than concentrating on a few. But increasingly the boundaries have been pushed out and (for example) Māori language has been woven into radio and television, into education and health promotion, and more recently into popular music including rap. Those innovations are consistent with the view that a resilient language is one that is used in both contemporary and customary contexts.

Indigenous resilience cannot be solely measured by indigenous participation in the dominant society since resilience is also about the way in which indigenous philosophies, styles of thinking, conceptualising, and turns of phrase are expressed in schools, at work, and in leisure time. Aligning indigenous people's cultural world views and indigenous knowledge with other knowledge systems and exploring the interface between them has unrealised potential.

'Living at the interface' was a theme at the first PRIDoC conference in 2002.[15] A tendency to appreciate indigenous knowledge and culture only because of its historic associations would miss any relevance for today and fail to capture the potential for knowledge expansion. In medical practice there is the opportunity to expand the basis for medicine by creating foundations drawn from the scientific tradition as well as the indigenous traditions. In that process indigenous doctors are well placed to show leadership and a capacity to work within two systems.[16]

Over the past decade progress in aligning indigenous cultures with professional development has occurred in several areas. For example, environmental protection, based on cultural perspectives of sacredness and identity has been discussed in relationship to health in Palau[17] and the integral significance of culture to health research has been emphasised in Pacific community based research proposals.[18] Repositioning traditional healing within a social science context has also been seen as an important step to improving health services in Tongan communities and the grouping of this healing with conventional health services has been postulated as a useful approach.[19]

Attitudinal bias

Although the pathways to success are complex with multi-determinants, there is empirical evidence that indigenous achievement (or non-achievement) is very often a product of the attitudes of others

– professional bodies, national organisations, state governments, international agencies, non-indigenous members of society, and indigenous peoples themselves. Expectations for indigenous peoples, especially where they are minorities in their own lands, are seldom high or indeed afforded priority and are not infrequently negative and disparaging. Many indigenous communities also have low levels of ambition and do not expect that their own people will be able to rise above adversity and exercise both leadership and control over their future directions. Lack of success becomes a self-fulfilling prophecy.

Reversing entrenched attitudes is no mean task. But there are encouraging examples where major attitudinal changes have occurred in recent times. The 1984 Hui Taumata[20] led Māori to refocus energies away from state dependency towards self-management, economic self-sufficiency and self-determination. Expectations of failure, trapped lifestyles and mediocrity are now increasingly balanced with expectations of success, innovative discovery, and collective wellbeing. In Australia, the establishment of an Indigenous Higher Education Advisory Council in 2005 has provided a vehicle for the advancement of indigenous students and academics through improved policies and strategies. The motivation for PRIDoC has similar objectives – the creation of a forum where indigenous doctors from the Pacific can anticipate success on dual fronts: success in professional and technical spheres and success in realising indigenous goals. Moreover a standard of excellence has been promoted.

The economy

Resilience is more likely where economic circumstances are favourable and the indigenous resource base is strong. Many indigenous peoples have experienced serious erosion of customary resources, especially land. Currently, for example, Māori own around 5 percent of the total New Zealand land mass, much of which is scarcely arable. Over a century and a half, and by one means or another, some 25,415,029 hectares were lost. The massive alienation of a once substantial estate was the product of imposed reformation of land tenure, a shift to a cash economy, large- and small-scale pastoral farming, mining, new perspectives on the value of land, urban development, tourism, conservation measures in the name of national interest, and an element of avariciousness. Moreover, alienation of Māori land did not apply only to surface rights but also came to include sub-surface rights to minerals, gas and geothermal energy.

Natural resources, including forests and fish as well as land, are important contributors to indigenous resilience. Partial restitution of resources through the settlement of grievances has improved the economic circumstances of some tribes and as Treaty settlements and fisheries investments mature, the Māori economy shows signs of gaining strength.[21] But increasingly Māori are looking to other resources to provide economic security, and resilience is being linked to exploration of the knowledge society and participation in the knowledge economy. Because the population is expanding at a faster rate than the physical resource base, that trend is likely to continue, not only for Māori but for Pacific peoples whose island-based resources are similarly unable to provide sustainable economic growth into the future.

Lifestyle environments

A common characteristic of indigenous peoples is a capacity to relate to the natural environment. All indigenous people perfected the art of adaptation in order to live in harmony with nature. In Aotearoa for instance the laws of tapu constituted a type of public health code which minimised risk and promoted an ethos of sustainability. But synergy with the natural environment has become less relevant in urban environments, and increasingly the challenge has been to adjust to new, man-made environments and their associated non-communicable diseases.[22] There are many examples where adjustments have been successful though not necessarily before considerable damage was inflicted. Overcoming endemic tuberculosis and, in recent times, reducing the incidence of meningococcal meningitis are examples of successful adaptive processes.

However, other environments remain to be harmonised. The rate at which carbon fossil fuels are burned has created a global warming problem with climatic change, threats of a greenhouse environment, and the emergence of new sets of health problems on a scale that has not been previously known.[23] There are also new social and cultural environments that predispose to mental disorders such as depression, alcohol and drug misuse,[24] and increasingly urban populations are faced with consumer environments that foster, among other things, type 2 diabetes. Speaking at the International Diabetes Federation's Diabetes in Indigenous People Forum in Melbourne in November 2006, Professor Zimmet from the International Diabetes Institute showed that diabetes had become a major and deadly threat to the continued existence of some indigenous communities throughout the world as a result of western lifestyles and diet.

Predictions of extinction are not new to Māori. By 1874 the *New Zealand Herald* was convinced the end was nigh: 'That the native race is dying out in New Zealand there is, of course, no doubt …. The fact cannot be disguised that the natives are gradually passing away; and even if no cause should arise to accelerate their decrease, the rate at which they are now disappearing points to their extinction in an exceedingly brief period.'[25] But by failing to take into account Māori resilience and adaptability, reports of extinction have been remarkably inaccurate. While recognising the seriousness of diabetes, and its increasing prevalence, the facts point to a resilient people with a capacity to adapt and succeed. The rate of adaptation and the expression of resilience in response to the threats of diabetes and other lifestyle disorders, will not only depend on the quality of information, access to early intervention, and the strength of indigenous leadership, but also on the development of a code of living that is comparable to codes that were fashioned when Māori learned to live harmoniously with the natural environment. It is perhaps a task for PRIDoC.

Policies of the state

Key to preparing for the future are policies that will facilitate resilience and the realisation of indigenous potential. Policies that recognise indigenous peoples as risks will do little to actively promote strengths or encourage innovation, and in fact increase those risks.

The ways in which states value indigeneity can often be clouded by two issues. First, the position of indigenous peoples within a state is not solely about socio-economic disadvantage, or health risks. Those considerations are germane to all people.

Second, addressing cultural diversity is not the same as recognising indigeneity or agreeing about the place of indigenous peoples within the modern state. Equal rights for all cultures endorses cultural respect but does not address the issue of indigeneity which is only partly about culture. Indigeneity is essentially about a set of rights and responsibilities that embrace economic, social, environmental and cultural dimensions, and the nature of the indigenous people's relationship to the state.

The distinctions between a celebration of culture and indigeneity are clear in the Draft Declaration of the Rights of Indigenous Peoples.[26] 'Culture refers to language, customs, and social protocols of any social or ethnic group while indigeneity refers to the status of indigenous peoples within their traditional territories. Culture is only one aspect of indigeneity.'[27] After twenty years of negotiation the Draft Declaration was widely supported by indigenous peoples from around the world, had been adopted by the UN Human Rights Council in June 2006, and was recommended for adoption by the General Assembly. But a 'no action' motion was advanced in the Third Committee of the UN General Assembly at the November 2006 session. African states, as well as Samoa, Micronesia, Kiribati, New Zealand, Australia, Canada and the United States of America were opposed to some aspects of the Draft and led the move to stall it. Other states including Tonga and Vanuatu abstained. In the event, a global opportunity to facilitate indigenous resilience was put on hold for further consideration before the end of the sixty-first session of the UN General Assembly (September 2007).[28]

Lack of state support for indigenous causes is not new. New Zealand, for example, has been through a two decade process of settling claims between Māori and the state. The injustices that are the basis of these claims were brought about by disregard for indigenous property and cultural rights. And some states have found it difficult to distinguish between indigenous rights and interests on the one hand and ethnic interests on the other. As societies become increasingly multicultural, the recognition of ethnic diversity will become more important and the celebration of their various cultures will add to the wealth of each nation. But important as ethnic and cultural rights are, indigenous rights constitute another dimension and require responses from states that are not based solely on cultural difference or ethnic diversity.

Indigenous mobility

A primary characteristic of indigenous peoples has been a longstanding relationship with land, forests, waterways, oceans and the air.[29] That characteristic is expressed in language, song, dance, and gatherings where tribal customs and aspirations can be shared. Increasingly, however, indigenous peoples have migrated away from homelands, either through a process of urbanisation or migration to other countries. Māori, Australian Aborigines and Torres Strait Islanders have moved in large numbers from rural areas to reside in towns and cities. Though still linked to traditional lands, and often retaining strong interests in them, their lives are largely shaped by metropolitan environments. Pacific peoples have also moved to new environments. When island economies have been unable to sustain expanded populations, families have migrated to neighbouring countries such as New Zealand and Australia, where work and education can be obtained.

The diaspora – whether urban or transnational – has sometimes been seen as a weakening of indigenous identity and potential. However, over time it has become apparent that many tribes in New Zealand, and many Pacific nations, have remained resilient not in spite of the diaspora but because of the diaspora. While those who leave home do not necessarily retain the same idiom or the same values as those who remain behind, a commitment to their own people may be no less and reconnections will be valued. The capacity to contribute to indigenous resilience may be increased by new skills, expanded networks, different organisational arrangements, and fresh visions acquired in distant environments.

Leadership – indigenous doctors and indigenous resilience

By virtue of their training and standing in the community, indigenous doctors can contribute to the promotion of resilience in two ways. Most obviously, improving health status will increase levels of resilience; but in addition doctors are well placed to participate in the conversion of environments that diminish resilience into environments that can enhance resilience.

Apart from public health physicians who have professional interests in whole populations, most doctors are concerned with the treatment of injury and disease for individual patients. In that respect the possible contribution to indigenous resilience is high, at least for individuals. But the promotion of resilience is likely to be even greater if the diagnostic and treatment process can address human potential as well as human pathology. While time spent with patients is valuable and inevitably never long enough, and notwithstanding the energies and costs required to establish a diagnosis and devise a treatment plan, should a medical examination also attempt to identify pathways that will lead to positive lifestyles and success in terms that are relevant to indigenous resilience? Is there a case for indigenous doctors to take a lead in the development of schedules and instruments that are capable of revealing the foundations of potential alongside the foundations of pathology?

Moreover, when considering resilience from the perspective of indigenous peoples as whole populations, there is another role for doctors, not necessarily as healers but as part of an indigenous leadership network. Leadership remains fundamentally important to indigenous development in modern times. Indigenous leaders need to be expert in navigating modern environments while remaining in touch with indigenous realities, indigenous aspirations and indigenous culture. As leaders, health professionals need to be able to establish positive relationships with a variety of institutions, communities, sectors, tribes, and systems of knowledge. Independently and collectively their influence with governments, professional bodies and their own people could be instrumental in converting hazardous environments to environments that are conducive to the emergence of resilience and potential.

While elders exercise leadership roles on the basis of a broad understanding of the overall aspirations of their people, indigenous doctors have professional and technical skills that are the product of lengthy training. But they will also need to be comfortable working at the interface between indigenous worlds and worlds dominated by global science, law and economic theory and will need to be equally comfortable working with indigenous colleagues from other disciplines and callings. Leadership embraces diverse skills and knowledge sets and is a major contributor to resilience. The establishment of academies for indigenous leadership could serve a useful purpose. Leaders in a range of endeavours such as education, commerce, the law and environmental management might join with leaders in health to learn skills relevant to indigenous futures, and to deliberately foster a climate of resilience.

Summary

Exploring indigenous resilience is an alternative way of understanding indigenous health. A number of determinants impact on resilience including demographic transitions, human capability, cultural affirmation, attitudinal biases, the economy, lifestyle environments, policies of the state, indigenous mobility, and indigenous leadership. To a large extent those determinants, together and individually, mediate between successful outcomes and outcomes where disease, disadvantage and deficit prevail.

Success refers to individuals, groups, tribes and the indigenous population as a whole. A successful person whose success is not mirrored in the success of others does not necessarily contribute to indigenous success. Success is a precursor of resilience and has at least three core characteristics. It is reflected in the quality and quantity of indigenous engagements with wider societies as well as with indigenous societies; and is further characterised by a high degree of autonomy and a capacity for self-management, self-governance, and collaboration.

Where there is success there is likely to be sufficient resilience to overcome adversity and disadvantage and to prepare the way for other individuals and groups to follow similar successful pathways. The task is to reduce adversity where it can be reduced and to build resilience so that any consequences of adversity do not outweigh the capacity of indigenous peoples to thrive and prosper.

Epilogue

If there were a central lesson from Pūkawa in 1856 it was that resilience must be nurtured and actively led. In November 2006 more than 5000 Māori gathered at Pūkawa to open a new tribal house and to remember the gathering that had taken place 150 years earlier. The event was led by descendants of Te Heu Heu and Potatau te Wherowhero. Not only had the lineages survived but there was evidence that they had prospered, grown in size and attracted wider support. Tumu te Heuheu was the host and Tuheitia Paki, who had been anointed the seventh Māori King only three months earlier, was the guest of honour. Together they, and their people, epitomised the spirit of Māori resilience.

CHAPTER 3

Indigenous Transformations in Contemporary Aotearoa

The J C Beaglehole Address, presented at the Conference of the New Zealand Historical Association, Wellington, November 2007.

Professor J C Beaglehole

Writing New Zealand's history so that it makes sense to New Zealanders and to a worldwide readership, requires a deep understanding of landscape, people, and the journeys they have made separately and together. More than an exercise in amassing evidence, it necessitates a capacity to analyse the sources, written and oral, and to construct a framework within which the evolution of nationhood, community and identity can be accommodated, capturing in the process the dynamic interplay between ideologies, constructions of knowledge, multiple perspectives, and the relationship of a past to a future.

Professor John Cawte Beaglehole became a champion for New Zealand history. Firmly grounded in Aotearoa, and keen to connect with the emerging New Zealand tradition, he set the stage for later scholars to engage with the past in a Pacific-centric manner, without being entirely influenced by insights and priorities from the northern hemisphere. The methodologies he used were not necessarily different from those employed by scholars in Europe or the Americas, and in that respect he gained a much deserved reputation as an international historian; but the subject material he chose was decidedly local and from that perspective he was essentially a scholar of New Zealand and the Pacific.

His example and his determination to investigate New Zealand's past came at a time when New Zealand as a South Pacific nation was greatly overshadowed by a colonial legacy that afforded more recognition to New Zealand as a far-flung outreach of the British Empire. Beaglehole set in motion an approach to history and scholarship that would eventually, some decades later, see historians not only focusing on the Pacific as the natural context for understanding New Zealand, but also engaging with a body of knowledge that was premised on indigenous concepts and methodologies on the one hand, and western intellectual traditions on the other. It is likely that the interface between the two bodies of knowledge will, in time, provide further fertile ground for a distinctive New Zealand historiography that will take Professor Beaglehole's pioneering work to new levels.

Transformations

The interface between two bodies of knowledge, two approaches to development, and two sets of understandings about the past as well as the future has meanwhile led to a significant transformation of New Zealand society. In the twenty-five year period 1982–2007, and despite elements of reluctance and intermittent retrenchment, New Zealand has given greater acknowledgement to Māori as indigenous New Zealanders, and to New Zealand as a Māori home. While the rationale for recognising indigeneity remains to be clarified, including whether or not it creates a parcel of rights not available to other groups or populations within New Zealand, there has nonetheless been a substantial shift in the life of the nation that has seen a Māori dimension included on the agendas of a range of social, economic, cultural and environmental policies and programmes.

These transformations are at odds with popular predictions made at the end of the nineteenth century and early in the twentieth century, when a different type of transformation was envisaged. In 1907 the New Zealand Institute, founded in 1867,[1] published a lengthy article which reaffirmed a widely held view that Māori were inevitably headed towards extinction. The author, Archdeacon Walsh, disputed early signs that Māori depopulation had been arrested, and in 'The Passing of the Maori' painted a grim future.'That the Maori is gradually though rapidly passing away there can be no doubt .... Finality has now been reached, and the next census will show that the Maori population, instead of increasing has been diminishing all the time, and that if the present rate of declension continues, it must soon reach the vanishing point.'[2]

The evidence accumulated over the preceding fifty years seemed to support the Archdeacon. In 1856 the Māori population was clearly in a state of decline and as early as 1836 there were reports that the population had been reduced by more than a quarter. In 1906 it was estimated at 45,000 – a decrease of more than 75 percent from 1806. However, Walsh had not taken early signs of a reversal seriously, nor had he taken Māori resilience into account. Determination to seek redress and gain greater autonomy, coupled with adaptation by tribal leaders, greater Māori influence in Parliament, and new professional capability proved to be a powerful formula for successful recovery, evident in emerging demographic patterns.

Demographic trends

Even though the methods used for classifying Māori have changed over time, making exact comparisons difficult, far from Māori declining in numbers, periodic census takes have shown a steady growth in the population dating from at least 1900. Most recently, in the 2006 Census, 565,329 New Zealanders identified as Māori and 643,977 claimed descent from a Māori.[3] The Māori population is larger than it has ever been and even over the past fifteen years has increased by 30 percent, now representing some 15 percent of the total New Zealand population. Further, by 2051 the Māori ethnic population will almost double in size to close to a million, or 22 percent of the total New Zealand population. Even more significant, by 2051 of all children in the country 33 percent will be Māori and the percentage of the Māori population over the age of sixty-five will steadily rise from 3 percent (1996) to 13 percent (2051) as life expectancy increases.[4]

Markers of post-1982 transformation

Apart from the demographic trends, evidence to support the notion of significant Māori transformations since 1982 comes from a number of sources. Educational access, Māori workforce development, the provision of services 'by Māori for Māori', entrepreneurship, economic growth, cultural affirmation, the settlement of historic grievances and political influence at local and national levels have all been areas where major gains for Māori can be demonstrated. Essentially, however, transformation can be represented by the extent of Māori participation in te ao whānui (the wider society), and Māori participation in te ao Māori (the Māori world). The two markers, te ao whānui and te ao Māori, recognise the reality of being Māori in modern times. At the Hui Taumata Mātauranga in 2001, that reality was expressed as a capacity to 'live as Māori and be citizens of the world.'[5]

Prior to 1982, Māori participation in both areas was limited, often to the point of exclusion. Māori children were scarcely visible in early childhood education, there were few Māori among major service providers in health, justice, education, or social welfare, the number of Māori professionals was small, employment in low-skilled occupations was high, and despite substantial increases in the population, designated Māori representation in Parliament had remained static. Moreover, there was concern that Māori children and many adults were very often excluded from those institutions which fostered Māori language and culture, and even greater concern that te reo Māori could join the ranks of extinct languages.[6] A double jeopardy existed: generations of Māori faced exclusion from active participation in wider society, compounded by exclusion from participation in Māori society.

Māori participation in te ao whānui

Education

However, since 1982 Māori participation has undergone significant transformation. Education for example has been transformed in two respects. First, the education system has recognised Māori language, knowledge, and culture as core elements of the curriculum. Second, participation rates in non-compulsory education have escalated in an unprecedented manner. While the level of participation is uneven, and many Māori learners still remain outside the reach of effective education, there has been a remarkable turnaround. By coupling early childhood education with Māori language revitalisation, whānau enthusiasm for preschool education escalated, not only through kōhanga reo but also through conventional early childhood services. By 2001, 45 percent of all Māori children under five years of age were enrolled in early childhood services, nearly one-third in kōhanga reo[7] and by 2005 around 90 pecent of Māori children entering primary school had experienced some form of early childhood education.[8]

For older learners there have also been significant gains. Retention rates for sixteen year olds at secondary school increased from 47 percent (in 1987) to 63 percent (in 2003). Although achievement levels remain a point of concern, especially for Māori boys, between 1983 and 2000 the percentage of all Māori students who left school with no qualifications decreased from 62 percent to 35 percent.[9]

At the tertiary level, gains have been more spectacular: between 1993 and 2004 Māori participation increased by 148 percent. By 2006 Māori had the highest rates of participation in tertiary education at 18 percent, though had lower rates of participation for eighteen to twenty-four year olds.[10] Most of the recent tertiary education growth has occurred through accredited wānanga, which increased enrolments from 26,000 students in 2001 to 45,500 in 2002.[11]

As well as a larger number of students enrolled in sub-degree programmes there has also been a demonstrable increase in the number of Māori with doctorate degrees (since 2000 around twenty or thirty graduates each year) with a corresponding increase in Māori research capacity.

Human services delivery

Gains in educational participation have been mirrored by active Māori participation in the delivery of human services. In the health sector, for example, workforce development became a high priority for improving Māori standards of health. An important component of a workforce strategy was the engagement of cultural advisors and Māori community health workers to work alongside health professionals, bringing first-hand knowledge of community, culture, and a capacity to engage diffident patients. Of critical importance, however, has been the recruitment of more Māori into the health professions. Affirmative action programmes – or programmes that have similar aims – have been significant vehicles in developing a workforce that is more representative of New Zealand's communities. Similar trends have been seen in the qualified medical workforce. From an estimated medical workforce of around sixty in 1984, there are now (as of 2006) over 200 Māori medical practitioners across a range of specialties, accounting for 3 percent of the total active medical workforce. The number of Māori dentists has increased from four or five in 1984 to forty-four in 2005. In the addiction treatment workforce there are more than 300 Māori practitioners, representing 25 percent of the entire addiction treatment workforce.

The most dramatic changes, however, have been in the number of Māori health provider organisations. Prior to 1980 there were only three or four Māori health providers but by 2007 nearly 300 Māori heath providers offered a range of services, and Māori language and culture had become more or less accepted as part of the operating norm in schools, hospitals, state agencies, the media, and community centres.

Participation in the economy

Greater Māori participation in the economy has been integral to the transformative experience and was one rationale for launching the Decade of Māori Development in 1984. Māori economic growth was boosted by Treaty of Waitangi settlements but earlier had been kindled by a scheme to encourage Māori organisations into commercial ventures. MANA Enterprises was a Māori business scheme initiative by the government in 1985 to facilitate the entry of Māori into business. From that beginning, Māori participation in the commercial sector escalated at a number of levels: several iwi have developed large-scale operations; a range of Māori providers have created successful businesses largely through state contracts; entrepreneurs in music, art and media have joined business networks; and at a national level organisations such as Te Ohu Kaimoana have been successful in entering the fishing industry as a major player.

The Māori economy is made up of the assets owned and income earned by Māori. This includes collectively-owned trusts and incorporations, Māori-owned businesses, service providers, housing owned by Māori and the wages and salaries earned by Māori. The Māori economy benefits the New Zealand economy. Māori collectively-owned assets and businesses produce $1.92 billion per year which amounts to 1.4 percent of New Zealand's economy, and Māori households and businesses pay $2.4 billion in tax per year.[12]

The Māori asset base (total Māori-owned commercial assets) is a key economic resource for individuals, whānau, hapū, iwi, and for New Zealand as a whole. The Māori asset base comprises Māori trusts, Māori trustee land assets, Māori organisations, iwi Treaty settlements, Māori trust boards and Māori businesses. In 2001 the Māori asset base was estimated to be $9 billion of which the assets of Māori businesses made up 63 percent or $5.7 billion.[13] By 2004 the Māori asset base was estimated to be $9.4 billion.[14] Māori assets and business activity are concentrated in the primary sector (agriculture, forestry and fishing: $3.1 billion assets) and the property and business services sector ($2.4 billion assets).[15]

Participation in Parliament

In 1867 the Māori Representation Act created four Māori electorates and four seats in the House of Representatives, giving Māori the option to enrol on a separate Māori electoral roll. For over 100 years the level of representation remained unchanged despite a changing demography. However, a new formula for deciding the number of Māori seats was contained in the Electoral Reform Act 1993. Whereas previously the number of seats had been fixed at four, regardless of the total Māori population or the number of voters, under the new Act the number of seats would be a function of the number of people enrolled on the Māori roll. By 2006 the number of seats had increased to seven. Electoral reform has led to a larger number of Māori in Parliament, seven representing the Māori electorates and some fifteen others representing general electorates or party lists.

The new Act also provided for mixed member proportional representation so that smaller parties could have a more effective voice in Parliament and could join larger parties in a governance role. The emergence of the Māori Party in 2005 was to be an indicator of the potential for Māori to play a significantly different role within mainstream politics.

Participation in the academy

From a position of virtual exclusion three decades ago Māori now make up around 8 percent of university student enrolments and over 90 percent of wānanga students. But apart from a strong visible presence, the academy has also been influenced by Māori world views and an indigenous knowledge base. Departments of Māori Studies, formerly considered subsets of Anthropology have become established academic units in their own rights. They teach across a range of disciplines including te reo Māori but are distinguished as much by the pedagogies they employ as by the subject areas they cover. Their research endeavours similarly reflect Māori methodological approaches.

Māori culture, language, and contemporary issues are also taught within other academic units; schools of education for example frequently teach courses in te reo Māori, and the entire degree curriculum is taught in Māori to students planning to teach in Māori immersion schools such as kura kaupapa Māori. In addition, Māori issues have become embedded in the curriculum of law schools, business programmes, and service professions such as nursing, social work and psychology.

Māori participation in te ao Māori

Te reo Māori

Apart from increased participation by Māori within wider New Zealand society there has been even greater participation in te ao Māori. Māori language has become an integral part of the school curriculum and opportunities for students to be taught entirely within a Māori language medium have increased from early childhood to tertiary levels. Surveys indicate that although levels of fluency are variable, te reo Māori has become an accepted spoken language and less endangered than it was when the Wellington Māori Language Board took a claim to the Waitangi Tribunal on the grounds that the government had failed to protect the language and may have contributed to its near demise. Māori television, radio, newspapers and magazines, as well as Māori language resources in conventional print media and electronic form, and a major Māori language publishing company (Huia Publishers) have enriched the language environment. Older people are still more likely than the young to speak Māori but there are many more young people who are able to converse in Māori than there were in 1982.[16]

Iwi

Closely linked to Māori participation in te ao Māori has been the reconfiguration of tribal structures. Rūnanga, legal entities that provide a developmental focus for tribes, are actively involved with service delivery, environmental management, and revitalisation of language and culture. Although the Iwi Rūnanga Act 1990 was repealed less than a year after it was enacted, rūnanga and related bodies have demonstrated how tribes can successfully engage in commercial activities without necessarily abandoning customary values and obligations. Tension between commercial objectives and cultural imperatives have been not infrequent but there have also been an increasing number of examples where the two goals have not only proved compatible but also mutually reinforcing.[17]

Because many whānau had lost contact with tribal authorities and were either unsure about tribal origins or uncertain how to reconnect with iwi, active outreach programmes were developed by iwi and also by national organisations such as Te Ohu Kaimoana. In part the reconnections were necessary to meet the terms of Treaty of Waitangi settlements but were also in response to whānau who were keen to make connections, access tribal services, and participate in sporting, cultural, and educational programmes organised through iwi. In addition, because provision of services and allocation of resources, especially fishing quota, depend on the number of tribal affiliates, it has been necessary for iwi to compile registers. Census data has also been expanded so that iwi affiliation can be recorded at a national level.

Rangatahi

For many Māori, however, especially younger age groups, participation in tribal activities has been less important than participation in Māori cultural, sporting, and musical events within their own communities. Kapa haka festivals for primary and secondary schools, speech competitions (Ngā Manu Kōrero) and sporting fixtures where other Māori are involved, including touch rugby and mau rākau, have become integral to the school year and markers of youthful enthusiasm to celebrate being Māori in modern times. A new dimension to a Māori identity has emerged, based less perhaps on whakapapa, marae and iwi, and more on peer associations, Māori innovation in contemporary music and performance, the use of te reo Māori, adaptation of electronic communication to accommodate Māori language, and a bias towards Māori broadcasting media. This new dimension not only reflects the realities of being youthful in a Māori community but also being Māori in an urban situation. In this context, participation in te ao Māori is linked to entry into a pan-tribal community where Māori idiom distinguishes young Māori from their non-Māori counterparts.

Tino rangatiratanga

A common theme underlying Māori development since 1982 has been independence, tino rangatiratanga. The theme encompasses a wide range of meanings ranging from greater authority for Māori organisations such as marae, service providers, or sporting organisations, to self-governance at tribal or national levels. On the one hand, tino rangatiratanga is a catch-cry that signals a determination to retain a level of autonomy, especially in dealings with government or government agencies, while on the other it represents defiance of government and the courts and a determination to establish an infrastructure that allows for self-management as well as self-government. Both ends of the tino rangatiratanga spectrum share a rejection of assimilation and a conviction that Māori futures will be best served by Māori leadership and control. They differ, however, in the extent to which autonomy is sought and whether or not it can be accommodated within a unified New Zealand society.

Catalysts for change

Transformations in Māori society over the past two decades have depended on five major catalysts: transformational leaders, investments in positive developments, legislative endorsement, the global indigenous peoples' movement, and recognition of the Treaty of Waitangi.

First, Māori leadership emerged in the 1980s as a network formed around the common goals of increased autonomy, economic self-sufficiency, tribal redevelopment, and cultural affirmation. Their task was not about survival as it had been for Māori leaders a century earlier, but about transforming society so that systems and institutions would be accessible, relevant to Māori, and able to lead to the best possible outcomes. Transformational leaders promoted sustainable and distributive leadership so that the benefits were widespread rather than localised, triggering and enabling different types of transition in society.[18]

Transformational leaders also have a capacity to straddle an interface. Māori, like other indigenous peoples in developed countries, live in two worlds – an indigenous world where one set of values, customs and expectations prevail, and a global world where there are other norms. Straddling the interface required policies and programmes that could balance two sets of values, two foundations for knowledge (science and indigenous knowledge) and two histories that did not always coincide. The challenge was not to dismiss either knowledge base, nor to explain one according to the tenets of the other, but to embrace both in order to reach fresh insights that might accord with the day-to-day experiences of contemporary Māori.

The second catalyst for Māori transformations concerns investments in positive development. Investments in Māori development have been derived from three main sources: government programmes for positive development, tribes, and Treaty of Waitangi settlements. In the economic restructuring that commenced in 1984, the government introduced policies of devolution and decentralisation, and facilitated the development of organisational arrangements that would allow for Māori governance and management. Economic restructuring and reducing the size of the state were important precursors for increased Māori autonomy and self-determination. More recently, especially for tribes and organisations with substantial turnover, investments from the private sector have become increasingly important.

A third catalyst has been legislative endorsement of Māori development. While many laws in the past were used to restrict Māori interests, there has been an increasing recognition of Māori rights in statute, particularly since 1975 when the Waitangi Tribunal was established under the Treaty of Waitangi Act. However, the special position of Māori within statute is only sometimes linked to the Treaty of Waitangi (when it appears to suggest a special relationship between Māori and the Crown, for example the Resource Management Act 1991, and the Public Health and Disability Act 2000). Sometimes this special position seems to stem from Māori as a disadvantaged minority (for example the Health and Disability Services Act 1993), or a culturally different client group (for example the Children, Young Persons and their Families Act 1989), or an indigenous people with a distinctive culture (for example the Maori Language Act 1987), or a group with a unique constitutional right (for example the Electoral Reform Act 1993).

A fourth catalyst was the global indigenous peoples' movement. Māori were especially involved in helping to shape the Draft Declaration on the Rights of Indigenous Peoples[19] which codified a set of rights based on indigeneity and the terms of indigenous participation in modern societies. After twenty years the Draft Declaration was widely supported by indigenous peoples across the world and had been adopted by the UN Human Rights Council in June 2006. But a 'no action' motion was advanced in the Third Committee of the UN General Assembly at the November 2006 session. In the event further consideration occurred at the sixty-first session of the UN General Assembly in 2007 and the Declaration was finally approved. New Zealand was one of four countries that continued to vote against approving the Declaration, largely on the grounds that some provisions, such as an indigenous right to traditional lands and territories, were inconsistent with New Zealand law.[20]

Nonetheless, New Zealand has been seriously influenced by the indigenous movement which has strengthened the Māori case for reform. Importantly, despite the relevance of ethnic and cultural rights, indigenous rights constitute another dimension and require responses from states that are not based solely on cultural difference or ethnic diversity.

Finally, recognition of the Treaty of Waitangi has been an important catalyst for the raft of transformations; and the inclusion of the Treaty in some statutes has been a significant development – indeed the Treaty is not legally enforceable unless it is incorporated into legislation. Recognition of the Treaty, however, is not confined to the statutes. Policies in most government sectors endorse the principles of the Treaty even in the absence of legislative requirements. Further, there appears to be a constitutional understanding, a convention, that issues of particular importance to Māori will not be progressed without some measure of Māori agreement. In the case of the Electoral Reform Bill, for example, representation from Māori reversed an earlier proposal for the abolition of the Māori seats.

After 1990 the focus of the Treaty of Waitangi shifted to the settlement of Treaty claims. Progress in settling claims has been considerable over the past ten or twenty years, at least compared to the previous 100 years. But many commentators including some politicians have seen a link between a successful end to settlements and the final demise of the Treaty itself. In that view a treaty will no longer be necessary since claims will be settled. Similarly there is a view that the elimination of disparities between Māori and other New Zealanders could be used as a powerful argument to make the Treaty obsolete. In that case, there is a presumption that equity as between Māori and non-Māori is the major aim of the Treaty, and once assured, the Treaty can be rested. Those arguments suggest a lack of understanding about the purpose of the Treaty; progressing settlements and relieving inequalities between different population groups within New Zealand are important matters but are not identical to discussions about the constitutional position of Māori as an indigenous population in society – which is the Treaty's main point.

Measuring the impacts

The transformation of Māori society over the past twenty-five years has been at least as significant as the transition from rural to urban environments that occurred after World War II, though cannot be measured in the same way. The extent of urbanisation can be quantified through census data that identifies usual place of residence. Measuring the transformation associated with positive Māori development, however, requires multiple measures.

Disparities

Disparities between Māori and non-Māori have become a major instrument for measuring Māori progress. Disparities in educational achievement, standards of health, levels of income, home ownership and offending, for example, are regularly reviewed to determine Māori advancement. On almost all indicators disparities exist. However, in some key areas, such as life expectancy and rates of mortality, disparities are less than they were prior to 1982. For non-Māori New Zealanders there was a steady increase in life expectancy at birth over the period from 1985/7 to 2000/2. For Māori there was little change for males or females during the 1980s but a dramatic improvement in the five years to 2000/2. Between 1984 and 2002 the life expectancy increased from sixty-five years for Māori males to sixty-nine years while for Māori females it increased from seventy to seventy-three years. Notwithstanding the eight year gap between Māori and non-Māori, in the five years to 2000/2, the gap reduced by 0.6 years.[21]

There is also recent evidence of a reduction in mortality disparities. Although Māori experienced the highest mortality rates in the period 1981–2004, the rate of decline in Māori mortality has increased, compared to a slowing in the European/other rate of decline. In the late 1990s and early 2000s relative inequality (mortality rate ratios) between Māori and European/other ethnic groups reduced slightly while absolute inequality (mortality rate difference) declined more notably. While much of the difference appears to be a function of socio-economic circumstances, other factors operating independently of socio-economic factors are relevant – such as racism, access to quality care, tobacco, diet and other lifestyle factors.[22]

Being Māori

However, disparities do not represent a comprehensive measure of Māori development since they presume a goal of equity with non-Māori. While attaining similar standards of living as other New Zealanders is an important consideration, a significant goal has also been to 'live as Māori.' Measuring the level of engagement with te ao Māori requires an estimation of the degree to which Māori are able to share in the cultural, social and economic benefits that accrue from being Māori. In turn that requires Māori-specific indicators which not only measure individual characteristics such as fluency in te reo Māori but also the value of Māori resources such as land, the number and quality of marae, and the strength of tribal and community entities that provide specifically for Māori.

Further, in addition to measuring resource and organisational capacity, the measurement of groups such as whānau, hapū and iwi allows the strength of Māori collectives to be assessed alongside the status of individuals.

Because there is no single indicator that can accurately reflect the state of Māori wellbeing, more than one set of indicators should be employed. The sole use of narrow single-dimension measures ignores the several dimensions of Māori wellbeing. For individuals those dimensions reflect spiritual, physical, mental and social parameters; while for whānau they include the capacity for caring, planning, guardianship, empowerment, cultural endorsement, and consensus. For the Māori population as a whole, measurements than can gauge the overall wellbeing of human capacity (individuals and groups) and resource capacity (intellectual and physical resources) are necessary. Some of these measurements will employ economic measures, others will be measures of social and cultural capital, and yet others will be linked to measurements of environmental sustainability. To assist in the identification of specific outcomes and indicators that can be used as a global measure of Māori wellbeing, an outcomes schema that incorporates multiple sets of indicators, Te Ngāhuru, has been developed.[23]

The New Zealand ethos

A further impact of the decades of transformation has been felt by New Zealand society generally. Sometimes unenthusiastic responses have accompanied Māori endeavours. The possibility that New Zealand has become 'a divided nation' as a result of the more visible Māori dimension has been voiced and concerns have been raised about the intrusion of Māori language and culture (such as the haka) into mainstream institutions. There have also been accusations of bias, Māori individuals seeming to have greater access to public funds and receiving special exemptions not available to others. Moreover the settlement of Treaty of Waitangi claims has often been depicted as a giant waste of public money for claims that have dubious validity while

Māori providers of health and social services have not infrequently been characterised as unqualified and unprofessional.

Yet although change in attitudes, knowledge and practice has been uneven and often slow, there has been a progressive re-indigenisation of the nation over the past twenty-five years. Te reo Māori, for example, has a place in the curriculum in primary and secondary schools and has increasingly become part of the wider New Zealand vernacular; large societal institutions such as hospitals and universities frequently employ cultural advisors or kaumātua; contemporary and customary Māori music, art and design have become national icons, and a growing awareness of tribal endeavours has resulted from hundreds of school visits to marae as well as increased media portrayal of contemporary tribal activities.

Local authorities have established working relationships with Māori groups, partly in response to a requirement to consult and partly to ascertain Māori interests in land, waterways and special sites. Māori perspectives on health, conservation, cooking, and technology have been added to existing conventions; Māori television has entered living rooms across the country; Māori commercial practices have found their way to board rooms; Māori-dominated sports such as waka ama and touch rugby have become sporting exports; and Māori phrases to introduce and close formal and not so formal speeches have become commonplace.

In short, a Māori dimension to New Zealand is now more obvious than it was for most of the twentieth century.

Transformed

Māori potential meanwhile has never been higher and it is likely that the next decade will see further transformations shaped around the four key goals that have crystallised over the past two decades: a goal for full participation in education, the economy and society; an indigeneity goal that includes certainty of access to Māori culture, networks, and resources; a goal of balanced outcomes that reflects spiritual, emotional/intellectual, physical and family dimensions; and a goal related to the relationship of Māori to each other, to the state, to other New Zealanders, and to other indigenous populations.[24]

Transformations in the decades ahead will bring new challenges. Among other things they will test the parameters of Māori self-determination and the extent to which Māori aspirations can be met within the confines of a single unitary state. At the heart of the matter is whether indigeneity confers rights and creates special obligations on states. In the New Zealand context the Treaty of Waitangi strengthens the position of Māori as an indigenous people but the Treaty itself is not enshrined in constitutional arrangements and there has been inconsistency in the recognition of indigenous rights. Reducing socio-economic disparities, remedying past injustices, recognising cultural diversity, guaranteeing human rights, and developing equal employment opportunities all provide some justification for encouraging active Māori participation in society but do not entirely capture the essence of the indigenous arguments for autonomy and a distinctive place within the country.

It is unlikely that the issue will be resolved without a more focused debate on the future of New Zealand's constitutional arrangements. At a constitutional conference held in Wellington early in 2000, the position of Māori and the ongoing relevance of the Treaty of Waitangi proved to be a major topic of debate, but without any clear resolution being gained.[25]

While increased Māori participation has occurred over the past two decades, it would be simplistic to imply that there is a formula to guide the process or that there is a fixed endpoint towards which the country is moving. Instead the developments are subject to a wider context based not only on structural arrangements but also on the dynamic nature of the Crown's relationship with Māori.[26] It is not unlikely that the focus for the relationship will shift, from a preoccupation with levels of representation to the development of mechanisms for creating effective partnerships. In the future Māori participation in governance may be less about inclusion within a unitary system of control and authority than about the establishment of Māori governing bodies to control Māori resources and provide a fulcrum for interacting with the Crown. Integral to that shift will be the formation of a national Māori body that has the capacity and the mandate to act as a governing body and to interact with the other governance structures in the nation. This does not mean the splintering of a single nation state but, in line with the emergence of a Scottish Parliament, a Welsh Parliament, and a Saami Parliament in Norway, it allows for the creation of systems of governance that have different jurisdictions but close ties, and ongoing relationships.

The main impetus for launching a Decade of Māori Development was directly linked to the economic position of Māori people compared to other New Zealanders. To some extent Māori can still be regarded as a marginalised population insofar as there are significant disparities in educational and health outcomes, with lower standards of material wellbeing and lower incomes.[27, 28] But measured against progressive participation in education and the economy, a growing workforce capability, cultural and language revitalisation, legislative change and greater political influence, it is clear that a major transformation has occurred over the past twenty-five years. In addition, quite apart from gains made by Māori, New Zealand as a whole has absorbed Māori values, culture, aspirations and ways of doing things that have substantially changed the national ethos.

CHAPTER 4

Global Transitions: Implications for a Regional Social Work Agenda

Key note address, Asia Pacific Social Work Conference 2009, Auckland, November 2009.

'Whakarongo, whakarongo, whakarongo
Whakarongo ki te tangi a te manu
Tūī, tūī, tūī tūīa
Tūīa ki runga, tūīa ki raro
Tūīa ki roto, tūīa ki waho
Ka rongo te pō, ka rongo te ao
Ka rongo hoki te kāwai tangata i heke mai i Hawaiki-nui,
Hawaiki-roa, Hawaiki-pāmamao
Ki te whei ao, ki te ao mārama.'

The verse 'Whakarongo, whakarongo whakarongo', reminds us that we are all connected to a wider world; we are not isolated from our natural environment; instead there are close and enduring bonds between people, the land, and the sky, between night and day and between the spiritual and the material. And when the voyages from 'Hawaiki-nui, Hawaiki-roa, Hawaiki-pāmamao' are recalled, there is recognition of distant shores from which journeys began and the common starting points that were home to the many peoples of Asia and the Pacific. Essentially the verse is an endorsement of the aim of this conference: to create an opportunity for delegates across Asia and the Pacific to identify common ground and to unite under a mantle of collegiality, a shared vision, and a shared sense of place.

On September 30 [2009], as a result of a major earthquake in the Pacific, tidal waves, tsunami, swamped parts of Samoa and Tonga. The same day a typhoon swept across Vietnam. The following day [New Zealand time] an earthquake of exceptional force left its mark on Padang in Sumatra. Together these events accounted for the loss of thousands of lives, wreaked havoc on buildings and whole villages, destroyed resources, left families homeless and destitute, and greatly aggravated already strained local and national economies.

Across the Pacific and into Asia there was an outpouring of both shock and disbelief as the extent of damage became apparent. The region was united in its grief and also the feelings of powerlessness in the face of such powerful forces of nature. Many Pacific people and Indonesians living in Australia and New Zealand were intimately caught up in the disasters and immediately set in train a set of actions to bring some relief to relatives and friends across the seas. And their concerns galvanised others, including governments and aid agencies to move quickly to reduce pain and suffering and restore normality. If there were an upside to the tsunami and the earthquakes it was the concerted response from across the region. Suddenly the vast stretches of ocean that separate the countries of Asia and the Pacific were reduced; distance gave way to affinity and difference took second place to humane concern.

Emerging from the destruction was the realisation that the corner of the globe we know as East Asia and the South Pacific has a distinctive character and a set of commonalities. We share the same unstable tectonic plates, the same ocean currents, the same hurricanes and the same potential for cataclysmic events. In addition, and perhaps more significantly, the links between the countries of Asia and the Pacific have a history that extends back much further than September 2009. It now seems fairly certain that Pacific inhabitants entered the Pacific by way of Asia. Having originated in Africa they travelled through the Persian Gulf, into the Indian Ocean, landed on the west coast of India, spent time in Malaysia and Taiwan and then entered the Pacific Ocean through the east, arriving in Aotearoa about a thousand years ago. The epic voyaging is recalled in fragments of modern culture: Māori and Malaysians vocabularies for example have many words in common such as ikan, (ika, fish), dua (rua, two), and khabapai (kei te pai, I am well).

In modern times, a regional identity has been strengthened by increasing economic interdependence. For many reasons Australia and New Zealand now rely less on northern hemisphere markets and more on the markets of Asia. Moreover there is a two-way flow of travellers and migrants between countries; students are increasingly studying in other countries within the region and a corresponding cultural diversity is emerging. Auckland is now not only the city with the largest Māori population (over a quarter of all Māori live in the greater Auckland region) but it has a larger Pacific population than any other city in the world, and has assumed a strong Asian character. The main point I am making is that on the basis of a shared history, connecting cultures, international travel, joint economies and exposure to similar climatic threats, there is justification for describing East Asia and the South Pacific as a well-connected region.

By the same token, the challenges facing countries in the Asia Pacific region will increasingly be shared challenges. Global climate change, global overpopulation and global food shortages, global inequalities, global colonisation, and global competitiveness will impact across the region demanding concerted responses and joint strategies. Impacts in the southern hemisphere will be different from those in northern countries and impacts on any one part of Asia Pacific will have consequences for other parts.

The Samoan and Tongan tsunami experiences, coupled with the Sumatra earthquake, are vivid reminders that no one part of the region will be immune from natural disasters, nor for that matter from economic fluctuations, epidemics, or demographic changes. Whether occurring in Thailand, Indonesia, Australia or Tonga, the ripples outwards will be felt in neighbouring countries and on distant shores.

The 2008 global economic recession originated in the northern hemisphere but soon reached nations to the south and will continue to impact disproportionately on many states within the Asia Pacific region. It is also clear that global inequalities between rich nations and poor nations will become progressively more visible. Already over 130 million people live in extreme poverty and as a result many children will never reach adulthood. A rapidly growing world population coupled with a worldwide food shortage will greatly exacerbate the extent of their plight. Inequalities between nations is a global problem, impacting directly on Asian and Pacific nations and it is a problem that will of necessity involve New Zealand, Australia, and indeed all countries in the Asian-Pacific region.

In addition to global inequalities and widespread malnutrition, a further challenge will come from the effects of global climate change. There is now clear evidence that without worldwide agreements to reduce carbon emissions and re-vegetate denuded landscapes, the planet will be seriously compromised and as a consequence humanity will suffer. Not only will previously controlled diseases such as malaria and tuberculosis reappear but global changes in climate will result in more cataclysmic events including droughts, cyclones, gales and floods leading to serious loss of life and property. The chances of some low-lying Pacific states disappearing completely are high and other states will find the progressive encroachment of the sea on land masses an ever-present reminder of insecurity. As a developed nation New Zealand contributes disproportionately to global warming, but even greater impacts will come from those parts of the world where population densities are high. In any event unless there are collective agreements on strategies to reduce carbon emissions and move towards carbon neutrality, the survival of future generations in their ancestral homes is doubtful.

Another challenge that will confront the region over the decades ahead has a double edge. Global colonisation, a process already in train, brings with it entry to worldwide markets, international educational prospects, access to unprecedented volumes of knowledge and information, and exposure to the world's music, art and literature. The opportunities will be unlimited; though will not be without compromise. Increased globalisation may mean that the customary ways of life in countries across the Pacific and in Asia will be submerged by other customs, and in the process cultural uniqueness will be transformed into a bland adaptation of a global norm. Language specialists are already predicting that up to 95 percent of the world's 7000 languages are likely to become extinct by the end of the century.[1] There is a real risk therefore that local distinctiveness will be lost to whatever global fashion holds dominance in the world at any particular time.

A consequence of overpopulation, limited resources, and global travel will be increased competition between nations. Superpowers will compete for markets where there are large numbers of consumers and where there is access to scarce natural resources such as water, and renewable energies derived from the wind, tides, and waterways. Global competition will see a shift in world political alliances from west to east and from the northern hemisphere to the southern hemisphere. The global economic policy coordinating body, the Group of 8 (G8), for example, has been replaced by the Group of 20 (G20), and whereas only one Asian country, Japan, was in the G8 around one-half of G20 members are Asian states.

It may not be entirely clear how the challenges I have mentioned will be relevant to social workers. Financial recessions are frequently regarded as tasks for economists, and climate change is often delegated to scientists and politicians to manage. The reduction of global overpopulation might similarly be seen as a job for religious and political leaders or for firm state intervention. There might also be widespread expectation that agriculturalists and food technologists will take the lead in addressing food shortages.

But the scale of the challenges facing the region and the failure of groups working in isolation to make substantial gains requires new approaches that are not handicapped by sectoral limitations or simplistic conclusions that one body of knowledge or one professional group has all the answers. Separating economic policies from social and environmental policies has been unhelpful and shortsighted. Expecting molecular scientists and economists to work in isolation from social scientists ignores the connections between people, the economy, and the environment. In that regard, the contribution of indigenous knowledge to environmental management and food production has been scarcely tested. Yet indigenous peoples have had first-hand experiences with land and water for thousands of years and have developed systems of management that have been both sustainable and practical.

Global transitions that threaten the integrity of the planet must become part of a regional social work agenda. Social workers need to be part of the solution. The problems are too complex and too far reaching to imagine that answers can be fashioned from technological advances or economic wizardry alone.

While all states represented at this conference have social work programmes that address internal domestic priorities, a regional agenda for social work presupposes that there will be opportunity for inter-state collaboration and the development of cross-regional social work strategies. Social workers will continue to address local and domestic matters but in addition to 'business as usual' there must be a readiness to shift the focus so that a meaningful social work perspective is felt at a regional level and alongside other groups and professions.

Social work engagements

In this respect it is possible to consider a regional agenda for social work. Bearing in mind the future regional threats arising from global climate change, global overpopulation, global inequalities, global colonisation, and global competitiveness, it is imperative that social workers across the region are ready to actively engage with these issues. Regional strategies for eco-engagement, engagement with demographic transitions, economic engagement, border engagements, and collegial engagements will become increasingly important as the threats draw closer.

Eco-engagement

Eco-engagement is about reducing global warming and at the same time being ready to respond to catastrophic events such as tsunamis, hurricanes and droughts. As community leaders, policy makers, and family advisors, social workers are well placed to assume active roles as protectors of the environment and champions for reduced carbon emissions. The human face of climate change and the potential of families and communities to diminish carbon impacts fall well within the scope of social work. While carbon neutrality might seem a low priority in the day-to-day involvement with drug abuse or access to adequate housing or recreational facilities for young people, all professionals have some responsibility to the planet and to the natural environment and social workers have much influence in local communities as well as in the formulation and implementation of social policies.

In the foreseeable future, however, it is highly likely that, despite best efforts, further regional disasters will occur. Eco-engagement is also about being ready to address the social needs that will inevitably accompany disasters. Disaster-readiness requires a thorough knowledge of existing community strengths as well as knowledge about situations in neighbouring countries. It is not unreasonable to expect that a disaster of serious magnitude in one country might be best managed by sending children and older people to another country in the region until normality is restored. Such a plan would necessitate close cooperation between workers in both countries and a capacity to respond quickly.

Demographic engagement

Unlike eco-engagement where the focus is on the relationship of people to their environment, demographic engagement is more concerned with population transitions – the impacts of a rapidly expanding world population and a rapidly ageing population. Social workers can make major contributions to both trends. The finite resources of the planet are such that continuing population expansion is unsustainable and the case for more active family planning is gaining in strength. Community leaders will be pivotal to those discussions and must be ready to mediate between religious, cultural, economic, and scientific perspectives. For many communities compulsory limits on family size will not be an acceptable answer to the world's population explosion, any more than euthanasia for the chronically sick or aged would be tolerable across the region. But it is abundantly clear that greater life expectancy coupled with reduced mortality rates will result in a population that is too large for this planet and social workers will inevitably be part of a nexus that must address this concern before it is too late.

Balancing population growth with the resources necessary for wellbeing will require greater attention to infrastructural regulations, governance and planning. An associated task and one that is already on social work agendas is linked to positive ageing. In all developed countries, greater longevity has led to new ways of conceptualising old age as well as the provision of a greater range of services. Meeting the needs of the well elderly and the not-so-well elderly will likely demand even more social work attention in the years ahead.

Economic engagement

Inequalities between nations warrant social work intervention; engagement with economies is a priority for a regional social work agenda. Social workers and economists have often been on opposite sides of the debate, the one promoting quality of life and the other affordability. Both dimensions, however, are equally important and it makes little sense to address them as if they were separable entities. While finite resources and maldistribution of resources are parts of the same debate, they are seldom argued together. In this respect economic and social policies are inextricably bound by the twin pillars of want and need. Social workers cannot by themselves address modern economic complexities; but neither can economists. Joint efforts based on agreed common goals rather than philosophical differences will be essential if future recessions are to be avoided and economic growth is to become meaningful for all. Reducing inequalities between nations in the Asia Pacific region will present particular challenges. But they need not be insurmountable.

This conference provides a platform for identifying starting points and aligning an agenda so that broad agreements might be forged and regional priorities for reducing inequalities agreed. Meanwhile the longstanding role of social workers as agents for the alleviation of poverty will continue and actions to reduce illiteracy will be a related goal.

Border engagement

Border engagements will be increasingly necessary as inter-state migrations increase and global travel becomes a way of life. The trend has two dimensions. First, the collective opportunities across the world should be accessible to all countries in the region. Both technology and air travel have been able to shrink distance to the point where the world has become everyone's oyster. Secondary and tertiary education in other countries is already a reality and both New Zealand and Australia have regional reputations as educational providers. A second dimension to globalisation, however, has less attractive implications. There is the very real threat that local distinctiveness will give way to global mimicry.

Countries in the Asia Pacific region will be driven as much by international brands as by their own traditions and in the process valuable heritage will be lost and the strength of diversity will be diminished. Social workers will be caught in both dimensions. On the one hand they will be expected to reduce barriers across borders so that travellers can move easily in two directions, but on the other they will be expected to defend local culture and local pride. The latter task will be especially important to indigenous communities, many of whom have struggled to revitalise language, culture, and native leadership, only to see them again threatened by a new wave of colonisers – online as well as on the ground.

Collegial engagement

In response to global competitiveness, a movement towards collegial engagement might be led by social workers. Collegial engagement implies a readiness to work collaboratively across states so that social work practices can be focused on common priorities. But it also implies a readiness to work with other professional groups – economists, lawyers, health practitioners, environmentalists, teachers – and with other sectors. Approaching social and economic problems from sectoral perspectives as if health, social welfare and economic and environmental sustainability could be considered in isolation overlooks the realities within which families and communities live. Social workers are sufficiently aware of those realities to promote integrated delivery options that focus on best outcomes rather than provider positioning.

A regional social work agenda

Delegates, I am grateful for the opportunity to share some views with you at the beginning of this conference. Although you will each bring different perspectives that have evolved in your own countries and within your own traditions, as social workers working in this part of the globe you will also have much in common. The challenge will be to harness the collective knowledge and skills you bring so that the Asia Pacific region can advance in a cooperative and integrated way in order to face the challenges ahead. That does not mean abandoning domestic priorities or disregarding cultural protocols at home, but it does mean actively promoting a level of regional awareness and ensuring that social work education can foster the development of skills that will be relevant to the wider region and to the future.

The main point I wanted to leave with you is that a regional social work agenda is needed. A focus on economic development alone, as a key to regional planning, runs the risk of ignoring the lives of real families and communities and reducing sustainability to a question of affordability and revenue. On the other hand, a strong united voice from the region's social workers will add balance and increase the chances that affordability will be matched with human dignity, cultural integrity, and social justice.

Essentially I have explored four key platforms relating to the broad themes of this conference. The first platform is the region itself. The Asia and Pacific region has unique characteristics. Not only is the region linked by the same unstable tectonic plates and atmospheric vagaries, but cultural similarities and DNA resemblances are reminders of ancient shared origins. And in modern times increasing migration between states and a growing Asia Pacific economy has added to the region's emergence as a functionally distinctive part of the globe.

The second platform is about global shifts. The countries in Asia Pacific will be increasingly exposed to major global transitions that will impact disproportionately on the region. Global climate change, global overpopulation, global inequalities, global colonisation and global competitiveness will present new challenges that will demand cooperative region-wide responses.

The third and fourth platforms are about social work engagement and social work actions. Engagements at macro-levels (social policy formulation) will contribute to broad regional policies while micro-engagements (social work actions) will strengthen families and communities as they move into the future. Eco-engagement – engaging with global climate change – will challenge social workers to develop programmes and practices that reduce carbon emissions while also being prepared for natural disasters that will inevitably recur across the Asia Pacific region. Engagement with overpopulation could encompass regional approaches to family planning but at a local level also address the social and economic consequences of an ageing population. Inequalities between nations within the region require social workers to actively engage with national and regional economies. While working to alleviate the plight of those living in poverty will continue to be a major task for social workers, working with economists to develop sustainable economies where inequalities are eliminated will be even more pertinent.

So too will engagement with the impacts of global colonisation have macro and micro opportunities. Social work engagements at borders can both facilitate policies for rationalised inter-state migration and also protect local distinctiveness. Ensuring access to wider regional resources and facilities will bring advantages to many families in different countries within the region. At the same time social workers will have a major role to play by ensuring that regional migration is not at the expense of indigenous culture and resources. Balancing the two directions – inter-state migration and cultural preservation – will present a number of dilemmas not the least of which will be comparing the gains made by opening up the region for regional exchanges against any loss of local distinctiveness or threats to national cultures.

Key to influencing future directions will be collegial engagement to counter the aggressive trend towards global competitiveness and western and northern hemisphere exploitation of Asia and the Pacific. Collegiality implies collaborating with social workers in other parts of the region and also working with other professional and sectoral groups so that there is an integrated approach to social, economic, environmental, and cultural interventions.

On the basis of these four platforms a framework for a regional social work agenda can be constructed. The framework is built on the distinctiveness of the region, the impacts of global transitions, opportunities for social work engagement at a policy level, and social work actions at family and community levels (Table 4.1).

TABLE **4.1** A framework for a regional social work agenda.

Global transitions	Social work engagements (Macro-interventions)	Social work actions (Micro-interventions)
Global climate change	Eco-engagement: policies that reduce carbon emissions	Energy sources that can be utilised by families and communities
Global overpopulation	Engagement with demographic transitions: policies that reduce the population explosion	Programmes that address the needs of an ageing population
Global inequalities	Engagement with economies: policies that reduce inter-state disparities	Programmes that alleviate poverty and illiteracy
Global colonisation	Engagement at borders: policies that rationalise inter-state migration	Programmes that protect indigenous cultures and local distinctiveness
Global competitiveness	Collaborative engagement: policies that foster international social work collaboration	Programmes that link social, economic, environmental, cultural interventions

Regional Distinctiveness

Shared natural environment   Common cultures   Inter-state exchanges   A regional economy

CHAPTER 5

Towards Social Cohesion: The Indigenisation of Higher Education in New Zealand

Presented at the Vice-Chancellors' Forum (VCF2009), Kuala Lumpur, Malaysia, June 2009.

Abstract

Since 1999 indigenous participation in tertiary education in New Zealand has been transformed. From a position of relative exclusion, multiple levels of Māori participation have evolved, reflected in the curriculum, the student body, the academic workforce, tertiary education policy, the establishment of tribal tertiary education institutions, and indigenous research. The impacts of the transformation have not only been apparent in educational institutions but have also been evident across society, especially in relationship to Māori capability in the professions, a greater understanding between Māori and other New Zealanders, and a stronger sense of shared nationhood. A conclusion is that universities have the potential to demonstrate social cohesion and also to prepare graduates for leadership roles in promoting a society that can model inclusiveness without demanding assimilation.

Transforming higher education

Accelerated indigenous participation in higher education in New Zealand has occurred since 1999.[1] Māori involvement in all aspects of tertiary education, including student enrolment, curriculum development, and the management and strategic development of educational institutions, has transformed New Zealand's education sector to the point where a palpable indigenous dimension can be felt both within and beyond the sector. The transformation has seen a shift from relative Māori exclusion in higher education to new levels of inclusion where, far from being discounted, cultural identity has been recognised as an important catalyst for learning. Moreover, the resulting increase in Māori capability has enhanced Māori professional, business, technical, research, and academic leadership, necessary for social, economic and cultural advancement. While significant gaps remain between Māori and non-Māori participation across most tertiary institutions and across particular academic disciplines, the progress has been sufficiently sustained to conclude that indigeneity (a distinctive indigenous perspective) has become embedded within higher education in Aotearoa New Zealand.

Intermittent Māori participation in universities began in the 1890s but generally with scant regard for learning preferences shaped by culture or by bodies of knowledge built on indigenous experience and indigenous ways of knowing. Nor was there previous involvement of Māori community leaders in university management or governance. In contrast, the modern era has seen the juxtaposition of universal approaches alongside the distinctive elements that make up Māori methodologies, pedagogies, and learning networks in modern times. The overall aim has not been solely to enrol more Māori students. Instead there has been a deliberate attempt to build on those indigenous foundations that have continuing relevance for new generations of Māori living in urban situations, and to reshape higher educational institutions as places where Māori culture, learning and aspirations can flourish.

In a UNESCO symposium of higher education, social cohesion was recognised as a reasonable goal for universities, and eleven characteristics necessary for cohesion to occur were identified:

Each university should have:

- publicly available standards of student and faculty conduct
- a transparent process of adjudication for misconduct
- students and faculty broadly representative of the wider population
- curriculum which reflects social problems
- empirical research particularly on social issues

- commitment to forging linkages with the wider community
- multiple sources of finance aside from government
- proactive leadership that explains and defends the role of the university
- public debate over sensitive issues
- academic freedom to ensure open debate and prevent retribution
- institutional autonomy so that it takes responsibility for its own policies.[2]

Among the characteristics, the symposium recommended that each university should have student bodies and faculties that were broadly representative of the wider population, a curriculum that reflected social problems, and a commitment to forging linkages with the wider community. Increasing levels of indigenous participation in university is consistent with all three of those characteristics and, in addition, has implications for three other characteristics: public debate over sensitive issues, academic freedom to ensure open debate and prevent retribution, and institutional autonomy so that universities can take responsibility for their own policies.

However, while social cohesion is an important goal, universities, at least in the western world, generally have a bias towards students and faculty members who subscribe to western academic conventions. Moreover, quite apart from financial barriers, entry depends on high achievement at secondary school; there is a tendency towards a self-selecting process that favours students who have succeeded in a system of education premised on the cultural norms of the west. In effect, without deliberate policies and measures, the people who make up university communities run the risk of being homogenous rather than 'representative of the wider population'.

Global under-representation of indigenous populations in higher education is the consequence of a multitude of obstacles that count against academic achievement. Not only do the obstacles reflect financial hardship aggravated by lower standards of health and education, but also a conflict between world views.[3] Indigenous peoples adhere to world views where knowledge is elaborated within an ecological framework built around relationships with both the natural environment and human environments. Though not all indigenous peoples subscribe to the same beliefs or ways of understanding, typically meaning comes from understanding connections and associations rather than focusing on an analysis of component parts studied in relative isolation from a wider perspective. Universities frequently have different starting points from such indigenous views.

Reducing indigenous barriers to education can be approached from two directions. First, efforts can be made to reduce socio-economic inequalities so that hardship is alleviated and students are able to contemplate deferring the need for an immediate income in favour of higher education and longer term benefits. Second, barriers can be reduced by ensuring that tertiary education institutions are able to embrace indigenous world views so that pedagogies, research methodologies, campus facilities, and the academic staff can endorse cultural identity and inspire students.[4] Māori experience in New Zealand has shown that both approaches are necessary: reducing inequalities is a critical determinant of full participation in higher education while expanding the context for higher education institutions is an essential prerequisite for students whose world views are not entirely shaped by western academic conventions. Moreover, the outcomes of participation go beyond indigenous students; there are benefits for the nation as a whole and for the broad goals of creating and transferring knowledge.

Evidence of transformation

Increased Māori participation in higher education can be measured against several outcome areas: tribal participation in higher education; the number of students studying for higher education qualifications; curriculum development; campus facilities that have cultural relevance; Māori research capability; staff profiles; and effective policies and strategies (Table 5.1). In this approach participation is defined as a level of inclusion where representivity occurs in association with changes to the culture of an organisation. The terms of participation become as important as the extent to which individuals participate.

Wānanga

A significant factor leading to increased Māori participation in tertiary education has been the establishment of wānanga. The Education

TABLE **5.1** Measures of Māori participation in higher education

Outcome areas	Indicators
Tribal participation in education	Establishment of wānanga; tribal partnerships with tertiary education institutions
Māori student participation	Student enrolments; levels of study; spread of academic programmes, successful completions
Curriculum development	Māori-centred programmes; Māori relevant programmes
Campus facilitation	Cultural 'space'; cultural endorsement; cultural protocols
Māori research capability	Research mentoring; indigenous methodologies; research capability funding
Staff profiles	Māori academic staff; Māori support staff
Effective policies, strategies, & decision-making	Māori participation in governance and management

Amendment Act 1990 provided for wānanga to be included as tertiary education centres eligible for state funding alongside universities and polytechics. In the legislation a wānanga is 'characterised by teaching and research that maintains, advances, and disseminates knowledge and develops intellectual independence and assists the application of knowledge regarding āhuatanga Māori (Māori tradition) according to tikanga Māori (Māori custom).' In fact, Te Wānanga o Raukawa had been established as an incorporated body in 1984, but had not previously qualified for funding, nor was the suite of qualifications offered recognised within an approved framework. But after registration as a statutory body, state funding and pathways for gaining academic course approvals were possible.[5] Three wānanga – Raukawa, Awanuiārangi and Aotearoa – are now integral to the New Zealand tertiary sector, offering a variety of accredited sub-degree and degree programmes, mostly built around indigenous world views and tribal knowledge but also addressing contemporary Māori society. Opportunities for second-chance learners, together with the inclusion of older people who had high cultural and tribal knowledge but little formal education, have characterised wānanga as niche educational providers within a Māori framework. Together the three wānanga account for some 60 percent of all Māori tertiary students and have been largely responsible for the transformational increase in Māori participation in tertiary education since 2000.[6]

Student enrolments

Between 1983 and 2000 the numbers of Māori students leaving school with no qualification decreased from 62 percent to 35 percent.[7] Over the same period, Māori enrolments at the tertiary level increased by 148 percent – and by 2003 the Māori participation rate in formal tertiary education was over 20 percent, higher than the national average. Most of the growth occurred for sub-degree programmes, largely through wānanga where enrolments increased from 26,000 students in 2001 to 45,500 in 2002 (though not all were Māori).[8] In 2003 the provider with the most Māori equivalent fulltime students (EFTS) was Te Wānanga o Aotearoa. Massey University had the second largest number of Māori EFTS while the Open Polytechnic was the polytechnic with the largest number of Māori EFTS.[9] In the two latter institutions, distance education remains an important delivery mode for Māori suggesting that many Māori students are part-time and actively engaged in the paid workforce or parenting.[10] Since 2006, the growth in numbers of Māori students at wānanga has levelled off, or even declined, but there has been a corresponding increase at polytechnics.

Although there has been an overall increase in Māori participation in tertiary education, the proportion of Māori students at universities has not increased to any great extent, remaining around 10 percent since 2004, with successful completion rates of around 62 percent.[11] However, the Māori university student profile is distinctive in three significant ways. First, compared to other student profiles, Māori students tend to be older (than twenty-five years) when they first enrol and are more often studying on a part-time basis.[12] Second, Māori students have now engaged in a wider range of academic programmes than two decades ago. Fewer are pursuing degrees in Māori Studies but more are studying Business, Education, Social Sciences, Law, Medicine, Nursing and the Applied Sciences. In part the trend points towards current career opportunities, but it may also suggest greatly increased pre-university levels of competence in Māori language and culture, so that having already been exposed to Māori language and culture, students proceeding to university are more inclined to explore other options. Third, proportionately more Māori students are now studying at the postgraduate level. In 2006, for example, for all New Zealand domestic university students Māori accounted for 12 percent studying at the master's level and 6 percent at the doctoral level.[13] Of particular note has been the increase in successful doctoral studies.[14] In the six years since 2002, when the Māori Academic Excellence Awards were initiated, more than 200 students have obtained PhD degrees.[15] In the six years prior to 2002, however, there were fewer than fifty Māori doctoral graduates.

Academic and support staff

Apart from wānanga, where most staff members are Māori, Māori are generally under-represented in the academic staff of tertiary education institutions.[16] However, two trends point towards new patterns of participation. Whereas most Māori staff once tended to be concentrated in Māori Studies, there are now significantly large concentrations in the Health disciplines, Education, Social Sciences, Fine Arts, Law, and Business Studies. Second, an increasing number of Māori academics have doctoral qualifications and strong research portfolios. Although an overall low level of Māori staff representation in higher education remains, the foundations for future development are strong and increasingly focused on subject areas where Māori students are studying.

An increase in the number of Māori students, many new to tertiary education and often unsuccessful at school in earlier years, has led to a range of support mechanisms within universities. Some, such as Te Rau Puawai (Māori Mental Health Workforce Development) at Massey University, are based around a bursary programme and adopt a proactive approach to student support. The programme has demonstrated that despite competing priorities such as employment, family obligations, and community commitments, high levels of academic achievement are attainable for more than 85 percent of students, even where earlier educational efforts have been unspectacular. An important factor in generating success has been the deliberate promotion of a group approach to learning. Communities of learning where students studying similar programmes can meet together, either face-to-face or online, increase motivation and foster high personal expectations. Other learning support programmes have focused on the first year student experience and especially on the provision of sound pre-enrolment academic advice so that courses of study are realistic and more sharply attuned to career prospects.

Māori university liaison officers provide ongoing linkages with secondary schools, especially those with high Māori populations, and are able to engage with wider Māori communities at regional and national events where large gatherings are occurring for particular events such as cultural festivals and inter-school sport and cultural competitions. Effectiveness of Māori advisors, mentors, counsellors, and liaison officers is closely linked to being able to communicate in Māori, participate in Māori networks, and mediate between Māori world views and the conventions associated with higher education. In this connection, dedicated funding for supporting Māori learning has been shown to have positive outcomes.[17]

The curriculum

Further evidence of a significant transformation of higher education can be found in the extent to which Māori knowledge and culture has been included in the curriculum. Māori Studies had been a university subject area since the 1960s but was associated with Anthropology. By 1995, however, most universities had established independent departments of Māori Studies where Māori language and culture were taught. Over the next decade the Māori Studies curriculum expanded to include visual and material arts, Māori history and politics, Māori health, and the application of the Treaty of Waitangi to contemporary times.[18] But by then, students were accessing the wider university and looking for a Māori perspective in a range of subject areas. As a result, courses with a Māori focus emerged outside Māori Studies. Some, but not all, were delivered in Māori language. At the University of Waikato, for example, a Māori Language BA degree covering a range of subject areas was introduced and at Massey University a Baccalaureate of Education degree (Te Aho Tātairangi) taught entirely in Māori was offered as a teacher education option. More frequently, courses with a Māori dimension have been included in undergraduate and postgraduate programmes in Business, Social Work, Psychology, Environmental Studies, Nursing, History, Science and Political Science.

Campus endorsement

Changes have not only been evident within the curriculum. Universities in New Zealand have also adopted Māori names and have incorporated Māori themes into university branding. Marae – traditional cultural meeting places with carved meeting houses – have been constructed on all North Island campuses and are used by staff, students, and local communities for cultural events as well as academic pursuits and formal university occasions such as welcoming new students, 'stay-overs' for visitors, teaching activities and, on occasions, funerals. Marae have added new dimensions to campus life, providing Māori students with a stronger sense of identity and reducing the monocultural bias of universities. In the process other students have had opportunities to participate in marae events, engage with Māori culture, and importantly, establish relationships with Māori students and communities.

Research

Indigenisation of higher education in New Zealand has also led to a vibrant research culture where indigenous methodologies and ethical principles are intertwined with universal approaches. A critical aspect of developing Māori research capability has been the establishment of some twelve Māori research centres in universities, many focused on health research but also on the Māori economy and other facets of Māori development. Training scholarships for emerging Māori researchers have been provided by the Health Research Council of New Zealand and the Foundation for Research Science and Technology since 1993. As a result there is now a critical mass of researchers who have expertise in both Māori research methods and methods derived from western science.

One of the seven centres of research excellence in New Zealand, Ngā Pae o te Māramatanga, is totally committed to developing Māori research capability and conducting multidisciplinary research relevant to Māori communities. Hosted by the University of Auckland, the centre funds a range of research projects and has forged alliances with Māori researchers in other universities as well as national and international research agencies.[19]

At a national level an academic academy, MANU-AO (Māori Academic Networks across Universities in Aotearoa), was launched in 2009 to encourage the elaboration of Māori scholarship and engagement between Māori academics. Senior Māori academics from New Zealand's eight universities jointly oversee the academy. Programmes include weekly video seminars accessible from all campuses, a prestigious lecture series, seminars for academic managers and programmes for Māori professionals, including postgraduate courses.

Governance and management

At the governance level there have also been significant changes. Councils for most tertiary education institutions have Māori members who represent the interests of tribes in the catchment area, or bring a wider Māori voice to the strategic and policy-making functions of councils. The University of Waikato also has a tribal forum, Te Rōpū Manukura, made up of representatives from the eight major tribes in the region. The forum acts as an advisory body to the university council and ensures that there are open conduits between the several Māori communities and the university.[20] In an effort to facilitate maximum entry to higher education, the three South Island universities are also part of a consortium, Te Tapuae o Rehua, made up of tribal representatives and senior managers from tertiary education institutions.

Although Māori make up the entire governance and management structures for wānanga, universities and polytechnics have more recently appointed Māori managers at the corporate level and to a lesser extent at the faculty level. Moreover, at a national level the New Zealand Vice-Chancellors Committee has established a Māori standing committee (Te Kahui Amokura) made up of the senior Māori managers from all eight universities and there is strong interest in establishing a similar body for polytechnics. Meanwhile the wānanga have formed an association (Te Tauihu o ngā Wānanga) where the respective executive officers and council chairs can jointly plan programmes and strategies relevant to all three wānanga. Typically the agenda includes research development, accreditation of qualifications, and funding arrangements.

The context for change

New directions

Transformations in New Zealand's higher education system have occurred in parallel with wider societal changes. Although Māori students have graduated from universities for more than a century, during most of that time the numbers had been disproportionately low and little acknowledgement, academic or institutional, had been given to the significance of being Māori.

Notwithstanding those limitations, the earliest Māori graduates were exceptionally high achievers who played major leadership roles in the life of the nation. Apirana Ngata, the first graduate, obtained a Bachelors Degree in Arts in 1894 and completed a double degree in Arts and Law from the University of Canterbury in 1897.[21] He subsequently entered politics, rising to the position of Acting Prime Minister and Minister of Native Affairs. Ngata was a prolific writer whose literary works retain high significance for modern scholars. Maui Pomare, the second university graduate, obtained the MD degree from an American medical school in 1899. He had a distinguished career in public health and later in politics as Minister of Health.[22] Te Rangi Hiroa (Peter Buck), also a medical graduate, was awarded the degrees of Bachelor of Medicine and Bachelor of Surgery in 1904 and obtained a Doctorate in Medicine in 1909 from the University of Otago. He worked with Pomare in the Department of Public Health, then after spending a brief period in politics became an anthropologist and was eventually appointed Director of the Bishop Museum in Honolulu.[23] His anthropological research in the South Pacific has been widely read and remains in print more than sixty years after being first published.

Others followed, and a cadre of graduates slowly emerged with a sense of commitment to higher education and to Māori. The formation of the Māori Graduates Association in 1965 not only signalled a critical mass of scholars but also gave some indication of how few there actually were; probably less than 100. In contrast, since the mid-1990s, around

1200 Māori students graduate each year from New Zealand universities and other tertiary education institutes.

The obvious transformation in higher education can be largely attributed to wider societal changes (Table 5.2). Having experienced high levels of state dependency following the Great Depression in the mid-1930s, and weathered severe social disruption following urbanisation between 1950 and 1975, a trend towards assimilation into wider New Zealand society and culture seemed inevitable. But a significant shift in aspirations accompanied by parallel changes in policy and practice occurred in the mid-1980s, propelling Māori into a determined effort to participate fully in the economy and in education while at the same time remaining Māori. The assimilatory pathway was rejected and a changing demographic that saw an expanded Māori population added weight to the new direction.

TABLE 5.2 Determinants of change

Catalyst	Impact
Demographic transitions	Increasing proportion of Māori in the total population with larger youthful cohorts
1975 Treaty of Waitangi Act	Legislation and policies draw attention to obligations on the Crown and Crown entities to recognise the principles of the Treaty
1981 Kōhanga reo – Māori language immersion early childhood education	Māori language becomes a spoken language in schools, tertiary education institutions, and in broadcasting and television
The 1984 Hui Taumata – Māori Economic Summit	A shift from state dependency to positive Māori development, self-determination and self-management
1993 Electoral reform	Increase in the number of Māori in Parliament; the emergence of the Māori Party
2002 Tertiary Education Strategy	University have obligations to improve Māori academic achievement

Demographic transitions

A major factor associated with increased Māori participation in higher education has been an increase in the size of the Māori population and a proportionate increase of Māori in the total New Zealand population. After prolonged depopulation and near extinction in the late nineteenth century, a reversal occurred after 1900 and led to a sustained increase in the Māori population which is likely to continue for several decades ahead.[24] Although accounting for some 15 percent of the total New Zealand population in 2006, by 2051 the Māori ethnic population will almost double in size to close to a million, or 22 percent of the total New Zealand population. Even more significant, at least for educational planning, by 2051 of all children in the country 33 percent will be Māori. By then Māori in the working age group, fifteen to sixty-four years, will have increased by 85 percent. Yet although the younger age groups will continue to grow, the population will begin to age, the proportion of men and women over the age of sixty-five years increasing from 3 percent in 1996 to 13 percent in 2051.[25]

Māori development

A renewed determination by Māori to embark on a journey of positive development had been heralded in 1975 but it was more patently evident in 1984 when a Māori economic summit was convened for Māori leaders and tribal elders.[26] The outcome was an agreement with the fourth Labour Government to shift the directions of Māori policy away from state dependency and menial labouring, to economic self-sufficiency, active roles in the delivery of health, social, and educational services, and a commitment to cultural endorsement. Strengthening the cultural base was a major focus that had particular implications for education. Within two decades, for example, Māori language which had been under the threat of extinction became a spoken language for new generations and a medium for education at primary, secondary and tertiary levels.

Language revitalisation was catalysed by the rapid spread of Māori-speaking early childhood centres, and cultural affirmation became an important rationale for the proliferation of Māori service providers. The number of Māori health providers, for example, increased from one in 1984 to over 270 in 2009. Business acumen, managerial skills and experience in governance followed so that by the end of the decade, in 1994, there was strong evidence of a societal transformation characterised by new levels of Māori economic, social, and cultural capability.

Political influence was also boosted following a change in the electoral system in 1993. The first-past-the-post system, which was associated with four Māori electorates regardless of the size of the Māori population, was replaced by mixed member proportional representation and opportunities for minor political parties to enter into coalition with major parties. More than a 100 percent increase in the number of Māori members of Parliament occurred after the 1996 general election, from six Māori members to fifteen.[27] By 2008 Māori political voice had become strong enough for the relatively new Māori Party to enter into a coalition arrangement with the National Party Government.

Treaty of Waitangi

But the societal changes since 1984 have also been influenced by a new Crown commitment to the Treaty of Waitangi. Signed in 1840 by tribal leaders and the British Crown, the Treaty guaranteed tribes the right to retain their own properties, including cultural properties, and to have a degree of autonomy over their own affairs. The fact that the Treaty was largely dismissed by successive governments did not diminish Māori resolve to have it restored as a foundation of New Zealand society, and the passage of the Treaty of Waitangi Act 1975 provided a mechanism for redress and restitution. In addition the Treaty's relevance to social policies, including educational policies, was emphasised in 1988 by the Royal Commission on Social Policy.[28] The Crown's Treaty obligations were seen to apply to all sectors and to extend to agencies funded by the government such as public schools and universities. By 1990, university charters, for example, were expected to show how they would recognise the principles of the Treaty of Waitangi. However, by 2004 there was also a suggestion that quite apart from any Treaty obligation, indigeneity itself was reason enough for government commitment: '... and for these reasons government has policies and programmes that explicitly address the needs of Māori as people who are indigenous to New Zealand'.[29]

Tertiary education strategies

Importantly, government policies for tertiary education have also placed emphasis on Māori academic achievement. In the *Tertiary Education*

Strategy, six strategies were proposed for tertiary education between 2002 and 2007, including a strategy for Māori tertiary achievement. Strategy Two, 'Te Rautaki Mātauranga Māori', prescribed a five year transformational period during which tertiary education contributions to Māori would be reflected in 'a holistic vision of wealth that is cultural, social, economic, environmental and spiritual'. [30]

The subsequent *Tertiary Education Strategy* for the years 2007–12 identified specific implications for Māori across the range of contributions expected from tertiary education – success for all New Zealanders through lifelong learning, creating and applying knowledge to drive innovation, and strong connections between tertiary education organisations and the communities they serve. Similarly it also drew attention to the implications for Māori of the four priority outcome areas: increasing educational success for young New Zealanders, increasing literacy and numeracy levels for the workforce, increasing the achievement of advanced trade, technical and professional qualifications to meet regional and industry needs, and improving research connections and linkages to create economic opportunities. Māori research and Māori enterprise were seen to hold unique opportunities of differentiation in a global market. [31]

Although there was little focus on tertiary education, four areas where Māori educational success could be accelerated were identified in Ka Hikitia: foundation years (early childhood); young people engaged in learning (years 9, 10); Māori language education; and organisational success. [32] Underlying all four were themes of shared responsibility (educators, students, families, government agencies), broad outcomes (the realisation of potential and cultural distinctiveness) and participation (in Māori communities, and national and global communities).

Change and challenge

While Māori continue to have significantly poorer educational outcomes than other New Zealanders, the trend towards a progressive increase in participation in higher education has been apparent for over two decades. The evidence also shows that the transformations in universities and polytechnics have been substantial and pervasive rather than cosmetic and peripheral. However, the extent of change has been accompanied by debate about the implications of indigenisation and concerns about a perceived bias that favours Māori over other groups. While there is fairly widespread agreement that higher education should be available to all sections of the community without prejudice or discrimination, there is less agreement that higher education institutions should make particular provisions for indigenous peoples, at least not without similar provisions being made for other sub-populations.

There are several layers to the debate. At one level, indigeneity is seen to be an ethnic argument and from that perspective the position of Māori is regarded as a variant of wider concerns about the participation of all ethnicities, including Pacific peoples, Asian immigrants and new settlers from other countries. The proposition is that arrangements for Māori should not be different from provisions for other ethnic minorities.

Another argument is built around socio-economic circumstances. Lower levels of Māori participation in higher education are seen to result from cumulative disadvantage rather than cultural, ethnic or racial factors, and in that respect any special provisions for Māori should be based on the same principles of equity that are applied to other groups who are disadvantaged by social adversity.

In a third argument, the lower levels of Māori participation in higher education are described within a context of intelligence, motivation and personal ambition. Individual merit rather than group alliance is seen as the proper concern of universities, and social class, ethnicity and other group characteristics should not intrude on individual worth.

All three arguments have relevance. Māori are an ethnic minority, they often come from disadvantaged backgrounds, and on standard tests do not always meet the usual criteria of merit. Nor would there be serious disagreement with propositions of fairness, equality, and ability to benefit from higher education. However, the indigeneity argument does not hinge on all or necessarily any one of those propositions. Instead, in addition to embracing all three propositions (Māori as an ethnic minority, Māori socio-economic disadvantage, individual Māori motivation), the unique position of indigenous peoples in their own territories has been a major reason for transforming higher education. A strong sense of unity with the environment,[33] a system of knowledge built around experiences with the environment, and a language that is not spoken as a first language elsewhere in the world are the more fundamental characteristics of indigeneity.[34]

From that perspective, fairness is about ensuring that indigenous peoples can participate in higher education without needing to abandon customary approaches to knowledge and scholarship. Moreover, in the pursuit of knowledge, a case can be made for states to have some responsibilities to ensure that languages and cultures native to their own countries are not assimilated or ignored but are afforded some priority. The rationale is less about disadvantage or equity and more about fostering the retention and development of systems of knowledge that are unique within the world.

Successful outcomes for higher education depend on many factors apart from high academic achievement. Education has both personal and public benefits and the charters of tertiary educational institutes in New Zealand accord high priority to the public good. One element of the public good is indigeneity. The Auckland University of Technology (AUT), for example, states that AUT will strengthen its research and workforce capacity in order to 'work alongside Māori communities to identify and provide solutions to the issues, challenges and needs they might have'. There is also an explicit link made to support Māori postgraduate success to progress to academic careers.[35] Similarly the university of Otago has a Māori Strategic Framework which is the key linking point with the wider strategic goals of the university. The university has specifically identified the development of its Māori staff as an area for focus in its Profile for 2008 to 2010.[36] Massey University has adopted a strategy, KIA MAIA, for investing in quality academic outcomes for Māori, building Māori professional capability, increasing Māori research capability and engaging with Māori communities and tribal organisations. The investment strategy is based on the principles of equity, demographic transitions, indigeneity, and Māori potential.[37]

Defining merit solely in terms of the academic merits of individual students, in isolation from other students or the institution's broader social goals, is seriously limiting. In addition to recognising individual qualities, the profile of the total student population must be considered so that the institution as a whole can foster academic advancement, provide society with leadership for the future, and utilise campus diversity to actively create opportunities for inter-ethnic learning experiences.[38] Taking account of ethnic populations helps institutions achieve their mission of promoting academic advancement, having diversity on the campus, and attending to long term societal needs.[39] Factoring indigeneity into the institution's goals and objectives provides a vehicle for addressing the several facets of need associated with indigenous populations and the nation.

In addition to concerns about placing too much emphasis on a Māori dimension within higher education, and from quite another perspective, a number of Māori are uncomfortable with the incorporation of indigenous studies into universities. Along with other indigenous groups they have raised two major concerns.[40] First, because other knowledge systems hold greater sway in academic circles, there is a concern that the integrity of indigenous knowledge will be at risk if it is part of university teaching and research agendas. There is a likelihood that analysis and interpretation will be guided by criteria normally applied to other bodies of knowledge such as science; in the process the underlying veracity will be misrepresented.

A second concern is that indigenous intellectual property will be appropriated by universities. Rights to tribal histories, resources, art, language, poetry, songs and philosophies run the risk of being assigned to researchers and teachers who have 'discovered' them, with little regard for the rights of traditional owners.[41] The possibility of university appropriation is greater because the actual traditional owners are unlikely to be identifiable on a register and there may be an assumption that the lack of clear ownership rights means ownership lies in the public domain.

While both concerns are founded on actual experience and evoke earlier memories of alienation of physical resources such as land, risks can be minimised by the introduction of organisational policies and protocols. In some universities there are already policies that require academic staff to consult with Māori colleagues when Māori data sets are analysed or Māori-centred teaching material is introduced. Moreover, human ethics committees now routinely consider the impacts of research from Māori perspectives and have Māori members who can provide expert opinion. In addition, many research programmes, especially those that have high Māori relevance, employ

Māori researchers or research consultants to assist with both research design and data analysis. To reduce the possibility of appropriation of indigenous knowledge, university policies on intellectual property rights generally provide protective mechanisms that require academics to ascertain ownership. Senior Māori staff are frequently engaged to assist in the process.

Finally, another reason for encouraging the inclusion of indigenous students and indigenous knowledge is related to contemporary indigenous development. Largely as a result of settlements for past injustices, many tribes have acquired substantial land interests, fishing quota, cash investments, and shares in forests. The need for a well qualified workforce that can add value to those assets has never been higher. Universities have the opportunity, if not the obligation, to provide a learning environment where Māori can acquire the knowledge and skills necessary for leading development in the years ahead. Importantly, Māori leaders in the future will need to be well versed in Māori culture and lore, as well as in the universal disciplines of science, business, law and the humanities. In that respect, the most convincing justification for a strong Māori presence in higher education is linked to the national benefits likely to accrue from knowledge creation at the interface between indigenous knowledge, science, philosophy and commerce.

The parameters of social cohesion

Concerns about indigenous inclusion pose important questions about the roles of universities and the parameters of social cohesion. Primarily universities deal with the elaboration of knowledge and are concerned with human beings in all their manifestations. They seek to establish what is common to all groups and what distinguishes one group from another.[42] Social cohesion is a reminder that universities do not exist in isolation of their own distinctive environments. If a main objective of social cohesion for universities is to have a student body that is representative of the community, then an equity perspective can offer a relevant framework. Affirmative action programmes, the provision of scholarships, and focused support services will be useful. If, however, in addition to having students from all sections of the community, a social cohesion goal is about having a university-wide culture that can reflect the values, customs, interests, and aspirations of groups within society, then a framework broader than equity is necessary.

Higher education in New Zealand has adopted the second goal, at least in respect of Māori. Social cohesion has been defined broadly so that a Māori student presence is only one measure of inclusion. Other measures are reflected in university policies and programmes that provide space in the curriculum for Māori knowledge, campus facilities and events that endorse Māori culture and values, Māori staff on the faculty and within support services, research methodologies that incorporate Māori world views, and Māori participation in tertiary education governance and management. Further, the provision of multiple pathways towards higher education have shown that Māori-centred institutions, wānanga, have been able to greatly increase the scope of Māori involvement in tertiary education and offer prospects of progression to higher degrees and research competencies that are distinctly Māori.

The increased social cohesion within higher education has also had impact beyond the campus. While the results of indigenous inclusion in universities and other tertiary education centres have been felt at a number of levels, they have been especially obvious in the expansion of the Māori professional workforce. The number of Māori medical practitioners, for example, has increased from less than fifty before 1984 (0.5 percent of the total medical workforce), to more than 250 in 2008 (2.6 percent) while the number of dentists has increased from four to sixty over the same period of time. The emergence of a large cadre of Māori lawyers, including several judges (two of whom are High Court judges) and the establishment of a Society of Māori Accountants, as well as a Māori Psychologists' Forum, a Māori Nurses' Council, and a Māori Social Workers' Caucus, add further evidence of Māori success in higher education.

But a second major impact of Māori participation in higher education has been the increased interaction between Māori academics and professionals and their non-Māori counterparts. There has been a renewed sense of partnership built around two sets of traditions, two bodies of knowledge and two cultures. The interface between the two approaches has become a rich ground for the expansion of knowledge and enhanced understanding, without assumptions that one approach is necessarily more worthy than the other. As it is for universities, social cohesion within New Zealand communities is premised on wider goals than equity and unqualified inclusion in a homogenous society; there is now evidence that Māori participation in society *as Māori* is also valued. In this respect the foundations have been laid for a society where indigenous perspectives can be factored into the heart of the nation. While the determinants of societal change are many, and include both state policies and global influences, universities have nonetheless played some part in nudging society towards a greater level of cohesion.

Having regard for the relative under-representation of Māori in universities, and especially in the sciences, it is clear that much remains to be done. Yet over the past two decades Māori inclusion has transformed higher education, not only by the greatly increased numbers of students completing postgraduate qualifications, including doctorates, but also by the expansion of knowledge constructed at the interface between western science and indigenous knowledge. The recognition of wānanga as core elements of the tertiary education sector, the establishment of a national Māori centre of research excellence, Ngā Pae o te Māramatanga, and the launch of a national inter-university academy, MANU-AO, to strengthen Māori scholarship, are additional signals that Māori participation in higher education has the potential to add new horizons to tertiary education in New Zealand. In the process, there will be significant gains for wider society and for New Zealand's identity as a modern state within the Asia-Pacific region.

CHAPTER 6

Indigenous Partnerships: The Academy as a Site for Enduring Relationships and the Transmission of Old and New Knowledge

The Inaugural Narrm Oration presented at the launch of the Murrup Barak Melbourne Institute for Indigenous Development, University of Melbourne, Australia, 5 November 2009.

Dual persuasions

The Narrm Oration coincides with the launching of Marrup Barak, the Melbourne Institute for Indigenous Development, and presents an opportunity to consider the more recent journeys of indigenous peoples, and the mutual benefits that might arise from partnerships with universities. Although much can be said about the themes of indigeneity, partnership, academia, knowledge, and leadership, a single conclusion underlies the oration. Simply, bringing together two bodies of knowledge offers better prospects than either one could achieve alone. The concurrence of the two will afford greater opportunities for indigenous peoples to participate in global economies while retaining those elements of custom and culture that will be important to future generations; and in parallel there will be greater incentives for the academy – the university – to create a type of scholarship that will be distinctive, grounded in the Australian landscape, helpful to all learners, and relevant to national if not global goals. In a world where technological innovation and scientific discovery are proceeding at unprecedented rates, the appreciation of different systems of knowledge will be increasingly important so that balance and perspective might accompany approaches to human advancement.

Bringing different bodies of knowledge together does not infer an amalgamation or a fusion of traditions but recognises that together, the elaboration of old knowledge and the creation of new knowledge have the potential to offer fresh insights at a time when communities are struggling to adapt to change and are questioning the whole point of change.

In many ways the coexistence of two bodies of knowledge reflects wider societal changes across all countries. Multinational incursions into Asia, Africa and, closer to home, the small Pacific Island states, have brought with them the prospect of quick fixes but also the risks of submersion in a global net of consumer enticement and a dwindling attachment to the principles that have been at the heart of endurance for earlier generations. Moreover, in the great cities of the world cultural diversity is increasing at a rapid pace but without any clear insights as to how different customs, languages, religions and world views might be reflected in civic, mercantile and educational endeavours, other than by responding to crises and protest. In that respect the deliberate inclusion of indigenous peoples and indigenous knowledge in the academy could bring with it the chance to fashion a model of engagement where the politics of difference can be transformed into the spirit of partnership and the old and the new can be seen as allies rather than adversaries.

It could be argued that in a new world there is no place for old knowledge or that because indigenous knowledge often defies scientific measurement it amounts to little. But the perception of indigenous knowledge and culture as applicable only to the distant past ignores the thrust for development that is part of the indigenous journey and similarly discounts indigenous systems of measurement that can gauge both impact and effectiveness.

The conclusion from this oration, that bringing together two bodies of knowledge offers better prospects than either one could achieve alone, is built around the observation that current models of teaching and research have yet to achieve coherence between disciplines and across subject areas. Too often, for example, economic growth and environmental sustainability have travelled in opposite directions, social equity and individual freedoms have not always reached the same endpoint, enhanced educational achievement has been the preserve of the few, and cultural richness has frequently fallen prey to financial incentive. As institutions that shape attitudes and mould societies, universities are well placed to lead an integrated approach to development and the promotion of social cohesion. The inclusion of indigenous peoples and indigenous knowledge within the academy will represent an important step towards achieving those goals.

Indigenous transitions

From some perspectives, there might be a degree of community scepticism about a partnership with a university but it is as well to remember that the resilience of indigenous populations owes much to an ability to adjust to changing circumstances. The possibility of extinction, widely predicted for Māori in New Zealand towards the close of the nineteenth century, for example, was met by a major rejuvenation of political and tribal leadership, better access to secondary and tertiary education, and a strong network between a small number of Māori graduates from three different universities. Similar demographic trends have also been witnessed in Australia: a rapid decline of the pre-contact population, estimated to be more than a million, followed by a dramatic increase during the twentieth century.[1] As in New Zealand, education has played a major role in the demographic reversal.

In more recent times the vulnerability and the rights of indigenous peoples have taken on a global theme and have become part of a worldwide agenda. In 1949 the UN General Assembly identified a number of characteristics shared by indigenous populations and emphasised the importance of reclaiming native languages and cultures.[2] But for indigenous peoples themselves the retention of indigenous values and customs was not necessarily the most significant goal. Protests in many countries, including the United States of America, Norway, and Canada, highlighted concerns about land ownership, political representation, waterways, and social equity, and made the case for a substantial degree of autonomy over indigenous affairs. Progressively there has been a shift in indigenous aspirations from the 1949 focus on language and culture to a broader platform where the relevance of indigeneity to modern times has been articulated, and the rights of indigenous peoples to participate fully in society, the economy, and education have been championed.

While they constitute approximately 5 percent of the world's population, indigenous peoples made up 15 percent of the world's poor, and are at greater risk for losing their native cultures. Commenting on the prediction that 95 percent of the world's languages will become extinct by the end of the century, Sha Zukang, UN Under-Secretary-General for Economic and Social Affairs, who is also the Coordinator for the Second International Decade of the World's Indigenous People, noted 'That would be a tragedy for indigenous peoples and indeed the world. More than 4000 of the approximately 7000 languages are spoken by indigenous people.'[3]

The modern agenda for indigenous advancement across the globe is probably best reflected in the Declaration of Indigenous Rights. After twenty-two years' preparation the UN General Assembly finally approved the Declaration in 2007. The Declaration addresses both individual and collective rights, cultural rights and identity, rights to education, health, and, among other things, rights to employment. It explicitly encourages harmonious and cooperative relations between states and indigenous peoples, prohibits discrimination against indigenous peoples and promotes their full and effective participation in all matters that concern them. It is a 'fundamentally remedial' instrument that aims to overcome the marginalisation and discrimination that indigenous peoples have systematically faced across the world due to colonisation, conquest and dispossession.

Although the Declaration does not override domestic law it is nonetheless an aspirational statement against which all states, including Australia, Canada, the USA, Samoa and New Zealand, all of whom did not sign it,[4] can measure progress within an international framework. Subsequent to 2007 both Australia and Samoa have endorsed the Declaration.[5] Indeed Australia went further. On 13 February 2008, Prime Minister Kevin Rudd offered an apology to Australia's indigenous peoples that recognised the legacy of trauma and grief they had suffered. That apology marked a beginning in which new hope was possible.

As part of the process of locating indigenous peoples within the context of contemporary societies, rather than within the confines of traditional communities, there has been much legal debate especially in regard to territorial rights, constitutional status, and claims to ownership of physical resources. However, legal criteria by themselves have been found wanting insofar as they are not generally based on indigenous understandings of ownership, entitlement and customary law. In this respect there appears to be a disjunction between common law rights and native title rights.[6]

Rather than seeking redress and recognition only within courts of law, many indigenous peoples are now seeking other avenues that will lead to the recognition and endorsement of their own language, culture and custom, the forward development of their resources, and acquisition of the tools necessary for global citizenship. Building on the foundations laid over the past half century, a new age is looming. In the new era, indigenous participation in modern societies will not only reflect indigenous values, cultures and styles of leadership but will also be measured by high levels of inclusion in the professions, in a wide range of industries, service providers and the arts. The new phase of development will not be premised on socio-economic disadvantage, ethnic minority status, or past grievances but on a capacity to contribute to national and international development in ways that provide a sense of continuity with the past, an ethical framework relevant to addressing tomorrow's challenges, and a sense of place in an increasingly globalised environment. At a time when the globe is threatened by climate change, indigenous world views have the strong potential to add insights into environmental management and eco-conservation, and to refocus the balance between economic and social policies.[7] A transformative spiral that links people closely with the land[8] will provide a new socio-political-economic ontology of 'what is possible' and in the process will lead to gains for nation states and future generations.

A transition from marginalisation to a position of strength in wider society will not reduce the need for greater accommodation of indigenous custom within statutes and policies. But in addition to refocusing the law to meet the diverse customs of increasingly complex modern nations, a significant extension of indigenous engagement with other institutions will also be required. Direct negotiation with government (outside the court room), for example, may be more rewarding than attempting to interpret indigenous knowledge, traditions and aspirations within laws derived from other customs and traditions. Beyond engagement with government, engagement with the private sector, industry, the health and education sectors and the

NGO sector offers greater prospects than always regarding the state as the most appropriate arbiter of indigenous futures.

Understanding partnerships

Importantly, Marrup Barak, the Melbourne Institute for Indigenous Development, is founded on the concept of partnership rather than on one-sided authority or narrowly-defined expertise. A partnership is different from a merger insofar as it does not demand any loss of independence or identity; and a partnership is the antithesis of a takeover where equality is sacrificed for dominance and difference is transformed into sameness. In contrast, partnerships carry the promise of mutual benefits based on mutual contributions. There is a commitment to respect the integrity of the other and to avoid compromising the core values and ideals that are dear to the traditions of each partner. Equality of voice, mutual trust, frequent and regular opportunities for dialogue, and the identification of common goals will strengthen partnerships. But partnerships will be weakened by the expectation of adversarial bargaining or unattainable expectations that must inevitably fail. In the past, indigenous interaction with the state and, for that matter, with other institutions, has not infrequently been marred by patronising assumptions of superiority and the imposition of criteria and standards that lack relevance to the indigenous partner. A shift away from a claims-based model, in which the superiority of the state is assumed, towards a relational model where mutuality prevails, should characterise government relationships with indigenous peoples in the future.[9]

Challenges to effective partnership will not necessarily arise as a consequence of any lack of goodwill or a shortage of adequately worded memoranda, but simply as a result of different understandings about cause and effect, different priorities about what is needed and why, and different aspirations for the future. World views of university academics, for example, rely heavily on measurable evidence, the intrinsic nature of structures, and global validation; whereas the world views of indigenous peoples rely more on the nature and quality of relationships, and consistency with local tribal traditions and values.

In New Zealand, the Waitangi Tribunal introduced partnership as a key principle underlying the Treaty of Waitangi[10] and partnership was also a key principle in the application of the Treaty of Waitangi to social policies.[11] When the Treaty was signed its partners were the Māori tribes and the Crown, each bringing different contributions but united by a determination to work together to build a modern New Zealand as a modern state. Subsequently the partnership model was to be applied to relationships between a wider range of Māori groups (such as urban authorities and Māori schools) and non-governmental agencies such as the churches, research organisations, and the voluntary sector. Inevitably all partnerships have taken time to construct an agenda that addresses both sets of ambitions while recognising the distinctiveness and the benefits that each partner brings. Since 1990 a number of state agencies, including those in health and education, have been required to form partnerships with tribes or other Māori groups and a Treaty compliance clause has been added to many government contracts. However, although partnerships operate within the law they are not necessarily driven by the law; indeed their sustainability may be more a function of the strength of the relationship than any sense of obligation or statutory requirement.

Experience in New Zealand has shown that partnerships have often been confounded by uncertainty as to the most deserving partners. The settlement of Treaty of Waitangi claims, for example, brought forth a host of groups who claimed to have the authority to represent a tribe or a sub-tribe. Although all groups were required to conform to a set process for obtaining a mandate, the process did not always conform to tribal ways of determining authority or representation. As a result Crown processes often led to legitimate tribal representatives competing with splinter groups who had little customary standing and often little direct interest in a particular claim. For its part, the Crown's processes seemed unable to distinguish between legitimate claimants and entrepreneurial dissidents. A related question is whether a partnership makes more sense if it were based on a Māori community group, rather than a tribal group, and if that is the case, which of a number of community groups would be the more relevant.

In similar vein, it has been difficult for Māori to decide the most relevant government agency to partner, and to know whether a national office or a local branch is more logical. Moreover, must a relationship with the Crown be expressed as a series of partnerships with each of the many government departments or is a whole-of-government approach possible? A number of Māori authorities currently labour under a requirement to complete reports for several government departments and to enter into a number of contracts with a range of government services, while dealing with different templates, unsynchronised reporting time frames and repetitive requests for material already submitted to another department. Māori uncertainty about the Crown partnerships is further increased when there are competing interests between similar providers. In the tertiary education sector, for example, Māori communities need to decide the relative merits of partnerships with universities, polytechnics or private academies. Further, given their complexities, does a university partnership encompass all aspects of the university including cross-disciplinary teaching and research or only one or two functions? Is a whole-of-university partnership possible?

Unpacking knowledge

Despite these difficulties and uncertainties, engagement with the knowledge sector can be expected to deliver substantial benefits to indigenous populations in the twenty-first century.[12] The advancement of knowledge over time owes much to four universal tracks: the fight for survival, intuitive trial and error, building on the foundations already established, and the urge for discovery. Advancement over time has been about converting accumulated knowledge into intergenerational wisdom, and fashioning new knowledge to navigate distant horizons. Both of those processes – the application of old understandings on the one hand, and the creation of new pathways on the other – have the potential to heighten appreciation of the nature of the world and to offer greater insights into human potential in the decades ahead. Regrettably, however, pairing bodies of knowledge so that both can be appreciated within their respective paradigms has not always been an academic goal. Instead, as often as not, different systems of knowledge have been subject to suspicion and preconceived assumptions either because they have posed threats to prevailing beliefs or because they have challenged the power hierarchies that assume ownership over knowledge.

More than 400 years ago, for example, the accepted wisdom was that the earth, not the sun, was at the centre of the solar system and everything revolved around our world. But in 1610, a young Italian scholar, Galileo, published a book that seemed to confirm a new theory: the earth was not stationary but travelled around the sun. His conclusions were aided by careful observation of the movements of heavenly bodies using his own invention – the telescope. The views of Galileo, however, were regarded as sacrilege by the Church; they were offensive to the theological teachings about the central place of humans in the grand scheme of things, and as a result he was tried and convicted of heresy, being forced to spend his latter years under house arrest.

The reason for highlighting Galileo's predicament was not to discredit the Church and its teachings but to illustrate that there is more than one way of looking at the world or, for that matter, acquiring knowledge. Galileo was caught in the middle of two knowledge systems. As a scientist he went headlong into conflict with the guardians of the prevailing great body of knowledge, religious faith, and was forced to curtail further experimentation. Now, some four centuries later, the situation has been largely reversed. The world of science has advanced so rapidly that in the twenty-first century scientific knowledge has gained greater credibility than religious knowledge, at least in the western world. At the same time, dismissing religious knowledge as irrelevant or out of touch with current realities, simply because it does not conform to the same rules as science, would be as short-sighted as dismissing Galileo because he had used a telescope to make a fundamental discovery about the dynamics of the solar system.

There is no single body of knowledge that can provide the total insights necessary for human advancement. Moreover, there are few opportunities to study at the interface between bodies of knowledge. Even when interface learning does occur it is all too often accompanied by vigorous efforts to apply the criteria of one system in order to rationalise the basis for the other. In the process validity and integrity are distorted, if not lost. That point was well made by Professor Ian Anderson in the 1993 Boyer lecture: 'Koori life experience and medical practice are not diametrically opposed.... However, the skills required in getting consensus are not intuitive. Nor are they necessarily facilitated by traditional modes of clinical interaction.'[13]

The establishment of Marrup Barak, the Melbourne Institute for Indigenous Development, therefore represents a significant development in the search for knowledge. It signals a move away from a parallel approach where different bodies of knowledge are locked into trajectories that never meet, towards a set of interacting pathways where a mix of ideas, values, and methodologies become available to accelerate inventiveness and add perspective to the human condition. An institute built on the several strands of indigenous knowledge together with the several disciplines of science, economics, jurisprudence, medicine, and the humanities, will have the potential to shape knowledge and inspire discovery in ways that have hitherto been unrealised.

Untangling the interface

Debates about the relative validity of science or indigenous knowledge are usually conducted on the assumption that one is inherently more relevant than the other. In practice, however, it is not unusual for scientists or indigenous peoples to live comfortably with the contradictions of different bodies of knowledge. Many scientists subscribe to religious beliefs that cannot be explained by science, and many indigenous people use scientific principles in everyday life while at the same time holding fast to indigenous values. There are an increasing number of indigenous researchers who use the interface between science and indigenous knowledge as a source of inventiveness and, rather than seeking to prove the superiority of one system over another, are more interested in identifying opportunities for combining both.

For example, the outcomes of new knowledge are most often measured by gains in economic growth, environmental sustainability, social wellbeing, and cultural integrity. However, the same outcome indicators are not necessarily applicable across all populations or cultures. While some indicators, such as life expectancy, have universal relevance, there are also outcomes that can only be measured by taking account of indigenous perspectives. If, for instance, land is valued simply as a function of market prices or economic yield, the indigenous values attaching to land and land tenure will be marginalised. The application of economic models to assess health outcomes may also be limited when it comes to evaluating indigenous health programmes.

Building social infrastructure and increasing social cohesion are important aspects of indigenous health services but economics are not good at measuring social networks. There may be no measurable health outcome but a coherent social infrastructure will increase access to services and a positive response to health messages.[14] Yet despite the difficulties in measuring outcomes, Māori-specific outcome measures have been developed for health interventions[15] as well as wider developmental programmes that impact on the human domain and the resource domain.[16]

Principles

A number of principles underlie 'learning and research at the interface' but based on Māori experience, four principles have particular implications for both policy and practice: mutual respect, shared benefits, human dignity, and discovery.[17]

The first principle, mutual respect, endorses the world view of each partner. Essentially mutual respect recognises the validity of both knowledge systems – indigenous knowledge and science – and accepts that each needs to be given its own space. Practitioners of one system are not necessarily equipped to interpret meanings that arise from the other, but can agree to have a collaborative relationship whereby each adds original and different dimensions in order to jointly create a new construct. Mutual respect extends to recognising different levels of expertise and alternate credentialing processes as well as different appreciations of evidence and information transfer.

A second principle, shared benefits, reverses outmoded assumptions about learning and research that often left indigenous peoples as passive respondents who derived little or no benefit from the research.[18] Regarding indigenous peoples as active participants in educational and research processes, however, requires that short and long term benefits for their communities are given explicit consideration. A major loss of confidence in higher institutes of learning such as universities occurred when the benefits were not clear, except to academics, and indigenous communities felt both exploited and devalued in a process that disregarded their own views and their own autonomy. A share in the benefits of new knowledge also has particular implications for the assignment of intellectual property and commercialisation of research findings.

Human dignity is an important principle for both teaching and research.[19] While often discussed in connection with research participants, it can also be applied to relationships between teachers and learners, to research teams and communities, and between members of research teams. The principle of human dignity implies that although world views may not be shared, or might be challenged, personal integrity and cultural identity should not be devalued or lightly dismissed because they do not accord with the belief systems of some academics.[20] Human dignity takes into account the world views of individuals and populations; it has ethical connotations and particular implications for the way teaching and research programmes are designed, implemented, and applied without compromising spiritual beliefs.[21]

The fourth principle, discovery, emphasises both exploration and invention. Discovery of new knowledge is at the heart of all research endeavours. In research at the interface, however, discovery owes its innovation to insights drawn from two knowledge systems that have moved together in directions not possible by recourse to one system only. As well, in addition to the notion of breakthrough, discovery also carries the concept of future. Sometimes indigenous knowledge is regarded as unchanging and essentially relevant to the past. That view, however, is often a product of attempts to relegate first peoples to a pre-colonial era and overlooks the expansion of knowledge by indigenous peoples as they explored their environments, developed theories about social relationships and drew conclusions about the nature of the universe. No culture is static and indigenous knowledge systems carry a formula for exploring the future, for understanding the nature and origin of phenomena, the connections and relationships between phenomena, and the trends that occur with phenomena.[22]

Indigenous capability

The application of partnership principles has the potential to generate new levels of indigenous capability – university graduates who will take their places in the several professions of teaching, medicine, business, the law, environmental management – while at the same time remaining close to their own people and contributing to their advancement. To a large extent the realisation of that potential will depend on wise leadership and trusting relationships between leaders. In turn, effective leadership requires courage to move beyond institutional conventions whether they be exercised within indigenous zones of comfort or inside the hallowed halls of learning, and to embrace difference as a source of inventiveness rather than a cause for suspicion. Indigenous partnerships have sometimes faltered because leaders have not been ready enough to acknowledge the parameters of effective leadership in other cultures or to recognise the tensions imposed between leaders and their followers when relationships outside the accepted norm are being established. Leaders must be wise on two fronts: they must be able to establish relationships with each other; and they must be able to persuade their own people that a partnership with another group will bring beneficial results not otherwise attainable.

Moreover, the days of charismatic leadership, focused on one or two leaders, have increasingly given way to leadership networks, distributed leadership, and strategic leadership where the future rather than the past is afforded greater attention.[23] Indigenous leadership networks extend across tribes, mobs, and communities and also across sectors, disciplines and subject areas. Sectoral development that places health, education, justice, housing and the environment in discrete silos is antithetical to cultures where holism is the basis for world views. Indigenous leadership networks also have a strong international basis; partnerships between indigenous groups across the globe have already demonstrated how common philosophies, histories, and aspirations can be harnessed to create new pathways and a sense of global solidarity.

As leaders in the academy, indigenous teachers and researchers play crucial roles in straddling the divide between western academic teaching and research and indigenous knowledge.[24] They have access to indigenous populations, and also to two systems of knowledge. They are equally aware of the rules for engagement with indigenous communities and the demands of robust methodologies.[25] At the same time they face potential criticism from two fronts. Indigenous communities may feel that indigenous academics are tainted by western academic conventions and have become somewhat detached from actual indigenous experiences.[26]

Academics, on the other hand, may complain that indigenous approaches introduce unnecessary variables such as ethical requirements which limit the integrity of their studies and confuse scientific principles with political imperatives. Both criticisms imply that pluralism at the interface will weaken integrity and undermine identity. However, provided there is sound grounding in the two methodological streams, and clarity about the contribution that each can make, the risks can be minimised.

In addition to academic staff who can relate to the indigenous situation and to indigenous students, success will also be determined by the overall campus experience. Unless the wider culture of the learning environment can impart a sense of home, it will fail to capture sustained indigenous attention. Strengthening identity and developing a sense of empowerment can be facilitated through designated physical spaces, social events, and counselling programmes that aid the transition from native communities to university and later to professional life.[27]

Building a strong professional indigenous workforce has been an important goal in New Zealand especially in health, law, business, and teaching. While there is no guarantee that a Māori professional practitioner will necessarily be wise in indigenous ways, there is a greater likelihood of the practitioner being part of indigenous networks and therefore being in a position to appreciate indigenous values and to work comfortably with indigenous peoples as well as professional communities.

Similar efforts have been directed at increasing the Māori academic workforce and establishing a network of well qualified researchers. Although recruiting indigenous health researchers is difficult, especially in areas such as health economics, substantial gains have been made in recent years.[28] A major milestone for New Zealand research was the establishment of two Māori health research centres in 1993 at Massey University and the University of Otago. Both addressed health concerns of high relevance to Māori and both afforded priority to doctoral training for Māori researchers. In 2002 a further milestone was the establishment of Ngā Pae o te Māramatanga, a centre for research excellence at the University of Auckland. The centre provides a focus for interface research across a number of tertiary educational institutes and is actively promoting the development of a large cohort of Māori doctorate graduates. More recently, in 2009 an inter-university academy for Māori academics was established. MANU-AO (Māori Academic Networks across Universities in Aotearoa) is governed by senior Māori managers from each university and organises weekly live video seminars to all campuses as well as sponsoring a prestigious lecture series, hosting subject area seminars, promoting collaboration between Māori professionals (in for example health, education, law, and accountancy), and conducting professional development courses for career academics. MANU-AO has been especially important for academics working in relative isolation and provides entry into a wide network of Māori scholars. It has the active support of all university vice-chancellors.

The promise of partnership

This oration has touched on some of the considerations that will be important to indigenous development in the future and especially indigenous partnerships that might accelerate development. In summary, five key themes have been advanced: indigenous transitions, enduring relationships, knowledge creation, leadership, and participation.

The first theme, indigenous transitions, recognises that over the past twenty-five years strong foundations have been laid for major transformations of indigenous communities, capabilities and economies. States have progressively recognised the special significance of indigenous populations, not only as bridges to past traditions and ancient wisdoms, but also as contributors to future development.

While retaining a level of autonomy is a high indigenous priority, the second theme revolves around an increasing realisation of the benefits that can accrue from indigenous relationships with other entities within the state and beyond. Especially important has been the development of relationships with the knowledge sector. Education in all its forms and with all the accompanying technology has been identified as a major highway for the next phase of indigenous development.

In that respect, the third theme, indigenous partnerships with universities, is about unleashing potential and promoting sustainable social, cultural, economic and environmental transformations. The Melbourne Institute for Indigenous Partnerships is well placed to play a leadership role by providing a forum where the knowledge resources of the university can be brought alongside the knowledge resources of indigenous communities.

The fourth theme identifies the interface between the two knowledge systems as a rich source of discovery and innovation with mutual gains and flow-on benefits to wider society. It also offers benefits to the nation and in that respect will contribute to the Australian Prime Minister's aspiration for 'a new era of relations between states and indigenous peoples'.[29] A key to success will be the way in which leaders in the institute can gain the support of their followers and build enduring relationships with leaders in other parts of the university, with other indigenous community leaders and indigenous leaders in other countries.

Finally, the fifth theme considers the future. While the past twenty-five years have been about securing a place in modern societies, the next twenty-five years will build on those foundations so that indigenous peoples, as members of increasingly global societies, can retain the customs and resources which are at the heart of their culture while at the same time participating fully in education, the economy and the development of a national agenda for the future.

'Kia tau hoki te marino
Kia tipu ake te mātauranga,
Kia puāwai ngā moemoeā ā rātou mā,
i roto i te kotahitanga me te whakapono.'
'May peace and calm always be with us,
May knowledge and learning forever grow,
And may the dreams of those who have since departed, be realised
In a spirit of unity and trust.'

Māori Development

CHAPTER 7

Race and Ethnicity in Public Policy: Does it Work?

Presented at the Social Policy, Research & Evaluation Conference 2004, What Works?, Wellington, 25 November 2004.

What works?

In keeping with the theme of the Social Policy, Research and Evaluation Conference 2004, 'What Works?', this paper asks a single question: do policies based on race or ethnicity work? It is unlikely to produce a straightforward or unequivocal answer, not because there is a dearth of research about the impacts of policies on race and ethnicity, or any lack of experience with race-based policies in New Zealand, but because 'what works' depends as much on who asks the question as who answers it. How should a good result be measured? Does it 'work' if it meets the objectives of the policy? Or should it be assessed according to a set of higher order principles capable of transcending political ideologies and good intentions? Or should the question have been asked from another perspective: do policies that purport to be neutral to race and ethnicity work?

Although race and ethnicity are often used interchangeably they are not identical in meaning. Whereas race has connotations of biological variation and genetic determinism, ethnicity emphasises social and cultural distinctiveness and places greater importance on world views, lifestyles and societal interaction. Furthermore, a particular type of race and ethnicity is indigeneity. There are some 5000 indigenous groups around the world with a total population of about 200 million, or around 4 percent of the global population. A long-standing bond with the land and the natural environment is the fundamental feature of indigeneity, and arising from that ecological relationship it is possible to identify five secondary characteristics of indigeneity – time, culture, an indigenous system of knowledge, environmental sustainability, and a native language.

Before attempting to answer the question about the effectiveness of race-based policies, it is worth recalling that 2004 is a significant year for New Zealand. It marks the 150th anniversary of the opening of Parliament. After the signing of the Treaty of Waitangi in 1840 when Britain assumed sovereignty and tribes ceded the right to govern to the Crown, New Zealand initially became a Dependency of New South Wales. But the following year, in 1841, the constitutional position changed from a dependency to a Crown colony, governed now by the British Parliament. Further constitutional change was heralded in a British statute, the New Zealand Constitution Act 1852, which provided for New Zealand to establish its own legislature and act as a self-governing colony. Two years later, in 1854, Parliament opened in Auckland and in 1865 was relocated to Wellington.

The English Laws Act 1854

One of the first pieces of legislation passed by the new settler Parliament was the English Laws Act. In a single statute the Act made all English laws binding in New Zealand with a proviso, introduced in 1858, that the English laws applied only so far as they were applicable to the circumstances of New Zealand. (In fact throughout the nineteenth century there were few cases where English law was held to be inapplicable unless the New Zealand legislature had specifically enacted contrary legislation.) It was an economic use of parliamentary time that spared the colonial politicians the task of developing a whole raft of laws specific to the new colony. Instead it was largely taken for granted that if the laws worked in England, they should work in New Zealand. New Zealand therefore not only inherited aspects of the British legal and constitutional systems, but common law and statute law also. Thus, although the Imperial Laws Application Act 1988 clarified which Imperial/United Kingdom statutes should continue to have legal force in New Zealand, acts such as the Habeus Corpus Act 1679, and the Bill of Rights 1688 are still applicable to New Zealand.[1]

Part of the Crown's rationale for assuming sovereignty over New Zealand had been expressly to institute British law so that Māori tribes would be protected from unruly settlers and settlers would be forced to live up to their obligations as law-abiding British subjects. As it transpired, however, British law was less protective than well-intentioned humanitarian officials in the Colonial Office had contemplated; if anything the law was to be used as a mechanism to advance settler interests regardless of impacts on Māori.

But in 1854 when Parliament opened, the prospect that Māori understandings of justice and fairness would be different in any way from those held by the English did not enter parliamentary conscience. The English Laws Act represented a peculiar mixture of patronage and arrogance. On the one hand it implemented a goal identified in the preamble to the Treaty of Waitangi to 'establish a settled form of Civil Government with a view to avert the evil consequences which must result from the absence of the necessary Laws and Institutions, alike to the native population and to Her [Majesty's] subjects.' Yet on the other hand there was no indication that tribal lore might be based on alternate concepts of right and wrong, or different approaches to ownership, civil responsibility and societal decision-making.

English laws are founded on notions of the common law. And the common law is simply an expression of community regard for right and fair. In that sense the common law is a measure of English culture as it has evolved over centuries. English common law today differs from what it was in 1840 so that the death penalty could hardly be regarded now as an expression of common law or contemporary English culture. But the point is that law and culture are intimately linked and English law in 1854 was as much a product of an ethnic English culture as Māori lore was a product of tribal world views. From that perspective the English Laws Act 1854 was New Zealand's first race-based policy. Built on the presumption that English common law had a universal dimension, the culture, customs and conventions of Britain were imposed on all New Zealanders to the benefit of a few (at that time Māori outnumbered settlers).

This might be a good time to return to the earlier question. Do policies based on race and ethnicity work? From the perspective of the coloniser the English Laws Act worked very well. It introduced a series of racially inspired reforms into New Zealand and laid the foundations for a policy environment within which English common law was the norm and Māori common law (culture) was the problem. Land tenure, criminal law, taxation policies, fishing policies and the authority of the Crown had more or less worked in Britain and were now to work in New Zealand. Even before a decade after the introduction of the Act, however, Māori had concluded that the new policies were not working for them. They protested that their understandings of land ownership, customary fishing, and tribal authority were at odds with the new laws. But their protest was interpreted as defiance of the very law they opposed. It was not entirely surprising therefore that war should break out, which it did in 1860.

Māori-specific policies

In order to address Māori custom that was at odds with English custom/common law, successive parliaments introduced legislation and policies that were race-based. Māori-specific legislation can be categorised according to the objectives of policy and the impacts on Māori. Whether the laws worked or not depends on whether they are measured against the achievement of parliamentary objectives or against the impacts as experienced by Māori.

Three major objectives and three domains of impact can be identified. Broad objectives of Māori-specific policies have included the limitation or extinguishment of Māori interests, the restoration of Māori interests, either through compensatory payments or the return of resources, and the protection of Māori interests. The domains of impact on Māori encompass impacts on property, culture and a Māori polity.

An analysis of Māori-specific policies and legislation based on an objectives/impact matrix shows that inconsistent political priorities for Māori have resulted in oscillations between policies of assimilation, and policies that support the retention and development of Māori interests (Table 7.1).

However, by far the greatest impact of Māori-specific provisions in legislation, mostly enacted in the nineteenth century, has been to limit or extinguish Māori interests. As a result a range of compensatory mechanisms became necessary more than a century later. Some of the motivation for limiting Māori interests can be tracked to different

TABLE **7.1** Māori-specific legislation, domains of impact and objectives

Objectives	Domains of impact (examples of legislation)		
	Property	*Culture*	*Polity*
	For example land, forests, waterways, fisheries.	Māori values, custom, language, knowledge, and social arrangements	Māori tribal and political organisation.
Provisions that limit or extinguish Māori interests	Maori Affairs Amendment Act 1967 Coal Mine Act 1903 Oyster Fisheries Act 1866.	Tohunga Suppression Act 1907	Maori Representation Act 1867
Provisions that restore or compensate for losses	Treaty of Waitangi (Fisheries Claim) Settlement Act 1992	Maori Language Act 1987	Te Runanga o Ngai Tahu Act 1999
Provisions that protect and develop Māori interests	Ture Whenua Māori Act 1993	Children Young Persons and their Families Act 1989 Resource Management Act 1991	Runanga Iwi Act 1990 Electoral Act 1993

understandings of customary rights and the relative bluntness of a system of law, derived from English cultural experience, to address Māori systems of tenure and organisation. Even in modern times there is a great deal of uncertainty as to whether a determination of Crown ownership over natural resources based on the English common law is consistent with interpretations of indigenous property rights.

A number of social policy statutes including the Education Act 1989, the Broadcasting Act 1989, and the Mental Health (Compulsory Assessment and Treatment) Act 1992 make specific provisions for Māori, and the Public Health and Disability Act 2000 contains a Treaty of Waitangi provision. But the inclusion of a Treaty clause into legislation or the addition of another Māori-specific reference is not generally based on granting additional rights to Māori individuals, but is rather to ensure that the same rights (such as the right to receive a sound education that does not sideline Māori perspectives, or to enjoy television programmes in one's own language, or to receive an adequate psychiatric assessment) can be guaranteed, taking into account Māori cultural values, processes, and protocols. For the most part, the majority population takes those rights as givens.

Socio-economic disadvantage and ethnicity

Recent debate about race-based policies in New Zealand has revealed a general lack of understanding about the objectives of policies, their application, and measures of effectiveness. Two sets of policies linked to social service delivery, and affirmative action programmes respectively, illustrate some of the misunderstandings.

First, policies that provide for Māori – or other ethnic groups – to deliver social services to their own people or to target ethnic groups have been criticised on the grounds that they lead to a form of advantage which other New Zealanders do not have. The argument against specific ethnic provision is based on the goal of equity as between individuals and makes a case for a needs-based approach which is race and ethnic neutral. Within the needs-based approach universality is emphasised and contextual variables are minimised or dismissed. Each person is to be treated equally according to 'need', regardless of wider societal associations.

In practice, however, the distinctions between individual needs, wider societal contexts, and ethnic affiliation are not so clear. The association between material disadvantage and ethnicity, especially among some ethnic minorities, has been well established in a number of studies. Compared to other New Zealanders, Māori and Pacific peoples have higher rates of unemployment, smaller household incomes, lower participation rates in early childhood and university education; their children are more likely to live in a lone parent family, not to be immunised, to have no parent in paid work and to live in a household in the lowest income quintile. In addition, life expectancy is significantly lower and mortality rates are higher. However, the strong relationship between ethnicity and adverse socio-economic circumstances has sometimes led to an assumption that one is a proxy measure for the other. Being Māori, for example, is often seen as a synonym for being poor, and being poor is sometimes seen as the distinguishing characteristic of Māori and Pacific peoples.

While there is a significant correlation between the two measures – ethnicity and socio-economic status – they do not measure the same phenomena. Needs-based policies and policies of equity as between individuals have tended to regard ethnicity and race as significant only insofar as they might be subsumed under universal indicators such as social class, life expectancy, and educational achievement. Recent research, however, has demonstrated that not only is class distinguishable from ethnicity, but that universal indicators by themselves are insufficient measures of need and outcome. Moreover, as one of five features of best practice in health policies and programmes, a World Health Organisation paper stresses the importance of ethnicity by recognising benefits to, and empowerment of, ethnic communities. (The other four features of best practice are health sector involvement in the policy process, civic society leadership and participation, financial sustainability, and a comprehensive health perspective basis.)[2]

Based on an analysis of socio-economic and ethnic data, three types of ethnic inequalities in health have been described: the distribution gap (Māori are not distributed evenly across all deprivation deciles and are overly represented in the very deprived neighbourhoods [deciles 8-10]); the outcome gap (Māori health outcomes are worse even after controlling for deprivation); and the gradient gap (socio-economic hardship impacts more heavily on Māori).[3] Māori who live in the most affluent areas, for example, have health outcomes that are similar to non-Māori living in the most deprived areas. The study confirms that quite apart from social class, ethnicity is a determinant of health outcomes. An intervention framework to improve health and reduce inequalities therefore recommended structural interventions that affirm power relationships as well as Māori health provider development; health and disability services that recognise cultural needs; and improved ethnic data collection.[4]

In a report on mental health outcomes, it was also shown that deprivation (socio-economic disadvantage) did not entirely explain the greater severity of mental disorders among Māori. Despite having similar levels of deprivation, Māori consumers were more likely than other groups to have higher levels of severity and lower levels of functioning. Further, in contrast to the general population, Māori who were living in areas of least relative deprivation were more likely to have higher levels of severity and lower levels of functioning than those living in areas of greater deprivation. Although bias on the part of researchers could have contributed to that unexpected finding, it might also have reflected a greater sense of cultural dislocation by Māori living in more affluent areas where there was less close contact with family networks and community support agencies.[5]

The relative roles of material circumstances and ethnicity have also received attention in respect of Māori educational outcomes. Family income and associated social and economic factors are significant determinants of outcomes and many researchers have concluded that once socio-economic differences are taken into account, there are no differences between Māori and other New Zealanders. However, instead of focusing on socio-economic differences, other researchers have examined the role of culture and language in outcomes and have concluded that there is often a mismatch between the culture of the school and the ethnic cultures of learners.[6] Both learners and teachers may make assumptions about 'normal' that implicitly exclude Māori while processes such as assessment can provide legitimisation for deficit views effectively 'disabling' minority children.[7] Evidence therefore suggests that difference in the educational outcomes of Māori children cannot be explained entirely on family incomes or class; the centrality of ethnicity and culture to outcome is a factor in its own right.[8] Deficit assumptions by teachers towards Māori have hampered progress but when they have been addressed higher levels of achievement have been demonstrated even in low decile schools. In other words while family income, poverty, and social class have a confounding effect, ethnicity is also a relevant determinant of outcome.[9]

Ethnic explanations for disparities may be grouped into two major categories. First, there are explanations that arise from the characteristics of ethnic groups themselves – genetic predisposition (though relatively few differences are determined by genetics); customary beliefs, and cultural practices. Second, however, there are a group of explanations that arise outside ethnic groups, and reflect the way society reacts to people who are different from the majority. They may show discriminatory behaviour in the provision of services and access to economic opportunities, or reactions based on stereotyped preconceptions, or frank rejection of ethnic cultural values and aspirations. All of these factors will influence social outcomes.[10]

Affirmative action

A second area of contemporary debate concerns the maintenance of affirmative action programmes based on race and ethnicity. There are a number of programmes that provide targeted assistance to Māori and Pasifika students either through government scholarships and bursaries, operational grants to tertiary education institutions (for example, the 'Special Supplementary Grant'[11]), or preferential entry into academic programmes. As a matter of interest, it is worth noting that 2004 is the centennial year of the graduation of Te Rangi Hiroa (Peter Buck) who was the first Māori to graduate from the University of Otago. Along with Tutere Wirepa, he was a recipient of a government grant made available specifically for Māori who wished to study medicine. The purpose of the grant was primarily to improve Māori health. Both the Otago and Auckland universities still have entry schemes that enable a limited number of Māori and Pacific students to enter medical school without necessarily having the same academic profiles as other students.

Criticism of programmes such as these has been made on two grounds. First, there has been a suggestion that Māori and Pacific students who enter tertiary education under a preferential scheme are allowed to graduate with lesser standards. Clearly that view represents a gross distortion. While different criteria might be used to justify admission, once admitted, students undertake similar course work, sit the same examinations and meet the same qualifying standards.

Second, the case has been made for all students to be admitted on 'merit'. Merit appears to mean that academic criteria should be the sole determinant of admission. The need for a non-Māori student with high grades to forfeit a place to a Māori student with lower grades seems wrong to those who associate academic performance with academic right. However, successful educational outcomes depend on many factors apart from earlier academic achievement. Moreover, the purpose of ethnically-based preferential entry schemes is not simply to have more Māori or Pacific doctors but for educational institutions to make a contribution to society.

Education has both personal and public benefits and the charters of many tertiary educational institutes accord high priority to the public good. In the University of Otago charter, for example, 'the enhancement, understanding and development of individuals and society' is part of the university's mission and a contribution to both Māori development and the development of Pacific peoples is highlighted.[12] In addition, in a discussion document on tertiary education priorities, the Tertiary Education Commission has identified 'working to national goals' as one of three major themes.[13]

While it makes sense to ensure that students accepted into a programme are going to be able to meet the required academic standards, it may be more meritorious to admit students who will help institutions achieve their public goals and meet charter obligations to provide for future societal leadership. It is both simplistic and short-sighted to define merit solely on the academic merits of individual students, in isolation from other students or the institution's broader social goals. In that respect it may be perfectly fair to reject a student because too many others like him or her have already been enrolled at the expense of diversity and institutional goals for a better society.

There are, therefore several criteria that should be considered in educational admission policies (Table 7.2). In addition to recognising individual qualities, the profile of the total student population must be considered so that the institution as a whole can foster academic advancement, contribute positively to the campus learning experience, and provide society with leadership for the future. Taking account of race and ethnicity helps institutions achieve their mission of promoting academic advancement, having diversity on the campus, and attending to long term societal needs.[14]

TABLE **7.2** A 'merit matrix'

The institutional mission:	Priority for students who will:		
	succeed academically	contribute to the campus learning experience	provide societal leadership in the future
• individuals			
• campus			
• society			

Conclusion

There are two main reasons why, alongside other factors (such as socio-economic status, government goals, equity and fairness), race and ethnicity should be identified as rationales for policy in their own right. First, there have been recent suggestions in New Zealand that a needs-based formula centred on individuals and their socio-economic status will suffice to meet policy requirements in health, education and social policy generally. Clearly that approach is inconsistent with the evidence and tends to assume that ethnicity is a function of economic need rather than a determinant of lifestyle, culture, and social organisation. Second, an increasing diversity of ethnic affiliations is a characteristic of modern New Zealand. Because race-based policies in the past have been used to disadvantage Māori more often than to create advantage, race-based policies need not be unfair. Instead, while race and ethnicity play such large roles in societies like New Zealand, it is illusionary to act as if they were non-existent.

To return to the question asked at the beginning of this paper as to whether policies based on race or ethnicity work, the answer largely depends on the identification of policy goals and the instruments used to measure impacts. A framework for considering race and ethnic based policies can be shaped around goals and indicators (Table 7.3). Three broad goals can be identified in current ethnic and race-based policies: full participation in society, education and the economy (the participatory goal); certainty of access to indigenous culture, networks and resources by indigenous people (the indigeneity goal); and fairness between members of society (the equity goal).

TABLE **7.3** Goals and indicators

	Individual indicators		Population indicators		Comparative indicators	
	Universal	*Specific*	*Universal*	*Specific*	*Inter-population*	*Intra-population*
Participatory goal						
Indigeneity goal						
Equity goal						

In practice, indicators tend to be based on aggregated individual measures and often use the Pākehā population as a benchmark for inter-ethnic comparisons. However, three shortcomings arise from those approaches. First, while many indicators such as life expectancy have universal application, others are specific to particular populations or groups. Health outcome measures, for example, should not only reflect clinical indicators, but also the health perspectives arising from specific ethnic world views. Second, while measurements based on individual circumstances such as educational experience are in common use, less use has been made of collective measures whether they are linked to groups such as families or to whole ethnic populations. Third, comparisons between Māori and non-Māori populations may not be the most useful set of measures. Instead comparisons over time or comparisons between urban migrants and rural Māori communities may be more informative. Comparing the health of Pacific peoples in New Zealand with health standards on Pacific islands may also provide more useful indicators of adaptability than comparisons with non-Pacific New Zealanders.

In short, indicators should be able to capture both the individual and the group; they should include universal measures and population-specific measures; and the comparative indicators should be capable of reflecting the significance of ethnicity.

Political ideologies that promote individual freedom as the foundation of modern society fail to acknowledge that societies are built on individuals who belong to groups – families, iwi, communities and races. Socialists, on the other hand, see society through different eyes – but although they are more inclined to recognise that groups are foundational to society, they have tended to place greater emphasis on class than either race or ethnicity.

For whatever reason, it is misleading to develop policies, programmes and practices that purport to be 'blind' to race and ethnicity. Unless ethnicity is explicitly acknowledged, covert policies will mask diversity, compromise best outcomes, and foster an assimilatory approach. The New Zealand reality is that an increasingly large number of people have an indigenous or ethnic orientation that underlies both personal and collective identity, provides pathways to participation in society, and largely influences the ways in which societal institutions and systems respond to their needs.

CHAPTER 8

Māori Achievement: Anticipating the Learning Environment

Presented at the fourth Hui Taumata Mātauranga, Taupō, 5 September 2004.

The Hui Taumata Mātauranga

The year of the fourth Hui Taumata Mātauranga, 2004, coincides with the 150th anniversaries of two of New Zealand's long-standing institutions. The first session of the New Zealand Parliament was held in 1854, and Te Aute College, the oldest surviving Māori school, also took its first pupils in 1854. In quite distinctive ways both institutions have contributed to Māori development and their paths have crossed on many occasions. The Young Māori Party for example, which arose out of the Te Aute Students' Association, actively encouraged its members to seek political office, and three members, Apirana Ngata, Te Rangi Hiroa and Maui Pomare successfully won seats between 1905 and 1911. The year 2004 also marks the centennial of the graduation of Te Rangi Hiroa from the University of Otago, the first Māori to graduate from that university.

One hundred and fifty years later, this hui has had the opportunity to view success from different perspectives and from different generations, and to consider how Māori and the Crown, together, might make a difference for future generations.

In February 2001 the first Hui Taumata Mātauranga provided a framework for considering Māori aspirations for education. It resulted in 107 recommendations based around the family, Māori language and custom, quality in education, Māori participation in the education sector and the purpose of education. There was also wide agreement about three goals for Māori education:

- to live as Māori
- to actively participate as citizens of the world
- to enjoy good health and a high standard of living.

The second hui, in November 2001, discussed leadership in education and examined several models for Māori educational authority. In addition, the contribution of other sectors to Māori educational success – and failure – was acknowledged. At all hui participants agreed that education could not be considered in isolation of other sectors and other aspects of positive Māori development. Five platforms for educational advancement were identified:

- educational policies of the state
- broader social and economic policies and a mechanism for assessing the educational impacts of all social and economic policies
- the relationship between Māori and the Crown
- Māori synergies
- leadership.

In March 2003, the third Hui Taumata Mātauranga focused on the quality of teacher education and the tertiary education sector. In addition, the interface between te ao Māori (the Māori world) and te ao whānui (the global world) was contextualised as a place where the curriculum, workforce development, quality assurance and relationships were shaped by:

- the exercise of control
- the transmission of world views
- participation in decision making
- multiple benefits.

Hui Taumata Mātauranga IV

Whereas the three earlier Hui Taumata Mātauranga had been led by education planners and providers, and as a result emphasised the views of parents, teachers, community leaders, policy analysts, academics, and politicians, this fourth hui of September 2004 has centred on the views of rangatahi, young Māori learners. Prior to the hui a number of regional hui canvassed the views of a range of young people, most still attending secondary school. The themes raised during discussions and in video interviews have then been used as a basis for identifying the determinants of success.

To complement the views of rangatahi, and to expand on the themes raised in a series of video interviews, a panel of young adults and another panel, of kaumātua and kuia, discussed the factors that had been important to them in their years at school.

Themes for success

Although the distance in age between the three generations spanned some sixty or seventy years, the themes raised by all three groups were not dissimilar. In response to questions about the ingredients of success, external factors that contribute to success and advice that might be given to new generations of learners, two major conclusions emerged. First, it was clear that Māori learners, from all three generations, were articulate, thoughtful, concerned about the learning process, and mindful of the importance of education to Māori futures. Second, it was also clear that they wanted the best, not only for themselves but also for those who might follow.

Of the several themes explored, five were given particular emphasis:

- relationships for learning
- enthusiasm for learning
- balanced outcomes for learning
- being Māori
- preparing for the future.

Relationships for learning

All three groups were unanimous that learning does not occur in a vacuum nor is it indifferent to interpersonal exchanges. Three sets of relationships were identified: relationships with teachers, peers, and whānau. Across all three, a climate conducive to asking for help and raising questions was important. Isolation, fear of ridicule, and insular thinking are not compatible with the best possible educational results.

Learning is more likely to occur where there is a positive relationship between teacher and learner; where aspirations overlap; and where teachers can engage with learners at a personal level. Though aware that teachers had professional roles to play (and in that sense were not to be confused with 'friends') there was a preference for a relationship that went beyond the narrow tasks of information transfer to encompass personal interest and respect. Teachers did not need to know everything, however, and there are times when students might be in a better position to answer a query or take the lead. Kaumātua and kuia remembered their teachers with exceptional clarity, evidence of the key roles teachers play and the lasting influence they can leave. The relationship with teachers, however, has not always been positive. Much depends on clear communication, mutual trust and a sense of equality.

Relationships with peers were also considered important. Where peers have a common attitude towards learning, are similarly focused on high attainment, and share enthusiasm for school, outcomes are likely to be better – in short, students who want to learn contribute to each other's success. Large classes are often a drawback to positive peer participation and too wide a range of interests and levels of learning within one class does little to promote an attitude of collective engagement.

Whānau relationships were valued by learners from the three generations, not only for social and family reasons but also because of the potential of whānau for improving educational success. Good and positive feedback from parents or older whānau members could make the difference between persevering with studies and abandoning them altogether. At the same time students agreed that despite the value of guidance and encouragement, in the end personal commitment and personal energy might be the most significant determinants.

Enthusiasm for learning

Education and learning should be enjoyable. An approach that is excessively task-oriented or is more concerned with compliance than discovery will quickly turn potential excitement about learning into an ordeal that must be endured. Converting a sense of burden into an opportunity for enjoyment is a challenge for learners and equally for teachers. Good teachers have passion and are committed to their subject, and their students. Poor teachers fail to convey enthusiasm for their subject, or their students, place undue emphasis on conformity, and give more emphasis to getting through the curriculum than to understanding the curriculum. Some students learn better in relaxed settings; most are more likely to make progress where there is a close alignment of cultural values within the classroom and across the school.

Balanced outcomes for learning

Learners from the three groups agreed that success depends to a large extent on the expectations of themselves as well as others. The expectations of teachers were especially important. Among some teachers, however, there was, and still is, an assumption that Māori learners would not do well, or at least not as well, as Pākehā and Asian students. Career choices were sometimes permanently compromised by those attitudes. Whānau expectations were also crucial in shaping pathways to success. Where whānau encouragement was not forthcoming, learners felt less inclined to aim high and were even ambivalent about continuing school beyond the absolute minimum number of years. Success, however, needs to be measured by more than one indicator. This point was well established by the kaumātua panel. Although NCEA is a relevant measure of success it is not, by itself, a sufficient measure. Success means that a learner has been well prepared for life beyond school, for civic responsibility, and for balancing work with recreation, leisure, and positive participation with whānau and friends.

Being Māori

Though eager to succeed and to enter rewarding careers, learners were also adamant that being Māori was integral to success. Kaumātua recalled with regret the requirement that they leave a Māori identity at the school gates. Education then was about transforming Māori into Pākehā. Indeed the Young Māori Party is sometimes criticised because it appeared to place greater emphasis on western values and ideals than on tikanga Māori. In fact, tikanga Māori was already an integral part of their lives and did not need to be reinforced within a school setting. But over time the education system as well as wider pressures within society did little to value being Māori.

As a result some panel members regretted not having had the opportunity to engage in Māori endeavours while at school. But for those who did, there was no question that time spent on te reo Māori, whakairo, waiata, kapa haka and tikanga was as important as other parts of the curriculum. And, contrary to views that are still prevalent in New Zealand, being Māori is not incompatible with aspirations for high levels of achievement in Science, Economics, Marine Biology, Art or History. Many learners maintain that competence in one area has implications for other areas: cultural confidence goes hand-in-hand with accomplishments in sport, study, and personal development.

Preparing for the future
Rangatahi, mātua and kaumātua saw schooling as a step towards preparation for life rather than an end in itself. Some rangatahi felt that schools were insufficiently focused and by offering a wide curriculum sacrificed depth and concentration. The schools should be more attuned to vocational and professional needs. But there was also a view that careers in the future might require broad knowledge and competence across several subject areas. It was a mistake to specialise too early in the educational process. While those two views express contradictory perspectives, there appears to be agreement that relevance to the future needs to be factored into education and the curriculum so that Māori learners can take their places in an increasingly competitive world. The point of agreement was that the learning environment had dual responsibilities to Māori learners: to prepare students for full participation in wider society, and to prepare students for full participation in te ao Māori.

Transformation in the education sector

During the Hui Taumata Mātauranga IV it has become obvious that across a range of ages, from sixteen to eighty-five years, Māori have reasoned and fervent views about education. It is unlikely, however, that many of the views discussed at this hui in 2004 would have been seriously entertained even twenty years ago. Then, the inclusion of Māori-specific items in the curriculum or within the culture of the school was the exception rather than the norm. When the Hui Taumata

– the Māori Economic Summit - was held in 1984 kōhanga reo was only just about to emerge as a system of early childhood education that could be applied on a national scale. Critics were concerned that a generation of Māori children might grow up unable to speak the language of commerce or science and would be seriously disadvantaged. Similar arguments were heard when kura kaupapa Māori were launched. And jibes of separatism were added. The conservative call was for New Zealand to have a single system of education, and a curriculum that the majority approved. But not only did both kōhanga and kura flourish, they also gave rise to whare kura, wānanga and a range of whānau, hapū and community educational initiatives.

An apparent irony is that Māori were able to assert demands for an education system that supported Māori values and ideals within a market-driven environment. The welfare state had presumed that its duty to Māori was discharged when the worst features of poverty had been eradicated. Being Māori meant being poor, not necessarily being indigenous or being able to live as Māori. Although the economic and government reforms instituted in the 1980s impacted heavily on Māori, causing unemployment to suddenly escalate, they were also accompanied by a fresh spirit of independence and a renewed determination to retain those elements of indigeneity that were essential to being Māori in a complex and modern society.

As a consequence, when the twenty-first century dawned, Māori were in a stronger position to be Māori than they had been two decades earlier. Prior to 1980 there were only a handful of Māori service providers and they often had to contend with dogmatic assumptions that all New Zealanders shared the same cultural values, aspirations and histories. In contrast, after 2000, there were several hundred Māori providers of health, education, and social services and Māori language and culture had become more or less accepted as part of the operating norm in schools, hospitals, state agencies and community centres.

Although the reformation over the past two decades has not been as even, or as extensive, as many would wish, it has nonetheless represented a major transformative experience for the education sector. Not only has it led to flourishing networks of Māori-centred educational institutions, it has also been instrumental in increasing Māori participation in early childhood education to around 50 percent and has seen Māori emerge with the highest rates of participation in tertiary education of any group aged twenty-five years and over. Consequential changes have also been evident in the primary and secondary curriculum, teacher training programmes, school cultures, and education policies. These changes would have been difficult to predict twenty years ago.

Transformations of systems and practices do not occur often, especially in the education sector; instead change tends to be gradual and incremental. When first introduced, compulsory education that was free and secular was a significant transformation and it could be argued that 'Tomorrow's Schools' has some aspects of transformation. But the inclusion of Māori concepts, processes and values within the education sector has even more obvious features of a major educational transformation in New Zealand. That transformation has had multiple impacts, but importantly it has led to improved access for Māori learners to te ao Māori, the Māori world, and has improved access to early childhood education, tertiary education and policy-making arenas.

The question now arises as to whether a further transformative experience is needed over the next twenty-five years or so to move beyond a focus on access and pockets of success, towards a focus on greater consistency, the realisation of the dual goals of living as Māori and being citizens of the world, and attaining uniformly high levels of accomplishment that will provide sound platforms for full participation in a world that is likely to be equally transformed.

Secondary Futures

Anticipating the future is a difficult task and has not been given great attention in New Zealand. Instead there has been a tendency to plan for short time-spans – three to five years ahead. But in 2003 a project called Hoenga Auaha Taiohi – Secondary Futures – was launched by the Minister of Education. Its aim is to encourage debate and discussion about schooling in twenty years' time and to identify the implications for learners and others involved in the education sector, including whānau. The project is led by four guardians, while a sector-wide advisory group – the Touchstone Group – provides oversight and opportunities for networking. Through the OECD, Secondary Futures has close ties with similar projects in Great Britain, Toronto, the Netherlands and Australia, and has been actively encouraging schools, communities, teacher organisations, and boards of trustees to become more involved in planning for the future.

Although some determinants of change can be estimated, by and large it is not easy to predict the future with a great degree of accuracy. One of the ways in which the future can be better contemplated, however, is through the use of scenarios that map what could be possible (rather than what is probable). The OECD has developed four types of scenarios that might well have universal application by 2020 – schools as social centres, schools as focused centres for knowledge transfer, schools that are part of a networked learning society, and a model for education that revolves around individual choices rather than schools.

Mapping the future for Māori learners also requires that changes within te ao Māori are considered. Some of these changes will be in the broad field of Māori social, economic and cultural development and are likely to be debated at the Hui Taumata planned for March 2005. Other changes will have more direct impact on education and learning and the early trends can already be identified. Māori demographic change is an important consideration. The Māori population will continue to expand; there will be proportionately more children, and more older people; and there will be greater ethnic diversity among Māori.

Having witnessed a rapid rate of depopulation in the latter half of the nineteenth century, the population in the twentieth expanded to the extent that it had reached half a million by the year 2000 and is likely to be approaching a million by 2051. Increases in the school age population will be particularly obvious, so that by 2031 about one-third of all learners will be Māori.

The wider scene will also change. Globalisation will make the world into a marketplace for Māori and all New Zealanders and will dictate fashion, music, food preferences, scientific discoveries and new technologies. National sovereignty will be balanced by international collegiality and interdependence and New Zealand will be kept constantly aware that it is a Pacific nation in close proximity to Asia.

The Māori economy is also likely to change over the next two decades. Treaty settlements will provide iwi with capital to enter the commercial world. Household incomes are likely to increase, less and less transfers from the state to individuals will occur, and land-based and resource-based economies will be increasingly supplemented by the knowledge economy.

Change will also affect Māori parents. By 2024 they will be older than they were two decades ago and may not have children until they are in their thirties. They will show greater socio-economic diversity and may have a wider range of affiliations with other ethnic groups, especially Pacific and Asian. Predictably they will have more disposable income; will be more likely to be competent Māori speakers than their parents and possibly their grandparents; will be expecting high levels of achievement from their children; and will want an education system that can accommodate unique aspirations.

Scenarios for Māori education

On the basis of the OECD experience and emerging trends in te ao Māori, it is possible to construct four scenarios for future educational environments:

- Whetū Marama – schooling through a range of centres of excellence
- Te Hononga Ipurangi – schooling through worldwide electronic networks
- Te Piringa – schools that are inclusive and comprehensive
- Te Ara Mātau – schools that focus exclusively on knowledge and knowledge transfer.

Whetū Marama

In this scenario, by 2025 schools as we know them will have virtually disappeared. Imagine that even by 2015, Māori, along with other groups, will have established a number of centres of learning where students can have access to the best possible tuition in specific subjects. Some of the centres will be marae-based, others located alongside rūnanga, others in shopping malls. Sporting academies, centres for te reo, intensive science programmes, mathematics, art and music will have all been developed to such high levels that instead of attending a single school and expecting that school to be expert at everything, students will now have the opportunity to mix and match their educational experience. In this scenario all learners will have been registered with approved educational advisors who will have brokered a suitable mix of programmes depending on individual need and preference. In the course of a single day a learner may attend three or four different settings and will also have spent quite a lot of time on the computer at home.

Te Hononga Ipurangi

Suppose, in this scenario, that Māori have embraced communication and information technology with enthusiasm. Imagine also that by 2015 Māori Television has become a major player in educational television, has formed a partnership with Te Huarahi Tika, the Māori Spectrum Charitable Trust, and also with CISCO which has by now overtaken Microsoft Word as leaders in academic networking. Together Māori Television, Te Huarahi Tika and CISCO will have created an environment where Māori learners can be part of national and international networks for learning. The virtual classroom pioneered through Kaupapa Ara Whakawhiti Mātauranga, CRS Education and Paerangi in the early 2000s will have become the norm. Though students will still attend schools, most learning will be through the internet. Being a small school will no longer prevent students from studying a wide range of subjects, including those where there is a national shortage of teachers. By then all teachers will have been required to obtain a first degree in CIT and will be expert in helping students gain maximum benefit from worldwide networks.

Te Piringa

A scenario such as Te Piringa had been seen as a distinct possibility as early as 2003 when it was noted, in the Māori Language Strategy Te Rautaki Reo Māori, that the education sector would play a major role in Māori language development. Hopes that whānau, hapū, and Māori communities would provide leadership in Māori language usage had unfortunately not been realised and it was clear by 2010 that schools needed to take a more dominant role. Moreover, many Māori initiatives in education had proven to be too small to survive the new economic climate and the political climate had shifted away from devolution and private provision to state monopolies. In most communities by 2025 state schools had become one-stop-shops. Almost all community activities were centred around the school. Not only did schools take full responsibility for programmes in te reo Māori and for delivering a complex curriculum but they also provided health services, recreation, leisure and sporting opportunities, counselling for families and individuals, career advice and access to community information. Most marae also had offices on the school campus.

Te Ara Mātau

In contrast to Te Piringa, in the scenario known as Te Ara Mātau, the role of schools is narrowed rather than expanded. Suppose that the Māori Language Commission had been able to increase funding for the active promotion of te reo in homes, on marae, and in sports clubs, and had shifted the learning emphasis away from schools. Whānau had been so successful in creating the home as a domain for te reo Māori that there was widespread reluctance for schools to have any involvement in teaching, or even using, Māori language. Hapū were adamant that te reo was a taonga that should not be promoted out of context or away from hapū control.

As a result by 2020 most schools had ceased to include te reo or tikanga in their programmes. It was part of a more general decision to narrow the focus and concentrate on transmitting knowledge about subjects that had international currency. Rather than attempting to be centres for social and community development, and for cultural activities, schools had been happy for sports academies to take responsibility for sport and recreation, for marae and whānau to assume guardianship of te reo me ona tikanga and for community centres to offer health services, career advice, homework centres, cultural programmes and counselling services. Schools had become experts at delivering a narrow curriculum and placed high emphasis on academic achievement, benchmarked against international standards.

Longer term planning

Although the four scenarios are very much for the future, and may never actually eventuate, in fact elements of all four are already evident in our communities. However, the reason for discussing them in the context of the Hui Taumata Mātauranga is not to encourage debate about a preferred scenario but simply to underline the importance of thinking about the future and considering the options that lie ahead. Too much planning for Māori development has been in response to a crisis or on the basis of short term goals. As a consequence, initiatives, while valuable in their own right, have not been integrated into a wider schema.

For many reasons the fourth Hui Taumata Mātauranga has greatly added to our knowledge of the opportunities and obstacles that impact on Māori success. Importantly the five themes emerging from three generations have added focus and sense to the debates about success:

- relationships for learning
- enthusiasm for learning
- balanced outcomes for learning
- being Māori
- preparing for the future.

The voice of rangatahi has been loud and clear and has raised challenges that should not be ignored. Nor should the views of kaumātua and the wisdom that has accompanied their own reflections on success be overlooked. Though reflecting on former times, the issues they have raised are not fundamentally different from those faced in contemporary times.

The four Hui Taumata Mātauranga have been favoured by the support and attention of Ministers Mallard and Horomia, and other Cabinet Members and Members of Parliament, all of whom have shown a keen interest in deliberations. The assistance of officials from the Ministry of Education and Te Puni Kōkiri has also been quite pivotal to the smooth running of each hui. But without the patronage of Ngāti Tuwharetoa, and te ariki, Tumu te Heuheu, it is unlikely that they would have been successful, at least in terms of the level of Māori participation and the credibility which they have rightly earned.

The year 2024 may seem a long time away but if there is to be a further transformative experience for Māori education so that access to quality education can be extended to the majority of Māori learners, and excellence can be seen as an outcome that is attainable by most if not all Māori learners, then there is an obvious need to actively engage with the future. As learners have emphasised, education should be relevant and useful, not only to today but also to the realities of tomorrow. To that end Secondary Futures will play a catalytic role as a vehicle for contemplating the future and steering a course towards it. But, essentially, anticipating the future is a matter that Māori need to progress. At present there is no obvious Māori capacity to advance that cause or to examine the implications of long term change in a deliberate and systematic manner. To that end the Hui Taumata Mātauranga team may wish to consider how a dedicated Māori capacity to explore longer term Māori futures might best be developed so that success in two worlds and across several domains can be shared by all Māori.

CHAPTER 9

Te Tai Tini: Transformations 2025

Key note presentation to the Hui Taumata 2005, Wellington, March 2005.

Māori potential

The potential within the Māori population has never been greater. According to the 2001 Census, 604,110 people are descended from Māori, and of those, 526,281, identify as Māori.[1] Further, high growth rates over the next fifty years will continue. Although accounting for some 15 percent in 2001, and notwithstanding trans-Tasman movement, by 2011 a population of 700,000 is predicted and by 2021 perhaps 770,000 or 17 percent of the total New Zealand population, rising to 800,000, or 22 percent of the total New Zealand population (and there could be more than 100,000 living abroad) by 2051. Even more dramatic, by 2031 of all children in the country 33 percent will be Māori, and Māori in the working age group, fifteen to sixty-four years, will increase by 85 percent. But at ages sixty-five and over the growth is projected to be in excess of 300 percent and there will be substantial increases in the very old, that is people over the age of seventy-five years. The two trends – a higher proportion of Māori in the school age population, and a rapidly increasing older cohort – mean that the dependency ratio will be altered, imposing additional burdens on the working age group. But it will also mean that Māori will have the potential to face the future with both the freshness of youth and the wisdom of age.

A century of change

The Hui Taumata 2005 takes place twenty years after the first Māori Economic Summit, the Hui Taumata 1984. But it is worth remembering that Māori development has a long history and has been influenced by a range of actions and reactions – some predictable, others opportunistic, many imposed by external agencies, many generated by Māori explorers, leaders and innovators. Change has often brought benefits, but not infrequently there have also been catastrophic consequences. For the last half of the nineteenth century, for example, the level of devastation was so severe that it appeared Māori might not survive as a people beyond the twentieth century and the duty of the government was to 'smooth the pillow of a dying race'.[2] Māori, it seemed, would share a fate similar to the extinct moa bird.

Even allowing for inaccuracies in enumeration and inconsistencies in determining who was Māori, the Census in 1896 certainly raised serious cause for concern: the Māori population had declined from around 150,000 in 1840, to 42,000.[3] The decline resulted from a range of causes including short distance factors such as high mortality rates from infectious diseases, warfare, and poor nutrition; medium distance factors such as a rapidly changing economy aggravated by an alarming rate of land alienation and loss of customary lore; and long distance factors such as political oppression, and colonial assumptions of superiority.[4]

By 1905, however, it seemed that depopulation had been arrested and there were early signs of recovery: the population had risen from 42,000 to 45,000. A sense of cautious optimism was conveyed in several reports from Dr Maui Pomare to the government. In 1901 Pomare had been recruited into the Department of Public Health as 'Medical Officer to the Maoris' and in 1905 was joined by Dr Peter Buck (Te Rangi Hiroa). Together they trained and supervised a team of community leaders, Māori Sanitary Inspectors, in the art and science of public health and their collective efforts – a combination of professional expertise and wise community leadership – played some part in effecting the positive change.

Meanwhile other developments were also re-shaping the Māori world as hapū and whānau struggled to adapt to new lifestyles, new economies, and new social mores. Two significant events occurring in 1905 are especially worthy of note.

First, Turakina Māori Girls' College was opened. Sponsored by the Presbyterian Church, the new school was located in the small township of Turakina in the Rangitikei before it was moved to the present site in Marton in 1927. Like other Māori church boarding schools Turakina was small – an intake of thirty in 1905 – but increasingly it was to play a significant role in Māori development through a dedicated commitment to education, Christian principles and Māori values. Moreover, the college showed a capacity to adapt to changing times with a curriculum that kept pace with altered societal needs providing greater opportunities for Māori women. As a beacon for Māori education, Turakina still provides a sense of continuity and purpose and is part of a growing network of schools that offer niche programmes for Māori students.

Second, 1905 saw the passage of the controversial Maori Land Settlement Act, but it was also the year that Apirana Ngata entered Parliament as the member for Eastern Māori. In the election Ngata successfully defeated Wi Pere who by then was sixty-eight years old and, apart from one term (when the seat was taken by Carroll), had been in Parliament since 1884.[5] Pere had been an effective leader whose strength had been in his close affinity to conservative Māori networks. He had been an advocate for Māori autonomy and a Māori Parliament but had been less able to manage parliamentary subtleties or to enter into parliamentary debate in English. Ngata on the other hand represented a new type of politician – educated in two worlds, energetic, and ready to apply the values and aspirations belonging to one world to the conventions and technologies of the other. His tenure in Parliament lasted until 1943 and perhaps most importantly he is remembered for his inspirational leadership and his ability to integrate economic, social and cultural policies and programmes.[6]

The reason for recalling those events in 1905 is not necessarily to shed light on the issues facing Māori in 2005 but to underline enduring principles for Māori economic development. Demographic challenges and the inspirational work of the Māori Sanitary Inspectors have shown that Māori are resilient and have been able to respond to adversity with innovation, adaptation, determination, and strong leadership. The example of Turakina College is not only a reminder that Māori progress depends heavily on educational achievement but that effective Māori education cannot always be met within the rubric of a homogenous state system. Ngata's election to Parliament and his ballot box defeat of Wi Pere illustrates another point but one which also has continuing relevance. Modern Māori leadership requires a set of competencies that are necessary for today and tomorrow. Unlike Ngata whose skills, knowledge and charisma were germane to the twentieth century, Pere's leadership was for a different era and a different forum. And arising from Ngata's leadership is the further example of integrated development – Māori advancement is as much about language and culture as it is about land, social circumstances and economic growth.

Although emerging a century ago, these principles – resilience, educational achievement, skilled leadership, and integrated development – remain applicable to today and the decades ahead. They also demonstrate that development needs to be considered as a long term process, the fruits of which might not necessarily be enjoyed by those who pioneer change but by future generations who have not been part of the earlier struggle.

The Hui Taumata 1984

In that sense, twenty years later, it is perhaps easier to view the 1984 Hui Taumata with a greater sense of perspective. Although billed as an economic summit, discussions covered social, cultural and economic policies and marked the launch of a 'Decade of Positive Māori Development'. To some extent the new direction for Māori fitted well with the new Right agenda: the major goals of the government's economic reforms – reduced state dependency, devolution, and privatisation – were also seen as preconditions for greater Māori independence, tribal redevelopment, and service delivery to Māori by Māori. Deregulation, the introduction of market-driven policies, and a downsizing of the state were accompanied by a parallel devolution of many functions to tribal and community organisations. Mātua Whāngai, Mana Enterprises, and Maccess Training Programmes, for example, were government programmes managed and delivered by Māori using Māori resources and Māori expertise. They were consistent with Te Urupare Rangapū, a government policy sponsored by Hon. Koro Wetere that was designed to guide Māori towards greater self-sufficiency and reduced dependency on the state.[7]

Devolution coincided with Māori ambitions for greater autonomy and the re-establishment of social structures such as iwi (tribes). It appeared to offer a degree of self-governance although clearly it was a government agenda with limited Māori control and confused grounds for its justification. Sometimes devolution was promoted as a partnership between Māori and the state, sometimes as community empowerment, sometimes as de-bureaucratisation and sometimes, especially in Māori eyes, as government abandonment of responsibility for Māori affairs.[8] Māori saw the process from two quite different perspectives. In a positive sense, devolution presented opportunities for assuming new levels of responsibility, but there were also some disquieting signals that it was a government manoeuvre for economic reform and cost-cutting at Māori expense.[9]

In the event, within a decade Māori had become major players in service delivery and had effectively entered the health, education, social welfare and labour sectors as providers of a range of services that had previously been the province of the state or of professional enclaves. Often services became part of tribal systems though many non-tribal organisations, based on urban affiliations or communities of similar interest, also assumed major provider roles.

However it was not only the delivery of social services that enthused Māori. By acknowledging that the Treaty of Waitangi guaranteed Māori property rights, the government was also persuaded to see language and culture as a type of property that also deserved protection. In 1986 the Waitangi Tribunal had delivered a report recommending greater government resolve to protect a language that was headed for extinction.[10] As a result the Māori Language Commission was established and Māori was declared to be an official language of New Zealand. Seventeen years later a Māori television channel was launched.

During the Decade of Māori Development new approaches to education from early childhood to tertiary allowed for greater Māori participation and the reflection of Māori world views in the curriculum and in teaching practice. Although a number of studies have shown that Pākehā/European, Asian and 'other' European children perform better than Māori and Pacific children,[11] the substantial gains made by Māori should not be overlooked. The establishment of Māori alternatives such as kōhanga reo provided new incentives and even within the mainstream, higher Māori participation rates in early childhood education were evident, growing by over 30 percent between 1991 and 1993. By 2001, 45 percent of all Māori children less than five years of age were enrolled in early childhood services, nearly one-third in kōhanga reo.[12]

At secondary levels, between 1983 and 2000 the percentage of Māori students who left school with no qualification decreased from 62 percent to 35 percent, while at the tertiary level, Māori participation actually increased by 148 percent between 1991 and 2000. By 2002 Māori had the highest rates of participation in tertiary education of any group aged twenty-five and over. Most of the growth occurred through wānanga which increased enrolments from 26,000 students in 2001 to 45,500 in 2002.[13]

Transformations

These changes, and others like them, represent major transformations the extent of which would have been difficult to predict, even twenty years ago. Then, the inclusion of Māori perspectives within health services or in environmental management were exceptions rather than the norm. In the same year as the 1984 Hui Taumata, the Hui Whakaoranga, the first national Māori health hui, was held at the Hoani Waititi Marae, and the possibility of Māori health delivery systems was raised. Critics were concerned that any move away from conventional medical models of delivery would disadvantage Māori, creating a type of separatism. But others argued health statistics clearly demonstrated that a type of separatism already existed. Māori were simply not gaining adequate access to health services and facilities. The conservative call then was for New Zealand to have single systems of education, health and justice, based essentially on majority perspectives.

An apparent irony is that Māori were able to assert demands for social systems that supported Māori values and ideals within a market-driven environment. The welfare state had presumed that its duty to Māori was discharged when the worst features of poverty had been eradicated. Being Māori meant being poor, not necessarily being indigenous or being able to live as Māori. Although the economic and government reforms instituted in the 1980s impacted heavily on Māori, causing unemployment to suddenly escalate, they were also accompanied by a fresh spirit of independence and a renewed determination to retain those elements of indigeneity that were essential to being Māori in a complex and modern society.

As a consequence, when the twenty-first century dawned, Māori were in a stronger position to be Māori than they had been two decades earlier. Prior to 1980 there were only a handful of Māori providers and they often had to contend with dogmatic assumptions that all New Zealanders shared the same cultural values, aspirations and histories. In contrast, by 2000, there were several hundred Māori providers of health, education, and social services and Māori language and culture had become more or less accepted as part of the operating norm in schools, hospitals, state agencies and community centres.

Although the reformation over the past two decades has not been as even, or as extensive, as many would wish, it nonetheless represents a series of major transformations. Notwithstanding continuing inequalities between Māori and non-Māori, Māori experience has been radically changed in the direction of:

- greater involvement in the delivery of social services, including health care
- improved access to services
- a proliferation of semi-independent Māori organisations
- higher participation rates in the education system at all levels
- immersion Māori education programmes from early childhood to tertiary levels
- significantly raised membership in the legal and health professions
- escalating entry into the fields of commerce, business, and science
- a major increase in the number of children who are native speakers of Māori
- a re-emergence of hapū and iwi as agents for Māori development
- the settlement of major historic Treaty of Waitangi claims.

The question now arises as to whether further transformative experiences are needed over the next twenty years so that future generations can realise the dual goals of 'living as Māori and being citizens of the world'.[14]

Transformations for 2025

While the decades 1984–1994 and 1995–2004 were witness to significant changes for Māori, the directions set in train then may not necessarily be the best options for a world which will be radically different by 2025. Transformations are time-bound so that major advances in one era may be insufficient or even inappropriate for another. The 1984 Hui Taumata, for example, ushered in a decade of development taking Māori in new and positive directions. But beyond the developmental mode is a more confident mode where not only can Māori can build on gains already made, but also shape the directions to suit new times and rebalance some of the imperatives that were so necessary in 1984 (Table 9.1).

Table 9.1 summarises the perceived transformational shifts that will be necessary to navigate the next twenty years. They build on the gains

TABLE **9.1** Transformational shifts 1984–2025

1984–2004 Development	Gains	Limitations	2005–2025 Sustained Capability
Participation and access	Improved levels of participation in education, health, etc.	Marginal involvement Mediocrity Uneven gains	1. High achievement, quality, excellence.
Iwi development	Iwi delivery systems Cultural integrity Commercial ventures	Benefits not shared by all Māori.	2. Enhanced Whānau capacities.
Settlement of historic grievances	Major settlements completed	Energies absorbed into exploring the past.	3. Futures orientation and longer term planning.
Proliferation of independent Māori providers	Improved service delivery 'By Māori for Māori' Independence and autonomy	Reduced incentives for collaboration Dependence on state contracts Lack of readiness for multiple roles	4. Collaborative opportunities and networks 5. Multiple revenue streams 6. Quality governance and organisational leadership

made since 1984 but identify new emphases and new directions. Overall the significant shift will be a refocusing from developmental mode to a mode of greater confidence and certainty.

1. Quality and high achievement

During the Decade of Māori Development an emphasis on participation and access were important goals and there were spectacular increases in the levels of active educational participation, especially in the early childhood and tertiary years. Greatly improved rates of participation were also evident in health care, Māori language learning, business, sport, music, film and television, and information technology. However, while access to education and other endeavours must remain an important goal for Māori so that the benefits can be felt across all marae and in all communities, access by itself will not be a sufficient measure of quality for 2025. Increasingly the emphasis will shift from access and participation to quality and high achievement. That will be true equally for second language learners, consumers of health services and tertiary education students. Otherwise, high participation rates might simply denote marginal involvement and mediocrity with a lack of comparability to other groups, either within New Zealand or abroad.

2. Whānau capacities

Another transformation that occurred over the past two decades was renewed confidence in iwi to undertake functions across a broad spectrum of activities, including environmental management, tribal research, the delivery of social programmes, broadcasting, and fisheries management. Runanga demonstrated that in addition to reconfiguring tribal structures to meet modern needs and to operate within commercial and legal environments, they could also act as anchors for cultural revival and the transmission of customary knowledge. However, although iwi development will likely continue as an important pathway for Māori advancement, it is also likely that there will be an increasing emphasis on building whānau. Expectations that iwi gains might trickle down to whānau are probably unrealistic, given contemporary Māori affiliations and different priorities between small groups such as whānau and large groups such as iwi. Iwi may well contribute to whānau aspirations but for the most part the tools necessary for building iwi capacities will not be the same tools required for developing whānau capacities, including the capacities for caring, for creating whānau wealth, for whānau planning, for the intergenerational transfer of knowledge and skills within whānau, and for the wise management of whānau estates.

3. Future orientation

The settlement of historic grievances against the Crown, though still in progress and far from complete, has nonetheless also been a salient feature of the past two decades. Direct negotiations between Māori and the Crown, sometimes on the basis of a Waitangi Tribunal report, sometimes simply on agreement that an injustice occurred, have led to several momentous settlements. Most have been the result of individual tribal claims but at least in respect of the fisheries settlement, the Sealords agreement was 'ultimately for the benefit of all Māori'.[15] Settlements were seen as necessary steps before both parties could 'move on'. However, the process of negotiation, coupled with a rehearsal of past events tended to reinforce an adversarial colonial relationship between Māori and the Crown. Beyond grievance there is a need to focus less on the past and more on the future. Settlements have very often diverted Māori energies into the past, sometimes at the expense of the present and often away from considerations of the future. But the rapidly changing world with new values, new technologies and global communication, will require Māori to actively plan for the future so that generations to come will be able to stand tall as Māori and as global citizens.

4. Collaborations

Reference has already been made to the greatly increased number of Māori providers, operating either from a tribal base or from communities of interest. This has been especially evident in health and education and has greatly contributed to higher rates of Māori participation and improved access to services and facilities. But three aspects of provider development warrant closer comment. First, within a framework of commercial contestability, provider organisations have prized their independence and have been correspondingly suspicious of their neighbours. The resulting proliferation of independent, semi-autonomous Māori organisations has counted against collaboration, shared infrastructure, and economies of scale.

5. Multiple revenue streams

Another issue that needs closer examination is that for the most part providers, including some iwi, have depended almost entirely on state contracts for sustaining their business. Having contested the notion of state dependency and welfare benefits at the Hui Taumata in 1984, there would be an irony if provider development were to create another form of state dependency, albeit at another level. It is a reminder that multiple revenue streams embracing the private sector, combined perhaps with a system of user co-payments, might create more sustainable provider arms than total dependence on state contracts.

6. Governance and leadership

A third aspect of provider proliferation that requires comment is the steep learning curve that Māori community workers have experienced. The rapid growth of organisations in size and number has required workers to learn new skills and to straddle several positions, often without formal training in any. For many it meant fronting up in classrooms, offices, homes or communities with little more than raw talent and abundant enthusiasm. Sometimes there have been additional expectations of senior leadership responsibilities. Often those expectations have been unrealistic, highlighting the need for more dedicated training for both managerial and governance roles. While twenty years ago there was an acute shortage of front-line workers who could bring a Māori perspective to service delivery, there is now a shortage of skilled people who can offer sound governance advice and provide effective leadership for successful ventures.

Towards 2025: a futures framework

Arising from experiences over the past two decades, and in anticipation of a rapidly changing world, a framework for considering Māori in 2025 can be constructed. The framework contains five goals, and five themes, and identifies key areas where strategic direction is needed at both local and national levels. See Table 9.2 following.

TABLE 9.2 A framework for considering Māori transformations 2025

Themes	Goals			
	High achievement	*Whānau capacities*	*Collaborations and networks*	*Governance and leadership capacity*
Māori paradigm				
Outcome focus				
Futures orientation				
Flexible delivery				
Extended relationships				

Goals

Reference has already been made to goals that might be important for Māori over the next twenty years. They include:

- extending the emphasis on access and participation to **high achievement and quality** outcomes
- creating, alongside iwi and hapū development, a specific focus on **enhanced whānau capacities**
- developing **collaborations and clustered networks** between Māori organisations so that economies of scale can be realised and the best use made of resources
- building a strong **governance and leadership** capacity.

Themes

In moving towards those goals, five major themes will be important:

- a Māori paradigm
- an outcome focus

- futures orientation
- flexible delivery
- extended relationships.

A Māori paradigm

In many respects Māori individuals share similar aspirations to other New Zealanders. However, in addition they also subscribe to aspirations, values and affiliations that align them with each other and with the range of institutions that characterise the contemporary Māori world.

Although there is no stereotypical Māori, and even allowing for diversity among Māori, it is possible to identify a number of attributes that contribute to 'being Māori'. These include:

- identifying as Māori
- being part of a Māori network or collective
- participating in te ao Māori, and enjoying a closeness with the natural environment
- celebrating the use of Māori language
- possessing some knowledge of custom and heritage
- participating as a whānau member
- having access to Māori resources.

In addition, the Māori paradigm is reflected in the activities and aspirations of Māori collectives such as hapū, sports teams, iwi, church groups, land incorporations, communities of interest, whānau and musical groups.

Defining best outcomes for Māori requires that the Māori paradigm is well considered so that 'being Māori' is adequately recognised as a determinant of wellbeing, alongside health status, educational achievement and economic wellbeing.

An outcome focus

An outcome focus contrasts with a focus on processes. During the past two decades considerable emphasis has been placed on processes with particular stress on tikanga, bicultural procedures, and the creation of opportunities for active Māori involvement. While those processes have been useful, and should continue to be pursued, they should not be confused with endpoints. The practice of cultural safety in health services, for example, is not justified simply as a celebration of culture but as a means of achieving better health outcomes. Similarly, the involvement of whānau in meetings about child and youth welfare is not simply intended to fulfil a cultural preference but to ensure the best possible outcome for a child and the family. Because most measurements are process measures, rather than measures of outcome, it has been impossible to judge the effectiveness of a number of interventions. Detailed records may document the number of home visits made by a community health worker but are unlikely at present to note whether the visits have contributed to gains in health. Part of the difficulty lies in the complexities associated with outcome measurements: there is a time lag between intervention and result; many variables apart from a specific intervention may impact on the outcome; and a good outcome for one group may be regarded as an unsatisfactory outcome by another group.

Complexity, however, should not be used as a reason for avoiding a focus on outcomes. Promising Māori-centred measurement tools have actually been developed and trialled. An outcome measure for mental health interventions for Māori, Hua Oranga, employs a Māori health framework as the basis for measuring impact.[16] Similarly a Māori development outcome framework, He Ngahuru, recognises cultural identity, participation in te ao Māori, and access to cultural heritage as important indicators of outcome, alongside more conventional indicators such as material and social wellbeing and health.[17]

Futures orientation

Typically, planning occurs in time frames of three to five years. This short term approach encourages incremental change but runs the risk of being unable to respond to major societal or environmental changes and leans heavily on precedent, convention, and crisis management as the drivers of change. The planning process tends to perpetuate sameness. A futures orientation introduces longer time spans – twenty or twenty-five years – and the directions that Māori might take in order to be relevant to Māori society, New Zealand society and global society in 2025. A futures orientation means that the urgent and pressing demands of the moment will not totally obscure those issues that will assume importance in five, ten, fifteen or twenty years' time. Although some iwi such as Ngai Tahu have developed longer term plans,[18] there has been relatively little exploration of futures methodologies by Māori, nor is there a dedicated capacity to do so. Too much planning for Māori development has been in response to a crisis or on the basis of short term goals. As a consequence, initiatives, while valuable in their own right, have not been integrated into a wider schema that will be congruent with a changing world. To that end Māori capacity for serious futures planning is needed.

Mapping the future for Māori requires that changes within te ao Māori and beyond are considered. Some of these changes will be in the broad field of Māori social, economic and cultural development, others will be demographic. Predictably the Māori population will continue to expand; there will be proportionately more children, and more older people; and there will be greater ethnic diversity among Māori. The wider scene will also change. Globalisation will make the world into a marketplace for Māori and all New Zealanders and will dictate fashion, music, food preferences, scientific discoveries and new technologies. National sovereignty will be balanced by international collegiality and interdependence and New Zealand will be constantly made aware that it is a Pacific nation in close proximity to Asia. Technological changes will lead to revolutions that cannot yet be conceived.

The Māori economy is particularly likely to change over the next two decades. Treaty settlements will provide iwi with capital to enter the commercial world. Household incomes are likely to increase, less and less transfers from the state to individuals will occur, and land-based and resource-based economies will be increasingly supplemented by the knowledge economy.

Change will also affect Māori parents. By 2025 they will be older than they were two decades ago and may not have children until they are in their thirties. They will show greater socio-economic diversity and may have a wider range of affiliations with other ethnic groups, especially Pacific and Asian. Predictably they will have more disposable income; will be more likely to be competent Māori speakers than their parents and possibly their grandparents; will be expecting high levels of achievement from their children; and will want an education system that can accommodate unique aspirations.

Flexible delivery

There is no single pathway that will lead Māori towards high capability by 2025. Instead multiple pathways must be considered. Using educational pathways to illustrate the options, it is possible to identify Māori-centred pathways (kōhanga reo, kura kaupapa, whare kura, wānanga), bicultural pathways (bicultural units), and generic pathways (ostensibly 'neutral' as to culture though usually based on conventional western educational models). While those three broad options have allowed choice, the links between them have been relatively frozen. In the future, however, it is highly likely that parents will seek customised learning experiences and may wish to enrol their children in all three options at the same time. Or they may wish to access some programmes provided by one particular kura kaupapa while still enrolled in another kura. Institutional loyalty and institutional autonomy will be of less interest than gaining access to particular programmes, regardless of where they are offered. When coupled with online learning opportunities, students will be keen to extend the principle of choice from choice of institution to choice of modules with flexibility in delivery options. Similar principles will arise in the delivery of health services and other human development sectors.

Extended relationships

Over the past two decades Māori and the Crown have formed relationships to advance a wide range of issues, including Treaty settlements, education and health policy, environmental protection, land and fisheries policy, and heritage preservation. In working together, the Treaty of Waitangi has been an important touchstone that has allowed expressions of indigeneity to be realised within contemporary societies and within the context of a modern state. But a partnership with the Crown need not be the only partnership entertained by Māori. Indeed state dependency, whether through policies of benign paternalism or as a consequence of state contracts or prolonged negotiations, is unlikely to encourage innovation or enterprise. Rather there is room for a range of pathways and partners. The private sector, global partners and other indigenous peoples have the potential to open new doors and allow for diversification and increased sustainability. Those new relationships, whether with Cisco Systems Inc, Microsoft or First Nations, might well be ratified through formal agreements or treaties and in time might stand alongside the Treaty of Waitangi and the Māori–Crown relationship. It is a matter of some surprise that Māori, as a people, have not entered into a single treaty since signing the Treaty of Waitangi in 1840.

Strategic direction

Many of the goals and themes raised in this paper have already been embraced by iwi, whānau and Māori communities. However, there remains a place for a more dedicated commitment to longer term planning, both at local levels and nationally. To that end, it would be prudent for Māori organisations, especially those charged with shaping tomorrow, to add a futures dimension into developmental plans. A futures plan might encompass:

- a Māori workforce strategy
- a Māori high achievement strategy
- a Māori governance and leadership strategy
- a whānau capacity strategy.

At the same time, given the demands on Māori communities and an array of urgent short term matters, there is also a place for a national Māori futures group to provide leadership in futures planning by developing appropriate methodologies, creating a focus for futures thinking, and providing assistance to those groups who are keen to actively engage with 2025.

CHAPTER 10

Indigenous Higher Education: Māori Experience in New Zealand

An address to the inaugural meeting of the Australian Indigenous Higher Education Advisory Council, Canberra, 1 November 2005.

Indigeneity

While there are significant differences in the circumstances of indigenous peoples in various parts of the world, there are also commonalities in experiences and world views.

Māori experience has not been substantially different from other indigenous peoples except in three important respects. First, Māori demographic patterns are distinctive. Around 14 percent of the total New Zealand population is Māori and the percentage is likely to rise to around 20 percent by 2051. Second, the 1840 Treaty of Waitangi has created a special relationship between Māori and the Crown, with implications for education policy. Though largely ignored for some twelve decades after it was signed, and still a point of contention for some political parties, since 1975 the Treaty has come to occupy a more central position in New Zealand's constitutional conventions. Third, there has been effective Māori leadership in education for more than a century, initially the result of a deliberate effort by one school to promote engagement in university study.

Pioneers in tertiary education

Among the Church of England schools established for Māori in the nineteenth century, Te Aute College (1854) was to develop a reputation as an incubator for a new type of Māori leadership based on a fervent commitment to Māori advancement and improvement of spiritual and material conditions. In 1891 an 'Association for the Amelioration of the Māori Race' was established by the young advocates, but did not lead to further activity. In 1897, however, many of the same group, under the guidance of Apirana Ngata formed the Te Aute Association 'whose special aims were to improve health, sanitation, education, work habits, and family life'.[1] The Association became synonymous with the Young Māori Party.

Two of the Te Aute group, Maui Pomare and Peter Buck (Te Rangi Hiroa) were to become the first two Māori medical graduates (in 1899 and 1904 respectively) while Ngata, the first Māori graduate (1894), achieved distinction in law, politics, literature and land reform. Māori social, economic and cultural revival is often credited to this trio, Ngata, Pomare and Buck, and to the Young Māori Party that they helped to establish. Their philosophy was greatly influenced by their inspirational principal, John Thornton, whose religious convictions and social conscience acted as a catalyst and agenda.[2]

Ngata, Pomare and Buck were adamant that the answer to Māori survival lay in the need to adapt to western society and to do so within the overall framework imposed by the law. While strongly and emphatically in support of Māori language and culture they were equally passionate advocates of western democracy, and higher education. Although differing on what aspects of Māori culture should be retained, they all believed it was possible to maintain a secure Māori identity while embracing Pākehā values and beliefs. They became powerful role models for tertiary education and were living examples of how to integrate western and indigenous aspirations.[3]

Ngata was awarded an honorary doctorate for his contributions to Māori literature while Buck received many prestigious academic prizes. His university degrees included the MB ChB (University of Otago, 1904), MD (University of Otago, 1910), MA (Honorary, Yale, 1936), DSc (Honorary, NZ, 1937), DSc (Honorary, Rochester, 1939), DLitt (Honorary, University of Hawaii, 1948). All three men were elected to Parliament, Pomare and Ngata becoming cabinet ministers and Ngata serving as acting prime minister for a short time.

Educational transformations – a century later

If the beginning of the twentieth century was dominated by the emergence of three Māori academic giants who were later to become inspirational leaders, the beginning of the twenty-first century has been characterised by the emergence of large cohorts of Māori learners at all levels of the educational ladder. While the participation rates are uneven, and many Māori youngsters still remain outside the reach of effective education, there has been a remarkable turnaround. The establishment of Māori alternatives such as kōhanga reo (Māori language immersion centres) have provided incentives and within the mainstream system higher Māori participation rates in early childhood education have also been evident, growing by over 30 percent between 1991 and 1993. By 2001, 45 percent of all Māori children under five years of age were enrolled in early childhood services, nearly one-third in kōhanga reo.[4]

Between 1983 and 2000 the percentage of Māori students who left school with no qualifications decreased from 62 percent to 35 percent, while at the tertiary level, Māori participation actually increased by 148 percent between 1991 and 2000. By 2002 Māori had the highest rates of participation in tertiary education of any group aged twenty-five and over. Although the significant improvement masked the fact that Māori were still five times more likely to enrol in government remedial training programmes and three times less likely to enrol at a university,[5] around 7 percent of the total university population in 2005 is Māori. Most of the recent tertiary education growth has occurred through wānanga which increased enrolments from 26,000 students in 2001 to 45,500 in 2002.[6]

Wānanga were formally recognised as tertiary educational institutes in the 1989 Education Amendment Act and they are eligible for funding in the same way as other tertiary institutions. Wānanga students tend to be older and more likely to be enrolled in sub-degree programmes, though both undergraduate and postgraduate degree programmes represent a significant part of the offerings of Te Wānanga o Raukawa and Te Whare Wānanga o Awanuiārangi. These two latter wānanga are closely aligned to tribal development, while the third, Te Wānanga o Aotearoa, operates at a national level with as many non-Māori as Māori students.

As well as the larger number of students enrolled in sub-degree programmes, there has also been a sharp increase in the number of Māori with doctorate degrees (since 2000 around twenty or thirty graduates each year) with a corresponding increase in Māori research capacity. A major milestone for the New Zealand research community was the establishment of Ngā Pae o te Māramatanga, a centre for research excellence at the University of Auckland in 2002.[7] The centre provides a focus for interface research across a number of tertiary educational institutes and is actively promoting the development of a large cohort of Māori PhD graduates. In addition to Ngā Pae o te Māramatanga there are several other Māori centres for research including Māori health research centres, Māori business research, educational research, and an interdisciplinary Academy for Māori Research and Scholarship (Te Mata o te Tau) at Massey University.

A centre for research into customary law at the University of Waikato (Te Mātāhauariki) plays an important role in bridging the legal and philosophical differences between systems of law in New Zealand, while Crown Research Institutes, such as the National Institute of Water and Atmospheric Research (NIWA) have also sought to include Māori research and researchers, and Māori capability building is part of a deliberate planning process.

The major Māori educational transformations that have occurred since 1984 can be summarised as following:

- rapid uptake of early childhood education
- greatly increased participation in tertiary education
- educational policies recognise Māori aspirations and Māori knowledge
- multiple educational pathways (university, polytechnic, wānanga, private training organisations)
- higher participation rates in sub-degree programmes
- significant research capacity.

Explaining the transformations

There is no single explanation for the transformations that have occurred over the past two decades – and in any event many commentators would ask why change had not been more rapid and more extensive.

But leaving aside concerns about the challenges yet to be faced and focusing for the time being on explaining the substantial gains already made, it is possible to identify three broad areas that have contributed to change: political recognition of indigeneity; reforms within the education sector; and institutional reforms.

Political recognition

Political recognition of indigeneity stems from two sources, often confused with each other and often argued from the same basis, although clearly they have quite different origins. First, policies and programmes that target Māori are sometimes justified on inequalities in socio-economic circumstances and are rationalised from a social justice perspective. Second, however, government policies for Māori are sometimes based on the 1840 Treaty of Waitangi with a corresponding sense of responsibility to Māori as an indigenous people. Under the Treaty, Māori ceded sovereignty to the Crown (or, according to the Māori text, at least 'the right to govern') in exchange for certain guarantees regarding property and wellbeing.

For many years in so far as it was recognised at all, the Treaty was applied to physical resources such as land, but after the Royal Commission on Social Policy report in 1988[8] a case was made for the Treaty to be recognised in social, environmental, and economic policies. The combined arguments – social inequalities and indigeneity – have been applied to health, justice, social welfare, employment, so that tertiary educational policies have been part of a wider set of reforms. Not all political parties are convinced of the arguments in favour of recognising indigeneity, preferring instead to simply focus on need without reference to race. But the Draft Declaration on the Rights of Indigenous Peoples (1993) suggests that there is a more fundamental status acquired by indigenous peoples (as collectives) with significant obligations on states.[9]

Educational reforms

Although the sweeping economic and government reforms instituted in the 1980s impacted heavily on Māori, causing unemployment to suddenly escalate, they were also accompanied by a fresh spirit of independence and a renewed determination to retain those elements of indigeneity that were essential to being Māori in a complex and modern society. Before 1980 there were only a handful of Māori health and social services providers and they often had to contend with dogmatic assumptions that all New Zealanders shared the same cultural values, aspirations and histories. In contrast, after 2000, there were several hundred Māori providers of health, education, and social services and Māori language and culture had become more or less accepted as part of the operating norm in schools, hospitals, state agencies and community centres.

Prior to the 1984 economic and structural reforms introduced by the fourth Labour Government, the inclusion of Māori-specific items in the curriculum or within the culture of the school was the exception rather than the norm. Kōhanga reo, Māori language immersion early childhood centres, were the first major transformations in Māori education and quickly became part of the national scene. Critics were concerned that a generation of Māori children might grow up unable to speak the language of commerce or science and would be seriously disadvantaged. Similar arguments were heard when kura kaupapa Māori (Māori speaking primary schools) were launched. The conservative call was for New Zealand to have a single system of education, and a curriculum that the majority approved.

But over the next decade not only did both kōhanga and kura flourish, they also gave rise to whare kura (Māori-speaking secondary schools), wānanga (Māori tertiary educational centres) and a range of tribal and community educational initiatives. Consequential changes have also been evident in the primary and secondary curriculum, teacher training programmes, school cultures, and education policies. The New Zealand Qualifications Authority, for example, has a Māori field within which criteria for a range of Māori-focused qualifications can be found.[10]

In addition, the Tertiary Education Commission, which funds tertiary education institutions (TEIs), has required some demonstration that each TEI will have developed initiatives to address Treaty of Waitangi principles[11] and has expected institutions to report against Māori enrolments, course completions by Māori students, and staffing profiles. Responding to Māori is no longer an optional exercise or a question of goodwill but is closely linked to funding agreements.

Institutional reforms

The major educational, health, and social service institutions within New Zealand society were largely managed on the premise that entry into those institutions was uniformly fair, regardless of ethnicity. But the relative rates of participation for students, patients, and consumers did not match the practice, especially in tertiary education institutes.

Affirmative action

At institutional levels several initiatives have led to greater Māori access to tertiary education. There has been active recruitment in schools and in communities by Māori liaison officers, and other marketing efforts. There are also a number of programmes that provide targeted assistance to Māori students either through government scholarships and bursaries, operational grants to tertiary education institutions (for example the 'Special Supplementary Grant'[12]), or preferential entry into academic programmes.

Two students, Tutere Wirepa and Te Rangi Hiroa, were the first recipients of a government grant made available in 1899 specifically for Māori who wished to study medicine at the University of Otago . The purpose of the grant was primarily to improve Māori health. Both the Otago and Auckland universities still have entry schemes that enable a limited number of Māori and Pacific students to enter medical school without necessarily having the same academic profiles as other students.

Criticism of programmes such as these has been made on two grounds. First there has been a suggestion that Māori and Pacific students who enter tertiary education under a preferential scheme are allowed to graduate with lesser standards. Clearly that view represents a distortion. While different criteria might be used to justify admission, once admitted, students undertake similar course work, sit the same examinations and meet the same qualifying standards.

Second, the case has been made for all students to be admitted on 'academic merit' alone. The need for a non-Māori student with high grades to forfeit a place to a Māori student with lower grades is opposed by those who associate academic performance only with pre-entry academic merit. However, successful educational outcomes depend on many factors apart from earlier academic achievement. Moreover, the purpose of ethnically-based preferential entry schemes is not simply to have more Māori doctors but for educational institutions to make a contribution to society.

Education has both personal and public benefits and the charters of many tertiary educational institutes accord high priority to the public good. In the University of Otago charter for example, 'the enhancement, understanding and development of individuals *and* [author's emphasis] society' is part of the university's mission; and a contribution to both Māori development and the development of Pacific peoples is also highlighted.[13]

While it is important to ensure that students accepted into a programme are going to be able to meet the required academic standards, it may be more meritorious to admit students who will help institutions achieve their public goals and meet charter obligations to provide for future societal leadership.[14] It is short-sighted to define merit solely on the academic merits of individual students in isolation from other students or the institution's broader social goals. The profile of the total student population must be considered so that the institution as a whole can foster academic advancement, contribute positively to the campus learning experience, and provide society with leadership for the future. Taking account of race helps institutions achieve their mission of promoting academic advancement, having diversity on the campus, and attending to long term societal needs.[15]

Communities of learning

It has been increasingly recognised that the establishment of communities of learning provides many students with greater likelihood of success. Māori students have been particularly attracted to the notion of cohort learning, and various programmes have been established to foster a sense of whānau (family) and maximise the positive effects of peer support. Te Rau Puawai is a comprehensive programme for Māori students who are studying for a mental-health-related qualification at Massey University.[16] Funded by the Ministry of Health, 100 students each year are awarded bursaries, provided with customised learning support and opportunities to meet together as a group two or three times a year while maintaining close electronic links during the academic year.[17] In the first five years of the programme 103 students successfully completed qualifications at undergraduate and postgraduate levels, and in the first semester of 2005, 92 percent of all papers taken by Te Rau Puawai students were awarded pass grades.

Campus innovation

To create a culturally-relevant environment, many institutions have developed cultural centres on campus. Of particular note has been the establishment of marae (cultural meeting places). Unlike tribal marae, the functions of institutional marae tend to be shaped around institutional business rather than tribal priorities, but for many students they nonetheless represent a safe place where cultural identity can be endorsed and customary rituals rehearsed. They are also sites for learning, especially in subject areas that are closely aligned to Māori culture such as Māori language courses, and offer students opportunities to associate with other Māori students as well as becoming part of wider tribal and community networks. Although there are sometimes tensions between institutional conventions and the protocols adopted on a marae, the overall experience has been that marae have contributed to both student retention and completion, and other non-Māori students have benefited as well as staff and the institution as a whole.

Collaborations

Partly because of charters' requirements, but also to create active links into Māori communities and to attract Māori students, TEIs have established a range of collaborations. Formal agreements with tribes have been important at governance and operational levels and at the Waiariki Institute of Technology, for example, a Māori council, Te Mana Mātauranga, made up of tribal elders, has been established with delegated authority from the council. Collaborations with Māori interest groups, Māori professional bodies and Māori public servants have also provided mutual benefits, facilitating TEI access to research as well as recruitment opportunities.

A Māori tertiary education matrix

Arising from the Māori experience and previous efforts to build a Māori tertiary education framework,[18] it is possible to construct a matrix within which Māori tertiary education can be considered. The matrix comprises a set of four high-level principles, five platforms necessary for enabling progress, and a series of pathways through which measurable gains can be made.

Principles

The principles include the principles of indigeneity, academic success, participation, and a futures orientation.

Indigeneity

The principle of indigeneity refers to the recognition of indigenous peoples and their culture, language and knowledge. For effective indigenous participation in tertiary education, indigeneity should be evident in national policies, educational policies and programmes, and the academic curriculum. It requires a commitment that goes well beyond the confines of the education sector and reflects the ways in which states value indigenous cultures. At institutional levels, indigeneity is reflected through the campus culture, the curriculum, communities of learning, and leadership at academic and governance levels.

Academic success

Academic success is a further principle. While access to the tertiary sector is an important starting point, of greater importance is academic success. In this respect measuring the progress of indigenous participation in tertiary education should focus primarily on the completion of recognised qualifications rather than simply the number of enrolments per year. Although Māori participation rates are relatively high, completion rates leave room for improvement.

Participation

The principle of participation has three dimensions. First, it refers to full participation in the tertiary sector – student participation, staff participation, participation in management, governance and policy making. Second, it refers to an outcome of tertiary education – namely full participation in society and the economy. Higher education is not in itself an endpoint; instead it is a stepping stone that increases chances of successful participation. Third, the principle of participation is about readiness to participate fully in indigenous society. If education has not made some contribution towards indigenous participation in the indigenous world then it has not addressed indigenous realities which are about belonging to two worlds and being active in both.

A futures orientation

A futures orientation is a reminder that planning for full and effective involvement in tertiary education needs to take a long term perspective. The Māori experience is that gains occur incrementally over time and a long term vision is a necessary precursor. Otherwise there is the risk that a series of fragmented and unconnected initiatives will occur with little impact and bring about a consequent loss of confidence by indigenous communities. But typically planning occurs for relatively short terms – three to five years – and often in response to a crisis rather than as part of a strategic direction that is relevant to the next generation of learners.

Platforms

Five platforms have been important to Māori: national policies, educational policies and programmes, balanced tertiary options, campus innovation and indigenous leadership.

National policies

National policies that recognise indigenous peoples across all sectors are necessary precursors to full tertiary participation. The corollary is that an approach to tertiary education which is out of step with other sectoral directions or which occurs in a policy vacuum is unlikely to be sustained.

Educational policies

Similarly educational policies and programmes must be consistent across all levels of education. There is evidence that success in later years of schooling and education is more likely if there has been some experience of early childhood education. And decisions about higher programmes of study are probably made in high school years, well before eligibility to enrol. An integrated educational system with minimal disruption between high school and tertiary education is necessary.

Tertiary education options
Tertiary education options that reflect diverse capabilities and interests are a feature of the current tertiary system in New Zealand. Students seeking a tertiary education may choose between wānanga, polytechnics, private training establishments, and universities. Similar financial conditions such as fees and state subsidies apply but not all options offer qualifications that will have international currency. Although choice has been an important part of the Māori experience, there is also a need for ensuring optimal ratios between programmes and levels of study. Currently Māori tertiary education participation is heavily weighted towards certificate and sub-degree programmes and in that respect lacks balance.

Campus innovations
Campus innovations have been important to Māori experience in tertiary education.[19] While policy decisions determine broad directions, each campus can implement more specific programmes to facilitate higher education for indigenous peoples. The benefits are mutual. Māori gain from being able to participate within a learning environment that is culturally resonant and the campus stands to benefit from Māori input into academic programmes and research. Many campus managers have concluded that what is good for Māori is good for the institution as a whole, enabling the fulfilment of higher goals and aspirations. The development of Māori strategies that are endorsed by governance and senior management have been useful ways of gaining buy-in and commitment from the institution as a whole.[20]

Indigenous leadership
Indigenous leadership is a further platform.[21] Māori, like other indigenous populations, are keen to employ a degree of self-determination and to exercise leadership across the full range of endeavours. In tertiary education, indigenous leadership is a necessary

precondition with implications for academic direction, research, managerial responsibilities, policy making and governance. All North Island polytechnics and universities have senior Māori managers (in the case of universities variously known as assistant vice-chancellors or pro vice-chancellors) with responsibilities for implementing Māori tertiary strategies, and the New Zealand Vice Chancellor Committee has established a Māori standing committee (Te Kahui Amokura) made up of the senior Māori academics from the eight universities. Māori leadership is similarly included on all North Island TEI councils. Academic leadership at professorial levels and in research arenas provides important modelling for both students and staff. In wānanga, all senior positions are filled by Māori and most of the academic and support staff are Māori.

Pathways

Pathways to achieve indigenous participation in education are summarised in Table 10.1. They may be grouped into four areas:

- pathways that secure access to tertiary education,
- pathways leading to successful completion of qualifications
- academic excellence
- workforce development.

TABLE **10.1** Pathways to higher education

Access	Successful completion	High academic achievement	Workforce Development
Affirmative action	Communities of learning	Postgraduate qualifications	Identification of career academics
Bursaries, scholarships	Engagement with elders	Centres of excellence	Recruitment
Collaboration	Cultural learning centres	Research capacity building	Staff development that includes opportunities to engage with indigenous peoples & groups
Curriculum expansion	Collaboration	Indigenous methodologies	
Multiple delivery modes	Curriculum expansion	Collaboration	Competitive remuneration.

Some pathways, such as collaboration, are important to all four areas. Links with tribal elders, Māori networks, marae in the vicinity of the campus, and specific Māori interest groups such as providers of health and social services, will contribute to student recruitment, academic success, post-graduate degree completion and research outcomes by indigenous researchers.

Workforce development is particularly important for building a critical mass of indigenous scholars. The burden carried by a lone indigenous academic can be a heavy one and sometimes leads to an early exit. When Māori were struggling to find a place at TEIs, departments of Māori Studies were of critical importance in attracting academics and providing an environment where peer support was available. Now that is less critical since clusters of academics can also be found in faculties of law, health sciences, education, social policy, performing and visual arts, research centres, and, in some institutions, the applied sciences.

The principles, platforms and pathways can be represented diagrammatically as core components of a Māori tertiary education matrix (Table 10.2).

TABLE 10.2 Māori tertiary education matrix

Principles	Platforms				
	National policies	Education policies	Tertiary options	Campus innovation	Māori leadership
Indigeneity					
Academic success			Multiple Pathways		
Participation					
Futures orientation					

The matrix can also be shown as a hierarchy of three levels of priority (Table 10.3): principles, platforms and pathways.

Essentially, Māori participation in tertiary education has depended on five platforms: national policies that endorse indigeneity; educational policies and programmes that successfully engage Māori learners in all stages of the education process, commencing with early childhood education; options for tertiary education (including wānanga, polytechnics, private training establishments, and universities) that recognise a range of approaches and subject areas; the gradual indigenisation of the academy – through campus innovations, curriculum extension, and methodological developments based on indigenous knowledge; and effective indigenous leadership at governance, managerial, and academic levels.

TABLE **10.3** Māori tertiary education: three priority levels

Principles			
Indigeneity	Academic success	Participation	Futures orientation
Platforms			
National policies	Education policies	Campus innovation	
Balanced tertiary options		Indigenous leadership	
Pathways			
Affirmative action		Centres of excellence	
Communities of learning		Bursaries, scholarships	
Campus cultural learning centres		Elders on campus	
Postgraduate qualifications		Collaboration	
Research capacity building		Curriculum expansion	
Workforce development		Multiple delivery modes	

CHAPTER 11

Whānau, Education and Māori Potential

Presented at the fifth Hui Taumata Mātauranga, Taupō, 8 October 2006.

Hinana ki Uta, Hinana ki Tai

The fifth Hui Taumata Mātauranga occurred almost exactly 150 years after an event that shaped New Zealand's future. In November 1856, at Pūkawa on the banks of Lake Taupō, and on the invitation of Iwikau te Heuheu, 1600 tribal leaders gathered to discuss how they might address perceived threats to Māori survival.[1] At the meeting, to become known as 'Hinana ki Uta, Hinana ki Tai' ('search the land, search the sea'), a major goal was to elect a king who might act as an authority and unite the tribes.[2] Over the preceding two years the possibility had been canvassed around the country but the office of king had not been a post that all leaders sought. There were concerns that the position could impose too many demands on iwi, creating burdens for future generations, and that the notion of a national leader, a king, was not compatible with the style of leadership based around tribal structures and tribal authority.

At the same time there was unanimity that in view of the radically changing times the establishment of a united Māori nation could bring advantages to all tribes and there was agreement that the search for a king should be thorough. But when eleven chiefs at the hui were asked to accept the post, for various reasons they declined. Eventually, although Potatau te Wherowhero was not at Pūkawa, he became the unanimous choice for king and finally agreed to be anointed in 1858. The Pūkawa Hui had delivered a result.

Although the anointment of the king came at a time when there was growing Māori disquiet about the alienation of tribal lands and the loss of voice in decision making, the position of Māori king was not primarily a challenge to the authority of Queen Victoria. Instead it envisaged a high level of Māori authority to complement the authority of the Crown, and to cement a closer relationship with both parties under the protection of the same God. The Kingitanga was also intended to stop inter-tribal fighting and to place all tribal lands under the king's authority.[3]

Meanwhile, although finding a king had been an important task for the 1856 hui, a more fundamental goal at Pūkawa was to bring leaders of the day together so they might reach agreement and stand together in the face of mounting alienation of tribal land and a progressive undermining of tribal leadership.[4] As migration to New Zealand from England, Scotland and Australia escalated and Māori were soon to be outnumbered, it was clear to the leaders that the future would be dramatically different to the familiar past and a new approach was necessary. Rather than tribes competing with each other and acting more or less independently, the Pūkawa meeting resolved that a collective approach to planning for the future was necessary.

Even though the goals shaped at Pūkawa in 1856 were inspired by quite different threats from those operating in the twenty-first century, both goals – Kingitanga and Kotahitanga – remain high on Māori agendas in 2006. The wide level of support for Kingitanga for example was no more evident than at the death of Te Atairangikaahu and the anointment of her successor Tuheitia Paki in August 2006. Not only has Kingitanga survived into the twenty-first century but it has become a stronger force than it was during the nineteenth and twentieth centuries and has emerged as a powerful national and international symbol of indigenous autonomy and determination to resist assimilation.

The second goal of Pūkawa, Kotahitanga, also remains important for Māori in 2006, though is less easily evaluated than Kingitanga. Kingitanga has a structural foundation and is imbued with a personality, so that its progress can be visibly tracked. Kotahitanga, however, defies ready measurement and is often more evident when it is absent than when it is present. However, the goal has been kept alive, not only through Kingitanga but also through a number of efforts that have emerged from time to time in order to counter fragmentation and divisiveness. Importantly, just as they did in 1856, Ngāti Tuwharetoa have played a significant role in creating platforms for Kotahitanga. The National Māori Congress convened by Sir Hepi te Heuheu, and the Hui Taumata Mātauranga convened by Tumu te Heuheu have essentially been about the promotion of Māori accord. The Congress sought to promote consensus among tribes; the Hui Taumata Mātauranga have searched for Māori agreement on educational policy and the delivery of educational programmes.

The Pūkawa themes

Underlying the two broad goals of Pūkawa – Kingitanga and Kotahitanga – it is possible to distinguish four themes: a united iwi front for Māori advancement, the participation of iwi in the 'new' society, strategies for the retention of tribal economic resources, especially land, and the terms of Māori engagement with the Crown. Not only were the themes important to the economic and political climate in 1856 but they can be applied with equal relevance to the twenty-first century and to the five Hui Taumata Mātauranga held since 2001.

The first theme, 'a united iwi front for Māori advancement', recognised the advantages of collective agreement, a unified approach, and strengthened inter-tribal relationships. In 1856 negotiating a framework within which tribes might agree to cooperate and adopt a united stance must have required a major attitudinal shift and a readiness

TABLE **11.1** The Pūkawa themes

Themes	A united iwi front for Māori advancement	Iwi participation in the 'new' society	Retention of tribal resources	Engagement with the Crown
Results	Agreed directions for Māori advancement under the aegis of a King	A strong iwi voice in the economic and political life of the nation	Cessation of land sales Economic security	Terms of engagement between Māori and the Crown A model based on equality

to set aside animosities and rivalries that had dominated interaction for centuries. Agreeing on a king was a significant indicator of consensus and an important step towards Kotahitanga. But the land wars and other events prevented the Pūkawa delegates from meeting again to examine the theme of consensus in greater detail. Nor were they able to establish a permanent forum for negotiating inter-tribal relationships. In its place the Māori King and Tainui carried the dual burden of Kingitanga and Kotahitanga, at least until 1892 when Paremata Māori emerged.

'Iwi participation in the "new" society', the second theme, was a response to the introduction of settler economies, new laws, and limited tribal decision-making opportunities. Having previously acted in a more or less autonomous way, tribes now had to consider how they might best relate to a new environment, avoiding marginalisation, and instead having a degree of control over the development of the colony. A major shift in power relationships had occurred and the threat of being rendered poor and powerless was a matter of considerable concern. The question was how best to position tribes so that participation in the economy and in society could be strong. This presented a serious challenge in 1856.

Strategies for the 'retention of tribal economic resources' were a major discussion item at Pūkawa in 1856. Alienation of land, coupled with the introduction of a cash economy, discouragement of subsistence living, and exclusion from political and financial decision making added an element of urgency to the debates. Aware that tribal economic stability was under threat and iwi were unable to stem the rate of change or halt the sale of lands, it was increasingly evident that unless Māori took proactive steps from a position of collective strength, erosion of tribal estates would continue unabated with dire economic consequences.

'Engagement with the Crown', the fourth Pūkawa theme, is based around a model of equality between Māori and the Crown. Recognising that they were losing control largely through a 'divide and rule' tactic, the tribes agreed on an approach that would be considerably more authoritative than if they engaged with the Crown on a tribe by tribe basis. A king would provide some comparability with the British Crown, creating a more even relationship with equitable distribution of power. The aim at Pūkawa was not to pursue a totally independent pathway or to retreat from colonial society, but to engage with the government and the emerging settler society from the strength of a collective base and with a greater sense of purpose. The intention was to take back the initiative and to adopt a proactive stance rather than simply reacting to Crown proclamations. And underlying the theme was the determination that the Māori–Crown relationship would be consistent with the preservation of iwi integrity – a degree of autonomy, retention of iwi estates, observation of iwi custom and lore, and recognition of iwi as indigenous peoples in Aotearoa.

Whānau and education

The fifth Hui Taumata Mātauranga has centred on the role of whānau in education. Discussions have revolved around whānau contributions to Māori advancement through educational achievement, effective whānau engagement with schools, iwi strategies for education and whānau development, and trans-sectoral government policies that have had impacts on whānau. Opportunities for educational gains have been identified at several levels – effective schooling, iwi programmes, government policy, the wider economy. But the focus has come to rest on the contributions that whānau might make, not only to educational achievement at school but also as agents of education in the broader sense of gaining knowledge and applying it to economic, social and cultural advancement.

It also has become apparent that the themes canvassed at the Hui Taumata Mātauranga V are reminiscent of the discussions at Pūkawa. They reflect Māori advancement (through education), Māori participation in society (and especially education), iwi strategies for development and education, and government policies (Table 11.2). But unlike the Pūkawa discussions, where the focus was on tribes, the themes have been applied to whānau and the key areas where whānau influence is especially relevant to education.

Whānau as contributors to Māori education

In 1856 tribal leaders were searching for ways in which they could collaborate with each other in order to bolster the Māori position. In

TABLE **11.2** The Pūkawa themes 1856–2006

1856 tribes	**A united iwi front for Māori advancement:**	**Iwi participation in society:**	**Retention of tribal resources:**	**Engagement with the Crown:**
	agreed directions for Māori advancement under the aegis of a king.	a strong iwi voice in the economic and political life of the nation.	• cessation of land sales • economic security.	• the Crown–Māori relationship • terms of engagement with the state • a model based on equality.
2006 whānau	**Whānau contributions to Māori advancement through education:**	**Whānau engagement with education sector:**	**Iwi strategies for whānau development and educational gains:**	**Government policies for whānau across the sectors:**
	• promoting a culture of learning • intergenerational transfers • te ao Māori • access to the knowledge society • building positive relationships.	• whānau as learners • whānau as advocates • whānau partnerships with schools.	• strategic relationships with key agencies • brokering on behalf of whānau • facilitating whānau entry into te ao Māori.	• educational policies to 'live as Māori and be citizens of the world' • coherent policies across sectors • integrated whānau interventions.

modern times whānau also provide a basis for positive development and for promoting educational achievement. Whānau have a dual interest in education. Not only are they interested in outcomes for Māori learners, but they are themselves educators laying the foundations for a culture of learning. A primary whānau role is the transmission of culture, knowledge, values and skills. Intergenerational transfers encompassing cultural values and experiences, including associations with tūrangawaewae, are significant sources of identity and contribute to learning, development, and the realisation of potential.[5] While educational institutions have been major contributors to the revitalisation of te reo Māori and Māori culture, the shaping of language, values, and cultural world views is a fundamental whānau function. The fact that it is not always well executed does not reduce the expectation that whānau will be the primary carriers of culture, whānau knowledge, human values and life skills, and in that sense will themselves exercise an important educational role. Even when they live in different parts of the country, whānau are still able to maintain meaningful relationships, increasingly with the aid of modern communication technologies.[6]

Constructive relationships between parents and children and with grandparents, siblings, uncles and aunts, and cousins are important determinants of successful learning, and lay the foundations for positive relationships in later life. There is some evidence, however, that whānau relationships are often stressed to the point of abuse or neglect,[7] and there is further evidence that relationships between teachers and students,[8] and between parents and teachers, are often an impediment to good educational outcomes. Whānaungatanga, building relationships, is a critical whānau function that contributes to human potential and to successful engagement outside the whānau.

The depletion of tribal land holdings and an increase in the size of the Māori population has meant that the Māori economy can no longer depend on a physical resource base. Instead there is an increasing recognition that a knowledge-based economy will be important to Māori, and whānau will be significant points of access. 'Indigenising' entrepreneurship from a whānau base and greater whānau participation in the economy were each recommended at the Hui Taumata 2005.[9]

For many whānau the shift towards a knowledge-based economy has been rewarding. Māori have the third highest rate of early-stage entrepreneurial activity compared to thirty-five other countries and there are some 56,000 Māori entrepreneurs amongst the 444,000 entrepreneurs in New Zealand.[10] Whānau entry into small and medium sized businesses has also attracted attention. Collective whānau resources provide a significant catalyst for business success but business expertise and leadership are equally important ingredients.[11] In that respect opportunities for training and retraining remain critically important to whānau.

Whānau engagement with the education sector

Whānau engagement with the education sector has several dimensions, not always centred on a school or designed to support a school. Three levels of engagement can be identified:

- whānau as learners
- whānau as advocates for education
- whānau educational partnerships.

Whānau as learners

Entry into the knowledge economy requires provision of learning opportunities that are accessible to whānau. Although Māori participation in tertiary education is now at a high level, many whānau members have not previously been part of a knowledge society. 'Literacy Aotearoa' has therefore been important for large numbers of adult Māori, providing a first step towards greater literary and numeracy competence. Many whānau were introduced to new learning when their children entered kōhanga reo and in that respect kōhanga have acted as catalysts for whānau learning with benefits that extend well beyond a focus on the child.

Wānanga have also provided important opportunities for parents and grandparents to embark on journeys of learning. Unrewarding experiences in secondary school, and a lack of opportunity for tertiary education often confined whānau to occupations that depended on manual labour or seasonal work. The focus of wānanga on 'second chance' learning, however, has significantly expanded many Māori horizons. In 2004 almost a quarter of Māori adults (23 percent) were involved in formal tertiary education, many at wānanga, and most at levels one to three (equivalent to senior secondary school) where the average age was over twenty-five years.[12]

An important consideration for Māori adult learners has been choice as to provider and mode of learning. Distance education has also enabled mature Māori learners to undertake serious study while working, often in areas that are remote from universities or polytechnics. Apart from wānanga, polytechnics, and universities, Māori have also been learners in private training establishments (PTEs). Although the overall number of learners attending PTEs has declined, largely as a result of government policy to limit PTE enrolments, PTEs remain a significant portal to tertiary education for Māori, and Māori participation has been relatively steady since 1998. In 2003 there were 122 PTEs identifying as Māori providers with 3683 students, accounting for 30 percent of the total number of Māori students enrolled in PTEs.[13]

Whānau as advocates for education
The National Education Goals 2000 appear to have been successful in ensuring that schools consult widely with Māori communities.[14] The consultation has led to greater whānau involvement in surveys about student needs and learning experiences, whānau support groups, parent–teacher meetings, and contact with whānau for school cultural events.

Whānau are also keen that their children should have a range of options for schooling. Māori medium learning has become an important option and 16 percent of all Māori school children were enrolled in kaupapa Māori schooling in 2005, most in bilingual classes (34 percent) but also in immersion schools – kura kaupapa Māori (24 percent) (including designated character schools).[15] Enrolment in the Correspondence School is a further option for many Māori. More Māori learners are enrolled at the Correspondence School than at any other single school in New Zealand. In 2005 over 26 percent of all learners at the Correspondence School were Māori, accounting for some 1700 students. Reasons for the correspondence option include lack of access to local schools, greater subject choice, and an education programme that matches parental aspirations.

Often, being able to enrol in more than one school at the same time has been important to parents. It has enabled their children to pursue customised programmes especially where one school has not been able to meet all requirements. The trend is likely to increase in the future.[16]

Whānau educational partnerships

Motivation for learning comes from both internal and external sources. But allowing whānau and students to have a sense of ownership and control over 'what is learned, how it is learned and when it is learned'[17] has been shown to be a powerful motivating factor that transforms 'schooling as an obligatory activity' to 'schooling as a sought-after opportunity'. A customised pathway provides scope to include services beyond the traditional academic ones and identify solutions that allow all students to grow into confident adults. Co-construction is at the heart of customised learning. Whānau, student and teacher work together to develop a personalised programme of learning where the teacher's experience and knowledge combine with the goals and aspirations of whānau and student to create pathways for achievement.[18]

'Individual Education Plans'[19] have already been introduced in some schools, including Ngā Taiātea Wharekura in Hamilton, and have a longer history for students with special needs. Sometimes, however, Individual Education Plans, where they are currently in use, are limited in that they are designed around a narrow curriculum choice and must be applied within a constrained framework. 'Customised Learning Pathways'[20] envisage a more fundamental approach to individualised learning in which students, parents and teachers work together on constructing a learning pathway that is most appropriate.

For many whānau, contact with school only occurs when there is a crisis or a problem, or funds to raise or a hāngi to prepare. Parents are often placed in a defensive position which all too often leads to a deteriorating relationship with school. The crisis approach to whānau involvement is not one that will induce a sense of whānau enthusiasm for learning or for education. While it is important that parents are kept informed of difficulties, it is more important that parents are also able to work with schools to identify potential and then to jointly construct pathways that will enable promise to be realised.

Underlying the relationship between whānau and school should be the interests of the student. All students should be able to expect that the learning process will recognise their unique potential and play a constructive part in preparing them for the years ahead. 'Students

First' is about placing the goals, aspirations and context of each student at the centre of delivery; whānau and teachers working together to build a system around their futures, and expecting that they will succeed.[21]

Iwi contributions to whānau and to education

Many iwi have developed educational plans and some have whānau development plans. Although whānau plans have often revolved around the delivery of services such as health services, there has also been considerable interest in creating programmes of learning for whānau members to encourage return to work or entry into a knowledge society.

Three broad types of iwi contribution to education and whānau can be recognised. An important one has been the establishment of strategic relationships with school, educational agencies such as the New Zealand Qualifications Authority (NZQA) and local authorities. As agents for whānau and parents, iwi are in a position to provide advice, contribute to planning, and monitor progress, and to promote the inclusion of learning opportunities that will contribute to the wider goals of tribes and Māori communities. Formal partnerships between iwi and the Ministry of Education have allowed iwi to take up innovative roles to support Māori learners: mentoring and tutoring, programmes to reduce truancy, and social support to learners and their families.

A second educational contribution is more directly linked to the interests of whānau. Some iwi have established wānanga where parents and other whānau members can participate in learning programmes that will improve chances of full participation in the knowledge society. Programmes in communication and information technology, management, health promotion, tribal history and tribal research (often in association with a Treaty of Waitangi claim), for example, have provided whānau with opportunities to engage in learning and in the process to seed a culture of learning for whānau members. Other iwi have seen their role more as a broker of educational services rather than providers, and have used relationships with a range of providers to encourage whānau participation in private training establishments, wānanga, polytechnics and universities.

However, a more universal iwi experience has been the promotion of whānau entry into te ao Māori. Iwi efforts to revitalise te reo Māori and tikanga Māori have placed emphasis on marae hui, creating accessible learning opportunities for whānau. Although not all whānau have direct access to marae, or sufficiently strong iwi links to participate in iwi activities, nonetheless the influence of iwi on marae development and the promotion of te reo Māori, including through the medium of iwi radio and television, has been highly significant as a vehicle for learning and whānau educational gains.

Government policies for Māori education and for positive whānau development

Across its several agencies the government is in a position to develop strategies that will facilitate Māori success in education. There has been general acceptance of the recommendation from the first Hui Taumata Mātauranga that Māori learners should be able to 'live as Māori and be citizens of the world' and that schools and the curriculum should play a key role in that process. However, there is not always clarity about the significance of indigeneity – being indigenous – in educational policy, and how indigeneity differs from ethnicity. While ethnicity and cultural diversity are important to New Zealand society, and with demographic change are likely to become even more significant, indigeneity is not primarily about ethnic identity or cultural difference but about the position of Māori as an indigenous people. A practice in New Zealand, at least since 1984, has been to address the indigenous dimension by reference to the Treaty of Waitangi, both in legislation and in policy. Were references to the Treaty to be removed, other mechanisms for addressing indigeneity would need to be introduced, unless it were concluded that being indigenous did not warrant any particular consideration. But discounting indigeneity or disputing the validity of Māori as indigenous New Zealanders would run counter to the evolving New Zealand tradition and would certainly fly in the face of emerging world opinion about the position of indigenous peoples.

Within the education sector there are a number of government agencies, all of which have developed Māori strategies, though not necessarily from the same basis or intended to provide pathways that are in agreement with each other and easy for whānau to navigate. An overarching education policy that can provide a higher level of integration and a consistent approach to all phases of education would benefit whānau and Māori learners and add value to the efforts of government.

Similarly, although the education sector has a lead role in formal learning, education has a broader context that embraces many sectors and government agencies. The impacts of policy on whānau are obvious when there is a family-focused policy but all policies have the potential to affect whānau and perverse policy effects are not unknown. In considering whānau contributions to education, the importance of a cross-sectoral approach is especially significant. The Families Commission has investigated the possibility of a model of Family Impact Assessment that can be applied to all policies, including those that at first glance have little to do with families.[22]

At a community level a number of agencies from a range of sectors are often involved in whānau interventions but in a fragmented way. Health workers, well-child care workers, educational agencies, truancy officers, employment agencies and services for children and young people focus on particular objectives and interact with whānau to advance those goals. However, whānau do not live their lives in sectors and the uncoordinated approach from a variety of workers may ultimately bring more confusion than light.

Government proposals for 'Strong Connected Families', including the 'Early Years' project will provide integrated health, education, and social services for families in need. By adopting an inter-sectoral strategy, programmes such as 'Strengthening Families' are designed to create a consistent and coherent approach – but they tend to be the exception rather than the rule. The development of an integrated framework for whānau interventions and whānau policy is a priority for the Families Commission. Too often there is fragmentation of effort and a consequent risk of duplication or a failure to hone in on a major issue. Despite a variety of workers, each interested in a particular problem, the underlying whānau dynamics may be entirely overlooked. Nor should it be assumed that statutory agencies are necessarily the best to lead whānau interventions. Community groups with a proven track record in interacting with whānau may be more appropriate and more effective.

To overcome some of these difficulties, Te Puni Kōkiri has recommended a 'Māori potential approach' as a basis for Māori policy and development. The 'potential approach' encompasses wellbeing, knowledge, influence and resources; and the desired outcome is one where Māori succeed as Māori. Built on the complementary pillars of rawa (wealth), mātauranga (knowledge) and whakamana (autonomy and control), the focus is away from deficit and failure towards success and achievement. Whānau development has been identified as a Ministry priority for implementing the Māori potential approach.[23]

Whānau and education as keys to Māori potential

Māori futures are certainly linked to the notion of potential and especially to the potential within all Māori children and young people. Findings from neuroscience suggest that potential is shaped quite early in life, probably before five years[24] and in this respect whānau and education hold the key to Māori potential. Although many factors influence outcomes, whānau have the power to unleash or alternatively diminish potential. Unleashing potential does not necessarily mean having all the insights and knowledge to realise latent strengths but it does mean recognising inherent talents and skills and taking steps to launch a journey where they can find full expression.

Most parents are alert to potential in their children, often to the point of exaggerating capability. But even allowing for overestimates, Māori educational progress over the past two decades has been transformative. High participation rates in early childhood education and tertiary education suggest a new enthusiasm for learning while a parallel shift towards Māori medium education has resulted in new generations of Māori speakers who are competent in two languages to an extent that would have been difficult to predict even a decade ago. Rising standards of oratory at the Manu Kōrero competitions and brilliance in sport, music, commerce, and the professions such as law and medicine, as well as a rapidly increasing cohort of Māori who enter doctorate programmes,[25] are indicators that Māori potential is being realised in a number of areas.

But the greater challenge facing whānau is to unleash the potential of all Māori children. In 2004 a little over a half (58 percent) of Māori in year 11 met both literacy and numeracy requirements for a National Certificate in Educational Achievement (NCEA) level one, while fewer than half of all Māori students in years 11 and 12 gained a level 1 or level 2 NCEA qualification and only 12 percent of Māori school leavers had a qualification that allowed them to attend university. Further, although Māori participation in the tertiary sector is high, it is largely concentrated in sub-degree programmes and too many Māori learners experience unsatisfactory outcomes. While overall retention and completion rates for Māori are higher than for non-Māori in qualifications below degree level, they are lower for undergraduate degrees and postgraduate qualifications.[26] Currently completion rates (that is, the proportion of students who complete a qualification within a five year period) are less than 50 percent for all qualifications including levels 7, 8, 9, 10. For levels 1 and 2, trainees in industry training organisations (ITOs), completion rates are around 30 percent; and at level 4 are now closer to 40 percent.[27]

A failure to realise potential is also evident in the prevalence of poor health within some whānau. Relatively high levels of cigarette smoking, obesity, and youth suicide, for example, preclude the realisation of potential.[28] In addition Māori potential is greatly diminished by whānau abuse and violence, road casualties, and criminal victimisation.[29]

Whānau transitions: converting unrealised potential to potential realised

A major focus at the Hui Taumata Mātauranga V has been on the realisation of Māori potential and the conversion of unrealised potential to potential realised. Despite the pockets of brilliance, the level of unrealised potential remains sufficiently high to leave little room for complacency.

The hui has identified four broad strategies for addressing unrealised potential:

- changing perceptions and attitudes to whānau and Māori learners
- normalising success
- expanding options for schooling
- reconfiguring policies and programmes for whānau education.

Attitudinal shifts: from deficit to potential

Although the pathways to success are complex with multideterminants, there is empirical evidence that student achievement is very often a product of the attitudes of others – parents, teachers, whānau, peers – and self-expectation. It is also apparent that expectations for Māori learners are not always high and in some situations are greatly diminished. The stereotypic low-achieving Māori student becomes a self-fulfilling prophecy, compounded by policies that place greater emphasis on access to education rather than excellence in education, and policies that target Māori because they are 'at risk' rather than because they have potential.

A deficit model assumes that Māori are problematic and energies should be focused on uncovering problems, or making a diagnosis, or identifying areas where family dysfunction blocks progress. Moreover, the preoccupation with disparities and comparisons between Māori and non-Māori, as if that were the most significant indicator of progress, creates a distorted picture of actual progress and assumes that the non-Māori benchmark captures whānau aspirations.

Reversing entrenched attitudes will be no mean task. Often potential may be so heavily masked by defiant behaviour or negative attitudes that both teachers and parents never catch any glimpse of latent potential. Similarly a tendency to focus on problematic behaviour rather than potential is often mirrored by agencies who are involved in supporting whānau. While many whānau interventions are concerned with the identification of problems such as learning difficulties, conduct disorders, truancy and obesity, few agencies or workers focus on the detection of potential.

Ignoring problems as if they did not exist is not a sensible answer but balancing problem detection and problem solving with equal weighting on identifying promise and potential could create another level of engagement that leads to longer term positive outcomes. In other words, solving the problem may only be a first step in encouraging the realisation of potential. The challenge, for whānau, schools, and for those who provide whānau support, is to shift from a paradigm of deficit and risk to one of potential and discovery.

Normalising success

For many whānau success, especially educational success, is sufficiently exceptional to warrant celebration even for quite small accomplishments. Celebrating success, no matter how small, is always worthwhile but success should become less and less the exception and more and more the whānau norm. Success is sometimes measured by entry into an educational system – participation being seen as a sign of accomplishment. However, while participation has been an important step towards the realisation of potential, it is not itself an endpoint. Instead, successful completion should be the goal, and the reason to celebrate.

Whānau and schools need to work together to improve Māori educational outcomes at primary, secondary, and tertiary levels. Moreover, success should be benchmarked against high achievement rather than merely satisfying minimal requirements. 'Centres of excellence' where potential in academic accomplishment or sport or music or art, might well be considered as part of the educational landscape for Māori learners, providing additional options and increasing delivery options to maximise opportunities for success.

Extended options for schooling

Māori educational success has been bolstered by increasing the options available for schooling and aligning options with Māori aspirations. Most whānau access local primary and secondary schools, not necessarily because they provide the best option, but because they are the only option. For many students, the result is satisfactory but for many others a 'one size fits all' approach fails to meet particular needs or to assist whānau meet their own goals.

Māori medium schooling including kura kaupapa, whare kura and bilingual classes have become embedded in the Māori educational landscape, and long-standing alternatives such as the Paerangi cluster of integrated Māori boarding schools offer another environment. Niche learning communities that can accommodate curricular and extra-curricular interests together with flexible school hours have been usefully applied in some areas. The Tu Toa Trust, for example, offers a supervised distance education programme (through the Correspondence School) for a limited number of students who are involved in high level sport.

An important task for whānau is to match aspirations, skills and potential with the learning environment that will unleash potential. Distance education may be a more viable option for students who do not adjust well to regimented programmes, or who for one reason or another cannot attend regular classes; and there is largely unexplored opportunities in e-learning for Māori learners.

Reconfiguring whānau policies and programmes

All policies impact on whānau and families, some more directly than others. Often, as already noted, whānau impacts are disadvantageous and emerge as unexpected consequences. But if, as the Families Commission maintains, whānau and families are the foundations of New Zealand society, then it goes without saying that all policies should determine the possible impacts on families. Taking whānau into account not only requires an assessment of household impacts but also the impacts on the educational outcomes of family members – young and old – health outcomes, environmental outcomes and outcomes related to full whānau participation in society.

Part of whānau policy assessment also includes a consideration of the way whānau participate in te ao Māori, Māori society. Will a policy facilitate or diminish Māori language use by whānau? Will whānau access to customary resources such as Māori land be eased or impeded? Will whānau choice as to schooling be constrained or expanded? Will whānau aspirations for future generations be seriously entertained or glossed over? The fact that there is no reliable whānau assessment tool that can be reliably applied to all policies is insufficient reason not to examine all policies for their likely impacts on whānau.

Policies that have direct applicability to whānau should also be consistent with each other. Whānau do not lead their lives in sectorised silos but as dynamic units where health, education, employment, recreation and leisure are intertwined. Policy coherence within sectors, especially within the education sector, and between sectors is of major importance. So too is coherence in the delivery of whānau services. Several case studies have shown that multiple agencies are often involved with a single whānau but in a fragmented way so that a piecemeal approach emerges and the main point may be lost. An integrated framework for whānau intervention at community levels is needed and the most appropriate agency for leading the intervention requires more consideration.

A specific focus on whānau development will be a useful way of addressing the needs of Māori children in the future.[30] It will need to include opportunities for growing expertise in whānau relationship building, effective parenting of Māori children, and providing clear pathways for young children who can benefit from preventative programmes. Within this approach there is a place for increasing the skills of kōhanga reo teachers, teachers at primary schools including kura kaupapa Māori, and professional and community Māori health workers. Implicit is a shift away from training a workforce to address specific disorders or problems such as truancy, and focusing instead on skills needed to address the developmental needs of whānau.

Effective whānau-centred interventions will require a rethink about the way services are funded and measured, greater coordination between providers so that duplication and confusion are avoided, and the systematic development of educational and training programmes to prepare whānau practitioners from a variety of backgrounds for improving whānau outcomes. Māori agencies, whether urban authorities or runanga-ā-iwi, have major roles to play in developing whānau relevant intervention methodologies that can traverse sectoral interests and address whānau potential.

Unleashing Māori potential

The Hui Taumata Mātauranga V has demonstrated that many factors determine the realisation of Māori potential. It is possible to group the determinants into those which operate from a distance (long distance factors that provide context), factors that are more obviously related to whānau wellbeing but not in a direct one-to-one way (medium distance factors) and factors that have immediacy for whānau (short distance factors).

Among the long distance factors, demographic change will be a significant determinant. Over the next three or more decades there will be an increasing Māori population relative to other populations, an ageing population, and an ethnically diverse population. Similarly macro-economic trends, trends for the Māori economy, and global economic trends will ultimately impact on whānau. And new technologies along with new patterns of work and leisure will have some influence on whānau though what that influence will be is not yet clear.

Medium distance factors are related to the policy environment – policies that will affect the way whānau participate in education and in the economy, and policies that will determine how whānau might participate in te ao Māori.

Short distance factors are those that have immediacy for whānau, and the Hui Taumata Mātauranga has focused on the intersection between whānau and education.

The whānau–education interface provides a site where Māori potential might be advanced in a direct and meaningful way. Where whānau and school can share positive attitudes, aspirations and expectations for students, success will be more likely. Parental involvement in schools can occur at many levels but it is especially important at the level of educational planning. The co-construction of an educational plan involving parents, student and teacher will make it possible to customise learning in a way that matches whānau aspirations and student potential. It will also indicate whether learning needs can be met in a single situation or whether the student's interests might best be served by enrolling in another centre of learning if only for a particular subject. The other centre of learning might well be web-based, though could equally be on a marae or through distance learning.

The realisation of Māori potential then, depends on multiple pathways and is influenced by a range of variables, some acting at a distance, others more direct, some linked to te ao Māori, others to te ao whānui – wider society. But the most immediate factors revolve around whānau and education and the interface between family and school. The ways in which the two institutions – whānau and school – relate to each other will have a profound effect on Māori potential.

If there is a single conclusion to the Hui Taumata Mātauranga V it is that Māori potential in the future will be strongly influenced by relationships – relationships between Māori and the Crown, between iwi and the state; relationships within whānau; between whānau and schools; and between whānau and wider society. Whānau relationships are three dimensional insofar as different generations carry messages about the past, the present and the future. Whānau provide continuity with the past but must also grapple with the present and at the same time anticipate the future. And, importantly, through a series of extended relationships whānau are gateways to education, the economy, society, and Māori potential.

This is not new. In 1856 the Pūkawa debate was along similar lines. It was essentially about building consensus, strengthening relationships, providing continuity with the past, and creating new approaches to anticipate the future.

CHAPTER 12

From Indigenous Exclusion towards Full Participation: The Māori Experience

Address to the Human Resource Development Forum, World Bank, Washington, DC, 30 October 2006.

Indigeneity

There are significant differences in the circumstances of indigenous peoples in various parts of the world, manifest by varying degrees of dispossession, different health and education experiences and diverse political relationships.[1] However, although colonisation and globalisation have often undermined indigenous culture and economies, global forces and electronic communication have also provided greater opportunities for indigenous communities to enter a worldwide network and to engage with each other. In that process the commonalities between indigenous peoples have become more apparent.

In defining indigenous peoples in 1949, the United Nations General Assembly noted several characteristics:

> Among the peoples of the earth, indigenous people constitute a vulnerable group which has long been neglected. Their social structures and lifestyles have suffered the repercussions of modern development. They have been subject to growing pressure to bring their languages, religions, knowledge, arts and oral traditions, and the other manifestations of their ways of life, into conformity with those of the majority social groups around them.[2]

In the definition, however, the General Assembly had not given weight to indigenous aspirations for self-determination and repatriation of resources. Although conforming to wider society has not been irrelevant, a primary aim of indigenous peoples has been to regain indigenous values, properties, and language and to exercise a degree of autonomy.

Most indigenous peoples believe that the fundamental starting point is a strong sense of unity with the environment.[3, 4] Arising from the close and enduring relationship with defined territories, land, and the natural world, and exemplified by the pattern of Māori adaptation to Aotearoa (New Zealand), it is possible to identify five secondary characteristics of indigeneity[5] (Table 12.1).

TABLE 12.1 Characteristics of indigeneity

Features	Key elements
Primary characteristic: an enduring relationship between populations, their territories, and the natural environment.	An ecological context for human endeavours.
Secondary characteristics (derived from the relationship with the environment):	
• the relationship endures over centuries	Time.
• the relationship is celebrated in custom and group interaction	Identity.
• the relationship gives rise to a system of knowledge, distinctive methodologies, and an environmental ethic	Knowledge.
• the relationship facilitates balanced economic growth	Sustainability.
• the relationship contributes to the evolution and use of a unique language.	Language.

The first secondary characteristic reflects the dimension of time and a relationship with the environment that has endured over centuries; the second, also derived from the environmental relationship, is about culture, human identity, and group structures and processes that celebrate the human–ecological union. The third characteristic is a system of knowledge that integrates indigenous world views, values, and experience, and generates a framework for a distinctive environmental ethic. Application of that ethic to natural resources provides a basis for the fourth characteristic, economic growth balanced against environmental sustainability. Finally, indigeneity is also characterised by a language so strongly influenced by the environment that it is not spoken as a first language in other parts of the world.

Indigenous exclusion

Despite differences in the standards of health of indigenous peoples, there are similarities in post-colonial experiences – patterns of disease, socio-economic marginalisation and political impotence. In the eighteenth and nineteenth centuries, for example, groups as diverse as Māori in New Zealand, Australian Aborigines, Native Hawaiians, the Saami of Norway, Native Americans and the First Nations of Canada, were nearly decimated by infectious diseases including measles, typhoid fever, tuberculosis and influenza[6]. For the First Nations, smallpox epidemics produced even greater suffering[7].

Higher levels of morbidity and mortality have continued among indigenous peoples.[8] Indigenous populations generally have lower life expectancy than non-indigenous populations, a higher incidence of most diseases, (for example diabetes, mental disorders, cancers) and experience of third world disease in first world nations (tuberculosis, rheumatic fever).[9] Similarly participation in education is often jeopardised by limited access to quality schooling, low expectations, and a failure to secure positive engagement with students and their families.

Recognising the marginalised position of indigenous people, and their exclusion from key societal institutions, four key factors have been recommended for indigenous participation in society and the economy in Latin America. First, since it is the most significant driver of income, more and better quality education for indigenous peoples is critical. Second, improving health status, especially malnutrition in children, can lead to better education outcomes. Third, social services should be more accountable to indigenous peoples and better attuned to indigenous world views and aspirations; and fourth, consistent data collection that enables indigenous peoples to be identified is a prerequisite for planning and action.[10]

Māori demographic trends

As the indigenous people of New Zealand, the Māori experience has had similarities with some indigenous populations in other countries. In 1905, the Māori population was estimated at 45,000 and close to extinction. However, not only did it survive, within a century it had become more numerous than at any other time in history. Even though changes to statistical definitions of Māori make it difficult to draw comparisons, there is strong evidence of a substantial and sustained increase in the Māori population. In the 2001 Census 526,281 New Zealanders identified as Māori (of which 85 percent were classed as urban dwellers).[11]

Although accounting for some 14 percent of the total New Zealand population in 2001, by 2051 the Māori ethnic population will almost double in size to close to a million, or 22 percent of the total New Zealand population. Even more significant, at least for educational planning, by 2051, 33 percent of all children in the country will be Māori.[12] By then Māori in the working age group, fifteen to sixty-four years, will have increased by 85 percent.[13] Yet although the younger age groups will continue to grow, the population will begin to age, the proportion of men and women over the age of sixty-five years increasing from 3 percent in 1996 to 13 percent in 2051.

Like many New Zealanders, Māori are mobile. Following World War II, urbanisation resulted in major migrations from country areas to towns and cities, and by 1976 more than 80 percent of Māori were living in urban settings, a quarter in the greater Auckland area. Emigration overseas has also become a significant trend, some 30,000 Māori now being recorded as residents in Australia.

Positive Māori development

From 1984, and for reasons beyond the scope of this paper, the process of dismantling the welfare state began in New Zealand. The new free market approach required reduced state expenditure, a radical restructuring of the economy, deregulation and wherever possible the introduction of competition. Driven by economic expediencies that included the removal of state subsidies from the agricultural and forestry sectors, 'temporary' stress on all New Zealanders was seen as inevitable. Māori, however, carried an excessive share of the burden. Within five years Māori unemployment more than doubled to over 20 percent and in some areas was higher for school leavers.[14]

But just as the welfare state had a downside for Māori, the free market environment had unexpected benefits. The Māori Economic Summit meeting, the Hui Taumata held in 1984, prescribed a 'Decade of Positive Māori Development' premised on the themes of tribal development, economic self-reliance, social equity and cultural affirmation. In keeping with the wider national economic reforms, where a diminished role for the state was being paired with a greater role for enterprise, the new call was for 'Māori solutions to Māori problems'. Both the lack of confidence in the capacity of the state to offer positive solutions, and a desire to capitalise on existing Māori structures and values, combined to inject a sense of independence and renewed commitment to alternate approaches. Significantly, a sound economic base was seen as a crucial step towards achieving any real social or even cultural survival.

The main impetus for launching a Decade of Māori Development was directly linked to the marginalisation of Māori people compared to other New Zealanders. To some extent Māori can still be regarded as an excluded population insofar as there are significant disparities in educational and health outcomes, with lower standards of material wellbeing and lower incomes.[15,16] But measured against progress over time, and Māori participation in non-compulsory education and in the health workforce, it is clear that movement from exclusion towards full participation is in progress.

Moreover, in contrast to the measurement of exclusion, where disparities between population groups based on universal measures are important, the measurement of full participation for indigenous populations requires indicators that reflect participation in the indigenous world as well as in wider society. For most of the twentieth century policies for Māori were essentially premised on attaining equity with other New Zealanders and adopting the same values and world views as the majority population. It was not until 1984, and the launching of the Decade of Māori Development that the retention of Māori values and culture was seen as integral to socio-economic advancement.

In the new approach, there was a frank rejection of any notion of assimilation. Instead the expectation was that all Māori young people should be able to grow up as New Zealanders and as Māori. Full participation need not mean abandoning a Māori identity. A second point arising from a Decade of (positive) Māori Development was the desire of Māori people to develop their own economic and social systems in ways that were consistent with Māori aspirations and priorities. While the state as a provider had certain attractions, seldom was it inclined to recognise Māori preferences. In contrast, in the deregulated environment, large numbers of Māori health, education and social service providers emerged, enabling families (whānau), communities and tribes to steer their own courses.

The trend is consistent with article 21 of the Draft Declaration of the Rights of Indigenous Peoples:

> Indigenous peoples have the right to maintain and develop their political, economic and social systems, to be secure in the enjoyment of their own means of subsistence and development, and to engage freely in all their traditional and other economic activities. Indigenous peoples who have been deprived of their means of subsistence and development are entitled to just and fair compensation.[17]

The twin approaches, retaining a Māori identity while rejecting assimilation, together with a measure of autonomy, self-management, and Māori delivery systems, have been important in the Māori journey from exclusion towards full participation. Transformations have been evident in a range of areas, including entrepreneurship,[18] but there has been particular progress in non-compulsory education and health workforce participation.

Māori participation in non-compulsory education

Since 1984 Māori participation in education at all levels has been transformed in two respects. First, the education system has recognised Māori language, knowledge, and culture as core elements of the curriculum. Second, participation rates in non-compulsory education have escalated in an unprecedented manner. While the participation rates are uneven, and many Māori youngsters still remain outside the reach of effective education, there has been a remarkable turnaround. The initial establishment of Māori alternatives such as kōhanga reo (Māori language immersion centres) in 1981 have provided cultural attractions, and within the mainstream educational system higher Māori participation rates in early childhood education have also been evident, growing by over 30 percent between 1991 and 1993. By 2001, 45 percent of all Māori children under five years of age were enrolled in early childhood services, nearly one-third in kōhanga reo,[19] and by

2005 around 90 percent of Māori children entering primary school had experienced some form of early childhood education.[20]

For older learners there have also been significant gains. Retention rates for sixteen year olds at secondary school increased from 47 percent (in 1987) to 63 percent (in 2003). Between 1983 and 2000 the percentage of Māori students who left school with no qualifications decreased from 62 percent to 35 percent, while at the tertiary level, between 1993 and 2004 Māori participation increased by 148 percent. By 2002 Māori had the highest rates of participation in tertiary education of any group aged twenty-five years and over. Although the significant improvement masked the fact that Māori were still five times more likely to enrol in government remedial training programmes and three times less likely to enrol at a university,[21] around 7 percent of the total university population in 2005 is Māori. Most of the recent tertiary education growth has occurred through accredited tribal learning centres, wānanga, which increased enrolments from 26,000 students in 2001 to 45,500 in 2002.[22]

Wānanga were formally recognised as tertiary educational institutes in the 1989 Education Amendment Act and they are eligible for funding in the same way as other tertiary institutions. Wānanga students tend to be older and more likely to be enrolled in sub-degree programmes, though both undergraduate and postgraduate degree programmes represent a significant part of the offerings of two wānanga.

As well as the larger number of students enrolled in sub-degree programmes there has also been a demonstrable increase in the number of Māori with doctorate degrees (since 2000 around twenty or thirty graduates each year) with a corresponding increase in Māori research capacity.

A major milestone for the New Zealand research community was the establishment of Ngā Pae o te Māramatanga, a centre for research excellence at the University of Auckland in 2002.[23] In addition there are several other Māori centres for research including Māori health research, Māori business research, educational research, and an interdisciplinary Academy for Māori Research and Scholarship (Te Mata o te Tau) at Massey University.

The major Māori educational transformations 1984–2005 can be summarised as:

- rapid uptake of early childhood education
- greatly increased participation in tertiary education

- educational policies recognise Māori aspirations and Māori knowledge
- multiple educational pathways (university, polytechnic, wananga, private training organisations)
- higher participation rates in sub-degree programmes
- significant research capacity.

Māori participation in the health workforce

In 1984 the first national Māori health hui was held and the possibility of Māori health delivery systems was raised.[24] Critics were concerned that any move away from conventional medical models of delivery would disadvantage Māori, creating a type of separatism with a lowering of standards. But others argued that health statistics clearly demonstrated a type of separatism anyway and that a high quality service was of little value if it were not used. Māori were overrepresented in almost every diagnostic category and were not gaining adequate access to health services and facilities.

Prior to 1980 there were only three or four Māori health providers and they often had to contend with assumptions that all New Zealanders shared the same cultural values, aspirations and history. In contrast, by 2004 there were nearly 300 Māori health providers and Māori language and culture had become more or less accepted as part of the operating norm in schools, hospitals, state agencies, the media, and community centres.

As one way of addressing the disproportionate representation of Māori in most illnesses and injuries, workforce development has become a high priority for improving Māori standards of health. In 2000, Māori made up around 14 percent of the total population but only 5 percent of the national health workforce.[25] In order to increase the size of the workforce, two broad strategies were instituted.

First, efforts to recruit more Māori into the health professions have included affirmative action programmes – or programmes that have similar aims. In 1998 for example the University of Auckland launched Vision 2020, a programme designed to significantly increase Māori entry into the medical school. In 1984 there were five new Māori medical students but by 2004, the number of new Māori entrants had increased to twenty-four.[26] Similar trends have been seen in the qualified medical workforce. From an estimated medical workforce of around sixty in 1984, there are now over 200 Māori medical practitioners across a range of specialties, accounting for 3 percent of the total active medical workforce. In addition, scholarships have been offered from a number of sources as incentives to encourage enrolment in other disciplines such as nursing, social work, clinical psychology and dealing with addictions. The number of Māori dentists for example has increased from four or five in 1984 to forty-four in 2005.

A second workforce strategy has been to engage cultural advisors or Māori community health workers to work alongside health professionals, bringing first-hand knowledge of community and a capacity to engage diffident patients. Often the combination has been highly effective though there has also been concern that the two streams of workers – cultural and clinical – have created potential for professional and cultural interventions to diverge. An integration of cultural and clinical dimensions is one of the more pressing challenges facing Māori health care.

While the impact of workforce strategies on Māori health status has not been specifically determined, there have been significant gains in Māori health, especially over the past five years. For non-Māori New Zealanders there was a steady increase in life expectancy at birth over the period from 1985/87 to 2000/02. For Māori there was little change for males or females during the 1980s but a dramatic improvement in the five years to 2000/02. Between 1984 and 2002 the life expectancy increased from sixty-five years for Māori males to sixty-nine years while for Māori females it increased from seventy to seventy-three years. Notwithstanding the eight year gap between Māori and non-Māori, in the five years to 200/002, the gap reduced by 0.6 years.[27]

Transformations

These changes, and others like them, represent major transformations, the extent of which would have been difficult to predict, even twenty years ago. Then, the inclusion of Māori perspectives within health services or in environmental management were exceptions rather than the norm and the conservative call was for New Zealand to have single systems of education, health and justice based essentially on majority perspectives.

An apparent irony is that Māori were able to assert demands for social systems that supported Māori values and ideals within a market-driven environment. The welfare state had presumed that its duty to Māori was discharged when the worst features of poverty had been eradicated. Being Māori meant being poor, not necessarily being indigenous or being able to live as Māori. Although the economic and government reforms instituted in the 1980s impacted heavily on Māori, causing unemployment to suddenly escalate, they were also accompanied by a fresh spirit of independence and a renewed determination to retain those elements of indigeneity that were essential to being Māori in a complex and modern society. As a consequence, when the twenty-first century dawned, Māori were in a stronger position to live as Māori than they had been two decades earlier.

Although the reformation over the past two decades has not been as even, or as extensive, as many would wish, it nonetheless represents a series of major transformations. Notwithstanding continuing inequalities between Māori and non-Māori, Māori experience has been radically changed in the direction of:

- greater involvement in the delivery of social services, including health care
- improved access to services
- a proliferation of semi-independent Māori organisations
- higher participation rates in the education system at early childhood and tertiary levels
- immersion Māori language education programmes from early childhood to tertiary levels
- significantly raised membership in the legal and health professions
- escalating entry into the fields of commerce, business, and science
- a major increase in the number of children who are native speakers of Māori
- a re-emergence of tribal groups as agents for Māori development
- the settlement of major historic Treaty of Waitangi claims.

The question now arises as to whether further transformative experiences are needed over the next ten years so that future generations can realise the dual goals of 'living as Māori and being citizens of the world'.[28]

Transformations for 2014

While the decades 1984–94 and 1995–2004 were witness to significant changes for Māori, the directions set in train then may not necessarily be the best options for a world which will be significantly different by 2014. Transformations are time-bound so that major advances in one era may be insufficient or even inappropriate for another.

The 1984 Hui Taumata for example ushered in a Decade of Development taking Māori in new and positive directions. But beyond the developmental mode is a more confident mode where not only can Māori can build on gains already made, but also shape the directions to suit new times and rebalance some of the imperatives that seemed so necessary in 1984.

The Ministry of Māori Development, Te Puni Kōkiri, has recommended a 'Māori potential approach' as a basis for Māori policy and development. The 'potential approach' encompasses wellbeing, knowledge, influence and resources, and the desired outcome is one where 'Māori succeed as Māori'. Built on the complementary pillars of rawa (wealth), mātauranga (knowledge) and whakamana (autonomy and control), the focus is away from deficit and failure towards success and achievement.[29]

The potential approach requires substantial directional shifts for those who have been focusing on greater Māori autonomy and gaining access to language, culture, and societal goods and services. While those issues were largely concerned with building foundations and instituting processes, the focus must now shift towards result and outcomes (Table 12.2).[30]

Quality and high achievement

During the Decade of Māori Development an emphasis on participation and access were important goals and there were spectacular increases in the levels of active educational participation, especially in the early childhood and tertiary years. Greatly improved rates of participation were also evident in health care, Māori language learning, business, sport, music, film and television, and information technology.

However, while access to education and other endeavours must remain important goals for Māori so that the benefits can be felt

TABLE 12.2 Transformational shifts 1984–2014

1984–2004 Development	Gains	Limitations	2005–2014 Māori potential
Participation and access	Improved levels of participation in education, health, etc.	Marginal involvement. Mediocrity. Uneven gains.	High achievement, quality, excellence.
Tribal development	Tribal delivery systems; cultural integrity; commercial ventures.	Benefits not shared by all Māori.	Enhanced whānau (family) capacities.
Settlement of historic grievances	Major settlements completed.	Energies absorbed into exploring the past.	Futures orientation and longer term planning.
Protocols and processes	Māori perspectives incorporated into health, education etc.	Focus on process has diverted attention from results.	Focus on relevant outcomes that reflect dual aims.
Government contracts	Improved service delivery. 'By Māori for Māori'. Māori provider development.	Dependence on state contracts. A focus on state outputs.	Collaborative opportunities and networks. Multiple revenue streams. Multiple partnerships.

across all communities, access by itself will not be a sufficient measure of progress for 2014. Increasingly the emphasis will shift from access and participation to quality and high achievement. That will be true equally for second language learners, consumers of health services and tertiary education students. Otherwise, high participation rates might simply denote marginal involvement and mediocrity with a lack of comparability to other groups, either within New Zealand or abroad.

Pockets of brilliance and high achievement are sufficiently evident to warrant optimism but there is a need to instil the same levels of achievement across all Māori. Success should be the experience of the majority.

Enchanced whānau (family network) capacities

Another transformation that occurred over the past two decades was renewed confidence in tribes to undertake functions across a broad spectrum of activities including environmental management, tribal research, the delivery of social programmes, broadcasting, and fisheries management. Tribal authorities demonstrated that in addition to reconfiguring tribal structures to meet modern needs and to operate within commercial and legal environments, they could also act as anchors for cultural revival and the transmission of customary knowledge. However, although tribal development will likely continue as an important pathway for Māori advancement, it is also likely that there will be an increasing emphasis on building family capabilities. For the most part the tools necessary for building tribal capacities are not the same tools required for developing family capacities, including the capacities for caring, for creating family wealth, for family planning, for the intergenerational transfer of knowledge and skills, and for the wise management of family assets.

Futures orientation

The settlement of historic grievances against the Crown, though still in progress and far from complete, has nonetheless also been a salient feature of the past two decades. Settlements were seen as necessary steps before both parties could 'move on'. However, the process of negotiation, coupled with a rehearsal of past events, tended to reinforce an adversarial colonial relationship between Māori and the Crown. Beyond grievance there is a need to focus less on the past and more on the future.

Settlements have very often diverted Māori energies into the past, sometimes at the expense of the present and often away from considerations of the future. But the rapidly changing world with new values, new technologies and global communication, will require Māori to actively plan for the future so that generations to come will be able to participate as Māori and as global citizens.

Best possible, relevant outcomes that reflect dual aims

In many respects Māori individuals share similar aspirations to other New Zealanders. A good outcome is one where individuals reach their potential and are well placed to compete in a global economy. However, a good outcome for Māori also reflects Māori aspirations, values and affiliations. There is no stereotypical Māori, but even allowing for diversity among Māori, it is possible to identify a number of attributes that contribute to 'being Māori'. These include:

- identifying as Māori
- being part of a Māori network or collective
- participating in te ao Māori (the Māori world), and enjoying a closeness with the natural environment
- using Māori language
- possessing some knowledge of custom and heritage
- participating as a whānau (family) member
- having access to Māori resources.

Defining best outcomes for Māori requires that 'being Māori' is adequately recognised as a determinant of wellbeing, alongside the more conventional indicators such as health status, educational achievement and economic wellbeing.

An outcome focus contrasts with a focus on procedure. During the past two decades considerable emphasis has been placed on processes with particular stress on the incorporation of Māori values and protocols, and the creation of opportunities for active Māori involvement. While those processes have been useful, and should continue to be pursued, they should not be confused with endpoints. The practice of cultural safety in health services, for example, is not justified as a celebration of culture but as a means of achieving better health outcomes. Similarly, the involvement of family groups in meetings about child and youth welfare is not simply intended to fulfil a cultural preference but to ensure the best possible outcome for a child and the family. And while measures such as workforce participation can often be regarded as proxy measures for wellbeing, they do not substitute for indicators that have direct reflection on outcomes. The number of Māori adults who have no need to see a dentist because their teeth are strong and healthy might be more relevant than the number of Māori dentists.

Because most measurements are process measures, rather than measures of outcome, it has been impossible to judge the effectiveness of a number of interventions. Part of the difficulty lies in the complexities associated with outcome measurements; there is a time lag between intervention and result; many variables apart from a specific intervention may impact on the outcome; and a good outcome for one group may be regarded as an unsatisfactory outcome by another group. But outcome measures that are relevant to Māori health, and the broader field of Māori development offer some prospect of being able to capture progress from a Māori perspective.[31,32]

Collaborations, multiple revenue streams, extended relationships and partnerships

For the most part providers, including some tribes, have depended almost entirely on state contracts for sustaining their business. Having contested the notion of state dependency and welfare benefits at the Hui Taumata in 1984, there would be an irony if provider development were to create further state dependency, albeit at another level. It is a reminder that multiple revenue streams embracing the private sector, combined perhaps with a system of user co-payments and global commercial ventures, might create more sustainable provider arms than total dependence on state contracts. To that end tribes and Māori as a whole will need to consider the development of a raft of relationships that include, but are not limited to, the state.

Towards 2014: unleashing Māori potential

Importantly in a global economy, relationships with other indigenous peoples and international agencies should receive due attention. That observation is captured in the overall aim for the next decade for Māori human development that Māori should be able to 'live as Māori and be citizens of the world.'

Embedded in this aim are four key goals:

1. The participatory goal: *full participation in education, the economy and society.*
2. The indigeneity goal: *certainty of access to Māori culture, networks, resources.*

209

3. The goal of balanced outcomes: *outcomes that reflect spiritual, emotional/intellectual, physical and family dimensions.*
4. The anticipatory goal: *long term planning to prepare for a changing future.*

The realisation of Māori potential depends on multiple pathways and is influenced by a range of variables, some acting at a distance, others more directly, some linked to national and global forces, others to forces within the Māori world.

These goals are more likely to be realised if they are supported by key catalysts: effective Māori leadership; government policies that are conducive to the realisation of Māori potential, Māori perspectives and values; a Māori workforce that is doubly qualified (cultural qualifications, educational/technical/professional qualifications); extended relationships between Māori and the state, the private sector, international agencies and other indigenous peoples.

TABLE **12.3** A framework for considering Māori potential 2014

Catalysts for change	Goals			
	Full participation in society & the economy	Indigeneity	Balanced outcomes	Long term planning
Māori leadership				
Conducive government policies				
Māori perspectives and values				
A doubly qualified Māori workforce				
Extended relationships				

CHAPTER 13

The Treaty of Waitangi in New Zealand 2008

Presented at the Treaty Debate Series, Te Papa Tongarewa, Wellington, 21 January 2008.

Introduction

There are only three points I wanted to make tonight.

First, although the Treaty of Waitangi has been inconsistently recognised and at times dismissed altogether, it is nonetheless embedded in the life of the nation.

Second, over the past two or three decades the Treaty of Waitangi has contributed to a spectacular transformation of New Zealand society. As a result, despite unjust alienation of land, threats to cultural survival, and quite substantial matters yet to be resolved, Māori have faith in the Treaty as a confirmation of rights and an affirmation of status.

Third, while the significance of the Treaty has been argued from several perspectives – historical, legal, social, political and cultural – fundamentally it has come to be about the way in which New Zealand values its indigenous people and their participation in society.

The Treaty in the life of the nation

The first point, the Treaty is embedded in the life of the nation, could appear to be at odds with the Treaty's uncertain status and questionable relevance. The Treaty cannot, for example, be legally enforced unless it is contained in legislation; and even apart from appearing in relatively few statutes, its actual impact depends on how it is written into the law. A statutory Treaty provision can be so worded as to elevate Treaty principles above all else in an Act (as in the State Owned Enterprises Act 1986), or to simply acknowledge the Treaty but without creating any binding obligations (as in the Ture Whenua Maori Act 1993). In that respect Parliament can fortify or weaken the Treaty.

Nor does the Treaty have any consistent place within the major institutions of society. Schools and universities, hospitals and prisons, churches and local bodies have largely discretionary Treaty policies and practices. While frequently they display a Treaty conscience, in the event they are often uncertain about the application of the Treaty – if any – to their work. Moreover, the private sector carries no Treaty duty, unless contracted to the Crown to undertake specific tasks. The day-to-day practices of professional groups such as doctors, lawyers and accountants are essentially unencumbered by the Treaty and for builders, shop assistants, IT technicians, and shearers the Treaty has no obvious relevance.

The Treaty's uncertain status is further evident at national levels. In the absence of a written constitution there is no single document that makes a clear statement about the place of the Treaty in modern New Zealand. As a result, over the years successive governments have taken it upon themselves to either extend or diminish the reach of the Treaty to suit political agendas. For their part, the courts in the nineteenth century were inclined to dismiss the Treaty as 'a simple nullity' though in recent times they have interpreted the Treaty according to its principles and the weight given to those principles within statute. Essentially courts are still guided by the dictum that the Treaty can only be addressed if it is contained in municipal law. Rarely has a decision from the bench been based on the Treaty's wider constitutional significance as 'part of the fabric of New Zealand society' (as it was in Huakina Development Trust v. Waikato Valley Authority.

Given the lack of constitutional clarity, limited enforceability, and a degree of political and societal ambivalence, the conclusion that the Treaty of Waitangi is 'embedded in society' might well be contested. There are, however, two reasons for reaching that position. The first is related to time. Far from Treaty awareness diminishing over the years, the opposite has occurred: New Zealanders generally are more aware of the Treaty than were their parents and grandparents. Although they may not agree with its relevance or application, the level of understanding is high compared to fifty years ago and much higher than it was twenty-five years ago. Further, although the working lives of teachers, doctors, lawyers and employees in the commercial sector are not immediately touched by the Treaty of Waitangi, to some extent the scope and context within which their various businesses unfold intersect with both the Crown and Māori and are therefore not entirely divorced from the Treaty's application.

But a second reason for asserting that the Treaty is embedded in the life of the nation hinges on long-standing recognition of Māori as participants in the nation's constitutional processes. The absence of a written constitution does not necessarily mean that the Treaty is not part of New Zealand's constitutional conventions. When, for example, the Royal Commission on the Electoral System raised the possibility of abolishing the Māori seats if MMP (the Mixed Member Proportional electoral system) were introduced, a delegation of Māori leaders persuaded the government of the day to retain the seats. Even before then, however, political leaders, including the late Sir Robert Muldoon, had accepted a convention that the seats would never be abolished without Māori agreement. While unwritten undertakings do not carry with them the force of law, or for that matter the views of successors, they are based on well-established conventions, derived from the Treaty of Waitangi. Conventions that have lasted for 168 years cannot be lightly put aside.

The Treaty and societal transformation

The second point I wanted to make tonight relates to Māori faith in the Treaty of Waitangi. The Treaty remains a touchstone for Māori. It could be argued that Māori confidence in the Treaty is seriously misplaced, especially in light of the countless broken promises so vividly rehearsed in hundreds of claims against the Crown. Nor do lower standards of health, education and household incomes give Māori reason to have faith in the Treaty's guarantees of 'equal rights and privileges'.

But 168 years after it was signed, Māori remain convinced that the Treaty of Waitangi will be as critical for future generations as it was for those who actually signed it. The Treaty has the potential to protect resources, including cultural resources, but also to afford recognition to Māori as distinctive proprietors and partners in local and national development.

Ironically, the champions of the Treaty have switched places. In 1840 the Crown was enthusiastic about the Treaty, actively promoting it among the tribes. Tribes on the other hand were relatively uninvolved in the process and were somewhat bemused by the Crown's fervour; they were not at all convinced that there would be benefits. In modern times, however, it is Māori who are fervent about promoting the Treaty and frequently they accuse the Crown of indifference to it. The rationale for the Treaty has also undergone some reversal. In 1840, the essential reason for the Treaty, and the point which required tribal assent, was to give legitimacy to the Crown to colonise the country. In 2008, the right of the Crown is more or less taken for granted and the more frequent question is whether Māori can retain their customary rights and at the very least control and manage their own affairs without government prescribing how that should be done.

A significant factor in Māori advocacy for the Treaty is linked to the position of Māori in New Zealand generally. During the decades when the Treaty played relatively little part in the nation's affairs, Māori were increasingly excluded from the major institutions of society and the economy. Participation in non-compulsory education was low, decision-making roles at local and national levels were extremely limited, and active engagement in business was virtually non-existent.

Signs of change came after the establishment of the Waitangi Tribunal in 1975 and were accelerated after the raft of reforms in 1984 which saw the Treaty incorporated in both legislation and policy and extended to include areas that had not previously been emphasised. In contrast to the view that the Treaty's scope was primarily limited to land, the role of the Treaty in social policy formed a significant part of the work of the Royal Commission on Social Policy. The Commission found that the Treaty was highly relevant to health, education, broadcasting and other social services.

Notwithstanding the substantial areas where agreement has yet to be reached, more than two decades later it is possible to describe the resulting changes as transformational. From a position of relative exclusion Māori participation within society has undergone radical reform. There is now active participation in tertiary education, the governance and delivery of health services, parliamentary decision-making, economic growth, environmental management, conservation, heritage management, the IT industry, and the professions. Moreover, the settlement of Treaty claims against the Crown has given a number of tribes the means to embark on new journeys and to forge new partnerships with the private sector, local authorities and international corporations. Māori have become major players within the fishing industry and successful entrepreneurs in a range of small and medium business enterprises.

Equally significant, accelerated Māori participation in society has been matched by rejuvenated Māori participation in te ao Māori – the Māori world. The predicted extinction of te reo Māori as a spoken language has been averted; a new generation of fluent Māori speakers has emerged; a Māori television channel enables Māori viewers to be part of extensive tribal and community networks; Māori provider organisations incorporate cultural values and priorities into their practices; and rūnanga as well as other authorities provide focal points for tribal and community cultural, social and economic development.

Although many factors have contributed to the transformations since 1975, it is unlikely that they would have occurred to the same extent or at the same pace, were it not for the application of the Treaty of Waitangi to policy and practice. From that perspective, far from being misplaced, Māori confidence in the Treaty as a vehicle for change and positive development is well founded.

Indigeneity and the Treaty

The third point to be made tonight is that fundamentally the Treaty of Waitangi has come to equate with the way New Zealand values its indigenous people, their language, culture, resources, and the terms of their participation in society. This underlying rationale is frequently masked by a range of other perspectives that dissect the Treaty according to its historical significance, legal validity, human rights impact, or compatibility with the principles of democracy.

While there are a range of conflicting views about the importance of the Treaty, there is a very high level of agreement that the Treaty of Waitangi is a unique historical marker that signalled the emergence of New Zealand as a modern state. There is also, however, a widespread parallel view that the significance of the Treaty should be confined to the historical arena, if only because the terms of the Treaty are not able to address the complexities of global economies, emerging notions of reconfigured sovereignty, intermarriage, equal opportunities, and new technologies. The Treaty's historic emphasis is further reinforced by the recent weight given to the settlement of historic claims against the Crown for breaches of Treaty principles. Many New Zealanders now equate the Treaty with Treaty settlements. In that view, once claims have been settled then the Treaty might also be put aside.

A similar line of thinking is evident in connection with social justice. According to most socio-economic indicators there are disparities between Māori and other New Zealanders and the lower standards of health, education, housing, and income are regarded as evidence of unfulfilled Treaty guarantees. From this perspective the rationale for the Treaty is often presented as a mechanism to ensure equality and once inequalities have been overcome, the Treaty will have served its purpose, at least in respect of social policy.

That view of Māori, as a disadvantaged ethnic minority requiring additional state support, is sometimes used to counter the relevance of the Treaty to modern New Zealand. There are a number of other ethnic minorities who also require support and the proposition that Māori have a prior Treaty-based claim to government aid flies in the face of notions of fairness, social justice, and equality. As New Zealand's cultural diversity is reshaped by greater representation of Pacific and Asian ethnicities, the Treaty is sometimes seen as discriminatory insofar as it appears to favour Māori culture and wellbeing over the wellbeing and culture of other ethnic minorities.

These arguments, based on the assumptions that the Treaty is primarily about our history, or about uniformity and sameness, the celebration of cultural diversity, or ethnicity, overlook two important starting points. First, the Treaty was never intended to be a memorial to the past. A major objective was to set in place an agreement that would accelerate development and provide a basis for facing the future with greater resolve and consensus. Māori were intended to be part of that future and to play a role in shaping it. Second, as development occurred, Māori intellectual and physical resources would not be compromised and Māori people, as indigenous New Zealanders would not be unfairly disadvantaged. While the second point might be construed as a prescription for all subsequent ethnic minorities, the key underlying concern related to indigeneity rather than to culture or ethnicity.

Within a Treaty context, indigeneity refers to Māori language, custom, intellectual resources such as mātauranga Māori, physical resources such as land and waterways, and the exercise of customary socio-political powers. Article two contains some of the understandings of indigeneity but a more comprehensive approach is taken in the Declaration of the Rights of Indigenous Peoples, ratified by the United Nations General Assembly in 2007. Although New Zealand voted against the Declaration,[1] largely on the grounds that some provisions, such as an indigenous right to traditional lands and territories were inconsistent with New Zealand law, it is likely that the Declaration will be a global benchmark against which state support for indigenous peoples will be measured.

The question that New Zealand will need to ask is how indigeneity should be valued and recognised. By New Zealand's stepping aside from the Declaration of the Rights of Indigenous Peoples, other nations and other indigenous peoples might well conclude that this country intends to deny Māori any special recognition on the grounds that the passage of time has extinguished the relevance of indigenous rights. But given our history and the progress the nation has made in addressing the indigenous position, however incomplete, extinguishing indigenous rights is an unlikely scenario. It does nonetheless raise the further question as to whether New Zealand can adopt a proactive approach that does not depend on claims against the Crown, or judicial decisions, or socio-economic disadvantage, but is focused more on making certain that indigenous people, resources, culture and society can be strong into the future. That was of course an objective of the Treaty of Waitangi.

The future

You will recall that I set out to make three main points tonight. The first was that the Treaty is embedded in the life of the nation; the second was that over the past two or three decades the Treaty of Waitangi has contributed to a spectacular transformation of New Zealand society, regenerating Māori faith in the Treaty's promise; and the third was that fundamentally the Treaty has come to be about the way in which

New Zealand values its indigenous people, their resources, and their participation in society.

A fourth point might also be added. Simply, the Treaty is about future opportunities. In contrast to the view that the Treaty imposes a burden on the Crown and adds to the increasingly long list of risks that must be managed by Crown entities and public institutions, the Treaty also provides an opportunity to create a future together. Having developed understandings and forged new associations while hammering out Treaty settlements, it would be disappointing if those relationships were not further developed and transferred from an adversarial platform to an arena where the future can be contemplated with a degree of eagerness. Nor, by itself, does an analysis of the Treaty within a risk management framework lead to any useful endpoint other than satisfying key performance indicators. Clearly, opportunities for Māori and the Crown to jointly plan for the future and to do so within a climate of enthusiasm and trust have received much less attention than efforts to correct past mistakes or avoid any fiscal or legal risk.

Looking ahead, it is highly likely that New Zealand's way of life as we know it will be increasingly squeezed. Quite apart from the Australian influence, predictably the western traditions that came to New Zealand in 1840 will be modified by the cultures and traditions from the east. Eastern world views will be reflected in commercial practices, decision-making, the public-private balance, education, the media, and technology.

But the distinctiveness of New Zealand as a competitive economy will not depend entirely on either the west or the east.

There is the opportunity for the nation to be grounded in what might be called the Aotearoa tradition. In that tradition Māori will interact with other New Zealanders, not on the basis of grievance or insular thinking but on the skills, knowledge, resources and values that each can bring. In short, the yet-to-be-realised promise of the Treaty of Waitangi is about the way in which we will prepare for the future and the unique stamp we will place on New Zealand as a distinctive modern economy within the Pacific.

CHAPTER 14

The Treaty of Waitangi: Domestic Relations, Global Impacts and a New Zealand Agenda

Presented at the Treaty Debate Series, Te Papa Tongarewa, Wellington, 4 February 2010.

An evolving relationship

The year 2010 marks the 170th anniversary of the Treaty of Waitangi. Signed in 1840 by Hobson, on behalf of the British Crown, and over 500 chiefs representing most tribes, the Treaty was an international agreement intended to accelerate the forward development of New Zealand as a modern state. Competition between France and Great Britain for control of the South Pacific was an important ingredient of the international dimension and securing a resourceful southern base ahead of competitors was to be a strategic element in the future expansion of the British Empire.

Although in recent years the Treaty's importance has stressed the significance of internal arrangements, with a strong historic focus, over the next few decades international relationships and future developments will shift the debate away from a purely domestic orientation and a recital of historic injustices to a global arena and an agenda for tomorrow. The Treaty's application to the future will overtake its significance to the past.

A recent Treaty settlement highlights the point. In June 2008 the Crown and eight tribes from the central North Island – the Central North Island Iwi Collective – agreed on terms for settling longstanding grievances relating to unfair land alienations. Made up of 176,000 hectares of Crown land, accumulated rentals valued at around 250 million dollars, three million New Zealand units of carbon credits, and preferential rights to purchase certain Crown properties, the settlement is by far the largest in New Zealand's history. The Central North Island settlement (CNI) is also the most comprehensive insofar as it embraces the interests of eight neighbouring tribes and will lead to the establishment of a forestry company, a geothermal energy company, and a carbon farming company. Moreover, the settlement is premised on a 100 year developmental timeframe; not until the year 2109 will the collective's right to first refusal of Crown properties expire. On a continuum between the resolution of past injustices on the one hand and securing a sound economic platform for future generations on the other, the CNI agreement appears to be more strongly aligned to future need than to past grievances.

In that respect a new era of Treaty relevance could be emerging. Though the past two decades have largely located the Treaty dialogue within an historic context concerned with righting past wrongs, in the case of the CNI settlement, at least, a Treaty of Waitangi relationship between Māori and the Crown has the potential to shape the future of the nation on a scale that has not been previously contemplated.

A future focus, however, should not be altogether surprising. When the Treaty was signed it carried with it the expectation that New Zealand's forward development would see a transition from a tribal society to a modern nation ready to stand alongside the wider community of nations. Britain would gain new territory bringing both strategic advantages as well as new wealth, while the tribes would benefit from any economic, social and civic gains without disadvantage or loss of standing. The Treaty was essentially about facilitating a new future for New Zealand and its peoples.

In the event less than twenty years after signing the Treaty those expectations were being questioned by Māori and disputed by the settlers. In 1856 the tribes had participated in a hui at Pūkawa on the shores of Lake Taupō to share their fears about the erosion of tribal estates and their lack of voice in decision making. The Pūkawa discussions led to two major conclusions. First, Kotahitanga – unity between the tribes – was necessary in the new environment; and second, Kingitanga – the anointment of a Māori king – would be an effective way of gaining unity. Although neither conclusion was implemented in quite the way tribal participants had envisaged, there was a strong sense of urgency to address new times with new structures that would bring fresh opportunities and greater say in the nation's development.

Meanwhile the outbreak of hostilities between the Crown and Taranaki tribes at Waitara in 1860 highlighted both settler impatience for forward development and Māori dissatisfaction with a process that did not seem to bring the promised tribal benefits. Concerned about the possibility of further hostilities, 150 years ago this year, Governor Gore Browne convened a four-week conference at Kohimarama in Auckland. Apart from the iwi of Taranaki, who were otherwise engaged with surveyors and soldiers, and Waikato iwi who were in mourning for the loss of the first Māori king, Potatau Te Wherowhero, the 1860 Kohimarama conference was attended by representatives from most tribes.

In contrast to the Pūkawa hui where the focus was on a Māori response to colonising efforts, the Kohimarama conference was about the relationship between Māori and the Crown. Claudia Orange's research[1] suggests that Governor Browne wanted to impress upon the tribes their obligation to be loyal to the Crown, so clearly stated in the English version of article one. But it seems that Māori participants were more interested in the Māori version of article two with a guarantee of tino rangatiratanga. Possibly because the link between the two articles was not explored, Kohimarama had ended on a high note though each party was satisfied for different reasons. The Governor concluded that a pledge for loyalty had been obtained while iwi were now much more aware of the extent and the potential of article two.

But regardless of the goodwill generated at the month-long deliberations, the covenant written at Kohimarama was not able to provide a mutually agreed way forward. Iwi assumptions about tino rangatiratanga remained at odds with imperial notions of sovereignty, and tribal opposition to settler incursions was interpreted by the Crown as Māori disloyalty. Inevitably relationships between Māori and the Crown deteriorated. Land wars extended beyond Taranaki and calls to abide by the spirit of the Treaty of Waitangi were effectively offset in 1877 when the Treaty was declared a 'simple nullity' without binding legal consequences. Disillusioned with the relationship, iwi pursued other options for exercising authority, including the launch of a Māori parliament, Paremata Māori, in 1892. Fifty years after the Treaty had been signed at Waitangi, and despite the introduction of Māori electorates in 1867, the relationship between Māori and the Crown had failed to reach a sufficient level of accord that could bring certainty to both parties. The Treaty and the notion of partnership within the Treaty had been effectively sidelined.

Although Māori retained faith in the promises made at Waitangi for a better future, it was not until 1975 that there was any discernable public awareness of the implications of the Treaty to modern times. Simmering unrest about dwindling land holdings, marginalisation of Māori urban dwellers, and the strong possibility that the Māori language could become extinct, spilled over into more strident protest that culminated with the historic Māori Land March led by seventy-nine-year-old Dame Whina Cooper. The extent of the unrest caught many New Zealanders by surprise. They had been blissfully unaware of Māori discontent and the smouldering sense of injustice. Government, however, had not been entirely oblivious to Māori concerns and in that same year the Treaty of Waitangi Act 1975 established the Waitangi Tribunal as a Commission of Inquiry to investigate claims against the Crown for breaches of the principles of the Treaty of Waitangi. Claims were relatively few over the next decade but in 1985 an amendment to the Act extended the jurisdiction of the Tribunal from 1975 back to 1840. Large numbers of claims, small and large and covering lands, fisheries and forests, were to follow.

To speed up the settlement of claims the process of direct negotiation was introduced. Where there was agreement as to the facts, whether determined by the Tribunal or not, claimants and the Crown were now able to negotiate the terms of settlement and reach an outcome that would be both fair and durable. Notwithstanding the emphasis in the so-called fiscal envelope policy on compromise and affordability, rather than full compensation based on principles of justice and modern day values, the major claims have now been settled and many claimants are well placed to establish sustainable economies that will allow greater self-sufficiency. Māori economic investments are higher than they have ever been and continue to grow at unprecedented rates, perhaps best illustrated by the Ngai Tahu experience.[2]

The connection between events occurring 150 years ago at Kohimarama, or even twenty-five years ago with the Treaty of Waitangi

Amendment Act, may not at first glance seem related to New Zealand's future. Both have historic significance and cannot be separated from the times in which they took place. Both events, however, are also about the evolution of relationships between Māori and the Crown. Mistrust, misunderstandings, and misjudgements have all too often been part of the relationship and have left indelible scars. But if the CNI agreement is any guide, there are also increasing signs that Māori and the Crown are refocusing their mutual interests towards the future, rather than the past, and in that respect are returning to the broad point of the Treaty which was about the emergence of New Zealand as a modern state within the worldwide community of nations. The indications are that the post-settlement era which now contextualises many tribal plans, will see a shift, away from grievance and adversarial bargaining between Māori and the Crown, towards a relationship based on a futures agenda, the prospect of mutual benefits, and greater national prosperity. In turn, however, the post-settlement era will likely raise other questions for iwi including whether the relationship between Māori and the Crown will be the most relevant relationship for Māori in the decades ahead.

Global impacts

New Zealand in 2035 – twenty-five years hence – will predictably be subject to quite different pressures than those experienced in 1840 or even operating in 2010.

First, New Zealand's future will be significantly shaped by a changing demography. By 2035 Māori will make up a proportionately greater percentage of the total population, close to 20 percent. By then the ageing of the New Zealand population will be more apparent with a median age of forty-two years compared to thirty-six years in 2006. But within the total population there will be significant differences in age structures between ethnic groups. At the 2006 Census, the median age of the European population was oldest at thirty-nine years while for Māori it was significantly younger at twenty-three years. By 2021, the European median age will have increased to forty-four years, but Māori will still be a relatively youthful population with a median age of around twenty-four years. The lag for Māori reflects higher fertility rates, a younger population base, and lower life expectancy.

Apart from an ageing population, the other significant demographic transition will be an increase in New Zealand's ethnic diversity. Māori, English, Scottish, Welsh, Irish, and Dutch backgrounds will be complemented by larger numbers of Chinese, Indian, Korean, Malay, Philippine, Samoan, Tongan, Fijian, Rarotongan, Kiribati, and Niue Islander settlers, as well as comings and goings from Australia. The diversity will not only add to the country's skill mix but will bring new understandings of society, democracy, commerce and sovereignty. Importantly, New Zealand's colonial attachment to Europe and the northern hemisphere will give way to a southern hemisphere identity and greater pride in being part of the Asian Pacific region. Just as early settlers from Europe in the nineteenth century showed little regard for Māori systems of governance, new settlers in the twenty-first century will not necessarily carry a sense of loyalty to the monarchy or even to the Westminster system.

New Zealand's future, however, will also reflect other worldwide trends. The recent economic recession, for example, has shown how events in the USA can seriously pressure New Zealand industries, force higher levels of unemployment, and freeze real estate. Of even greater concern will be the effects of global warming and climate change. Already there is clear evidence that without worldwide agreements to reduce carbon emissions and re-vegetate denuded landscapes the planet and humanity will be seriously compromised. Not only will previously controlled diseases such as malaria and tuberculosis reappear but global climate changes may result in cataclysmic events including drought, cyclones, gales and floods leading to serious loss of life and property. The age of oil will come to an end and other forms of energy will need to be harnessed. Natural resources such as fresh water will become scarce commodities and their ownership will be a source of tension between iwi, farmers, commercial interests, local authorities and government, all vying for control.

Living in a global community has a double edge. Global colonisation, a process already in train, brings with it entry to worldwide markets, international educational prospects, access to unprecedented volumes of knowledge and information, and exposure to the world's music, art and literature. The opportunities for Māori and all New Zealanders, at home and abroad, will be unlimited. But they will also demand compromise. Increased globalisation may mean that te ao Māori, the Māori world, becomes submerged by other customs and in the process a distinctive way of life will be transformed into a bland adaptation of a global norm. There is a risk that tikanga, kawa, te reo Māori and those other markers that characterise Māori in modern times will be lost to whatever global fashion holds dominance in the world at any particular time.

Māori in a reconfigured world

But no matter how unpalatable that prospect, it would be short-sighted to assume that New Zealand is sufficiently isolated from the rest of the world to have immunity from wider global transitions. Indeed even when the Treaty of Waitangi was signed in 1840, global competitiveness between the powerful colonising nations of the world, and overpopulation in industrialised cities were reasons for Britain's interest in New Zealand.

Although forecasting the future is difficult, given the rate of change, the advent of new technologies, and the consequences of new epidemics and other calamities, there are trends that provide useful signposts. Demographic patterns, for example, as well as emerging political alliances and global climate change have impacts that can be largely anticipated.

Nonetheless, futures planning is an imperfect art and an additional way of considering the potential impacts of national and international events on Māori and on the Treaty is through the construction of scenarios. Scenario development is a method of exploring the future and takes into account already known trends, previous patterns of development such as nineteenth century colonisation, horizon scanning to detect, for example, the emergence of new technologies, and vigorous imagining. Three scenarios have been constructed to illustrate some of the possibilities for New Zealand by the year 2035.

Scenario 1: The Republic of New Zealand (RNZ)

The first scenario is about New Zealand's constitutional future. It assumes that by 2035 New Zealand has declared itself a republic, still part of the Commonwealth but with a new head of state. The possibility had been canvassed at a national conference in 2000 but no firm conclusions had been reached and because it all seemed too hard, the debate was shelved. But in the wake of developments in the European Union during the early 2020s and the consequent impositions placed on royalty in Scandinavia as well as Great Britain, constitutional monarchies had steadily fallen out of favour. In addition the large number of New Zealanders of Asian and South American descent had little or no interest in perpetuating a constitutional framework that emanated from the northern hemisphere.

In the event, transitioning towards a republic had been surprisingly uneventful except for three questions. First, should the president of the new republic be appointed or elected? Second, should there be a written constitution or simply a continuation of the nation's reliance on a series of conventions, supported by pragmatic innovation as required? Third, with a final exodus from a colonial past, what would be the status of the Treaty of Waitangi?

Of the three questions the third proved to be the least problematic. Despite a rearguard protest that the Treaty was an instrument of division and should be ignored, most Kiwis, including Pacific and Asian communities, thought that the rights of indigenous peoples should be maintained, and because it allowed for negotiated solutions rather than dogmatic assertions, the Treaty seemed to be the least difficult way of doing that. Moreover, in wake of highly successful Māori enterprises in a post-settlement environment, the Treasury, no less, had long since concluded that New Zealand's distinctiveness was a function of a vibrant Māori economy and an indigenous approach to climate change. Retaining the Treaty not only recognised indigenous interests but also affirmed the brand necessary for New Zealand to be competitive in a global economy.

Then, once agreement had been reached that the benefits of a written constitution far outweighed the dangers of having no constitution at all, the Treaty of Waitangi was integrated into the constitution as an overriding statement about New Zealand's indigenous peoples and the nation's indigenous resources. For the first time the Treaty now had explicit recognition as an entrenched constitutional element rather than existing solely as a part of a fuzzy national conscience. By 2035 the Republic of New Zealand was widely recognised as a champion for social cohesion and for indigeneity.

Scenario 2: The Confederation of the States of Australasia (CSA)

In contrast to the first scenario, in a second scenario by 2035 New Zealand has become integrated into the Confederation of the States of Australasia. Two factors had contributed to the formation of the Confederation. First, concerns about global warming and the high expenditure of carbon credits on long distance flying meant that northern hemisphere markets, including tourism, were less attractive. Second, strong Asian economies were competing with both Australia and New Zealand and effectively playing one off against the other. Largely in response to the new economic circumstances evident as early as 2015, New Zealand, Australia and some small Pacific nations agreed to explore the possibility of a new set of alliances with a single currency, a single passport and a single government.

New Zealand was generally enthusiastic about the proposition but a stumbling block had been the New Zealand Crown's commitments to the Treaty of Waitangi. Australia was reluctant to see any reference to indigenous peoples incorporated into the new arrangements for fear that it would unsettle the now 'settled' Aboriginal and Torres Strait Island populations. Despite having eventually agreed to the 2006 Declaration of the Rights of Indigenous Peoples, Australian states had effectively 'bought out' aboriginal demands through a system of compensatory payments that had expired in 2020. In their view all obligations to indigenous peoples had been met and adding the Treaty of Waitangi to the new Confederation's agenda could introduce an argument that the Australian government did not wish to revisit. New Zealand eventually complied with the majority view and reluctantly accepted that the Treaty status would be confined to cultural matters and would not impose obligations on the new federal government, thereby removing a constitutional encumbrance. By

2035 the State of New Zealand had taken its place as one of ten states making up the Confederation of Australasia and in the process the Treaty had been effectively consigned to history.

Scenario 3: Māori Integrated Economies Inc (MIE)

Unlike the second scenario, the third scenario expects that Māori will be leaders in worldwide indigenous networks. One network, Global Indigenous Systems (GIS) had been established in 2025, largely as an initiative of the Indigenous Peoples' Forum at the United Nations. The global economic recession which had started in 2008 and continued through to 2011 had unfortunate longer lasting repercussions for indigenous peoples in many countries. Further, although many nations had signed up to the Declaration on the Rights of Indigenous Peoples in 2006, few had actually encouraged indigenous economic development. The GIS goal was to advance indigenous economies through worldwide indigenous collaboration.

Meanwhile by 2020 it had become clear in New Zealand that Māori investments following Treaty settlements had led to new wealth, experience in economic development, and expertise in financial governance and management. The impact of the economic recession had not been as severe as for other indigenous populations and Māori were keen to maximise economic returns and build economies of scale. As a result, Māori Integrated Economies Inc (MIE) was established in 2022. It represented an amalgam of Sealords, Treelords (the collective CNI companies), Māori Providers Ltd, and the Ahuwhenua Trust – a consortium of Māori land incorporations.

MIE had provided a model for integrating economic and social capital and by bringing together a mix of resources had become a major player in the New Zealand economy and a world leader in indigenous economic development. When GIS was established by indigenous peoples in 2025, MIE was invited to provide overall leadership and to extend their model across global indigenous networks. By 2035, Māori had become masters in integrated solutions and MIE was the dominant economic force in New Zealand. The New Zealand government, aware of Māori wealth and commercial partnerships with international businesses, saw the Treaty of Waitangi as an important vehicle for the state to lever off Māori enterprise and gain entry into global markets. The Crown now seemed to place greater emphasis on the Treaty's significance than the tribes.

Tino rangatiratanga

The three scenarios are all possible though clearly not all would be equally popular. Scenario 2 (about the Confederation of Australasian States) would probably have least appeal to Māori while both scenario 1 (Republic of New Zealand) and scenario 3 (Māori Integrated Economies) would be more attractive options. However, the intention for sharing these scenarios was not to enter into a debate about which of the three would be more probable or even more desirable but to illustrate how the position of Māori in Aotearoa and the standing of the Treaty of Waitangi in the future cannot be contemplated without considering the global context and the inevitability of significant economic and political change in the future.

Importantly, it cannot be assumed that current Māori perceptions of constitutional rights will necessarily apply in the future. Take, for example, attitudes to the Treaty of Waitangi. While the Treaty has been both an enabling and a disabling instrument, it may also have inadvertently narrowed Māori horizons. The Treaty of Waitangi was essentially an understanding about the relationship between Māori and the Crown. Under the Treaty, sovereignty, or at least the right to govern, was exchanged for guarantees about property and citizenship. The Treaty gave some protections but also positioned Māori alongside the Crown. In a sense Māori had been captured by the state at the expense of other potentially more profitable relationships. There are no good reasons why the Treaty should be the single most important defining statement about the position of Māori or for that matter why Māori should not enter into other treaties.

Debates about the relationship between Māori and the Crown, which have occupied great legal and academic minds – both Māori and Pākehā – have tended to measure Māori political legitimacy against the criterion of sovereignty, a concept that is culturally bound and increasingly bounded by time. Not only will notions of sovereignty be subject to the permeation of global philosophies and global quests for power and wealth, as evidenced by multinational companies, but the sovereign boundaries between states will become blurred as digital technologies shrink distance, and public and private interests become increasingly intertwined. For those reasons, it could be unwise for Māori to measure tino rangatiratanga solely against the parameters of the Crown's sovereignty, whatever meaning sovereignty might have in the future. The Copenhagen climate change conference and the addition of folic acid to bread, both widely debated in 2009, are signs that New Zealand's sovereignty will come to reflect overseas pressures and trends as much as Kiwi aspirations for self-determined dominion.

In addition, in a post-settlement environment, it is likely that Māori engagement with the Crown will alter in both purpose and intensity. That does not mean there will be no relationship but a two-directional change in the nature of the relationship can be expected.

First, Māori involvement with the Crown will be increasingly focused on New Zealand's agenda for the future, rather than on compensation for the past. Recent discussions between the Crown and the Iwi Leadership Forum in relationship to water management provide an example of a new type of relationship, while the Central North Island Settlement is clearly aligned to the century ahead rather than the century past.

Second, Māori will predictably choose to spend more time and energy exploring relationships with the private sector, seeking investment opportunities with overseas companies, and playing leadership roles in global indigenous networks, while spending less time engaging with the Crown. To meet those changes it may be opportune for Māori to enter into a new set of treaties with other parties, beyond the Crown and beyond New Zealand, and geared to the twenty-first rather than the nineteenth century. A Treaty partnership with the Crown will remain important but the nature of the relationship will increasingly reflect mutually beneficial interests in the future, and in addition there will be greater Māori interest in other types of partnerships with the private sector, with overseas commercial interests, and with indigenous peoples across the globe.

The point is that the practice of measuring tino rangatiratanga against the single yardstick of sovereignty may already be outdated. The Treaty of Waitangi prescribes a relationship between iwi and the Crown that hinges on distinctions between sovereignty and tino rangatiratanga. That relationship will grow in importance as indigenous traditions and resources increase in value, and the eyes of the region come to rest on New Zealand's shores. However, the standing of Māori in Aotearoa and beyond will not be defined solely or even mainly by notions of legal sovereignty or rights conferred through the application of the Treaty of Waitangi. Many of those rights actually predated the Treaty. But in any event, rather than authenticating the Māori position only in the law, Māori authority will increasingly be a product of demographic significance, economic might, and international recognition.

Ironically, that position may not be too far removed from the situation in 1840 when Britain became conscious of the natural wealth of New Zealand, aware of iwi as proprietors, and hopeful that Māori might be strategic partners in a competitive world. Indeed they were the very reasons for signing the Treaty of Waitangi.

Health

CHAPTER 15

Indigeneity, and the Promotion of Positive Mental Health

Key note address to the Third World Conference for the Promotion of
Mental Health and Prevention of Mental and Behavioural Disorders,
Auckland, 15 September 2004.

Indigenous peoples

In the presence of so many indigenous peoples here today it is with
some hesitancy that I speak about indigeneity and indigenous values
as they might be applied to mental health. While I belong to the
indigenous Māori people of Aotearoa New Zealand, I am only too well
aware of the differences between indigenous peoples and the risks of
presuming that being indigenous is the same the world over. Clearly
between indigenous populations there are differences of colour, history,
language, size, and culture. Yet despite the differences there are also
common bonds that make it possible for indigenous peoples to break
through cultural barriers as well as the barriers imposed by geographic
distance and political alignments.

There are some 5000 indigenous groups around the world with a
total population of about 200 million, or around 4 percent of the global
population. While there is no simple definition of indigenous peoples or
the attributes that underlie indigeneity – being indigenous – it is possible
to identify a number of characteristics that are shared by indigenous
peoples and which add clarity to the so-called indigenous perspective.

First, indigenous peoples have very often experienced contact with
other cultures and civilisations and as a result have suffered a range of
unfortunate consequences including alienation from traditional lands

and properties, depopulation and serious health problems. While many of those experiences are in common, a more unifying characteristic is a sense of unity with the environment. The people of Whanganui have an expression which links them closely to their environment: 'We are the river, the river is us'.[1] And the North American Indians see themselves as inseparable from the land: 'We are the land the land is us'. The celebrated Native American scholar, Vine Deloria, stressed the nature of the connection in: 'Most tribes were very reluctant to surrender their homelands to the whites because they knew that their ancestors were still spiritually alive on the land.'[2]

A bond with the land and the natural environment is the fundamental feature of indigeneity. The land is an extension of tribal and personal identity and the relationship is reflected in song, custom, hunting, approaches to healing, and the utilisation of physical resources.

Common to indigenous peoples is a world view that locates people within the context of the natural environment, rather than apart from the environment. Māori refer to tribes that have a long association with a particular territory or locality as 'tangata whenua' – people of the land. Other tribes do not have the same relationship and even though they might have since moved into an area, they are not able to describe themselves as tangata whenua, at least not as long as the original inhabitants are alive. Back in their own territories, however, it is another matter. There, they too are tangata whenua.

The primary characteristic of indigeneity is therefore a close relationship with defined territories, land, and the natural world. Arising from that relationship it is possible to identify five secondary characteristics of indigeneity. The first reflects the dimension of time and a relationship with the environment that has endured over centuries; the second, also derived from the environmental relationship, is about culture, human identity and group structures and processes that celebrate the human–environmental union. The third characteristic is a system of knowledge – indigenous knowledge – that integrates indigenous world views, values, and experience and generates a framework for a distinctive approach to health and wellbeing, an approach that emphasises collectivity, spirituality, balance, and an ecological perspective within which human behaviour unfolds. Application of that perspective to natural resources and human endeavour provides a basis for the fourth characteristic, economic growth balanced against environmental sustainability for the benefit of future generations. Finally, indigeneity is also characterised by a language so strongly influenced by the environment that it is not spoken as a first language in other parts of the world.

These five secondary characteristics – time, culture, an indigenous system of knowledge, environmental sustainability, and a native language – as well as the primary characteristic, the overriding relationship with the natural environment, bring indigenous peoples into a circle of shared understandings.

To a large extent the aspirations of indigenous peoples can also be found in the Draft Declaration of the Rights of Indigenous Peoples.[3] It contains forty-five articles covering cultural, spiritual, economic, political and constitutional rights and has major implications for the terms under which indigenous people will live within states.

A second important document had its origins in 1999 when the World Health Organisation arranged an International Consultation on the Health of Indigenous Peoples in Geneva. A Declaration on the Health and Survival of Indigenous Peoples was subsequently prepared and endorsed at the UN Permanent Forum on Indigenous Issues in 2002.[4] Written in five parts, the Declaration affirms the links between culture, the wider natural environment, human rights, and health, and proposes a definition of health: 'Indigenous Peoples' concept of health and survival is both a collective and individual inter-generational continuum encompassing a holistic perspective incorporating four distinct shared dimensions of life. These dimensions are the spiritual, the intellectual, physical and emotional. Linking these four fundamental dimensions, health and survival manifests itself on multiple levels where the past, present and future co-exist simultaneously.'

In effect the two declarations suggest that indigenous peoples should have access to the indigenous world with its values and resources, access to the wider society within which they live, access to a healthy environment, and a degree of autonomy over their own lives and properties.

Indigenous health experience

Indigenous peoples, especially those who have become minority populations within their own lands, have suffered comparable patterns of disease. In the eighteenth and nineteenth centuries, groups as diverse as Māori in New Zealand, Australian Aborigines, Native Hawaiians, the Saami of Norway, Native Americans and the First Nations of Canada, among others, were nearly decimated by infectious diseases such as measles, typhoid fever, tuberculosis and influenza. For some, including the First Nations, smallpox epidemics produced even greater suffering.[5]

But by the mid-twentieth century, following the near-universal experience of urbanisation in the 1950s, other health risks emerged. In developed countries such as Canada, Australia, the USA and New Zealand, vulnerability to injury, alcohol and drug misuse, cancer, kidney disease, obesity, suicide, depression, and diabetes have become the modern indigenous health hazards.[6] Compared to non-indigenous members of the population, life expectancy is significantly lower for indigenous peoples and the incidence of most diseases is higher, sometimes by rates of two or three times (diabetes, mental disorders, some cancers).[7]

Health determinants

Leaving aside early colonists' views about 'constitutional inferiority', explanations for current indigenous health status can be broadly grouped into four main causes: genetic predisposition, socio-economic disadvantage, resource alienation, and political oppression.[8]

Possible genetic predispositions have been investigated in alcohol disorders, schizophrenia and bipolar disorders, though are generally regarded as less significant than socio-economic disadvantage, which is often central to contemporary indigenous experience. Poor housing, low educational achievement, unemployment and inadequate incomes, are known to correlate with a range of health problems and facilitate lifestyles that predispose to disease and injury.[9]

However, socio-economic factors by themselves do not explain health disparities between indigenous peoples and non-indigenous populations. For example when Māori and non-Māori at the same levels of deprivation are compared, Māori health status still remains lower than non-Māori: Māori patients are more likely to be admitted to a psychiatric inpatient unit (63 percent for Māori, 33 percent for European); Pacific inpatient episodes are 35 percent above the national average while Māori inpatient episodes are 22 percent above average.[10] While there has been some call for health policies that are race and colour-free, the reality is that ethnicity, race and colour are very much part of the epidemiological pattern and should not be simply regarded as proxies for deprivation.

Among other possible explanations for increased rates of indigenous mental health problems, alienation from natural resources along with environmental degradation have been identified as a cause of poor health in several countries. But it is not only alienation of physical resources that is important. Intellectual and cultural resources are also relevant to mental health to the extent that deculturation contributes to poor mental health and personal identity.[11] Several writers have also drawn a link between colonisation and poor health.[12] They argue that loss of sovereignty along with dispossession (of lands, waterways, customary laws) created a climate of material and spiritual deprivation with increased susceptibility to disease and injury.

All four positions can be justified and conceptualised as a causal continuum. At one end are 'short distance' factors such as the impacts of abnormal molecular and cellular processes, while at the other end are 'long distance' factors including governmental policies and the political standing of indigenous peoples. Values, lifestyle, standards of living, and culture, so important to mental health, lie midway.

Māori models of health promotion

Given the range of causative factors, mental health promotion requires a broad approach that covers a wide spectrum of interventions. To bring together the several components and to visualise the scope, a Māori model for mental health promotion has been developed in New Zealand.[13] It uses the imagery of Te Pae Māhutonga, a constellation of stars popularly referred to as the Southern Cross (Crux Australis) that is visible high in the southern skies and acts as a marker of the magnetic South Pole.[14] Te Pae Māhutonga has long been used as a navigational aid and is closely associated with the discovery of Aotearoa.

Because it is an indigenous icon, Te Pae Māhutonga can also be used as a symbolic chart for mapping the dimensions of mental health promotion[15] and the promotion of health for indigenous children and young people.[16] The four central stars can be used to represent four key foundations of health: cultural identity and access to the Māori world (mauriora), environmental protection (waiora), well-being and healthy lifestyles (toiora), and full participation in wider society (whaiora). The two pointers symbolise two key capacities that are needed to make progress: effective leadership (ngā manukura) and autonomy (mana whakahaere).

Mauriora: cultural identity and access to the Māori world

The first foundation concerns cultural identity and access to the indigenous world. Good health depends on many factors, but among indigenous peoples cultural identity is considered to be a critical prerequisite; deculturation has been associated with poor health whereas acculturation has been linked to good health.[17] In modern urbanised societies indigenous peoples often have limited access to their own worlds. The alienation of estates is common enough so that ongoing links with tribal land have very often been severed; but many indigenous languages have also been threatened or even lost altogether, and access to cultural institutions such as marae has often been restricted by geographic dislocation and cultural estrangement.

A task of health promotion therefore is to facilitate access by indigenous people to the indigenous world: access to language and knowledge; culture and cultural institutions; sites of heritage; and indigenous networks, especially family and community.

Waiora: environmental protection

The second health foundation, waiora, is linked more specifically to the natural world and includes a spiritual element that connects human wellness with cosmic, terrestrial and water environments. A central element of indigeneity is the close association between people and their accustomed environments – land, waterways, the air, beaches, harbours and the sea, native flora and fauna. Good health is compromised where there is atmospheric pollution, contaminated water supplies, smog, random mining activities, or commercial developments that exploit the land they cover; or where access to traditional sites is barred.

Toiora: healthy lifestyles

A third foundation for mental health concerns personal wellbeing and healthy lifestyles. Indigenous peoples have their own perspectives on health and wellbeing. A frequently discussed Māori health perspective is known as Te Whare Tapa Whā, a construct that compares good health to the four sides of a house and prescribes a balance between spirituality (taha wairua), intellect and emotions (taha hinengaro), the human body (taha tinana) and human relationships (taha whānau).

Major threats to health come from unbalanced lifestyles, products of contemporary living and modern societies such as the use of alcohol and drugs, unsafe roadways, tobacco use, disregard for the safety of others, unprotected sex, sedentary habits, social isolation, estrangement from family and friends, and risk-taking. Many indigenous peoples, young and old, are trapped in risk-laden lifestyles and have little chance of ever being able to realise their full potential.

Whaiora: participation in society

A fourth foundation for health, whaiora, is about indigenous participation in wider society measured against material circumstances, social equity, cultural affirmation, justice, and effective representation. Full participation is dependent on the terms under which people participate in society and the confidence with which they can access quality personal services, sport and recreation, meaningful employment or political voice.

Disparities between indigenous and non-indigenous populations are well documented and confirm gaps on almost every social indicator.[18] Health promotional goals need to consider ways in which indigenous participation in society can be increased, especially in relationship to the economy, education, health services, modern technologies, incomes, and decision making.

Ngā manukura: leadership

A common indigenous experience has been for public agencies and health professionals to assume positions of leadership on behalf of indigenous peoples. However, not only did that approach foster both dependency and assimilation, but it also undermined indigenous leadership, now generally regarded as an essential component of mental health promotion. Indigenous leadership should reflect a combination of skills and a range of influences and includes tribal leadership, community leaders, sectoral leaders (such as health professionals or teachers), elected representatives, and academic leaders. An indigenous workforce is critical for indigenous mental health promotion.

Non-indigenous health professionals have important roles to play but should not suppress the leadership that already exists in indigenous communities. While tribal and community leaders may not have technical and professional skills, they do possess an intimate knowledge of their people and have the advantage of being able to communicate in a vernacular that makes sense.

Mana whakahaere: autonomy

Colonisation very often supplanted indigenous forms of governance and management creating instead dependency and marginalisation. It is clear from the Draft Declaration of the Rights of Indigenous Peoples, however, that dependency is not compatible with human dignity or good health. Campaigns by indigenous peoples for greater autonomy have resulted in tension and sometimes open conflict with states. However, although disputes remain about property rights, control of resources, representation, and the manner in which goods and services are made available to indigenous peoples, a number of pathways are able to give expression to the spirit of self-governance. Some of these, such as tribal development programmes, assume a high level of indigenous control and leadership. Similarly, even though they operate within the framework of a state contract, a number of non-tribal community organisations have their own systems of governance and management.

But key to autonomy are the constraints of capability and authority. In many countries, including New Zealand, indigenous workforce development has been afforded some priority though not without creating controversy especially when affirmative action programmes have been introduced or indigenous world views have been woven into the curriculum, or indigenous values have been applied to clinical interventions and key performance indicators.

Implications

Te Pae Māhutonga is one way of bringing together the threads of mental health promotion. It is not so much a model for best practice as a schema to identify the parameters of practice, and to signpost the strategic directions that might be pursued by states, the health and education sectors, and indigenous peoples themselves. Most importantly, indigenous health issues cannot be seriously addressed unless they are part of a wider discussion that includes cultural identity, the natural environment, constitutional arrangements, socio-economic realities, and indigenous leadership.

Inevitably this broad approach raises challenges for the state, the professions, and of course for mental health practitioners, policy makers, and planners. A particular issue concerns the way indigeneity is recognised. While most governments are willing to recognise cultural diversity as a modern reality, not all are willing to accept indigenous peoples as populations with unique rights based not solely on cultural distinctiveness but also on a longstanding relationship with the territory, predating colonisation. Even when treaties have been signed to that effect, there has been debate about their enforceability in modern times.

Some political leaders are also inclined to view health spending entirely according to individual health need, and they dispute population-based funding as a rational basis for addressing health problems, especially when ethnicity or race is the population in question. But while the principle of equality as between individuals can be defended as a democratic principle, it is only one principle that underpins a modern democracy. Health policies based entirely on individual need run the risk of missing the contexts within which people live their lives and which are integral to good mental health. Equality as between populations must also be factored into health policies; and in that respect indigenous peoples have well-established claims for recognition as distinctive populations.

The interface

There is of course a vital role for indigenous practitioners of mental health promotion and health education. Their contribution to indigenous health and more broadly to indigenous development will stem mainly from being at the interface between two worlds: the indigenous world and the globalised world.[19] Living at the interface and inhabiting two spheres could be a source of confusion. But it can also be a site of potential. Wise leadership requires careful management of the interface so that the benefits of modern technologies and science can be transferred to indigenous people in ways that strengthen indigenous world views and contribute to good health.

For too many indigenous people the interface between the indigenous world and society at large has become a giant chasm within which human potential has been drowned. Indigenous workers have a special role to play in negotiating the interface. By virtue of their backgrounds and their professional training they have access to two bodies of knowledge. They are in a position to bridge the gap between the world where indigenous values dominate and the world dominated by science, technology and global imperialism.

Conclusion

There were only five points I wanted to make today.

The first was that indigenous peoples have not been shielded from mental ill-health and a host of accompanying behavioural disorders. There is conclusive and extensive evidence that for a variety of reasons they are overrepresented in hospital admissions, prison incarceration, school failure, unemployment and alienation from key societal and community pathways.

Second, there is an association between mental health and the world views that indigenous peoples hold dear. The indicators of 'good' mental health are not universal and indigenous peoples place particular emphasis on the quality of relationships with family, tribe, community, the land, sites of heritage, and traditional knowledge. Health risks appear to be greater where those world views have been fractured. However, there is also evidence that culture does not necessarily confer immunity. A range of mental health problems occur in people who are strong in their own culture and language. Sometimes the carriers and guardians of culture may be under more stress and pressure than others and consequently assume greater risk.

Third, socio-economic factors are important contributors to poor mental health among indigenous peoples. Measured against almost all socio-economic indicators, Māori, for example, fare less well than other New Zealanders. Educational outcomes are worse; standards of health are lower; unemployment is higher and incomes are correspondingly poorer. It is now well documented that there is a strong correlation between the prevalence and incidence of mental disorders and socio-economic deprivation.

Fourth, however, socio-economic disadvantage is not sufficient to explain the indigenous position. Even where there is equality of living standards, indigenous people suffer worse health and a greater range of mental disorders. Indigeneity appears to be a factor in its own right. However, the precise relevance of that factor is uncertain. While genetics may play a part, the evidence is not overwhelming to support a genetic basis for the disparities. Possibly genetic factors might play a contributing role in some disorders such as diabetes, alcohol disorders and possibly affective disorders, but generally genetic predisposition cannot be seen as the most important determinant. Other possibilities must also be considered including deculturation, societal prejudice, and the multiple impacts of a life lived at the interface between two worlds, without being firmly committed to either.

The fifth point, and it is amply illustrated in indigenous models of health promotion such as Te Pae Māhutonga, is that the prevention of mental and behavioural disorders, and the promotion of positive mental health requires approaches that are consistent with indigenous perspectives, values and world views, but also with best practice and evidence-based policies. The promotion of good health will be ineffective if it is based on an assumption that all people subscribe to the same views of health and aspire to similar goals. Insofar as most indigenous peoples live at the interface between two worlds, health promotion should be delivered in a way that aligns with the dual realties within which indigenous populations live in modern times.

CHAPTER 16

Impacts of an Ageing Population on New Zealand Society

Key note address to New Zealand Association of Gerontology 2007 Conference: Ageing: The Everyday Experience, Hamilton, 14 November 2007.

Demographic trends

Ageing populations are a characteristic of developed nations and New Zealand is no exception. For some decades the trend towards a higher proportion of older people has been apparent and has been further confirmed by the 2006 Census. A combination of lower fertility rates and increased life expectancy has led to a shift in the overall population profile so that the proportion of people over the age of sixty-five years has been steadily increasing while the proportion of people under the age of fifteen years has been gradually declining. In 1985 for example 25 percent of New Zealand's population was under the age of fifteen years compared to 22 percent in 2006. In contrast the population over the age of sixty-five years increased from 10 percent in 1985 to 12 percent in 2006.

The current pattern of ageing is also reflected in a rising median age. In the 2006 Census, the median age of the total New Zealand population was thirty-six years (that is, half the population were older than thirty-six and half younger). Projections indicate that the trend is likely to continue well into the future. By 2016 the median age is expected to be thirty-nine years and by 2026 it will be forty-one years.

Within the total population there are significant differences between ethnic groups. The median age of the European population in 2006 was oldest at thirty-nine years while for Asian, Māori, and Pacific populations it was younger, significantly so for Māori and Pacific. The median age of Asians living in New Zealand is twenty-eight years, for Māori twenty-three years and for Pacific peoples twenty-one years. However, all ethnic groups show a similar trend. By 2021, the European median age will have increased to forty-four years, Asian to thirty-six years, Māori twenty-six years and Pacific peoples twenty-four years. In effect, although the rates of ageing are different, all sub-populations in New Zealand are ageing. The lag for Māori and Pacific populations reflects higher fertility rates, a younger population base, and lower life expectancy.

Greater life expectancy is a further indicator of an ageing population. For non-Māori New Zealanders there was a steady increase in life expectancy at birth over the period from 1985/87 to 2000/02. For Māori there was little change for males or females during the 1980s but a dramatic improvement in the five years to 2000/2. Between 1984 and 2002 the life expectancy increased from sixty-five years for Māori males to sixty-nine years while for Māori females it increased from seventy to seventy-three years. Notwithstanding the eight year gap between Māori and non-Māori, in the five years to 2000/2, the gap reduced by 0.6 years, a further indication that Māori are also an ageing population.[1]

In addition to ethnic differences in life expectancy, there are also regional differences. Generally for both males and females life expectancy is higher in large urban areas and lower in some provincial areas. In Auckland, for example, men have a life expectancy of 77.5 years and women 82.1 years while in Gisborne, the corresponding figures are 72.6 and 78.9. Across all regions, men have lower life expectancy than women by some five or six years.

The reality of an ageing population, if not already evident, will become increasingly so during the next decade. Over the next fifty years the population aged over sixty-five years will more than double to 1.18 million, the largest increases occurring during the 2020s and 2030s. By 2050 only 28 percent of the population will be younger than forty years.[2]

Perspectives on ageing

Societal views on ageing are shaped by many experiences and prejudices. A shift towards an ageing population has resulted in a greater visibility of older people within communities, families and whānau and has challenged society to rethink traditional attitudes towards older members. It has also uncovered society's mixed attitudes towards older people, reflected in folklore, the literature and differing cultural perspectives.

Age has not always been well regarded in the Holy Bible and is not seen as a guarantee of good judgement: 'A young man who is poor and wise is better than a king who is old and foolish and will not be guided by the wisdom of others.' (Ecclesiastes 4:13).

But age, as distinct from youth, is also attributed with wisdom. 'There is wisdom, remember, in age and long life brings understanding' (Job 12:12).

By comparison, in *As You Like It*, the great English playwright, William Shakespeare, portrayed the seventh stage of life – old age – as an inevitable time of deficit and ineptitude.

'Last scene of all,
That ends this strange eventful history,
Is second childishness and mere oblivion,
Sans teeth, sans eyes, sans taste, sans everything.'[3]

The eminent psychoanalyst, Eric Erikson, developed an eight-staged framework for considering psycho-social development but concluded that within each stage there were psychological challenges that could result in either positive or negative outcomes. The central task in adolescence, for example, was to build a positive identity; the default position was a diffuse identity which compromised healthy adaptation to society. In his eighth stage of psycho-social development, Erikson describes ego integrity and despair as poles characterising successful or failed adaptation in old age. Ego integrity 'is a post-narcissistic love of the human ego – not of the self – an experience which conveys some world order and spiritual sense.'[4] Integrity in old age is a type of ecological experience where the significance of the individual is measured by relationships beyond the self; it is shaped by culture and transcends the limitations of personal concerns so that the self merges with the wider human condition. By way of contrast, despair represents a failure to transcend the limitations of body and to live in a world preoccupied with personal decline.

Erikson's eighth stage captures to some extent the expectations upon Māori elderly. When other New Zealanders might be contemplating withdrawing from public life, Māori elderly are often encouraged to accept new responsibilities expected by their own people. For some there may be little real choice. By virtue of genealogical descent, cultural competence, location (living near or on a marae), or family ties, they will inevitably be caught up in the nexus of Māori society; self-interest will give way to the interests of whānau and hapū.

Māori views on ageing and older people are especially evident on marae and in metaphor. They too illustrate mixed views on ageing.[5] 'He rākau tawhito, e mau ana te taitea i waho rā, e tū te kōhiwi' can be literally translated as an ancient tree with sapwood just adhering to the outside, while the heartwood stands firm. The tree is a metaphor for an older person: an infirm body but an indomitable spirit. 'Ka haere te mātātahi, ka noho te mātāpuputu' compares youth and age and concludes that youth rushes in where age deliberates.

A less positive view on ageing can also be found on the marae: 'Ka ruha te kupenga, ka pae kei te ākau' – literally when the old net is worn out it is cast upon the beach – is also a metaphoric way of saying that older people are less desirable once they have lost their youth. 'Me he ika kōharatia e te rā' has a similar meaning. The literal translation 'like a fish split open in the sun' stands for a person who has outlived usefulness and is no longer of value to others.

Measuring impact

The contrasting views on ageing and older people are also reflected in the ways that the impact of an ageing population on society is measured. Often indicators are selected entirely on economic considerations, based on the age-related costs. As the costs of hospital treatment for older people escalate, and the costs of care, whether in communities or at home, increase, concern has been expressed about the net debt on society that will accompany increased longevity. The dependency ratio, a measure of the working population against the population who are not in the paid workforce, will predictably narrow so that a proportionately smaller segment of society will support a growing number who are unable to work or who are not yet old enough to work. Moreover, as the personal income of older people declines, state support by way of universal superannuation or some similar scheme will add dollars to the tax take at the expense of the take-home pay for younger workers.

However, the depiction of older people as repositories for disabilities and diseases, confined to wheelchair or bedridden, and dependant on the care of others, does not constitute a valid way of assessing the net costs of ageing on New Zealand society in modern times. While older people are more likely to require hospitalisation, and to encounter age-related sensory and motor disabilities, as well as mental disabilities such as Alzheimer's disease, increasingly older people are also playing critical roles in society and adding value to communities, families, and the economy. The value-added components and the short and long term benefits to society are more difficult to measure than the economic costs of service utilisation and social transfers, but represent significant social and cultural capital that provide society with a sense of continuity and a more balanced perspective on development.

Too often the context for discussing the implications of an ageing population on modern society is shaped only by the costs. What also needs to be factored into the equation are the distinctive contributions of older people and the benefits that accrue to society as a whole. Costs incurred need to be balanced by contributions made. Impact is essentially a measure of both costs and benefits.

Far from benefiting society, the absence of a large cohort of older people creates a significant hiatus. World War II, for example, robbed Māori society of a generation of men who, in the fullness of time, would have become leaders on marae, in board rooms and in tribal runanga. Instead, of the 3578 volunteers in the 28th Māori Battalion, 70 percent became casualties. Hostilities in North Africa, Greece, Crete, Italy and Malta led to the deaths of 649 young Māori and many more suffered long term disabilities.[6] Two or more generations later many marae were to experience a serious gap with a lack of competent kaumatua able to provide cultural and strategic leadership. While younger men often stepped up to fill the void, the standing of marae and tribe was diminished by a lack of visible older men.

Older people as societal assets

Because the flip side of societal cost is societal contribution, the full impact of an ageing population on modern society requires an examination of the contributions made by older people as well as any burdens imposed on the nation. The costs of ageing are well documented but there have been fewer efforts to measure the contributions older people make to families, communities and future generations. A series of contributory roles can be identified and although many of them are more readily recognised within Māori society, all of them have some applicability to wider society and to all sub-populations within New Zealand.

Older people as carriers of culture

The standing of a tribe, its mana, as distinct from its size, relates more to the visible presence and authority of its elders than to the vigorous activities of its younger members. Executive and industrial leadership may well rest with the young and the middle-aged but it is the older generation who carry the status, tradition and integrity of their people. Without leadership at that level a Māori community will be the poorer and, at least in other Māori eyes, unable to function effectively or to fulfil its obligations. The roles ascribed older people are not only positive, they are critical for the survival of tribal mana.[7] Because much cultural knowledge is learned over a lifetime by watching, listening, and then emulating earlier generations, it is older people who come to carry the culture and pass it on to younger generations. Not only have they been able to absorb the examples of their own elders, but they have been able to marry knowledge with relevance, sense of occasion, and modern realities. In effect they are in a position to mediate culture so that it makes sense to contemporary times, while retaining a link with the past.

Moreover, older Māori are still more likely to converse in Māori than younger age groups and use dialectal phrases, not usually available to second language learners, as a matter of course.[8]

Older people as anchors for families

In many cultures, older people act as anchors for families. They are accorded positions of responsibility and in turn provide avenues for family connectedness even when family households are separated by geography or by international boundaries. Though they may have little active involvement in day-to-day activities, their contribution to family events and to the family identity has the potential of being a major source of strength to younger members and especially to families with children. Although there have not been a large number of studies into grandfathering, there is sufficient evidence to challenge the image of an austere and aloof figure; grandfathers and grandmothers are important to their adult children and to their grandchildren. Grandfathers can provide support (financial and emotional) at times of family crisis, and can act as surrogate male parents where fathers are absent.[9]

When the 'anchors' are gone, the dynamics within families undergo major shifts often leading to fragmentation and splintering. The respect accorded older people within families is not based on age alone but on their positive roles and the protection they give to families in the course of community interaction. In many Māori whānau older people are gateways to marae and to wider tribal society.

A survey of 400 kaumātua aged sixty years and over was undertaken from Te Pumanawa Hauora at Massey University.[10] The survey found that older Māori men and women live active lives, physically, socially and culturally. Contact with families is close and responsibilities and obligations are reciprocal. Far from being inactive, three-quarters of the older people interviewed provided support for other family members as well as enjoying high levels of marae and tribal participation.

Older people as models for lifestyle

Older people act as counters to younger generations especially those who are more inclined to adopt risk-laden lifestyles. For whatever reason, risk taking and risky lifestyles are less prevalent in later years. People aged over fifty years, for example, smoke less than younger people and have experienced the greatest decline in smoking prevalence over the past twenty years.[11] Similarly the prevalence of obesity declines after the age of sixty-five years; for over seventy-five females it is 17 percent and for males 19 percent, compared to 31 percent and 29 percent for people aged between fifty-five and sixty-four years.[12]

Despite lower levels of physical activity, older people are more likely to be satisfied with their leisure time and to be most satisfied with their work–life balance.[13] Levels of alcohol consumption are markedly lower in the over sixty-five years age group and the prevalence of marijuana abuse is similarly low. In the forty-five to sixty-four year age group the prevalence of any substance use disorder is 1.2 percent, but it is less than 0.1 percent for those sixty-five years and over.[14]

Older people are less likely to indulge in modern lifestyle risks such as 'P', binge drinking, street car racing, invasion of the privacy of others, and internet piracy. In this respect they can provide a perspective that is relatively independent, less entangled in a climate of urgency and immediate gratification, and more attuned to longer timeframes.

Older people as bridges to the future

Older people are not confined to living in the past. Laying the foundations for Māori health research, for example, was largely a function of older Māori women in the Māori Women's League. They wanted answers to questions about the health of Māori women that captured Māori values, ideals and actual situations. After an initial scoping exercise, the research was reformatted so that it aligned with Māori perspectives and had more relevance to Māori women and whānau. League members themselves undertook training and completed the field work, interviewing some 1200 women in their own homes. Many of the interviewers were seventy years or older and the project directors were also older women. Their efforts not only led to the publication of an influential report, *Rapuora*,[15] but also laid foundations for incorporating Māori perspectives into research methodologies. Later, kaupapa Māori research paradigms formalised the innovations but the earliest initiative had come from older members of the League, led by the Director, Erihapeti Murchie.

The kōhanga reo experience also illustrates the importance of older people as bridges to the future. Faced with possible extinction of the Māori language, older native speakers of Māori – men and women – were recruited into early childhood education centres, kōhanga reo, where they interacted with preschool children and adult supervisors, using everyday words and phrases that would normalise Māori as a language for modern times. Under the guidance of a small but energetic group of elders, including Sir James Henare, Sir John Bennett, Dame Te Atairangikaahu, and Iritana Tawhiwhirangi, the future of Māori language, as a spoken language, was implanted in young children as an investment for the future. Without leadership and guidance from older Māori, the efforts of the movement would have floundered.

Older people as bulwarks for industry

Compulsory retirement at sixty-five years robbed communities of accumulated expertise and wisdom. Skills gained over four or more decades were suddenly lost to the workforce and with them, product understanding, intuitive know-how, and sector networking. Legislative changes that no longer sanction age-related retirement have created opportunities for older people to choose when they will retire and to continue working alongside younger colleagues. Now around 40 percent of men and 20 percent of women aged between sixty-five and seventy years remain active participants in the workforce.

While there are benefits for older employees, there are also substantial gains for the workforce. No matter what the pace of change, the working environment benefits from a sense of stability and an institutional memory. Technological wizardry, the domain of the digital generation, needs to be balanced by human capabilities and workforce relationships. Older people provide guidance for younger workers, are able to balance innovation with the perfection of skills, can improvise, and are well placed to mediate between employers and employees. Moreover, loyalty to the product and to the employer, a characteristic of older workers, is very often associated with greater productivity across the whole workforce.

Older workers are said to be more reliable insofar as they have fewer interests that compete with work. Parental responsibilities, sporting engagements, and prolonged social activities create fewer distractions and intrude less on the working day. Given the contributions older people can make to the workforce, an ageing population does not necessarily mean a dependant population.

Older people as guardians of landscape

Attachment to the land underpins indigeneity, and in Māori society older people have responsibilities as kaitiaki, guardians, of the land. To many, the essence of being Māori is to be found in the nature of relationships with the environment, and the quality of those relationships is largely dependent on the ways in which elders act as guides so that the relationship can be experienced first-hand and better understood by whānau. Time and familiarity allow the environment to be soaked up, to be felt as an extension of self and to become part of living history.

In 1975 a land march saw 5000 Māori come together in an epic journey from Te Hapua in the Far North to Parliament to present a petition to Parliament about the retention of Māori land. Leading the march was Dame Whina Cooper, already in her late seventies. As an elder her participation and her determination to fight for land retention was inspirational to younger generations and to the nation as a whole.[16] Shortly after, a protest at the Raglan Golf Course aimed at seeking the return of golf course land to Māori was also led by an older Māori woman, Eva Rickard. And at Waitara, an older man, Aila Taylor, took the initiative to protest about proposed developments that would have seen a petro-chemical plant pollute the Taranaki coastline.[17] In all three instances, the role of older people as guardians of the land was pivotal.

Older people as leaders of communities and nations

The transformation of Māori health, education, communities and tribes over the past two decades owes much to older people. At an age when retirement from public life might seem an attractive proposition, Māori elderly often find that life becomes busier rather than quieter. Age by itself does not confer wisdom nor guarantee the skills necessary for effective leadership. Nor are the positive roles which older Māori men and women come to occupy necessarily unique to that age group. In contemporary Māori communities, however, there are particular roles which are enhanced if they are filled by older people. Those roles include speaking on behalf of the tribe, or family; resolving disputes and conflicts between families and between tribes; carrying the culture; protecting and nurturing younger adults and children; and recognising and encouraging the potential of younger members. With advancing years both men and women are expected to demonstrate spiritual leadership and to satisfy tribal needs in either religious or cultural contexts. It is still considered undignified for young people to travel to a Māori gathering without older people to guide them and to perform, on their behalf, the many necessary duties.

In recent years and in contemporary times there have been many examples where older people have been powerful and effective leaders in their own communities, at national levels, and on international platforms. The employment of cultural advisors and kaumātua in public institutions endorses older people as leaders, recognising the distinctive leadership that they can offer, not necessarily as executives or managers but as experienced mediators, who can strengthen relationships, build networks and reposition activities within a wider context.

Contributions to society and communities

Older people add distinctive elements to the life of the nation. As carriers of culture, anchors for families, models for lifestyle, bridges to the future, bulwarks for industry, guardians of landscape, and leaders of people, their contributions enrich the quality of life for younger generations. The ageing New Zealand population and the increased proportion of older people will bring consequential gains for the country as a whole.

Measuring the economic costs associated with an ageing population is complex but measuring the value of the contributions older people make to society is a great deal more complicated. It involves measuring the outcomes of paid and unpaid work as well as the value of social and cultural capital. Moreover, and even more difficult, it requires an estimation of contributions to environmental sustainability and an assessment of the value of transfers of knowledge, vision, and experience in order to benefit future generations. The point, however, is not that contributions made by older people are incalculable, but rather that they are immense, even if their precise quantification defies the present state of accounting knowledge.

To the extent that there is a need to measure the impacts of an ageing population on society, a valuation formula would need to show contributions as well as the more familiar costs, such as health care. Net contribution can be represented by the contributions, less the costs. Given the increasing number of older people and the greater number who reach old age in good health, the contributions to society as a whole are likely to exceed the costs to society.

In their professional capacities, gerontologists inevitably encounter problems associated with ageing more often than the benefits accruing from ageing. But in encouraging positive health, and the prevention of disease, whether physical or mental, gerontologists are also well placed to refocus the debate so that contributions as well as costs are duly acknowledged. In time this will require the development of measures that can quantify the social and cultural capital within older populations. To date, however, measures of pathology and the impacts of disease have been more precise than measures of potential and the impacts of multiple contributions by older people. The challenge meanwhile is to maximise opportunities for the realisation of the full potential of older people. Such opportunities may arise from the application of preventive medicine, clinical grading, and constructive counselling. But essentially the task is to recognise that from an ageing population, potential benefits will flow on to communities, society and the nation.

CHAPTER 17

Bioethics in Research: The Ethics of Indigeneity

Key note presentation to the Ninth Global Forum on Bioethics in Research (GFBR9), Auckland, 3 December 2008.

Similarities and difference

The ethics of research involving human subjects is largely about the quality of relationships between individuals and communities who participate in the research, and the researchers. Underpinning the relationship is an expectation that the research will not offend the ethics of participants and will bring benefit to them or their families, if not in the short term then in the fullness of time. While research should do no harm, more importantly it should do some good. In that respect it is not enough to simply acknowledge the views of others; instead pathways that can lead to gains in health and wellbeing should be evident within research goals.

In considering the values, beliefs and world views of participants, there are ethical principles that have universal application. Avoiding unnecessary pain and suffering, respecting property, protecting the young, abiding by accepted community standards and conventions, and valuing people, are ideals that transcend race, ethnicity, culture and nationality. Universal values are held in common by many populations though the commonalities can often be masked by the differences that exist between groups.

It is also important to recognise that within groups there is likely to be a diversity of views and values. Not all New Zealanders, for example, believe there is a 'New Zealand way of doing things', nor do all Māori people hold the same views about culture, relationships or a distinctive environmental ethic. Many will be influenced by Christian principles and ethics and their views may have more in common with other Christians than with other Māori. People living in urban environments may have quite different attitudes to the natural environment than their rural cousins, while the perspectives of Māori youth may well transcend race, religion and ethnicity to coincide with a global culture of youth.

Yet despite the diversity, and the universality, groups can bring a collective distinctiveness shaped by shared histories, common perspectives, settlements in a defined territory and a set of aspirations built around a widely held world view. Group distinctiveness can be manifest at several levels. Rural people, older people, nations, religions, colleagues often hold views that not only embrace their members but also distinguish the group from other groups. This paper is primarily concerned with group distinctiveness as represented by indigenous peoples. They share sufficient characteristics to distinguish them from other populations.

Indigeneity

There are some 5000 indigenous groups around the world with a total population of at least 200 million, or around 4 percent of the global population. Often the essential characteristics of indigeneity are linked to socio-economic disadvantage, post-colonial marginalisation, and cultural difference from the majority. Certainly, compared to non-indigenous populations socio-economic disadvantage is often severe; and colonisation has resulted in resource alienation, suppression of culture, and the imposition of foreign rule. A frequent outcome has been relative exclusion from wider society accompanied by higher rates of unemployment, lower standards of health and education, and lack of political voice.[1]

But despite socio-economic similarities and comparable experiences with colonisation and post-colonial development, the unifying feature of indigenous peoples has a more fundamental quality that depends on a sense of unity with the environment.[2] The individual is a part of all creation and the idea that the world or creation exists for the purpose of human domination and exploitation is absent from indigenous world views.[3] Instead, an ecological approach based on a synergistic relationship, has not only led to careful stewardship of the environment and natural resources, but also to a way of thinking within which health and illness are conceptualised as products of relationships – between individuals and wider social networks, and between people and the natural world.

Adaptation to the natural environment was not only necessary for food and shelter but also gave definition to social groupings, tribal identity and a philosophy of environmental sustainability within which human survival unfolded.[4] Language, culture, and a distinctive system of knowledge was a by-product of the environmental experience and the bond with the land was reflected in song, custom, approaches to healing, birthing, and the rituals associated with death.[5]

Modern understandings of indigeneity, at least as they apply to research bioethics, encompass both the old and the new realities (Table 17.1). While the ecological orientation remains a key marker, and can be regarded as the fundamental characteristic, the economic and cultural parameters associated with human encounters constitute another point of distinction. Meaningful engagement is more likely to occur when cultural protocols are observed and mutual benefits can be demonstrated.

TABLE **17.1** Three characteristics of contemporary indigeneity

Ecological synergies	Human encounters	Autonomy and self-determination
Human survival is a function of ecological balance. The natural environment contributes to defining human identity.	Territory confers authority and obligation. Cultural protocols facilitate human encounters and meaningful engagement.	Socio-economic disadvantage precedes marginalisation and vulnerability with unequal power relationships. Autonomy and self-determination strengthen capability and active participation.

Indigenous communities also value a third characteristic - autonomy and independence. Where there has been loss of self-determination, coupled with socio-economic disadvantage, vulnerability arises, generating potential for unequal power relationships with societal agents, including researchers.

Māori world views

Māori experience is not dissimilar from other indigenous peoples who have become a minority in their own country. From an estimated population of 200,000 in 1800, by 1894 the Māori population had dwindled to 42,000 and was close to extinction. But within a century it had become more numerous than at any other time in history. Even though changes to statistical definitions of Māori make it difficult to draw exact comparisons, there is strong evidence of a substantial and sustained increase in the Māori population. In the 2006 Census 565,329 New Zealanders identified as Māori with a median age of 22.7 years; of whom 85 percent were classed as urban dwellers.[6]

After some decades of assimilatory policies and programmes, by 1984 a positive approach to development had emerged. Māori language and culture were endorsed, Māori systems of service delivery emerged and despite an urban environment, new generations of Māori relished the opportunity to live as Māori. The introduction of Māori immersion education programmes, centred initially on early childhood education centres (kōhanga reo) has led to a generation of young people who are fluent in both English and Māori and a resurgence in Māori language usage by both young and old.

Rangi and Papa – the ecological dimension

However, despite new environments and lifestyles typical of contemporary New Zealand, there remains a Māori sense of attachment to the natural environment. The attachment is often presented as a family analogy within which relationships between the elements, natural resources, and people can be conceptualised.

Rangi and Papa, the sky father and the earth mother, were locked in an embrace which precluded daylight and threatened to smother their children. However, as the offspring matured they sought greater independence and decided to assert their powers by pushing the sky away from the earth so that light could penetrate and they could realise their full potential. As a result the forests were enabled to stand tall, the ferns spread, fish multiplied, crops flourished, the earth was warmed and humankind took its place alongside trees, birds, plants, waters, and the elements. The parents remained but were forced to sacrifice intimacy so that others could thrive.

There are three points to the story. First, it provides a framework within which environmental relationships can be better understood and the position of humans within a wider ecological context can be appreciated. Human privilege is constrained by responsibilities towards other players and by dependence on them. In this world view, human identity is grounded.[7] People cannot be fully understood without taking into account the natural environment which has nurtured their ancestors through childhood and into adult life. The phrase 'tangata whenua' captures some of the duality – people and the land – and recognises that in every region some people have longstanding bonds with the land that sets them apart from others who do not share those bonds.[8] The point is further emphasised by the concept of tūrangawaewae, a term linking individuals with a site or location that underpins their identity, as well as the identity of their relatives.

Second, the story of Rangi and Papa is predicated on an outward flow of energy. Underlying the world views of indigenous peoples and at the heart of indigeneity, is an 'ecological synergy spiral'. Basically about connecting relationships that are complementary and mutually reinforcing, the spiral moves from the small to the large, from individuals to groups, and from people, plants, fish and animals to the earth and the sky. It is based on an outward flow of energy, away from microscopic minutia, and towards an ever-expanding environment.[9] Ultimately the spiral moves towards the cosmos so that all objects, species, planets and stars can be incorporated in an interacting system that gives meaning and insight to existence. Within the spiral, knowledge comes from locating matter and phenomena within wider ecological contexts rather than attempting to understand and value objects and systems according only to their intrinsic component parts. The energy flow is centrifugal rather than centripetal.[10]

Third, just as people take on qualities derived from the natural environment, inanimate material objects possess a form of life, a mauri, which both distinguishes them (from other objects) but also unites them within a wider network of entities. Stone, for instance, cannot be fully understood without recognising the wider environment within which it lies. In an indigenous world objects that appear to be inanimate are not regarded as lifeless or static since they also possess an identity of their own and are part of a wider network. Belonging to that network creates a vibrant relationship that is at odds with the view that motionless objects lack life. In the language of global warming and climate change, so-called inert objects may well have carbon credits that ultimately add to the world's equilibrium. There are energy chains within, and dynamic relationships beyond.

Human encounters

While humans have close and synergistic relationships with the wider natural environment, land also provides a basis for protocols which guide relationships between groups. Formal exchanges, such as occur on marae (tribal meeting places), are premised on the relative roles of tangata whenua (belonging to a particular land-based territory) and manuhiri (visitors to that site).[11] Marae encounters demonstrate the distinctive psychological and behavioural activities that occur when discussions between groups commence.[12] Essentially those discussions are about negotiating relationships according to an accepted cultural format (or kawa – a consistent way of engaging in discussions). The terms of engagement are scoped in a series of speeches but are only implemented if there is general agreement.

Marae encounters also provide space and time to assess compatibility and to determine the extent of any risk. Risks do not necessarily mean that a relationship cannot continue, but they sound cautionary notes. On the other hand an encounter is more likely to have a good outcome if mutual benefits are on the agenda, agreement is reached about the terms, and when a koha (in modern times a monetary donation) is given and then accepted, and a commitment to a long term relationship is made.

Autonomy and self-determination

Vulnerability, an all-too-often marker of indigeneity in contemporary times, occurs when an indigenous population is excluded from full participation in wider society. Where colonisation has occurred, either through the aegis of a treaty (the Treaty of Waitangi for Māori) or by sheer force, indigenous alienation from traditional resources including language and culture has usually occurred. Loss of voice and political power has been an inevitable sequel.

Much Māori effort is directed towards regaining autonomy so that matters involving indigenous people can be decided by indigenous decision-makers. This quest for self-determination has been especially evident in the provision of services to Māori (health, education, social services), the governance of Māori resources including land, fish, and forests, as well as intellectual resources such as language, and the management of tribal affairs.

While absolute autonomy is neither realistic nor desirable in a nation where interdependencies are important, and where economies of scale largely dictate the options, the underlying principle advanced by Māori is that Māori roles in decision-making should be afforded priority where those decisions concern Māori people, resources, or intellectual property.

Implications for research bioethics

Arising from the three characteristics of indigeneity – ecological ties, human encounters, autonomy and self-determination – it is possible to identify three major ethical domains: eco-connectedness, engagement, empowerment (Table 17.2).

TABLE **17.2** Ethical domains and indigenous characteristics

Indigenous characteristics	Ethical domains
Ecological ties.	The ethics of eco-connectedness.
Human encounters.	The ethics of engagement.
Autonomy and self-determination.	The ethics of empowerment.

The ethics of eco-connectedness

In a Māori world view it is not possible to understand the human situation without recourse to the wider ecological environment.[13] The impacts of research on humans cannot be considered in isolation of intended or unintended consequential impacts on the environment. A number of ethical issues therefore require consideration by researchers. An important one is linked to the effect a project may have on environmental equilibrium. This applies especially in modern times to the acceleration of climate change. Even if the aim of the research is exclusively focused on human subjects and does not have an explicit environmental impact, consideration still needs to be given, for example, to the levels of carbon emissions generated during the research and how they might be minimised. Moreover, the methods by which humans adapt to their environment and manage environmental risks are matters that merit attention. An investigation into the ways in which the cells of Māori diabetics handle insulin, for example, should not be divorced from the wider question of how Māori handle contemporary food environments.

An equally challenging set of ethical questions revolve around the unique characteristics of species. Because all objects have a 'mauri', they possess an integrity that distinguishes them from other objects. Consequently many Māori have serious objections to procedures involving xenotransplantation.[14] Human integrity is compromised when the mauri from one species is introduced into another. In that view, in addition to any health risks or physical imbalances, 'cultural offence results from a mixing of genes between species and the generation of metaphysical imbalance.'[15] The debate is not necessarily about the sacredness of humankind but about the uniqueness of all species and the dynamic relationships that have developed between them over time.

On the other hand, an important consideration for Māori, in the past and equally in modern times is about survival and the quality of survival. Human behaviour often revolves around ensuring that future generations will be secure and continuity of whakapapa (genealogical lines) will be guaranteed. Many of the customs that evolved after Māori reached Aotearoa 1000 years ago were geared towards survival even if they jeopardised the lives of others. Warfare between tribes over territories and associated resources resulted in extensive loss of life and there were instances where children were sacrificed lest they cried and betrayed the whereabouts of a party intent on escape from an enemy. Further, early accounts of cannibalism often associated eating the organs of a captive (especially the heart) with gaining power from the victim so that the tribal superiority could be retained, both literally and symbolically. When group survival is under threat, the ends appear to justify the means.

Assisted reproductive technologies and organ transplants are sometimes seen as antithetical to Māori custom because they offend the 'principles of nature'. However, when the ethical focus shifts from attention to cellular details to the wider question of human survival, the debate takes on new dimensions.[16] Where family continuity is threatened, a new balancing point is introduced between what is 'natural' and what is possible. The balancing point is shifted even further when there are questions about survival of the tribe, or even the quality of survival of the whole population.

The possibility that diabetes will pose a threat to Māori survival, for example, was raised at the International Diabetes Federation's, 'Diabetes in Indigenous People' Forum in Melbourne in November 2006. Professor Zimmet from the International Diabetes Institute provided convincing evidence that diabetes had become a major and deadly threat to the continued existence of some indigenous communities throughout the world as a result of western lifestyles and diet. Media reports in New Zealand concluded that unchecked, the diabetes problem could lead to Māori becoming extinct. Even though the claim was extravagant, the case for reinforcing human pancreatic tissue with tissue from other species takes on a new meaning when population survival rather than individual relief is the objective.

The ethics of engagement

Engagement with Māori for research purposes is more likely to be effective when the terms of coming together are clear and when the accepted protocols for encounter have been met. The process requires time and space and is more likely to be successful when it is aimed at relationship building rather than recruitment of subjects. Preliminary discussions with community leaders may uncover impediments or potential difficulties but may also alert communities to the benefits, thereby increasing engagement with individuals and families. Moreover, there may be expectations that the relationship will continue long after the research has been completed.

The ethics of engagement are essentially based on the development of a relationship that enhances the standing of both parties. Although Māori have often felt used and taken for granted by researchers there are instances where benefits to Māori partners have extended beyond those intended in the initial research proposal.[17] The involvement of university researchers with an extended Māori family prone to hereditary diffuse gastric cancer for example, led to ongoing close and mutually supportive relationships between the research team and the whānau community.[18]

Integral to developing a positive research relationship is the need for clarity about the purpose of engagement. There are distinctions between gaining the views of a sample of Māori and gaining views about indigeneity. Not all Māori will be familiar with an underlying indigenous world view and in any event in most interview contexts they will be inclined to give a personal perspective, especially if the issue is related to personal health. Articulation of an indigenous perspective is more likely to come from a panel of 'experts', in much the same way a religious view might be expected to come from religious authorities rather than from those whose connection to a religion is simply based on a nominal affiliation.

The ethics of empowerment

Indigenous answers to disadvantage and vulnerability emphasise the empowerment of tribes, communities and families. Opportunities for empowerment occur across various phases of research. First, since it is a prelude to entering into a relationship, giving consent provides a space for an exchange of information, not only about the details of the research but also about the impacts of the research beyond human subjects and over a long period of time. Knowledge is power and researchers should be able to provide relevant information in ways that make sense to participants and lead to a state of enlightenment, rather than to mystification or confusion.

Second, active participation in research should not be confused with being an object of research. Māori are interested in research design, the choice of methodology, protocols for involving others, and procedures for engagement with Māori individuals as well as Māori communities. Active partnership is more empowering than passive participation. Moreover, engaging Māori as researchers and providing opportunities for Māori researchers to increase their knowledge and skills either through the acquisition of formal academic qualifications or working alongside experienced researchers will contribute to capability building, self-determination and greater autonomy.[19]

Third, Māori as guardians of research is a further step towards empowerment. Kaitiakitanga – guardianship – includes monitoring the integrity of the research process, and ensuring that stories, samples, and data obtained from Māori participants are protected and managed with both respect and care. A frequent concern of Māori is that the ownership of their contributions to research will be lost and that others will benefit at their expense.[20] The alienation of intellectual property, whether tribal and family narratives or detailed personal records, or the use of bodily samples for undisclosed purposes have occurred frequently enough to justify the appointment of Māori leaders as guardians of process and data.

During a national nutrition survey, for example, a Māori advisory group (the kaitiaki group) made up of eight elders, was appointed to assist the research team. The elders recommended changes to the research protocols by extending the food frequency questionnaire to include foods that had some special cultural value to Māori. In addition, two elders were designated as spiritual guardians for the blood and urine samples. They travelled with the specimens to the laboratories and once analyses were completed, they oversaw the burial of blood and urine remnants in the earth. In this way, the beliefs of participants were endorsed and anxieties about future misuse of bodily fluids were minimised.[21]

Māori advisory committees can also provide advice on an appropriate process for the dissemination of research findings so that indigenous communities are empowered, rather than disempowered. They can also assist in determining who might have access to research data and under what circumstances. Protocols for Māori guardianship of process and data were successfully instituted during the national mental health prevalence study that involved large numbers of Māori participants.[22]

An indigenous bioethics framework

Building on the characteristics of indigeneity a framework for considering indigenous bioethics can be constructed (Table 17.3).

TABLE **17.3** Indigenous bioethics framework

Ethical domains	Ethical principles	Ethical outcomes
Eco-connectedness	Mauri ake (integrity of species) Tangata whenua (people & environment) Matatū (endurance)	Integrity of ecological systems Balanced relationships between people & environment Resource sustainability
Engagement	Kawa ā-iwi (procedural certainty) Koha (reciprocity) Whakamārama (enlightenment)	Human dignity, safety & vitality Mutual regard Gains for future generations.
Empowerment	Rangatiratanga (retained authority) Kaitiakitanga (guardianship) Whakamana (capability)	Guardianship of data & processes Research partnerships Increased research capability Benefits from research

The framework is made up of ethical domains, ethical principles, and ethical outcomes. Ethical principles reflect indigenous values and world views. Arising from the ethics of eco-connectedness are the principles of species integrity (the mauri principle), the human–environment continuum (the tangata whenua principle) and the principle of endurance (matatū). Principles relating to human encounters include procedural certainty (kawa ā-iwi), reciprocity (koha) and enlightenment; while from the domain of empowerment, the key principles are retained authority (rangatiratanga), guardianship (kaitiakitanga) and capability (whakamana).

A third component of the framework comprises outcomes that might result from the application of ethical principles. For example, outcomes associated with the ethics of eco-connectedness include the retention of the integrity of ecological systems, balanced relationships between people and the environment, and resource sustainability. Emerging from the ethics of engagement, outcomes that can be expected relate to the preservation of human dignity, safety and vitality, as well as positive mutual regard, and gains for future generations. Finally, empowerment can lead to secure guardianship of data, samples and research processes, research partnerships, increased research capability and ultimately discernable benefits from the research.

Promoting ethically sound research

Because it accords with local custom and perspectives, research which is conducted within an ethical framework is more likely to be accepted by communities and families and therefore more likely to lead to better outcomes. But the promotion of ethically sound research that recognises and endorses indigenous world views requires an active commitment of both researchers and research agencies to high ethical standards. Importantly, quite apart from possessing knowledge about Māori cultural beliefs or the beliefs of other indigenous populations, researchers often carry attitudes which belie that knowledge. For many, ethical compliance is regarded as an intrusion on time, finances, and even academic freedom. What may not be appreciated is the opportunity to extend understanding by establishing links with people who bring other world views and other systems of knowledge to the research programme.

Similarly an undue focus on methodological issues, with increasing attention to smaller facets of the research at the expense of a bigger picture may fail to engage Māori minds because it focuses downwards and inwards (centripetal) rather than upwards and outwards (centrifugal). The intent of the research and its significance may be lost in the detail. At another level, researchers who set out to recruit Māori subjects may be less successful than those who wish to foster active participation within a climate of partnership. Recruitment provides less opportunity for empowerment and engagement than a relationship where the agenda is not already prescribed. By the same token, cursory consultation, as opposed to building a relationship based on trust and mutual interests, may be a deterrent to active involvement.

Researchers will be much concerned with scientific merit, but Māori communities may be more interested in indigenous gain and contributions to indigenous advancement. Whether the findings are accepted in a prestigious journal or are the subject of a conference presentation will hold less attraction than whether they can be translated into demonstrable benefits and inform an indigenous body of knowledge. Researchers who are ready to complement enthusiasm for scientific merit with enthusiasm for conventional indigenous ways of knowing, will encounter greater willingness for collaboration.

But rather than placing the onus on researchers to initiate protocols with Māori, recommendations have also been made that institutions involved in research should develop ethical procedures and clear guidelines to assist researchers and reduce the responsibilities on them.[23]

Indigenising ethical standards and protocols.

During the past two decades there have been positive responses to indigenous concerns about research ethics. In Canada, for example, the Institute for Aboriginal Peoples' Health, in association with the Canadian Institutes of Health Research, has produced ethical guidelines for health research involving aboriginal people.[24] In New Zealand, Māori participation in research and research ethics has been evident for more than two decades and owes much to the provision in the Health Research Council Act 1990 for the establishment of a Māori Health Committee. By 1993 two university-based Māori health research centres had been developed, and four others have been subsequently established.

Māori representation on health ethics committees is now the rule rather than the exception and two research funders, the Health Research Council and the Foundation for Research Science and Technology, have similarly recognised an indigenous dimension that warrants a tailored approach to research.

In *Guidelines for Researchers working with Māori* the Health Research Council has identified a number of factors that will enhance the engagement process including the appropriate use of Māori language, the appointment of Māori advisory groups, regard for the principles of the Treaty of Waitangi, especially the principle of participation, and respect for cultural views.[25]

The Bioethics Council has similarly urged that indigenous perspectives be accorded some priority in decisions about research involving human subjects. The Council has concluded that Māori ethical views on biotechnology are sufficiently important to warrant the establishment of a Māori expert group who could develop protocols based on Māori world views in order to make decisions about inter-species transplants and other related procedures.[26]

Māori decision making in respect of ethical issues involving Māori has also been raised in other fields of inquiry. For more than a decade, the Waitangi Tribunal has been investigating a claim into Crown policies regarding Māori and native fauna and flora.[27] More recently the claim has been extended to consider ownership of Māori intellectual property. At the heart of the claim is a concern that Māori guardianship of the natural environment, and Māori ownership of cultural property, are inadequately protected in law and practice. The possibility of a Māori commissioner has been raised in submissions. Among other things the commissioner would have a role in exploring the interface between Māori custom, science, and the environment.

Despite considerable progress, there is also ongoing concern about the adequacy of current forms of ethical review, largely on the grounds that ethics committees typically try to accommodate Māori perspectives within a review framework that marginalises Māori values. The development of a Māori ethical framework, based on Māori values and overseen by a national Māori ethics committee, has been recommended as a way of introducing a parallel Māori ethical review pathway.[28]

Conclusion

The ethics of indigeneity, as they might apply to research bioethics, stem from indigenous world views, indigenous cultures and contemporary indigenous realities. While there are elements of universality, and although not all indigenous individuals subscribe to identical beliefs or hold the same values, there are nonetheless distinctive indigenous approaches to the acquisition of new knowledge that have implications for researchers from the several disciplines of western science.

Three characteristics of indigeneity shape the ethical debate: the close and enduring relationships between people and the environment; the protocols associated with encounters between groups and ways in which relationships are cemented; and the indigenous quest for autonomy and self determination – a response to vulnerability and societal disadvantage. Arising from these characteristics are three sets of ethical domains: the ethics of eco-connectedness, the ethics of engagement, and the ethics of empowerment. Together they point towards the ethics of indigeneity (Table 17.4).

TABLE 17.4 The ethics of indigeneity

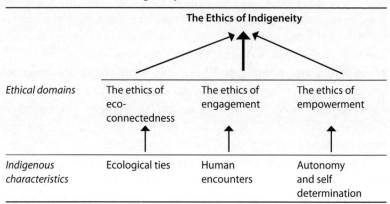

	The Ethics of Indigeneity		
Ethical domains	The ethics of eco-connectedness	The ethics of engagement	The ethics of empowerment
Indigenous characteristics	Ecological ties	Human encounters	Autonomy and self determination

CHAPTER 18

Quality Health Care for Indigenous Peoples: The Māori Experience

Key note address to the third Asia Pacific Forum: Quality Improvement in Health Care, Auckland, 3 September 2003.

Introduction

The Third Asia Pacific Forum on Quality Health Care provides an opportunity for communities within the Pacific, and those who live on its rim, to share ideas and to learn from each other so that high standards of health care might become a reality. It is a singularly important event bringing together views from several nations, many peoples, and diverse cultures so that the many guises within which quality health care takes shape can be revealed. However, while observations from the several perspectives may highlight differences in health care, it is also important to remember that the foundations of quality health care are firmly built on the human condition and on hopes that transcend nationhood and diversity. There is, so to speak, a common platform made up of universal human values.

Good health depends on many factors, most of which are well outside the health sector – quality housing, a decent education, meaningful employment, access to goods and services, opportunities for sport and recreation. But even if it is not the most influential factor, health care is a crucial determinant of good health, the more so where other factors create health risks and predispose to ill health.

The Asia Pacific Forum takes place in an era when technological advances have transformed health care from an essentially caring activity to one enriched by innovations in diagnostics, treatment, analysis, management and policy-making. At the same time, technology by itself is unlikely to lead to uniformly high standards of care. There is a human factor that cannot be simply reduced to technological opportunities or the mass application of scientific breakthroughs. While technology and science have a critical place in modern health care and offer fresh hope for the future, human feelings and beliefs are equally important to the healing process and need to be factored into the health care equation.

In that respect, indigenous health care is largely about the balance between scientific advancement and human spirituality.

Indigenous peoples

AD 2002 was an important milestone for indigenous peoples. First, after nearly eighty years of advocacy and negotiation, the United Nations established a Permanent Forum on Indigenous Issues. The inaugural session was held in New York in May 2002 during the 1995–2004 Decade of Indigenous Peoples and ten years after the launch of the Year of Indigenous Peoples in 1992. Those events represent significant advances in the struggle of indigenous peoples for recognition within their own lands and territories and have brought global attention to the impacts of colonisation, discrimination, ethnocide, and sometimes frank genocide.

While there are significant differences in the circumstances of indigenous peoples in various parts of the world, there are also commonalities in experiences and world views. Colonisation, for example, was a common experience, associated with epidemics of infectious diseases, depopulation and disempowerment at local, tribal and national levels. And it was followed by a common pattern of alienation: loss of culture, loss of land, loss of voice, loss of dignity, loss of health and loss of intellectual traditions.

In modern times the common threads that bind indigenous communities are linked to their similar socio-economic positions, their rejection of assimilation, their comparable aspirations for greater autonomy, and their similar experience of disease. However, the defining element of indigeneity is not colonisation, socio-economic disadvantage or political ambitions.

Instead, most indigenous peoples believe that the primary starting point is a strong sense of unity with the environment.[1] This appears to be the most significant characteristic of indigeneity at least according to indigenous writers.[2, 3] 'People are the land and the land is the people.' 'We are the river, the river is us.'[4]

Loss of that environment was associated with new patterns of disease. However, the infectious diseases that underlay much of the population decline in the nineteenth century gave way in the twentieth century to diseases associated with new social environments, the so-called lifestyle diseases of diabetes, motor vehicle accidents, alcohol and drug misuse, cancers, heart disease, depression and suicide.

The ecological approach is also evident in indigenous approaches to health. In 1999 at Geneva, the World Health Organisation arranged an International Consultation on the Health of Indigenous Peoples. Arising from the consultation a Declaration on the Health and Survival of Indigenous Peoples was subsequently presented to the UN Permanent Forum on Indigenous Issues in 2002.[5] The Declaration affirms the links between culture, the wider natural environment, human rights, and health, and proposes a definition of health: 'Indigenous Peoples' concept of health and survival is both a collective and individual inter-generational continuum encompassing a holistic perspective incorporating four distinct shared dimensions of life. These dimensions are the spiritual, the intellectual, physical and emotional. Linking these four fundamental dimensions, health and survival manifests itself on multiple levels where the past, present and future co-exist simultaneously.'

As part of a movement to reclaim culture and identity, indigenous peoples have fought to reshape health services so that they align more sensibly with indigenous world views and modern indigenous realities. They have urged the adoption of cultural protocols into health care, and are keen that greater recognition be given to socio-economic disadvantages as significant barriers to effective care. In some communities traditional healing has also been given new emphasis, though more often the call has been for the development of an indigenous health workforce that draws on indigenous values as well as the modern health sciences.

The Māori experience

Māori experience has not been substantially different from other indigenous peoples except in three important respects. First, Māori demographic patterns are distinctive; second, the 1840 Treaty of Waitangi has created a special relationship between Māori and the Crown with implications for health policy; and third, there has been effective Māori leadership in health for more than a century.

Leadership

The year 2003, for example, is the centennial year of the first recorded conference on Māori health. In 1903 Māori leaders who had been appointed as sanitary inspectors came together at Rotorua to discuss strategies and improve their own skills. They were leaders from their own communities and faced the daunting task of turning around a rapidly declining Māori population that had become victim to endemic tuberculosis, malnutrition, pneumonia, goitre, excessively high child mortality rates and a host of infectious diseases. The decision to engage Māori community leaders as health inspectors was made by Dr Maui Pomare, the first Māori medical practitioner who had been appointed to the Department of Public Health in 1901 as Medical Officer to Māori.

Other community leaders also emerged in that era including the much revered spiritual healer, Tahupotiki Wiremu Ratana, and Te Puea Herangi, a tribal leader who, after the 1918 influenza epidemic fought to establish a hospital where Māori values and customs could enrich conventional medical practices. She was unsuccessful but sixty-four years later in 1984, her tribe was among the first to pioneer a health centre that integrated Māori perspectives into practice in a modern primary care clinic. In the 1930s and again in the 1950s two influential women's organisations, the Women's Health League and the Māori Women's Welfare League respectively, provided leadership, largely on a voluntary basis. Both groups continue to make substantial contributions to Māori health advancement and have been staunch advocates for improved Māori access to health care.

Demographic change

When the conference of Māori sanitary inspectors was held in 1903, the Māori population was estimated at 45,000 and close to extinction. Even though changes to the definition of Māori have made it difficult to make comparisons, there is strong evidence of a substantial and sustained increase in the Māori population. In the 2001 Census 526,281 New Zealanders identified as Māori; of whom 85 percent were classed as urban dwellers.[6]

Although accounting for some 14 percent of the total New Zealand population in 2001, by 2051 the Māori ethnic population will almost double in size to close to a million, or 22 percent of the total New Zealand population. Even more dramatic, by 2051, 33 percent of all children in the country will be Māori.[7]

The Treaty of Waitangi

The Treaty of Waitangi is the third unique aspect of Māori health development. After nearly 100 years of legal and political dismissal the Treaty is now accorded greater respect as a source of constitutional rights for Māori. Signed in 1840 between Britain and most tribes, the Treaty provided for British governance, certain guarantees to the tribes relating to property rights and (at least in the Māori version) to continuing tribal authority, and the conferment of citizenship rights on individual Māori people. In the immediate years after its signing the Treaty and its lofty goals were taken seriously by the Crown but in 1877 the Treaty was declared by a court of law as 'a simple nullity' and more or less abandoned as a serious Crown obligation.[8]

Although the application of the Treaty to land and the physical environment was eventually established and even confirmed in legislation, it was not until the mid-1980s that there was also recognition of its relevance to social and economic domains.[9]

A commitment to the Treaty by the fourth Labour Government in 1984 gave it greatly increased prominence across the range of government activities and ushered in what amounted to a Māori constitutional revolution.[10] Three years later the Department of Health formally recognised the Treaty as important to health services and instigated initiatives aimed at giving Māori greater say in health policy and the delivery of health programmes.

The current legislative framework

Current health legislation, the New Zealand Public Health and Disability Act 2000, recognises the Treaty of Waitangi, the first piece of social policy legislation to do so. But when the legislation was first proposed, there was some concern about risks to the Crown and the litigation that might follow if Māori were to claim that the health sector had not delivered the best outcomes. By the legislation's having a Treaty clause, it was also argued that Māori might be able to make a demand on health services for preferential treatment.

Although it was unlikely that a Treaty clause could have overridden other aspects of the Bill or even overturned clinical common sense, the perceived clash between the principle of universality and the principle of indigeneity was sufficient to lead to a redraft. In the event, the statute now makes it clear that district health boards must address Māori health and must recognise the Treaty of Waitangi in decision making and priority setting. To emphasise the point, the Minister of Health appointed two Māori members to each of the twenty-one district health boards. The Act also requires that health disparities be decreased by 'improving the health outcomes of Māori and other population groups.'

Patterns of disease and disparities

In many respects Māori health is better than at any time in the past. Māori infant death rates, for example, as high as 94 per 1000 live births in 1929, had reduced to 54 per 1000 by 1959 and to 18 by 1991. Similarly Māori life expectancy increased from thirty-three (for males) and thirty (for females) in 1903 to sixty-six (for males) and seventy-one (for females) in 1996. As already discussed, these gains have been associated with rapid population growth, from 43,000 a hundred years ago to 526,000 in 2001.

The diseases that ravaged Māori communities in the late nineteenth and early twentieth centuries have largely disappeared, at least as major causes of death and disability. Early Māori had to contend with constant shortages of food, cold and damp conditions, pneumonia, gastro-enteritis, infant deaths due to infection, and accidents. By 1901 the main health risks were still largely related to malnutrition and infectious diseases but had come to include tuberculosis, typhoid, and diphtheria. The fact that those diseases are now consigned to history is cause for celebration.

But the reality is that the old threats to health have been replaced by modern health problems, less lethal perhaps but contributing to the disproportionately high rates of disease and disability for Māori and Pacific peoples. Whereas tuberculosis, diphtheria and malnutrition were major causes of ill health a century ago, the contemporary health problems for Māori now include rheumatic fever, sudden infant death syndrome, injury, diabetes, cancer, heart disease, depression and youth suicide. They comprise the most common causes of death and greatly inflate the burden of disease carried by New Zealand.

While Māori health status measured over time has improved, disparities in standards of health between Māori and non-Māori remain. Recent evidence suggests that over the past two decades the disparities are even growing. In the twenty years between 1980 and 1999 mortality rates for Māori men increased from 1.48 times higher than the non-Māori rate to 1.74 times higher, while for Māori women the disparity rose from 1.96 to 2.20. Similar trends can be observed for Pacific peoples living in New Zealand.

Ethnic disparities in life expectancy have also increased. While Māori male life expectancy increased from 64.6 years to 65.8 years in the twenty years between 1980 and 1999, non-Māori male life expectancy increased from 70.9 years to 75.7 years, a gain of 4.8 years compared to the Māori gain of only 1.2 years.[11]

There is also evidence that while access to health services is one important determinant of health status, structural causes account for much of the increasing disparities. [12] In 1984 New Zealand's major social and economic reforms impacted adversely on Māori and Pacific peoples with widening gaps in employment status, housing, education and income. Widening health inequalities were predictable outcomes.

Positive Māori development

Economic restructuring in 1984 was accompanied by new approaches to Māori policy. Positive Māori development, as the policy was known, prescribed a shift away from state dependency and a welfare mentality to a greater emphasis on self-determination, economic self-sufficiency, social equity, and cultural reaffirmation. The move was in part a response to free market policies, but also consistent with worldwide indigenous rejection of assimilation and submission. For Māori it was to lead to a revitalisation of Māori language, greater confidence in tribal systems of governance and management, increasing entry in the commercial world, and the establishment of distinctive Māori provider organisations for the delivery of education, social services, housing, legal services and health care.

Māori health development

In that context contemporary Māori health policy evolved. It has been characterised by six major themes. First, Māori perspectives of health have provided a philosophical basis; second, Māori cultural values and practices have been introduced into conventional health services; third, a range of Māori health care providers have established Māori-centred services; fourth, there has been a major focus on Māori health workforce development; fifth, a parallel Māori health research stream has emerged; and sixth, state policies and programmes for health have recognised Māori initiatives and aspirations for services that are responsive to Māori and, increasingly, delivered by Māori.

Māori model for conceptualising health

The promotion of Māori concepts of health was evident in the early 1980s. When the Māori Women's Welfare League was embarking on a survey of the health of Māori women, for example, a model of health known as Te Whare Tapa Whā anchored their study.[13]

The model's appeal was based on its holistic approach to health and the recognition of spirituality as a significant contributor to good health. Until then discussions about Māori health had dwelt on the rates and consequences of disease, creating a sense of disempowerment and passivity. But by reconfiguring health in terms that made sense to Māori, it was possible for Māori communities to experience a sense of ownership and to balance medical and professional dominance with community involvement and local leadership. Te Whare Tapa Whā was presented as a four-sided house, each wall representing one aspect of health – spirituality (taha wairua), the mind (taha hinengaro), physical health (taha tinana) and family and social relationships (taha whānau).

Taha wairua remains important to Māori since it captures the notion of a special relationship with the environment, as well as a Māori cultural identity. Taha hinengaro concerns the way people think, feel and behave and recognises that Māori patterns of thought value metaphor and allusion. Taha tinana is not only about physical illness but also fitness, mobility and freedom from pain; while taha whānau focuses on the nature of interpersonal relationships, within the family but also beyond into wider society.

While the model had some of the elements of the World Health Organisation's definition of health, it was embraced by Māori as a vehicle for exploring other ways of conceptualising health and delivering health care. Increasingly it is being used as a framework for the development of models of assessment, treatment, care, the measurement of outcomes and the formulation of health policies.

Māori health services

A Māori model for conceptualising health was followed closely by Māori health initiatives. At first they revolved around community liaison and health promotion and arose largely because of perceived gaps in arrangements for formal health care. Māori dissatisfaction often stemmed from concerns about cultural inappropriateness in health interventions as well as barriers to access. In contrast, Māori initiatives revolved around community workers who were well versed in Māori values, familiar with local Māori networks, and sufficiently aware of health systems to negotiate on behalf of consumers.

The 1993 health reforms provided an ideal opportunity for Māori health groups to tender for the delivery of services, mostly in primary health care, disability support and mental health. Quite quickly, provider organisations multiplied from as few as five or six programmes in 1984 to some hundreds of registered Māori provider organisations, tribal and community, by 2002. Their approach was typically based on Māori perspectives but also came to employ conventional methods and professional staff. In fact a criticism emerging by the late 1990s was that some Māori health services had become indistinguishable from conventional services. To some extent that criticism arose out of a contracting regime that required all providers to meet similar objectives, in effect squeezing Māori providers to trade cultural innovation for compliance with measures standardised against a wider 'norm.' The engagement of traditional healers in primary health contracts, for example, was hindered because some healers regarded the suggested performance measures as too intrusive.

But by 2002, when primary health care organisations (PHOs) were first established, the rapid growth of Māori health care providers meant there was a vigorous Māori health care infrastructure able to bring a dimension to health care that was not available in earlier conservative practices.

Health service responses

Although the rise in Māori health care organisations was rapid, most Māori people were, and still are, reliant on conventional primary and secondary care services. The Māori health message, however, had penetrated the prevailing health system and by 1995 most North Island hospitals had introduced a range of cultural initiatives to ensure that their processes, if not outcomes, were more able to address Māori concerns. Sometimes it was by using Māori words on public signage; sometimes by employing Māori staff; sometimes by requiring staff to attend cultural safety courses. In addition, the practice of cultural safety, introduced by the late Dr Irihapeti Ramsden, was being taken seriously by nurses and led to increased awareness of cultural difference as a factor in health care.

At a corporate level, the requirement to comply with Treaty of Waitangi obligations resulted in greater Māori representation on boards and committees, and formal links with tribal groups and Māori community organisations. Attitudes to care were also changed by the involvement of whānau (family) who pushed for more flexible visiting arrangements in hospitals and improved facilities to accommodate relatives who wished to stay close to their sick family member.

Workforce development

Workforce development is another common theme in indigenous health development. Māori make up around 14 percent of the total population but only 5 percent of the national health workforce.[14]

Two broad strategies have been used to address that situation. First, efforts to recruit more Māori into the health professions have included affirmative action programmes. Initiated at the University of Otago in 1900 when two positions were created for Māori students at the medical school, the policy has since been extended to the Auckland medical school and other tertiary educational institutions. In addition, scholarships have been offered as incentives to encourage enrolment in particular programmes.

The second workforce strategy has been to engage cultural workers or Māori community health workers to work alongside health professionals, bringing first-hand knowledge of community and a capacity to engage diffident patients. Often the combination has been highly effective though there has also been concern that the two streams of workers – cultural and clinical – have simply created potential for professional and cultural interventions to diverge. An integration of cultural and clinical dimensions is one of the more pressing challenges facing Māori health care.

Māori health research
Efforts to recognise Māori world views in research were greatly boosted in 1993 when the Health Research Council of New Zealand funded two Māori health research units and established a Māori Health Committee to support Māori-led research projects. In addition a series of scholarships and training fellowships have enabled more than twenty Māori researchers to seek advanced research qualifications. Māori health research objectives are two-fold: to increase the Māori research capacity, and to encourage the development of methodologies that reflect Māori world views and intellectual traditions.

Useful clinical applications have resulted. Te Taura Tieke, for example, is a three-part framework for describing health service effectiveness. It encompasses technical and clinical competence, structural and systemic responsiveness and consumer satisfaction.[15] Hua Oranga is a measure of outcome designed for users of mental health services. Based on a Māori health perspective, it assesses outcome from a holistic viewpoint and includes ratings from clinician, client and a family member.[16]

State policies and responses to Māori health challenges
When the New Zealand Board of Health promoted the Treaty of Waitangi in 1987 as a document that had relevance to health,[17] and then endorsed tribal authorities as agents for health,[18] a new era of health policy was launched. It recognised two approaches to Māori health: Māori delivery systems and state responsiveness to Māori based on the principles of the Treaty of Waitangi.

Since then successive waves of health reforms have recognised the significance of the Treaty and have recommended specific strategies for Māori health. While there has not been universal agreement with policies that identify Māori health as a focus, distinct from the health of other New Zealanders, there has been acceptance that quality health care for Māori requires a range of factors to be taken into account, including cultural competence and Māori health views.

Currently health system objectives for Māori are not only contained in legislation but appear in the New Zealand National Health Strategy, the Primary Health Care Strategy and the Māori Health Strategy. To a greater or lesser extent, district health boards have responded positively though have not always found it possible to provide the levels of resource sought by Māori nor to reconfigure health service compliance requirements so that they align with Māori health perspectives.

Results

Whether the new approaches to health care for Māori can be translated into health gains is a question of considerable importance. Any suggestion that continuing disparities in the health standards of Māori and non-Māori is evidence that the current approaches have been unsuccessful is a shallow analysis that fails to take account of the wider socio-economic context within which Māori live. It implicitly places an unfair burden on the health sector as a panacea for the ills generated within wider society.

Anecdotal evidence suggests that there have been demonstrable gains in some areas such as immunisation, smoking cessation, improved Māori self-management of diabetes, asthma and hypertension. Of equal importance, however, is the degree to which Māori health awareness has been raised. Active participation within the health sector by providers, consumers or advisors has been accompanied by a level of enthusiasm that augers well for positive change. Nonetheless the full impacts of the new approaches to Māori health care need to be formally assessed.

There are of course many other issues that need further discussion and investigation. Importantly the relationship between cultural interventions and clinical interventions is often ill defined and two parallel streams can easily be formed without adequate linkages or synergies. Contracts for health services may exacerbate that particular problem by separating cultural and clinical components, especially in disability support services. In some areas Māori providers are encouraged to take up cultural support contracts quite independently of associated clinical contracts.

A framework for considering quality health care for Māori

The main reason for discussing trends in Māori health care over the past two decades has been to identify key components of quality health care for Māori. It is possible, on the basis of the New Zealand experience, to construct a framework within which quality care can be assessed according to goals, principles, pathways and performance.

Goals

Three goals can be identified. The first is about equitable access. Quality health care amounts to little if it is not accessible. Financial, geographic, cultural, and information barriers can present formidable obstacles to care, especially if they are cumulative. Sometimes Māori access is blocked by exclusion criteria especially if those criteria are solely based on health risks and the likely, clinically-measurable, benefits.

A second goal, human dignity, is concerned with the process of care. Health interventions that do not afford due respect for human values, cultural world views and differing health perspectives, will undermine dignity and diminish self-respect. In an outcome-driven environment, health care must also be concerned with processes and the ways in which technology is applied.

Third, however, a goal of quality health care must be to produce the best possible health gains measured against reliable clinical benchmarks that accommodate differing health perspectives. Quality health care is not the same as patient satisfaction. Treatment that is comfortable but fails to improve health status to the degree it might, lacks quality.

The three goals – equitable access, human dignity and best outcomes – are all important, and should be reflected in health services.

Principles

Māori experience has acknowledged three key principles in quality health care: indigeneity, clinical expertise, and cultural competence.

The principle of indigeneity takes into account the determination of indigenous peoples to retain their own distinctive cultural identity, avoid assimilation and exercise a degree of autonomy. This principle goes beyond cultural recognition to claim a special place for indigenous peoples in the life of the nation. The principle of indigeneity does not mean other cultures should not also be duly recognised in health care, but it does acknowledge a unique position for indigenous peoples.

Clinical expertise is a second principle. Māori as much as other New Zealanders expect the best possible treatment using tried and true methods. They also hope they will not be subjected to unnecessary interventions and will have access to new technologies and developments benchmarked against the best in the world.

Cultural competence, the third principle, expects that health care workers will be competent at the interface between their own culture and the culture of others. Language barriers, differing codes for social interaction, variable community expectations and a willingness to involve friends or families in assessment, treatment and rehabilitation make important differences in the way care is experienced.

Pathways to health

Based on Māori experience three health pathways have been identified: Māori-centred pathways, Māori-added pathways and collaborative pathways. There is no single route that will satisfy the wide range of Māori health needs.

Māori-centred pathways

Of three possible pathways a Māori centred pathway is one that is largely under Māori direction and has an obvious focus on increasing access and human dignity. In these pathways Māori cultural revitalisation sometimes appears to be the uppermost objective – an objective which though laudable, is not the same as improved health status. More often, however, cultural objectives are secondary to health objectives. Generally Māori centred pathways are also closely linked to Māori communities and tend to be aligned with the broader goals of Māori development as much as the goals of the health sector.

Māori-added pathways

Most Māori are not cared for in Māori centred services. Instead they attend hospitals, clinics and surgeries. They might reasonably expect that a Māori dimension will be added – the Māori-added pathway. The Māori dimension may be symbolic (Māori signage for example) or an integral part of the treatment process. Some argue that it is too little, a token, while others complain that it is too much and forced on the wider population for little purpose.

But, compared to 1984, there has been a major attitudinal shift and a demonstration that a Māori agenda can be tolerated and even encouraged within conventional health services.

Collaborative pathways

A third pathway is concerned more with collaborative rather than solo effort. The collaboration might be between a Māori health service and a primary health care centre, or between a hospital and a Māori disability support service, or between a conventional mental health unit and a Māori community health team.

Institutional loyalty is a value worth promoting; but institutional solitude may not be in the longer term interests of clients or whānau. The collaborative pathway seeks to create a total picture out of several parts. It may well count against the ideological aims of absolute Māori independence or the conservative insistence on professional dominance, and it can be costly, but if excellent outcomes benchmarked against the best in the world are the aim, then increasingly collaboration of effort within and outside New Zealand will become an integral part of health care.

Performance

In order to support high quality health performance for Māori, it has become apparent that three preconditions are necessary. First, the legislative and policy framework must endorse best practice by recognising aspirations and involving Māori in decision making, priority setting and service planning.

Second, without a well-rounded workforce, quality care will never be possible. Workforce development is concerned with two main issues: the promotion of cultural competence and the expansion of the indigenous health workforce across professional disciplines and within their communities.

Third, there must be measures that can reflect Māori world views and realities. It is not sufficient to observe cultural practices and perspectives in the workplace without also ensuring that they can be measured in key result areas, using relevant targets and indicators – outcome measures, service performance measures and criteria for entry into treatment or care.

The twelve-point framework

Twelve points relating to a framework for Māori health have been discussed:

- three goals: equitable access, human dignity, best health outcomes
- three principles: indigeneity, clinical expertise, cultural competence
- three pathways: Māori-centred, Māori-added, collaborative
- three performance indicators: legislative and policy framework, workforce capacity, and indicators and measures.

The framework can also be represented as a matrix (see Table 18.1): the horizontal axis contains the broad goals – equitable access, human dignity, best outcomes – and the vertical axis contains the principles, pathways and performance indicators.

Many models and approaches to health will be discussed at the Third Asia Pacific Health Forum. This framework is but one and has been constructed on the basis of Māori experience over the past two decades. It needs to be seen alongside the others so that a comprehensive and clear picture of quality health care can emerge.

TABLE 18.1 Twelve-point matrix for quality health care

Goals ⟶	Equitable access	Human dignity	Best outcomes
Principles: • indigeneity • clinical expertise • cultural competence.			
Pathways: • Māori-centred • Māori-added • collaborative.			
Performance: • policy frameworks • workforce capacity • indicators & measures.			

CHAPTER 19

Māori Health Impact Assessment

Paper presented at the Symposium on Health Impact Assessment, Wellington, 30 March 2004.

Impacts

Māori health has often been shaped by events beyond expectation or their own control. Some impacts have been deliberate, some consequential though not necessarily intended, others perverse and quite unexpected. Impacts have arisen from local initiatives such as local authority decisions, and have impacted on specific groups of tangata whenua in quite direct ways. Others can be attributed to global processes and their less direct impacts might affect all Māori.

Harmful effects of impacts can be alleviated by modifying the source of impact (for example changing a policy) or strengthening the point of impact (for example ensuring ready access to goods and services). More often than not, however, impacts have been considered in hindsight, after the event. Indeed grievances relating to the Treaty of Waitangi are about the impacts of Crown policies or actions that occurred after 1840.

Avoiding undesirable impacts, rather than attempting to redress them after they have occurred, is probably a more constructive goal. But predicting the range of possible impacts, their effects, intensity and targets is not always straightforward and requires careful consideration of origins, pathways and destinations.

Economic, cultural, environmental, and social impacts can originate from a range of sites and through a variety of mechanisms. They can have multiple effects, on groups as well as individuals. Decisions under the Town and Country Planning Act 1962, for example, to restrict building permits according to a minimum size of land holdings, resulted in families who owned less than ten acres of land (or in some counties fifty acres) having to purchase urban sections in order to build their own homes. Both socially and economically they were penalised. The stated intention of the Act, however, was not to disadvantage Māori land owners, but to prioritise rural land for agricultural purposes. Consequential impacts on Māori could have been predicted but had not been given adequate consideration.

Social programmes can also have perverse effects. Adoption practices, for example, did not allow adopted children to know about their heritage or tribal affiliations. A policy of strict confidence was maintained by the Department of Social Welfare, ostensibly in the best interests of the child.[1] But in later years the same children were to learn that they had been effectively alienated from whānau and tribal resources such as land, educational grants and marae participation and had thus been disinherited. Similarly, the much publicised Matua Whāngai programme under which difficult-to-manage children and adolescents were transferred from the care of the Department of Social Welfare to the control of the wider whānau, underestimated the resources needed by whānau. Although the programme enabled the department to progress the incremental closure of residential care facilities, it passed the burden of care on to whānau but not the means to compensate for the additional demands.[2]

Impacts can be measured according to their influence on social, cultural, economic or environmental parameters (Table 19.1).

TABLE **19.1** Parameters and pathways of impact

Pathways	Parameters of Impact			
	Social	*Cultural*	*Economic*	*Environmental*
Legislation				
Policies				
Programmes and services				
Media				

Social impacts include the way people live and work and the relationships that they establish. The Town and Country Planning Act already referred to encouraged urbanisation for Māori families and as a result many links with wider whānau and communities were severed. At the same time, rural Māori were brought into closer proximity with other New Zealanders and were able to access a wider range of facilities than had previously been available.

Cultural impacts can arise when a development or a programme intrudes on cultural values or impedes the exercise of tikanga. An airport for example can have unwanted cultural impacts if flight pathways are directly above a marae, especially during tangi. Similarly a family welfare programme would have undesirable impacts if it led to reduced whānau cohesion, and if a health promotion programme had failed to take account of customary practices then it would be more likely to fail.

Economic impacts arise from programmes and policies that increase or decrease wealth, discretionary spending power, and national prosperity. During the years of major economic restructuring (post-1984), economic policies focused on reducing overseas debt by decreasing state subsidies, lowering interest rates and reducing inflation rates. Though successful when measured against the broad objectives, a consequence of the policy was high unemployment for Māori who had previously worked in areas where state subsidies were high. Between 1984 and 1990, Māori unemployment levels rose from 7 percent to 20 percent. Employment programmes to offset the trend were established, including the Maccess programmes aimed specifically at unemployed Māori. But they often delivered courses that were far removed from the requirements of the labour market and as a result did little to develop the type of skills that were needed to compete effectively in the new environment.

Environmental impacts refer to any development that has consequences for environmental sustainability. Unmonitored clearing of forests has led to disastrous consequences in many parts of New Zealand. Soil erosion, loss of bird life, and depleted stands of native trees have been all too common in the past. Moreover as the Waitangi Tribunal pointed out in the Motunui Report, industry has the potential to seriously pollute rivers and coastlines if waste products are discharged into water without adequate precautions.[3]

Pathways that lead from the source of an impact to a destination can take several forms (Table 19.1). Legislation is the most enforceable mechanism though may not be the most influential or may be at a level that is distant enough from community concerns to escape notice. On the other hand, government policies may be highly relevant and have great impact. For example the *Crown's Proposals for the Settlement of Treaty of Waitangi Claims* were not contained in legislation but became the framework for settling historic Treaty claims against the Crown.[4] Of the many impacts resulting from the policy, both beneficial and disadvantageous, the decision to focus on iwi (rather than hapū) initially created a climate of centralised control that left smaller hapū without effective voice. Only later were criteria for mandating refined so that any sense of exclusion could be minimised. Implementation of policies requires the institution of appropriate programmes and services.

Social policies have had mixed impacts. For example, to a large extent Māori tertiary education policies have relied on increasing Māori participation in polytechnics and wānanga and there has been a significant increase in tertiary enrolments by nearly 150 percent between 1991 and 2000.[5] But the policy has been less successful across all tertiary educational institutes: there have been no such dramatic increases in university enrolments.

It is possible to describe impacts as universal, selective, or specific according to their relevance and applicability (Table 19.2).

TABLE **19.2** Sites of impact

	Universal	Selective	Specific
Individuals			
Groups			
Populations			

Many impacts have universal application; they have similar effects and elicit identical responses from all peoples and populations. Immunisation against diphtheria, for example, has the same health impacts on all children regardless of race, ethnicity, or socio-economic variables. However, other impacts operate differentially. Selective impacts occurred, for example, in policies that introduced part charges for medical prescriptions. Some patients elected to forgo recommended treatment because they could not afford the medication. In that case the differential impact was a function of socio-economic circumstances.

Petrol rationing after the oil crisis in 1973 also impacted selectively. Some sections of society could obtain dispensations with relative ease, usually because of the nature of their work, while others were bound by the restrictions. Similarly very specific impacts arise when particular groups or populations experience them differently from society as a whole. A television company might impose a limit on the amount of spoken Māori during an evening's entertainment, a decision that would impact specifically on Māori since other viewers would be less likely to seek more Māori language programming.

A further factor that distinguishes impacts, however, is related to the emphasis placed on individuals, groups and populations. Personal injury, for example, is not evenly spread across the entire population. Forestry workers (where there are high concentrations of Māori) are more likely to sustain injuries than sedentary occupational groups, and rural populations are more subject to motor vehicle accidents than city car users. The impacts of safety standards and road maintenance therefore have greater significance for them.

Diverse populations may also experience environmental impacts differently. A government decision that restricted the clearing of scrub in preparation for forestry plantations satisfied 'green' advocates but did little to reassure Ngāti Porou about the future viability of their economic strategy and did not accept their views on environmental sustainability.[6]

Educational impacts are often measured according to their effect on individuals and the association between educational achievement, groups and populations can be easily overlooked. Success in education depends on multiple factors, many of which are outside individual control. When aggregated data sets are analysed, it quickly becomes apparent that specific groups (such as boys) or specific populations (such as Māori) each have similar experiences, sufficient to justify a population (rather than an individual) approach to impact assessment.

Causes of poor health

Given concerns about standards of Māori health, and the disparities that exist between Māori and other New Zealanders, the reasons for poor health have been the subject of considerable research and debate. Leaving aside early colonists' views about 'constitutional inferiority', explanations for Māori health status can be broadly grouped into four main causes: genetic predisposition, socio-economic disadvantage, resource alienation, and political oppression.[7]

Possible genetic predispositions have been investigated in diabetes, alcohol disorders and some cancers, though are generally regarded as less significant than socio-economic disadvantage, which is often central to contemporary indigenous experience. Poor housing, low educational achievement, unemployment, and inadequate incomes are known to correlate with a range of health problems and facilitate lifestyles that predispose to disease and injury.[8] Alienation from natural resources along with environmental degradation caused by destructive logging, dam building or oil spillage has also been identified as a cause of poor health for indigenous peoples in several countries, while cultural alienation is a further factor, of particular importance in the delivery of health services.[9] There is abundant evidence that where clinician and patient are from different cultural backgrounds there is greater likelihood of misdiagnosis and non-compliance.

A number of writers have also drawn a link between colonisation and poor health.[10] They argue that loss of sovereignty along with dispossession (of lands, waterways, and custom laws) created a climate of material and spiritual oppression with increased susceptibility to disease and injury.

All four positions can be justified and conceptualised as a causal continuum (Figure 19.1). At one end are 'short distance' factors such as the impacts of abnormal molecular and cellular processes, while at the other end are 'long distance' factors including governmental policies and the political standing of indigenous peoples. Values, lifestyle, standards of living and culture, so important to clinical understandings, lie midway.

Using a classification employed by Te Rangi Hiroa to distinguish illnesses that were of unknown origin (mana atua) from disorders that could be readily explained (mana tangata),[11] two broad sources of impacts can be identified: those that arise spontaneously or at least without obvious human encouragement, and those that can be attributed to the actions of people either directly or indirectly (Table 19.3).

Figure **19.1** Health impacts – a causal continuum

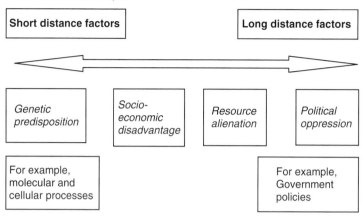

TABLE **19.3** Sources of health impacts

Mana atua	Mana tangata
Acts of nature, for example floods, earthquakes, cyclones.	Individual behaviour, for example careless driving, excessive childhood discipline.
Cosmic phenomena, for example eclipses of the moon.	Societal institutions for example arrangements for childcare.
Inborn errors of metabolism, for example type 1 diabetes.	Government policies, for example alcohol tariffs.
Microbial invasion, for example viral infections, meningococcal meningitis.	Legislation, for example Resource Management Act.
Deformity, for example talipes.	Political ideologies, for example free market policies.

Contrary to the views held in previous times, we now know that the impacts arising from 'mana atua' are capable of modification, and even sometimes prevention. Microbial invasion is less likely where there is adequate ventilation and an absence of overcrowding; inborn errors of metabolism can be prevented by genetic counselling or the effects minimised by early intervention; deformities can often be traced to intra-uterine toxins and avoided.

However, impacts due to human intervention are still more readily altered. Many of the factors attributable to mana tangata, that is, to human behaviours, are linked to national public policies, though policies at local levels are also important. For example a kōhanga reo policy on nutrition will have significant impacts on health, a marae policy on car parking will have implications for safety, and a wānanga policy on smoking will influence personal behaviours while addressing the wider campus environment.

Measuring the health effects of impacts

Three types of measures are useful in measuring health impacts on Māori – direct measures, proxy measures and population-specific measures.

Direct health measures include mortality rates, morbidity data, hospital admissions and discharges, disease prevalence surveys, and disparity measurements between groups. Some direct measures such as mortality rates are universal and can be applied to all peoples but population-specific measures focus on particular groups only. Rural injury rates, for example, are measures relevant to the rural population.

Proxy measures of health utilise indicators that have a strong association with health status but are not themselves measures of health. Unemployment rates, educational failure, poor standards of housing, and Māori ethnicity are known to correlate with poor health.

It is sometimes argued that proxy measures are 'colour-blind' in the sense that socio-economic measures are fully able to explain differences in health status without needing to make reference to ethnicity. However, there is evidence that both socio-economic factors and ethnicity are relevant and are not synonymous with each other. People with the same index of deprivation do not have identical patterns of health experience when they are from different ethnic backgrounds.

Population-specific measures of health are shaped not only by health experiences but by culture, values, and perspectives that underpin concepts of health and wellness. Indigenous peoples share a world view that emphasises a connection with the territories, land and the wider natural environment.

Arising from that relationship, it is possible to identify five major characteristics of indigeneity. The first reflects the dimension of time and a relationship with the environment that has endured over centuries; the second, also derived from the environmental relationship, is about culture, human identity and group structures and processes that celebrate the human–ecological union. The third characteristic is a system of knowledge that integrates indigenous world views, values, and experience and generates a framework for a distinctive environmental ethic. Application of that ethic to natural resources provides a basis for the fourth characteristic, economic growth balanced against environmental sustainability. Finally, indigeneity is also characterised by a language so strongly influenced by the environment that it is not spoken as a first language in other parts of the world.

This definition of indigeneity has implications for the measurement of Māori health. Health consequences arise when there are impacts on the human domain (individuals, groups) or on the resource domain (cultural resources, physical resources).[12] Measurements of the health of individuals should take into account Māori health perspectives by recognising and quantifying the impacts on taha wairua (spiritual health), taha hinengaro (mental, intellectual health), taha tinana (physical health) and taha whānau (family and social health). While some of those measurements (such as measurements of physical health) will be universal, others will be Māori-specific. The same is true for the proxy measures arising from impacts on collectives such as whānau or the resource domain. Where an intervention has led for example to alienation of language or land, or desecration of the natural environment, health consequences can be predicted.

A Māori health impact framework

A Māori health impact framework incorporates several dimensions that are necessary to measure Māori health impacts (Table 19.4) and encompasses domains where impacts are experienced and indicators that can quantify the experience. Two major sites of impacts are the human domain and the resource domain; and two broad groups of indicators are those that have universal application (such as mortality rates, access to cultural institutions; land holding) and those that are specific to Māori (for example cultural identity, whānau participation, marae access, access to tribal resources).

TABLE **19.4** A Māori health impact framework

	Human Domain		Resource Domain	
	Personal	Collective	Cultural, intellectual	Tribal and Māori estates
Universal indicators				
Māori specific indicators				

Conclusions

Health impacts have multiple origins and multiple destinations with consequences for people (individuals and groups) as well as the environment. Although universal measures can be applied to many situations in order to quantify impacts, population-specific measures are also necessary. They are likely to reflect world views, values and concepts of health that are not shared by all other populations. A Māori health impact framework provides for both universal and population-specific indicators; it scopes the parameters of health impact assessment; and identifies the human domain and the resource domain as sites where health consequences are generated.

CHAPTER 20

Indigenous Health: Catalysts for Innovation

Paper presented at the Innovation for Health Conference: Sharing
Knowledge and Building Relationships, Wellington, 10 October 2007.

Indigenous resilience

The capacity of indigenous peoples to survive and then prosper has
been a characteristic of post-colonial development. Not only have the
catastrophic impacts of infectious diseases, alienation from culture and
customary lands, and loss of autonomy been withstood but generations
later, indigenous peoples in the Pacific have endured and advanced to
the extent that they are now in significantly stronger positions than
they were 150 years ago.

Indigenous resilience has several dimensions but essentially
encompasses individuals and groups, a capacity for positive engagement,
and a level of autonomy.[1] Much of the literature on resilience centres
on the potential of individuals to overcome personal trauma and
succeed. However, resilience is also about the achievements of collectives:
families, whānau, communities, tribes, and whole populations. Success
in that sense is a shared experience which reflects an ability to adapt
and a propensity for turning adversity into accomplishment.

Two broad capacities underpin indigenous success. The first one is
the dual capacity to engage with indigenous culture, networks and
resources, and to engage with global societies and communities. The
duality recognises the two worlds within which indigenous peoples live
and the skills needed to negotiate both. Successful engagement with
the indigenous world is facilitated by spiritual and cultural competence
and acceptance by communities, while engagement with global societies

is eased by the acquisition of technical skills, educational qualifications, and a capacity to deal with bias and prejudice.

A second aspect of indigenous success is built around autonomy and self-management. Resilience is less likely if indigenous futures are premised on the aspirations of others. Instead indigenous success requires a capacity for indigenous approaches to governance and management that are compatible with the world views of families, tribes, and indigenous communities while at the same time being attuned to wider societal values and economies. Autonomy does not necessarily mean an independent pathway but opportunities for collaboration and cooperation on the basis of equality and shared goals.

Innovation is a third factor that can accelerate resilience. Clinging to the old ways without any adaptive capacity, or alternatively abandoning the past as if it had no implications for the future, will not be sufficient to prepare indigenous peoples for the future. Instead innovation that can harness the energy from two dimensions and two world views has been shown to enhance resilience and increase indigenous potential.

Two innovative approaches, separated by a century and each lasting for a period of twenty-five years, have made major contributions to Māori standards of health and provide a basis for understanding indigenous innovation. The first period, 1882–1907, was instrumental in reversing a steady population decline that might well have led to Māori extinction; while the second, between 1982 and 2007, laid the foundations for addressing health risks in the twenty-first century and enabling full Māori participation in the health sector.

Māori innovations
Period one: 1882–1907

Reversing a steep population decline was a major accomplishment initiated by Māori leaders in the 1880s. However, the publication of an article by Archdeacon Walsh in the *Transactions of the New Zealand Institute* in 1907 seemed to cast doubt on their efforts. Despite early signs that the depopulation process had been arrested, 'The Passing of the Maori' painted a grim future. 'That the Maori is gradually though rapidly passing away there can be no doubt. ... Finality has now been reached, and the next census will show that the Maori population, instead of increasing has been diminishing all the time, and that if the present rate of declension continues, it must soon reach the vanishing point.'[2]

The evidence accumulated over the preceding fifty years seemed to support the Archdeacon. In 1856 the Māori population was clearly in a state of decline. Even by 1836 there were reports that the population had been reduced by more than a quarter and by 1906 it was estimated at 45,000 – a reduction of more than 75 percent from 1806. By 1874 the *New Zealand Herald* was convinced the end was nigh: 'That the native race is dying out in New Zealand there is, of course, no doubt…. The fact cannot be disguised that the natives are gradually passing away; and even if no cause should arise to accelerate their decrease, the rate at which they are now disappearing points to their extinction in an exceedingly brief period.'[3]

Autonomy

However, neither the *Herald* nor Walsh had taken Māori resilience and Māori innovation into account. Determination to seek redress and gain greater autonomy, coupled with adaptation by tribal leaders, greater Māori influence in Parliament, and new professional capability proved to be a powerful formula for successful innovation. A delegation to London in 1882, led by Hirini Taiwhanga (later to become Member of Parliament for Northern Māori) sought a greater measure of autonomy for Māori and proffered the suggestion of a Māori Parliament to manage Māori affairs. Even though they received a sympathetic hearing from British officials, their efforts were not appreciated in New Zealand. But tribal leaders throughout the country were similarly concerned about loss of independence and were to join forces for a greater measure of control over their own matters. The earlier election of a Māori King (in 1858) was a clear sign of a desire for autonomy while the formation of the pan-tribal Kotahitanga movement led to the establishment of a Māori Parliament (Paremata Māori) in 1892.

At the same time, more astute Māori politicians were voted into Parliament, including James Carroll (1887), Hone Heke Ngapua (1893) and Apirana Ngata (1905). Well attuned to political processes and to Māori aspirations they became highly important conduits between legislative processes and Māori advancement. Both Carroll and Ngata were knighted and both were to attain eminence among politicians, Pākehā and Māori.

The Young Māori Party

Ngata had been part of a small but influential cohort of Māori secondary school students groomed for roles in the changing Māori world. Te Aute College in Hawkes Bay acquired a reputation as an incubator for a new type of Māori leadership based on a fervent commitment to Māori advancement and improvement of spiritual and material conditions. As students at school some had undertaken walking tours to rural communities where they met with tribal elders to advocate health and hygiene measures, taking upon themselves the task of reforming Māori communities, largely by promoting western lifestyles and standards. In 1891 an Association for the Amelioration of the Māori Race was established by the young advocates, and in 1897 many of the same group, under the guidance of Apirana Ngata, formed the Te Aute Association 'whose special aims were to improve health, sanitation, education, work habits, and family life'.[4] The Association became synonymous with the Young Māori Party.

Two of the Te Aute group, Maui Pomare and Peter Buck (Te Rangi Hiroa) were to become the first Māori medical graduates before they entered politics, while Ngata achieved distinction in law, politics, literature and land reform. Māori social, economic and cultural revival is often credited to this trio, Ngata, Pomare and Buck, and the Young Māori Party that they helped to establish. Their philosophy was greatly influenced by their inspirational principal, John Thornton, whose religious convictions and social conscience acted as a catalyst and agenda.[5]

Ngata, Pomare and Buck were in no doubt that the answer to Māori survival lay in the need to adapt to western society and to do so within the overall framework imposed by the law. Though strongly and emphatically in support of Māori language and culture they were equally passionate advocates of western democracy, education and modern health practices. They believed it was possible to retain a secure Māori identity while embracing Pākehā values and beliefs.

The appointment of Pomare as a medical officer to the Māori in the Department of Public Health in 1901 provided an opportunity for Drs Pomare and Buck to apply the Young Māori Party philosophy to health care. Consistent with that philosophy Pomare committed his energies to Māori community development and worked to empower Māori community leaders. He had decided to make the best of the Maori Councils Act 1900 which had established Māori councils, and recognised among the local councils a powerful army for health. That became his strategy, and his single most important contribution to Māori health – health could not be prescribed by the doctor; it should arise from within communities; and the leaders of health were not to be doctors or nurses, but community leaders who could use their influence and wisdom to alter lifestyles and living conditions. Pomare, later assisted by Buck, worked with every Māori council assisting them to identify problems and lending his medical knowledge and skills. When the task of visiting and assisting councils became impossible, he then appointed and trained a team of Māori sanitary inspectors as liaison officers. In effect, a team approach was instituted: an amalgam of medical knowledge and expertise, combined with tribal and community leadership, and supported by government through the fledgling Department of Public Health.

Although extinction had been widely predicted, not only did Māori survive, within a century they had become more numerous than at any other time in history. Even though changes to statistical definitions of Māori make it difficult to draw exact comparisons, there is strong evidence of a substantial and sustained increase in the Māori population. In the 2006 Census 565,329 New Zealanders identified as Māori, with a median age of 22.7 years.[6]

Further, although accounting for some 14 percent of the total New Zealand population in 2001, by 2051 the Māori ethnic population will almost double in size to close to a million, or 22 percent of the total New Zealand population. Even more significant, by 2051, 33 percent of all children in the country will be Māori and the percentage of the Māori population over the age of sixty-five will steadily rise from 3 percent (1996) to 13 percent (2051) as life expectancy increases.[7]

Period Two: 1982–2007

A second period of innovation occurred a century later and began with the promotion of Māori concepts of health. When the Māori

Women's Welfare League was embarking on a survey of the health of Māori women in 1982, a model of health known as Te Whare Tapa Wha anchored their study.[8] The model's appeal was based on its holistic approach to health and the recognition of spirituality as a significant contributor to good health. Until then discussions about Māori health had dwelt on the rates and consequences of disease, creating a mood of disempowerment and passivity. But by reconfiguring health in terms that made sense to Māori, it was possible for Māori communities to experience a sense of ownership and to balance medical and professional dominance with community involvement and local leadership. Te Whare Tapa Wha was presented as a four-sided house, each wall representing one aspect of health – spirituality (taha wairua), the mind (taha hinengaro), physical health (taha tinana) and family and social relationships (taha whānau).

Taha wairua remains important to Māori since it captures the notion of a special relationship with the environment, as well as a Māori cultural identity. Taha hinengaro concerns the way people think, feel and behave and recognises that Māori patterns of thought value metaphor and allusion. Taha Tinana is not only about physical illness but also fitness, mobility and freedom from pain; while taha whānau focuses on the nature of interpersonal relationships, within the family but also beyond into wider society. Increasingly the model is being used as a framework for the development of models of assessment, treatment, care, the measurement of outcomes and the formulation of health policies.

Further opportunities for adopting new approaches to health care came in 1984. Not only were major economic reforms introduced, but devolution of state-provided services followed, as well as deregulation of many industries that had previously been the province of protected groups. Driven by economic expediencies that included the removal of state subsidies from the agricultural and forestry sectors, 'temporary' stress on all New Zealanders was seen as inevitable. Māori, however, carried an excessive share of the burden and within five years Māori unemployment more than doubled to over 20 percent and in some areas was higher for school leavers.[9] Nonetheless the raft of reforms positioned Māori to move towards active roles in health and education, reinforced by renewed government commitment to the Treaty of Waitangi and the inclusion of a Treaty clause in several statutes.

Decade of Positive Māori Development

New directions were spelled out at a Māori Economic Summit meeting, the Hui Taumata held in 1984. A 'Decade of Positive Māori Development' was prescribed premised on the themes of tribal development, economic self-reliance, social equity and cultural affirmation. In keeping with the wider national economic reforms, where a diminished role for the state was being paired with a greater role for enterprise, the new call was for 'Māori solutions to Māori problems'. Both the lack of confidence in the capacity of the state to offer positive solutions, and a desire to capitalise on existing Māori structures and values, combined to inject a spirit of independence and enthusiasm for alternative approaches. Significantly, a sound economic base was seen as a crucial step towards achieving any real social or even cultural survival.

During 1984 a series of other important hui were held by Māori covering education, economics, the Treaty of Waitangi and health. The Hui Whakaoranga, the first national Māori health hui in modern times, began as a recital of Māori health problems but quickly became a platform for advocating Māori-led health initiatives. Inspired by the recently formed Māori Nurses' Council and the few Māori communities who provided health services, Māori enthusiasm for active participation in health care blossomed. Independent Māori health providers and Māori services within conventional institutions were soon to materialise. At Tokanui Hospital, for example, Whaiora was established as a Māori treatment centre within a major psychiatric hospital.

For most of the twentieth century policies for Māori were essentially premised on attaining equity with other New Zealanders and adopting the same values and world views as the majority population. It was not until 1984, and the launching of the Decade of Positive Māori Development that the retention of Māori values and culture was seen as integral to socio-economic advancement.

In the new approach, there was a frank rejection of any notion of assimilation. Instead the expectation was that all Māori young people should be able to grow up as New Zealanders and as Māori. Full participation need not mean abandoning a Māori identity. Moreover, there was a strong desire by Māori to develop their own economic and social systems in ways that were consistent with Māori aspirations and priorities. While the state as a provider had certain attractions, seldom was it able to recognise Māori preferences. In contrast, in the deregulated environment, large numbers of Māori health, education and social service providers emerged, enabling families (whānau), communities and tribes to steer their own courses.

Transformations in education participation

By the end of the twenty-five-year period major transformations had occurred. Māori participation in education at all levels was radically altered in two respects. First, the education system recognised Māori language, knowledge, and culture as core elements of the curriculum. Second, participation rates in non-compulsory education escalated in an unprecedented manner. While participation rates are uneven, and many Māori youngsters still remain outside the reach of effective education, there has been a remarkable turnaround. The initial establishment of Māori alternatives such as kōhanga reo (Māori language immersion centres) in 1981 provided examples of Māori innovation and were followed by higher mainstream Māori participation rates in early childhood education, growing by over 30 percent between 1991 and 1993. By 2001, 45 percent of all Māori children under five years of age were enrolled in early childhood services, nearly one-third in kōhanga reo[10] and by 2005 around 90 percent of Māori children entering primary school had experienced some form of early childhood education.[11]

For older learners there were also significant gains. Retention rates for sixteen year olds at secondary school increased from 47 percent (in 1987) to 63 percent (in 2003). Between 1983 and 2000 the percentage of Māori students who left school with no qualifications decreased from 62 percent to 35 percent, while at the tertiary level, between 1993 and 2004 Māori participation increased by 148 percent. By 2002 Māori had the highest rates of participation in tertiary education of any group aged at twenty-five years and over. Although the significant improvement masked the fact that Māori were still five times more likely to enrol in government remedial training programmes and three times less likely to enrol at a university,[12] around 7 percent of the total university population in 2005 is Māori. But most of the recent tertiary education growth has occurred through accredited tribal learning centres, wānanga, which increased enrolments from 26,000 students in 2001 to 45,500 in 2002.[13]

Transformations in health care

Transformations in health care have paralleled gains in the education sector. Greater emphasis on health promotion, primary health care and disability support has bccn possible with the steady growth of a Māori health workforce within Māori communities. New interest in traditional healing, as an adjunct to primary care and as part of a comprehensive health package has also increased Māori access to services and reduced the gap between healing and treatment.

As one way of addressing the disproportionate representation of Māori in most illnesses and injuries, workforce development became a high priority for improving Māori standards of health. An important component of a workforce strategy has been the engagement of cultural advisors and Māori community health advisors to work alongside health professionals, bringing first-hand knowledge of community and a capacity to engage diffident patients. Often the combination has been highly effective though there has also been concern that the two streams of workers – cultural and clinical – have created potential for professional and cultural interventions to diverge. An integration of cultural and clinical dimensions is one of the more pressing challenges facing Māori health care.

Of critical importance, however, has been the recruitment of more Māori into the health professions. Affirmative action programmes – or programmes that have similar aims – have been significant vehicles to develop a workforce that is more representative of New Zealand's communities. In 1998, for example, the University of Auckland launched Vision 2020, a programme designed to significantly increase Māori entry into the medical school. In 1984 there were five new Māori medical students but by 2004, the number of new Māori entrants had increased to twenty-four.[14] Similar trends have been seen in the qualified medical workforce. From an estimated medical workforce of around sixty in 1984, there are now over 200 Māori medical practitioners across a range of specialties, accounting for 3 percent of the total active medical workforce. In addition, scholarships have been offered from a number of sources as incentives to encourage enrolment in other disciplines such as nursing, social work, clinical psychology and addiction treatment. The number of Māori dentists for example has increased from four or five in 1984 to forty-four in 2005.

But the most dramatic changes have been in the number of Māori health provider organisations. Prior to 1980 there were only three or four Māori health providers but by 2007, nearly 300 Māori heath providers offered a range of services and Māori language and culture had become more or less accepted as part of the operating norm in schools, hospitals, state agencies, the media, and community centres.

Health gains

While the impact of workforce strategies on Māori health status has not been specifically determined, there have been significant gains in Māori health, especially over the past five years. For non-Māori New Zealanders there was a steady increase in life expectancy at birth over the period from 1985/7 to 2000/2. For Māori there was little change for males or females during the 1980s but a dramatic improvement in the five years to 2000/2. Between 1984 and 2002 the life expectancy increased from sixty-five years for Māori males to sixty-nine years while for Māori females it increased from seventy to seventy-three years. Notwithstanding the eight year gap between Māori and non-Māori, in the five years to 2000/2, the gap reduced by 0.6 years.[15]

Since the 1960s disparities between Māori and non-Māori have formed the basis for appraising Māori health. Generally disparities exist for almost all disease states and for levels of severity. However there is recent evidence of a reduction in mortality disparities. Although Māori experienced the highest mortality rates in the period 1981–2004, the rate of decline in Māori mortality has increased, compared to a slowing in the European/other rate of decline. In the late 1990s and early 2000s relative inequality (mortality rate ratios) between Māori and European/other ethnic groups reduced slightly while absolute inequality (mortality rate difference) declined more notably. While much of the difference appears to be a function of socio-economic circumstances, other factors operating independently of socio-economic factors are relevant – such as racism, access to quality care, tobacco, diet and other lifestyle factors.[16]

Catalysts for innovation

Although the two periods 1882–1907 and 1982–2007 witnessed widely different conditions and approaches to health care, it is possible to identify three themes common to both eras that accelerated action and contributed to positive outcomes: leadership, interventions at the interface, and investments in innovation.

Leadership

First, transformational Māori leadership emerged. At the conclusion of the nineteenth century, adaptive tribal leaders as well as political leaders and a new cohort of Māori professionals provided inspiration, guidance and commitment to Māori survival. Unlike an earlier generation of leaders who had literally fought to retain the old ways, the task of Ngata, Pomare and others was to guide Māori into a new environment, retaining useful cultural values and perspectives while embracing new technologies and a new economy. Similarly, as the twentieth century closed, a Māori leadership network formed around the common goals of increased autonomy, self-sufficiency, tribal redevelopment, and cultural affirmation. Their task was not about survival – by then an expanding population would assure Māori endurance for many generations to come – but about transforming society so that systems and institutions would be accessible, relevant to Māori, and able to lead to the best possible outcomes.

Transformational leadership demands a type of leadership that is essentially outward looking; integrative more than defensive; ready to cross institutional boundaries and institutions; and strategic rather than bound by a set of operational conventions. Transformational leaders promote sustainable leadership. Stand-alone charismatic leaders have less to offer changing environments than leaders who can weld together other leaders – from political, tribal, community and professional arenas and encourage a deliberate strategy of succession planning. Sustainable leadership develops leadership capacity and leadership networks where innovation, rather than standardisation, can flourish. Moreover, transformation requires a type of leadership that is distributed so that the benefits are widespread rather than localised, triggering and enabling different types of transition in society.[17]

Interventions at the interface

A second theme emerging from the two periods of Māori transformation is a capacity to straddle an interface. Connecting with indigenous people means being able to live in two worlds, simultaneously. Language, cultural values, cultural protocols and indigenous associations at community, tribal and even national levels will be important vehicles for communicating and assisting indigenous clients. But equally, interventions to promote good health need to take account of findings from science and technology, medical advancement and clinical expertise. Working between two bodies of knowledge – science and indigenous knowledge – recognises that neither indigenous knowledge nor science alone provides a universal answer. Health care is firmly premised on science and the medical model depends on evidence derived from scientific inquiry. In contrast indigenous knowledge is not fixated on science; instead it largely depends on a set of values and observations that link people into the wider natural environment. Unlike science, where explanations are constantly tested and revised, indigenous knowledge is all the more remarkable because it has endured over centuries. The challenge is not to dismiss either knowledge base, nor to explain one according to the tenets of the other, but to embrace both in order to reach fresh insights that might enrich the lives of those who are touched by both systems.

In contemporary health care the interface can take many forms: the interface between health and other sectors, between physical health and mental health; primary care and secondary care; wellness and disease; professional leadership and consumer perspectives; technology and human compassion; clinical skills and cultural paradigms.

Investments in innovation

A third theme concerns investments in innovation. Typically investments in Māori health innovation have been derived from three main sources: government, health agencies, and Māori tribes and communities. In 1901 the Department of Public Health invested in a 'medical officer to the Maoris', the Department of Native Affairs invested in Māori councils and, despite huge adversity, Māori communities invested time and expertise. In the economic restructuring that commenced in 1984, the Ministries of Health and Māori Development similarly invested in tribal and community organisations, and after the 1993 health reforms there were substantial investments by health funding agencies in the

Māori health provider organisations. Research funders have meanwhile provided major investments in innovation and the Health Research Council's innovative efforts to build Māori health research capacity as well as research at the interface between science and indigenous knowledge have been critical to strengthening Māori health capability.

A four-way investment pattern has required a series of partnerships at national, agency, local and community levels. Sometimes this has created confusion with the Crown's preferred model of negotiating with tribes, at least in respect of Treaty of Waitangi settlements, and the sectoral approach has also complicated investments that have inter-sectoral implications. Further, once established, innovative approaches to health care have often been quite quickly operationalised so that further innovation becomes compromised by a requirement to meet specified milestones.

Investments in innovation present a degree of risk to investors since the outcomes are not always clear or certain. During the period 1982–2007 a number of Māori health innovations did not survive or were criticised for not realising greater returns. While risk can be minimised by the provision of clear guidelines and specified indicators, an element of risk is part of the innovation reality. But leaving no room for innovation can also present risks especially where there is clear evidence that current practice does not meet actual need.

Preconditions for innovation

On the basis of Māori experience during the two periods 1882–1907 and 1982–2007, it is possible to draw some conclusions about the parameters of innovation in health and health care. Three broad preconditions can be recognised.

First, innovation arises in response to a need for change. Change is indicated when current approaches fail to address existing problems in health care, either because there is inadequate access and lack of perceived relevance, or doubts about quality and safety, or multiple problems that cut across disciplinary boundaries. And when participation takes a passive form rather than creating opportunities for active involvement thereby forcing consumers into states of dependency, or when diagnosis and treatment are compromised by a cultural mismatch, innovative responses are needed.

Second, innovation is more likely to occur when the right catalysts are present. Transformative leadership is a critical catalyst. Transformative leadership integrates rather than fragments, can be sustained even when the instigators have left, and can deliver widespread benefits that trigger other societal gains. Interventions at the interface can also catalyse innovation that will not occur within segmented silos. Interfaces can be found between different bodies of knowledge, different sectors, different levels of health care, and different areas of specialisation. Investments in innovation are also necessary catalysts requiring cooperation between investors, a degree of risk taking and a willingness to explore options that will improve health care and health status.

Third, an important precondition for innovation is an enthusiasm for change. Unless the enthusiasm is shared by the sector, the community, and government, it is unlikely that innovative changes will be sustained or even commenced. In effect an innovation climate is necessary for innovation to blossom.

Arising from these considerations and from Māori experience gained over a century it is possible to represent innovation as a process that occurs within an innovation-friendly environment where communities, the sector, and government find a measure of accord, unleashing catalysts for change and ultimately producing new knowledge, enhanced sector capability, and importantly, gains in health.

CHAPTER 21

Indigenous Responses to Health and Disease: Principles, Goals, and Pathways

The 2007 Wunderly Oration: presented at the Thoracic Society of Australia and New Zealand & the Australian and New Zealand Society of Respiratory Science Conference, Auckland, March 2007.

Dr Harry Wunderly

This oration is a tribute to Dr Harry Wunderly who died in 1971 after a lifetime of devotion to a cause dear to his own heart. His devotion inspired thousands of others in Australia and in the process generated a nationwide health movement that would lead to huge gains in the health status of the nation. Few people can claim to have effectively translated clinical experience into government policy, or beyond that to have significantly changed the course of history. Yet that is part of the Harry Wunderly legacy.

In his several roles as doctor, public health promoter, benefactor, mentor, educator and pioneer chest physician he energised the profession and the nation in a way that would eventually see a major breakthrough in the management of chronic disease. Having experienced tuberculosis first hand, his personal resolve to overcome the illness became transformed into a lifelong commitment to eradicate the disease on a national scale, and in the process to build a strong medical workforce with the capacity to address whatever respiratory illnesses might await future generations. On all counts he was highly successful. Although tuberculosis remains a global health problem, especially in developing countries, and in Eastern Europe and Asia where multi-drug resistant tuberculosis is common enough to warrant a global response,[1] the problem in Australia and New Zealand is largely contained. If tuberculosis has not been entirely eradicated, then at the very least it no longer has the endemic dimensions that threatened survival in many Australian and New Zealand communities during the nineteenth and twentieth centuries. Further, the two societies associated with this conference bear testimony to Harry Wunderly's determination to foster chest medicine as a modern medical discipline.

In recognition of his services Harry Wunderly was knighted in 1954. Rightly, even before his death in 1971, the Wunderly Oration provided an opportunity to reflect on his efforts and to celebrate a medical triumph. This year, 2007, Auckland has the honour of hosting the event.

Dr Maui Pomare

As it happens, 2007 is the 100th anniversary of an event not widely known in New Zealand but not unrelated to the work of Dr Wunderly and to the promotion of health. It concerned the enactment of a piece of legislation largely intended to address the increasing prevalence of tuberculosis in New Zealand, especially among Māori people. Whether or not the Act contributed to any diminution of the disease, whether it even improved health standards, or whether it was motivated by an undisclosed agenda remain points of debate. But for whatever reason the Tohunga Suppression Act 1907 sought to eliminate tuberculosis by outlawing 'Every person who gathers around him by practising on their superstition or credulity, or who misleads or attempts to mislead any Maori by professing or pretending to possess supernatural powers in the treatment or cure of any disease, or in the foretelling of future events.' The latter point, 'foretelling future events', was probably added to justify the arrest of a Māori prophet, Rua Kenana, who forecast that a Māori millennium was nigh and that all Europeans would be expelled from the country.[2] It added fuel to theories that the legislation had a primary political purpose far removed from tuberculosis.

A key figure in promoting the Act was a physician who had the distinction of being the first Māori medical practitioner. Maui Pomare had attended a private Māori boys' boarding school, Te Aute College, which was to play a significant role in developing a cohort of Māori university graduates who would lead a reformation to bridge the nineteenth and twentieth centuries and reverse the population decline that had characterised the half century from 1850 to 1900. With support from the Seventh Day Adventists' Church, Pomare attended an intermediate school for medical students at Battle Creek College in Michigan, and then enrolled at the American Medical Missionary College at Chicago. He graduated MD in 1899.[3]

Following a brief internship at Cook County Hospital in Chicago, and immediately after returning to New Zealand, at the age of twenty-five years Pomare was appointed to the new Department of Public Health in 1901 as the first Māori medical officer. His duties included 'visiting the natives in their villages; inquiring and investigating into their general health; the conditions of water supply; and the enlightening of the native mind by means of lectures on all points concerning sanitation and hygiene and any social questions materially affecting the welfare of the race.'[4]

Pomare himself was somewhat intimidated by the task ahead. 'It was with a heart full of fear and trembling that my mission was undertaken,' he wrote in his first report to the chief health officer.[5] He knew that while many medical advances would find favour with Māori, sooner or later his own views about health and development would take him into a head-on collision with his own people. He foreshadowed the clash with comments about tohunga (traditional healers) in his 1903 report. 'I have watched all these tohungas at work and have come to the conclusion that, unless Parliament passes a stringent law prohibiting the practice of any kind of tohunga, we shall always have a great many Maoris dying from the effects of tohungaism.'[6]

Despite the strong language Pomare was not opposed to Māori values or to his own people; on the contrary if there were ever dedication to Māori advancement and improved standards of health, then it was epitomised by him. His record in improved sanitation, better housing, health education, and vaccination is unparalleled; and his efforts to endorse the best of traditional culture important to Māori communities at a time when there was a strong move towards assimilation. In that respect his earlier years at Te Aute College had engendered a philosophical position endorsing the importance of technological and scientific advances though without abandoning a cultural past.

Pomare quickly came to recognise that health could not be detached from a wider environment and galvanised community leadership to endorse doctrines of health and hygiene. Taking advantage of the Maori Councils Act 1900 which had established Māori councils in several regions throughout the country, he worked with all the councils assisting them to identify potential and actual problems, and lending his medical knowledge and skills to create solutions. He then appointed and trained tribal leaders as Māori sanitary inspectors to monitor health status, water supplies, sanitation and food hygiene. That was probably his single most important contribution – health was not to be regarded as a medical condition, but a state which should arise from within communities; and the leaders of health were not to be doctors or nurses, but community leaders who could use their influence and wisdom to alter lifestyles and living conditions.

By 1909, Pomare could rightly claim some credit for the reversal of health trends that were in progress and it was clear that he had more to offer than could be realised within the Department of Public Health. Consequently, after approaches from Māori communities he accepted nomination for Parliament. Now as an Independent Member of Parliament for Western Māori his efforts were to be at another level and in 1923 he became Minister of Health in the first Reform Party Government. His service to his country was recognised in 1922 when he was made a Knight Commander of the British Empire.[7]

Pomare died in office at the relatively young age of fifty-four years in 1930. He had travelled to San Francisco to recuperate in a warm environment but it was too late. Nothing could actually be done to reverse the spread of pulmonary tuberculosis, the very disease that had focused his energies thirty years earlier.

Changing times and changing environments

Pomare and Wunderly were from different backgrounds, different countries, different ethnicities and different eras. Both, however, were knights of the realm and both tackled the problems of their times using their medical qualifications and skills to advantage while looking beyond patient management to address the environments that fostered ill health. In their own lifetimes they were able to witness major gains in health status and the way health services were delivered and to contribute to the substantial gains in health in Australia and New Zealand.

Health gains – and threats

One measure of gain can be found in Māori demographic transitions. In 1800 the estimated population was 200,000 but by 1894, and for a variety of reasons, it had dwindled to 42,000 and extinction was widely predicted. Instead, however, and because of the efforts of Pomare and other leaders, the decline was arrested at the turn of the century, to be followed by an increasing rate of growth so that by 2006 the population was in excess of 565,329 or 15 percent of the total New Zealand population.[8] And because the population is relatively youthful with a median age of 22.7 years, high rates of growth can be predicted to occur for four or more decades. By 2051 around one-third of all New Zealand school children will be Māori.

Gains can also be found in mortality rates and life expectancy. Infant death rates as high as 94 per 1000 live births in 1929 had reduced to 54 per 1000 by 1959 and to 18 by 1991. Similarly Māori life expectancy increased from thirty-three (for males) and thirty (for females) in 1903, to sixty-six (for males) and seventy-one (for females) in 1996, and to sixty-nine (males) and 73.2 (females) by 2002.

The diseases that ravaged Māori communities in the late nineteenth and early twentieth centuries have largely disappeared, at least as major causes of death and disability. From 1901 the main health risks were largely related to malnutrition and infectious diseases especially tuberculosis, typhoid, and diphtheria. The fact that those diseases are now largely consigned to history is cause for celebration.

However, although the management of tuberculosis owed much to Mantoux testing, the Heaf test, BCG vaccination, mobile chest X-rays, and specific anti-tuberculous agents such as Isoniazid, it was also boosted by better understanding of the environments within which people lived – damp and overcrowded housing, inadequate diets, interpersonal contagion, distance from amenities and services, and often attitudes of resignation. If those conditions continue to constrain the lives of some communities, Māori and Australian Aborigines are now also confronted by contemporary social, physical, and economic environments that are also hazardous to health and catalysts for new sets of health problems that have emerged or are about to emerge.

The old threats to health have been replaced by modern health problems, less lethal perhaps but contributing to the disproportionately high rates of disease and disability for Māori, Australian Aborigine peoples and Torres Strait Islanders. Whereas tuberculosis, diphtheria and malnutrition were major causes of ill health a century ago, the contemporary health problems for Māori and Northern Territories Aborigines now include sudden infant death syndrome, injury, diabetes, cancer, heart disease, chronic obstructive pulmonary disease, asthma, bronchiectais, and mental health disorders.[9] For Māori, *Te Rau Hinengaro* provides a comprehensive picture of the prevalence of mental disorders in New Zealand that will be useful for planning mental health services especially in the primary health care sector. A survey of 12,992 New Zealanders published in 2006 contained a sample of more than 2500 Māori participants and concluded that Māori were overrepresented in most categories including depression, minor anxiety disorders, and alcohol related disorders.[10]

Disparities in Māori health status

While Māori health status measured has improved over time, disparities in standards of health between Māori and non-Māori remain. Recent evidence suggests that over the past two decades the disparities are even growing. In the twenty years between 1980 and 1999 mortality rates for Māori men increased from 1.48 times higher than the non-Māori rate to 1.74 times higher, while for Māori women the disparity rose from 1.96 to 2.20. Similar trends can be observed for Pacific peoples living in New Zealand.

Ethnic disparities in life expectancy have also increased. While Māori male life expectancy increased from 64.6 years to 65.8 years in the twenty years between 1980 and 1999, non-Māori male life expectancy increased from 70.9 years to 75.7 years, a gain of 4.8 years compared to the Māori gain of only 1.2 years.[11] By 2000/2, however, Māori life expectancy had increased even further to sixty-nine years for males and 73.2 years for females and there were signs that the gap (vis-à-vis non-Māori) was decreasing, from 9.1percent (in 1995/7) to 8.5 percent (by 2002).[12]

Māori health responsiveness

In a climate where there is both cause for celebration of achievements in Māori health over the past century, coupled with concerns about disparities and the emergence of new epidemiological patterns, there has been major Māori engagement in addressing health problems. The Māori response, at least since 1990, has evolved around a series of principles, goals and distinctive pathways.

Principles

Although a number of principles underlying successful engagement have been identified, three stand out as especially important for health outcomes: indigeneity, dual competence, and human dignity.

The principle of indigeneity takes into account the determination of indigenous peoples to retain their own distinctive cultural identity, avoid assimilation and exercise a degree of autonomy. This principle goes beyond cultural recognition to claim a special place for indigenous peoples in the life of the nation. The principle of indigeneity does not mean other cultures should not also be duly recognised in health care, but it does acknowledge a unique position for indigenous peoples.

Dual competence, the second principle, refers to competence in both clinical and cultural dimensions. Māori as much as other New Zealanders expect the best possible treatment using tried and true methods. They also hope they will not be subjected to unnecessary interventions and will have access to new technologies and developments benchmarked against the best in the world. But there are also parallel expectations that health care workers will be competent at the interface between their own culture and the culture of others. Language barriers, differing codes for social interaction, variable community expectations and a willingness to involve friends or families in assessment, treatment and rehabilitation make important differences to the way care is experienced.

A third principle, human dignity, is concerned with the process of care. Health interventions that do not afford due respect for human values, cultural world views and differing health perspectives, will undermine dignity and diminish self-respect. Technology and cost containment do not replace human values as the marker of quality. In an outcome-driven environment, health care must also be concerned with processes, the ways in which technology is applied, and the regard which doctors have for their patients.

Goals

As steps towards the overall aim of improved Māori health outcomes, four major goals have been identified: the promotion of healthy lifestyles; equitable health outcomes; reduced socio-economic disparities between Māori and non-Māori; and self-determination and self-management.

The first goal, the promotion of healthy lifestyles, recognises the importance of families as vehicles for healthy lifestyles and the significance of a strong cultural identity for health. Indigenous writers have emphasised the link between cultural certainty and good health and many indigenous health programmes have been developed around strong cultural practices. Community leadership coupled with expert advice regarding sensible nutrition, sport and exercise and the avoidance of known health risks such as tobacco, alcohol and drugs, have also been influential in effecting changes, even in communities where unhealthy lifestyles were endemic. Although much remains to be done, there are encouraging signs that major modifications to day-to-day lifestyles and health-related practices are attainable by individuals as well as families and communities. Smoking uptake rates for Māori men, for example, have decreased significantly compared to Māori women.[13]

The goal of achieving equitable health outcomes recognises the disparities between Māori and non-Māori in respect of most disease categories and in levels of disability. Comorbidities occur with higher frequency in the Māori population and can diminish the prospect of equal outcomes because of a cumulative effect. Exclusion criteria can also count against Māori in so far as eligibility for selected interventions such as coronary bypass operations can eliminate a disproportionate number of potential candidates either because they are smokers or are obese. Equitable outcomes for health also require equitable access to services and funding arrangements which are based around results rather than processes, volumes or staff establishments. However, in current practice, outcome measurements are relatively unsophisticated, especially as they apply to indigenous peoples. While some outcome indicators are universal, and can be applied to all populations, measures of outcomes for Māori, especially in areas such as mental health, need to include Māori perspectives, world views and values. Opportunities for health promotion and enhanced wellbeing will have been lost if health interventions are measured only by symptom reduction.

A third goal is to reduce broader socio-economic inequalities for Māori. Substandard housing, poor educational attainment, low incomes, unemployment, and reduced access to key societal institutions all contribute to poor health.[14] There is now considerable evidence that while access to health services is one important determinant of health status, structural causes account for most of the increasing disparities.[15]

Self-determination and self-management represent a fourth goal that contrasts sharply with policies associated with colonisation – a known health risk.[16] But Māori communities also recognise that self-management requires access to information and technology, a level of expertise, and rather than absolute independence, opportunities to establish collaborative relationships with other Māori and with other health providers.

Meanwhile, not all states are sympathetic to the principle of self-determination. After twenty years the Draft Declaration on the Rights of Indigenous Peoples was widely supported by indigenous peoples from around the world, had been adopted by the UN Human Rights Council in June 2006 and recommended for adoption by the General Assembly. But a 'no action' motion was advanced in the Third Committee of the UN General Assembly at the November 2006 session. African states, as well as Samoa, Micronesia, Kiribati, New Zealand, Australia, Canada and the United States of America were opposed to some aspects of the Draft and led the move to stall it. Other states including Tonga and Vanuatu abstained. In the event a global opportunity to facilitate indigenous resilience was put on hold for further consideration before the end of the sixty-first session of the UN General Assembly (September 2007).[17] In that respect there is a constitutional dimension to the goal. Māori generally do not aspire to form a 'state within a state' but do want to be able to manage their own affairs and to provide for their own people.

Pathways

Six pathways have provided springboards for action to achieve Māori health goals: first, Māori cultural paradigms have provided a philosophical basis; second, health policies have increasingly identified gains in Māori health as a priority area; third, Māori leadership and Māori services have been important elements to achieving good outcomes; fourth, health services have been developed that are responsive to Māori; fifth, there has been coherent development with inter-sectoral collaboration based around positive Māori development; and sixth, a parallel Māori health research stream has emerged.

Māori health paradigms

When the Māori Women's Welfare League was embarking on a survey of the health of Māori women in 1982 a model of health known as Te Whare Tapa Wha anchored the study.[18] The model's appeal was based on its holistic approach to health and the recognition of spirituality as a significant contributor to good health. Until then discussions about Māori health had dwelt on the rates and consequences of disease, creating a sense of disempowerment and passivity. But by reconfiguring health in terms that made sense to Māori, it was possible for Māori communities to experience a sense of ownership and to balance medical and professional dominance with community involvement and local leadership. Te Whare Tapa Wha was presented as a four-sided house, each wall representing one aspect of health – spirituality (taha wairua), the mind (taha hinengaro), physical health (taha tinana) and family and social relationships (taha whānau). Similar perspectives have been described for Australian Aborigines and Torres Strait Islanders.[19]

Health policies

When the New Zealand Board of Health promoted the Treaty of Waitangi in 1987 as a document that had relevance to health,[20] and then endorsed tribal authorities as agents for health,[21] a new era of health policy was launched. It recognised two approaches to Māori health: Māori delivery systems and state responsiveness to Māori based on the principles of the Treaty of Waitangi.

Since then successive waves of health reforms have endorsed the significance of the Treaty and have recommended specific strategies for Māori health.

Current health legislation, the New Zealand Public Health and Disability Act 2000, recognises the Treaty of Waitangi, the first piece of social policy legislation to do so. But when the legislation was first proposed, there was some concern about risks to the Crown and the litigation that might follow if Māori were to claim that the health sector had not delivered the best outcomes. By having a Treaty provision within legislation, it was also argued that Māori might be able to make a demand on health services for preferential treatment.

Although it was unlikely that a Treaty clause could have overridden other aspects of the Act or even overturned clinical common sense, the perceived clash between the principle of universality and the principle of indigeneity was sufficient to lead to a redraft. In the event, the statute now makes it clear that district health boards must address Māori health and must recognise the Treaty of Waitangi in decision making and priority setting. To emphasise the point, the Minister of Health has appointed two Māori members to each of the twenty-one district health boards. The Act also requires that health disparities be decreased by 'improving the health outcomes of Māori and other population groups'.

While there has not been full agreement with policies that identify Māori health as a focus, distinct from the health of other New Zealanders, there has been acceptance that quality health care for Māori requires a range of factors to be taken into account, including cultural competence and Māori health views.

Currently health system objectives for Māori are not only contained in legislation but appear in the New Zealand National Health Strategy, the Primary Health Care Strategy and the Māori Health Strategy. For the most part, national policies for Māori health have obligatory consequences for district health boards which are required to report against progress made towards improved health outcomes for Māori and to indicate how their funding allocations have addressed Māori health issues. To a greater or lesser extent, district health boards have responded positively though have not always found it possible to provide the levels of resource sought by Māori nor to reconfigure health service compliance requirements so that they align with Māori health perspectives.

Māori health leadership

Māori leadership in the health sector owes much to Drs Pomare and Buck (Te Rangi Hiroa). But although there was a steady stream of health professionals who were Māori, the non-Māori professional and institutional domination did little to encourage leadership within Māori communities or to link health gains with wider aspirations for Māori advancement.

It was not until the mid 1980s that new forms of active Māori leadership re-emerged, largely as a series of Māori health initiatives. At first the initiatives revolved around community liaison and health promotion and arose largely because of perceived gaps in arrangements for formal health care. Māori dissatisfaction often stemmed from concerns about cultural inappropriateness in health interventions as well as barriers to access. In contrast to the prevailing health services, Māori initiatives revolved around community workers who were well versed in Māori values, familiar with local Māori networks and sufficiently aware of health systems to advocate on behalf of consumers.

The 1993 health reforms, with emphases on deregulation, devolution and contestability, provided a further opportunity for Māori health groups to tender for the delivery of services, mostly in primary health care, disability support and mental health. Quite quickly provider organisations multiplied from as few as five or six programmes in 1984 to some hundreds of registered Māori provider organisations, tribal and community, by 2006. Their approach was typically based on Māori perspectives but also came to employ conventional methods and professional staff. In fact a criticism emerging by the late 1990s was that some Māori health services had become indistinguishable from conventional services. To some extent that criticism arose out of a contracting regime that required all providers to meet similar objectives, in effect squeezing Māori providers to trade cultural innovation for compliance with measures standardised against a wider 'norm'. The engagement of traditional healers in primary health contracts, for example, was hindered because some healers regarded the suggested performance measures as too intrusive.

But by 2002, when primary health care organisations (PHOs) were first established, the rapid growth of Māori health care providers meant there was a vigorous Māori health care infrastructure able to bring a dimension to health care that was not available in earlier conservative practices. In many ways, however, workforce capacity still lagged behind Māori initiatives for more provider services.

Workforce development is another common theme in indigenous health development. Māori make up around 14 percent of the total population but only 5 percent of the national health workforce.[22] Two broad strategies have been used to address that situation. First, efforts to recruit more Māori into the health professions have included affirmative action programmes. Initiated at the University of Otago in 1900 when two positions were created for Māori students at medical school, the policy has since been extended to the Auckland medical school and other tertiary educational institutions. There are now over 200 Māori medical practitioners across a range of specialties. In addition, scholarships have been offered as incentives to encourage enrolment in other disciplines such as nursing, social work, clinical psychology and pharmacy.

The second workforce strategy has been to engage cultural workers or Māori community health workers to work alongside health professionals, bringing first-hand knowledge of community and a capacity to engage diffident patients. Often the combination has been highly effective though there has also been concern that the two streams of workers – cultural and clinical – have simply created potential for professional and cultural interventions to diverge. An integration of cultural and clinical dimensions is one of the more pressing challenges facing Māori health care.

Health service responsiveness

Although the rise in Māori health care organisations was rapid, most Māori people were, and still are, reliant on conventional primary and secondary care services. The Māori health message, however, has penetrated the prevailing health system and by 1995 most North Island hospitals had introduced a range of cultural initiatives to ensure that their processes, if not outcomes, were more able to address Māori concerns. Sometimes it was by using Māori words on public signage; sometimes by employing Māori staff; sometimes by requiring staff to attend cultural safety courses. In addition, the practice of cultural safety, introduced by the late Dr Irihapeti Ramsden, was being taken seriously by nurses and led to increased awareness of cultural difference as a factor in health care.

At a corporate level, the requirement to comply with Treaty of Waitangi obligations resulted in greater Māori representation on boards and committees, and formal links with tribal groups and Māori community organisations. Attitudes to care were also changed by the involvement of whānau (family) who pushed for more flexible visiting arrangements in hospitals and improved facilities to accommodate relatives who wished to stay close to their sick family member. But the impact of responsiveness on actual health outcomes has yet to be measured. Partly this is because it is not clear what ought to be measured. Suggestions that effectiveness could be gauged by reduced hospital admission rates for example, did not fully recognise the level of undiagnosed pathology existing in Māori communities so that increased admissions might actually reflect better utilisation of health facilities.

Coherent development

Economic restructuring in 1984 was accompanied by new approaches to Māori policy. Positive Māori development, as the policy was known, prescribed a shift away from state dependency and a welfare mentality to a greater emphasis on self-determination, economic self-sufficiency, social equity, and cultural reaffirmation. The move was in part a response to free market policies, but was also consistent with the worldwide indigenous rejection of assimilation and submission. For Māori it was to lead to a revitalisation of Māori language, greater confidence in tribal systems of governance and management, increasing entry in the commercial world, and the establishment of distinctive Māori provider organisations for the delivery of education, social services, housing, legal services and health care. Importantly, health initiatives were seen as integral to broader social goals as well as tribal economic development. In other words, an inter-sectoral approach was favoured by tribes. The state sectoral system, however, had difficulties accommodating that approach even though it was known that the determinants of health were multiple and linked to a range of social and economic conditions.

Māori health research

Efforts to recognise Māori world views in research were greatly boosted in 1993 when the Health Research Council of New Zealand funded two Māori health research units and established a Māori Health Committee to support Māori-led research projects. In addition a series of scholarships and training fellowships have enabled more than twenty Māori researchers to seek advanced research qualifications. Māori health research objectives are two-fold: to increase the Māori research capacity; and to encourage the development of methodologies that reflect Māori world views and intellectual traditions.

Useful clinical applications have resulted. Hua Oranga for example is a measure of outcome designed for users of mental health services. Based on a Māori health perspective, it assesses outcome from a holistic viewpoint and includes ratings from clinician, client and a family member.[23]

Results

Whether the new approaches to health care for Māori can be translated into health gains is a question of considerable importance. The fact that continuing disparities remain between Māori and non-Māori standards of health does not in itself negate the impact of current approaches. Health services cannot be expected to 'cure' the conditions that generate poor health such as economic disparities, alienation from society and racism.

Anecdotal evidence suggests that there have been demonstrable gains in some areas such as immunisation, smoking cessation, and improved Māori self-management of diabetes, asthma and hypertension. Of equal importance, however, is the degree to which Māori health awareness has been raised. Active participation within the health sector by providers, consumers or advisors has been accompanied by a level of enthusiasm that augers well for positive change. Nonetheless the full impacts of the new approaches to Māori health care need to be formally assessed.

There are of course many other issues that need further discussion and investigation. Importantly the relationship between cultural interventions and clinical interventions is often ill defined and two parallel streams can easily be formed without adequate linkages or synergies. Contracts for health services may exacerbate that particular problem by separating cultural and clinical components, especially in disability support services.

In some areas, Māori providers are encouraged to take up cultural support contracts independently of associated clinical contracts.

A framework for considering Māori health responsiveness

The principles, goals and pathways that have evolved over the past two decades constitute the elements of a framework for considering how to achieve best health outcomes for Māori. The framework can be represented as a matrix, the horizontal axis containing the four goals and the vertical axis containing three principles and six pathways.

This framework, the indigenous health outcomes framework, (Table 21.1) has been constructed on the basis of Māori experience over the past two decades. It needs to be seen alongside the other models and frameworks developed by indigenous workers in Australia and other states in the Pacific so that a comprehensive and clear picture of quality health care can emerge. Meanwhile, in the New Zealand context the several elements in the framework have positioned Māori to move forward with greater confidence and a clearer sense of direction than was evident in 1984 when the first Māori health conference was held (the Hui Whakaoranga).[24] The framework has also allowed Māori

TABLE 21.1 Indigenous health responsiveness framework

Goals ⟶	Healthy lifestyles	Equitable health outcomes	Reduction of socio-economic disparities	Self-determination & self-management
Principles: • indigeneity • dual competencies • human dignity.				
Pathways: • Māori paradigms • health policies • Māori leadership • health services • coherent development • research.				

aspirations for improved health outcomes to be addressed within the context of national health policies and strategies, policies for Māori development, and district health board priorities.

Working at the interface

From the framework it is clear that advances in indigenous health status will not come from any single strategy or from the health sector alone. Instead health gains will be linked to wider aspirations and a combination of forces that seek to combine social, cultural, economic and political dimensions. The goal of achieving good health is as much about improved standards of living as it is about healthy lifestyles, and it looks forward to outcomes that are relevant to being Māori and consistent with a degree of independence and self-direction. Of the several pathways that lead to good health, some depend on the policies and practices within public health services and in that sense are subject to government funding priorities. But others are within the reach of Māori individuals and collectives, and will depend on Māori leadership, Māori innovation, and holistic Māori services offered within a cultural context that resonates with Māori world views and contemporary Māori realities. Urban, mobile, technological, and rapidly changing environments add risks that will rival the environments from which tuberculosis here emerged a century ago. But unlike last century when Māori engagement with the health sector was largely confined to patient roles, the past two decades have seen the emergence of a Māori health workforce that is increasingly large and sufficiently well trained to provide effective leadership so that being healthy and being Māori can be synonymous.

Nor is the challenge only one for indigenous health leaders. In a highly mobile world where environments hazardous to health expand in an exponential manner and where interaction between different cultures, religions, ethnicities and systems of knowledge will interact as never before, a major challenge for all doctors will be to work with others recognising their expertise and contributions while at the same time offering medical knowledge and skills that can enrich communities. Moreover, though based on science and empirical evidence, medical effectiveness may also depend on being able to inject a large measure of humanitarianism and to acquire the capacity to read the environment, including the diverse cultural environments that underpin attitudes to health and health care. The study of human pathology and responses to pathogens needs to be balanced by an appreciation of the environments within which families live and grow, the insights that emerge from human experience over time, and the cultural understandings that give meaning to health and sickness.

Living and working at the interface between medical science and other bodies of knowledge, especially indigenous knowledge, will increasingly present new challenges – as well as opportunities – for doctors in Australia and New Zealand.[25]

CHAPTER 22

Indigenous Participation in Mental Health: Māori Experience

The Mark Sheldon Address. Presented at the Forty-third Royal Australian & New Zealand College of Psychiatrists' Annual Congress, 'Community and Politics', Melbourne, 29 May, 2008.

Technological advances are transforming the mental health sector. From their origins as an essentially caring activity, psychiatry and mental health care are being enriched by innovations in diagnostics, treatment, analysis, and management. At the same time, technology by itself is unlikely to lead to uniformly high standards of health or necessarily the best quality of care. There is a human factor that cannot be simply reduced to technological opportunities or the mass application of scientific breakthroughs. While technology and science have a critical place in modern health care and offer fresh hope for the future, human feelings and long-standing beliefs are equally important to the healing process and need to be factored into the health care equation.

In that respect, indigenous health care is largely about the balance between scientific advancement and human spirituality. Those sentiments were encapsulated by the late Dr Mark Sheldon who worked closely with Aboriginal communities in remote parts of Australia. His dissertation for Fellowship in the Royal Australian and New Zealand College of Psychiatrists, 'Psychiatric Assessment in Remote Aboriginal Communities in Central Australia' recognised the advantages of blending traditional methods and modern medicine and advocated interventions that embraced psychological and social dimensions.[1] Sadly, his professional career was cut short by an early death, but his contribution to indigenous health and his example remain a significant legacy for mental health workers in Australia and New Zealand.

As part of a movement to reclaim culture and identity, indigenous peoples have fought to reshape health care and health services so that they align more sensibly with indigenous world views and modern indigenous realities. They have argued for the adoption of cultural protocols into health care, and have identified socio-economic disadvantage as a significant barrier to effective care. In some communities traditional healing has also been given new emphasis though more often the call has been for the development of an indigenous health workforce that draws on indigenous values as well as the modern health sciences.

The Māori experience

Māori experience has not been substantially different from other indigenous peoples. First, although the scale is different, Māori demographic patterns show similar trends to many indigenous populations that have experienced colonisation. From an estimated population of 200,000 in 1800, by 1894 the Māori population had dwindled to 42,000 and was close to extinction. But not only did it survive, within a century it had become more numerous than at any other time in history. Even though changes to statistical definitions of Māori make it difficult to draw exact comparisons, there is strong evidence of a substantial and sustained increase in the Māori population. In the 2006 Census 565,329 New Zealanders identified as Māori, with a median age of 22.7 years; and of whom 85 percent were classed as urban dwellers.[2]

There are further similarities between Māori and other indigenous populations. Interventions with indigenous populations have typically employed a range of methods and approaches. The missionary approach, for example, was premised on an assumption of moral superiority: native people were uncivilised and were considered in need of Christian values and beliefs. Religious conversion followed, associated with major social changes and often the abandonment of indigenous culture, including language. But with the missionaries came education, compassion, new technologies and access to whatever medical advances were available at the time. Though often couched in patronising terms, the missionary influence had a profound and enduring impact on Māori. As a method for reshaping attitudes and lifestyles, moral persuasion could be considered effective. Nor was that approach to be the sole province of missionaries; some modern health promotion campaigns, such as nutritional advice, parenting, and tobacco cessation are executed with missionary zeal, drawing as much on a sense of moral right as scientific evidence.

In contrast to the missionary approach, the medical model is based on science and scientific evidence. While the model has contributed to major gains in health, an overly-zealous focus on the diagnosis and treatment of illness can lead to the depiction of indigenous peoples as a collection of syndromes and pathological processes. Moreover, the search for pathology, and psychopathology, runs the risk of attaching diagnostic labels to situations that might be better explained as cultural norms. Quite apart from mistaking parasensory experiences for pathological hallucinations, metaphorical allusions, for example, a characteristic of Māori communication, are sometimes regarded as evidence of tangential thinking or overt thought disorder.

A third type of intervention with Māori mental health hinges on conformity to a statistical norm. Mainstream benchmarking employs comparative methodologies to highlight disparities between indigenous populations and the majority. Differences in standards of health preoccupy investigations, rightly drawing attention to inequities and inequalities, but at the same time promoting a deficit perspective that sees Māori as a population in need of a 'catch up' with the majority. Although 'catch up' is a not an unreasonable goal, it may sometimes be confused with the pursuit of sameness or the intolerance of difference.

Unlike other models that attempt to explain indigenous 'difference' the MĀORI model is Māori-centric. Literally translated, Māori means 'normal' and was used by tribes to distinguish native New Zealanders from early settlers. However, MĀORI is also an acronym for a Māori Agenda for Optimal outcomes, Relevant processes, and Indigenous affirmation. Significantly, in this approach Māori interventions depend on a Māori framework – Māori culture, aspirations, and advancement. Rather than casting Māori as 'morally wanting', or disease-prone, or lagging behind the national average, the MĀORI model affords greater attention to positive results, the realisation of human potential, and a readiness to draw on customary concepts in order to explore new horizons.

Advances in Māori mental health services have not occurred in isolation. Beyond the health arena there have been wide-reaching changes across a range of sectors. In 1984 a Māori economic summit meeting, the Hui Taumata, prescribed a 'Decade of Positive Māori Development' premised on the themes of tribal development, economic self-reliance, social equity and cultural affirmation. The new call was for 'Māori solutions to Māori problems'. Gains on several fronts occurred. Māori participation in business, which had been critically low, escalated; state agencies developed closer working relationships with tribes and with Māori communities; independent Māori providers emerged in the education, health, and social service sectors; major claims against the Crown for historic breaches of the principles of the Treaty of Waitangi were settled; and the revitalisation of Māori language was to lead to Māori-speaking early childhood centres, two Māori television channels, and a new generation for whom Māori is a first language. In effect a major transformation of New Zealand society has occurred, characterised by greatly increased Māori participation in society and a widespread cultural renaissance that has touched not only Māori but all New Zealanders.

Transforming the mental health sector

During the same period (1983–2008), the transformations evident in society generally were also occurring in the mental health sector. Deinstitutionalisation during the 1970s had led to the development of community-based services underpinned by a philosophy of social integration so that the isolating features of institutional care might be avoided. In the new environment, increased Māori rates of admission to psychiatric facilities were coupled with a renewed determination by Māori to inject indigenous world views into societal institutions. Attention focused on four major goals: the promotion of healthy lifestyles, equitable health outcomes, reduced socio-economic disparities, and self-determination and self-management.

Goals for Māori mental health care

The first goal, the promotion of healthy lifestyles, recognises the importance of families as vehicles for healthy lifestyles and the significance of a strong cultural identity for mental health. Indigenous writers have emphasised the link between cultural certainty and good health, and many indigenous mental health programmes have been developed around strong cultural practices.

The goal of achieving equitable health outcomes recognises the disparities between Māori and non-Māori in respect of most disease categories and in levels of disability. Comorbidities occur with higher frequency in the Māori population and can diminish the prospect of equal outcomes because of a cumulative effect. Equitable outcomes require equitable access to services, interventions that take social and cultural factors into account, and choice for consumers.

A third goal is to reduce inequalities between Māori and other New Zealanders. Substandard housing, poor educational attainment, low incomes, unemployment, and reduced access to key societal institutions all contribute to poor mental health. There is now considerable evidence that while access to health services is one important determinant of health status, structural causes account for much of the increasing disparities.[3] In 1984 New Zealand's major social and economic reforms impacted adversely on Māori and Pacific peoples with widening gaps in employment status, housing, education and income. Widening health inequalities were predictable outcomes.

Self-determination and self-management represent a fourth goal. Māori communities recognise that self-management requires access to information and technology, a level of expertise, and, rather than absolute independence, opportunities to establish collaborative relationships with other Māori and with other health providers. The goal of self-determination is viewed cautiously by some states which fear that cession will be an ultimate outcome. In that respect there is a constitutional dimension to the goal. Māori generally do not aspire to form a 'state within a state' but do want to be able to manage their own affairs and to provide for their own people. In their view a level of autonomy is guaranteed in the Treaty of Waitangi.

Platforms

Six platforms have provided springboards for action to implement those health goals: first, Māori cultural perspectives have provided a philosophical basis; second, improved opportunities for the dissemination of information and the generation of new knowledge have led to greater levels of awareness among Māori families and communities; third, government health policies have explicitly identified Māori health as a priority area; fourth, innovations in the delivery of health services have increased accessibility as well as effectiveness; fifth, independent Māori mental health providers have created choice for service-users; and sixth, active Māori mental health workforce development has led to a greatly expanded workforce in the mental health system.

Māori health perspectives

When they were introduced in 1982, conceptual foundations for Māori mental health, based on indigenous world views, were viewed with scepticism. The prevailing view, that health was a universal concept, transcending culture, gave little recognition to the fact that the 'norm' was actually based on Eurocentric philosophies, culture, and methods. Māori health perspectives challenged the monocultural assumptions and introduced other ways of considering health. Te Whare Tapa Wha, for example, was a construct that compared good health to the four sides of a house with balance between spirituality (taha wairua), intellect and emotions (taha hinengaro), the human body (taha tinana) and human relationships (taha whānau).[4] It was a holistic prescription that resonated with Māori communities not only because it was consistent with indigenous world views but also because it created an opportunity for active engagement with health services at a time when health care was regarded as the province of health professionals. Moreover, the Māori perspective was consistent with an emerging view of health care that questioned the increasing reliance of western approaches to mental health on medication and a parallel rejection of spirituality and ecological relationships.

Mental health information

More comprehensive information about Māori mental health has depended on greater consistency in recording and publicising ethnic data, better understandings of the characteristics of Māori service users,[5] and evidence of the extent of mental health problems within Māori communities. Research into several aspects of Māori mental health were greatly boosted in 1993 when the Health Research Council of New Zealand funded two Māori health research units and established a Māori health committee to support Māori-led research projects. Four other academic Māori health research centres had been established by 2004. Meanwhile *Te Rau Hinengaro*, a survey of 12,992 New Zealanders containing a sample of more than 2500 Māori participants, revealed that Māori were overrepresented in most categories including depression, minor anxiety disorders, and alcohol related disorders. Even after adjusting for socio-economic correlates, Māori had higher rates of prevalence over a twelve month period than others and were more likely to have bipolar disorders.[6]

Health policies

Since 1984 successive waves of health reforms have identified Māori health as a priority area. Current health legislation, the New Zealand Public Health and Disability Act 2000, makes it clear that district health boards must address Māori health and must recognise the Treaty of Waitangi in decision making and priority setting. The Act also requires that health disparities be decreased by 'improving the health outcomes of Māori and other population groups'. There has been considerable debate about the extent to which Māori health should be prioritised and whether policy should simply focus on socio-economic disadvantage rather than ethnicity. However, there is also accumulated evidence that socio-economic disadvantage by itself does not fully account for disparities between ethnic groups.[7] A series of health strategies developed by the Ministry of Health, including the National Health Strategy, Primary Care Strategy, Disability Strategy, Mental Health and Addiction Strategy, and the Māori Health Strategy, place high priority on improving health outcomes for Māori.

Health service re-alignment and innovations

By 1984 a small number of Māori health initiatives had been established within conventional health services. Essentially they pioneered a system of health care that incorporated Māori knowledge, Māori models of practice, and Māori staff. Whaiora, for example, was the prototype for a mental health service where Māori values permeated the milieu. As a mental health facility within a large psychiatric hospital, it was developed around Māori values and philosophies, staffed by Māori nurses and a Māori psychiatrist, but also incorporated conventional methods of treatment.[8] The distinctiveness arose from the observance of customary ceremonies to receive new patients and their families, the incorporation of spiritual encounters into patient management, the inclusion of families in aspects of treatment, and the employment of tribal elders to oversee the cultural milieu. While western treatment methods, including standard pharmacological regimes were used, much emphasis was placed on relationship-building and strengthening cultural identity.

Currently government-funded district health boards have taken two broad approaches to addressing Māori mental health needs. Contracts have been awarded to Māori providers for community-based services – by Māori for Māori – and conventional services have developed protocols that reflect Māori values and Māori communication processes as well as linking more directly to Māori networks.[9] Elders, kaumātua, are sometimes employed to oversee cultural interventions and there have been deliberate efforts to employ qualified Māori staff as well as Māori support staff.

Māori providers

From as early as 1899 Māori leadership in the health sector has owed much to a steady stream of Māori health professionals who have maintained a small but significant presence within the professions and health institutions. It was not until the mid 1980s, however, that new forms of active Māori leadership re-emerged, largely as a series of Māori health initiatives. At first the initiatives revolved around community liaison and health promotion and arose largely because of perceived gaps in arrangements for formal health care. Community health workers were well versed in Māori values, familiar with local Māori networks and sufficiently aware of health systems to advocate on behalf of consumers. The 1993 health reforms, with emphases on deregulation, devolution and contestability, provided further opportunity for Māori health groups to tender for the delivery of services, mostly in primary health care, disability support and mental health. Quite quickly provider organisations multiplied from as few as five or six programmes in 1984 to some hundreds of registered

Māori provider organisations by 2008, including 144 Māori providers of mental health and addiction treatment services. Their approach is typically based on Māori perspectives but contracting regimes often squeeze them to use measures standardised against a wider 'norm' and to trade cultural innovation for compliance.

Culturally inspired interventions have become integral components of New Zealand's mental health services.[10] Aspects of traditional healing, including the use of rongoa (remedies derived from plants), have been incorporated into some mental health programmes, usually alongside other approaches. Although varied, ranging from distinctive counselling programmes to activities such as mau rākau (a type of weaponry drill), cultural interventions are underpinned by the common objective of strengthening identity and in the process enhancing wellbeing. Strengthened identity does not necessarily protect against mental disorders but appears to facilitate the healing process.[11] Unlike treatments that are based on biological dysfunction or inner psychological conflict, Māori cultural interventions tend towards an ecological approach where understanding and assurance come from building links beyond the individual. In mau rakau, for example, the immediate objective is to develop sufficient discipline and skill to manipulate a wooden weapon (taiaha), but the wider goal is to work in concert with a team of others. Similarly, Māori counselling methods place emphasis on the acquisition of cultural knowledge and skills and also on relationships with whanau and cultural institutions.

Māori mental health workforce development

The Māori mental health workforce has expanded rapidly over the past twenty-five years. There has been a significant increase in the number of Māori professionals including mental health nurses, clinical psychologists (4 percent) social workers, and, to a lesser extent, medical practitioners (3 percent). But the greatest increase has come from the engagement of cultural advisors or Māori community health workers to work alongside health professionals, bringing first-hand knowledge of community and a capacity to engage diffident patients. Some 22 percent of addiction treatment practitioners and more than 30 percent of support workers in 2004 were Māori.[12] *The National Māori Mental Health Workforce Development Strategic Plan* sets a ten year goal of 20 percent across all occupational categories, based on a workforce to population ratio aligned to the projected Māori population in 2011.[13] As already noted, the expanded Māori mental health workforce has been accompanied by the establishment of a number of Māori provider organisations. Most offer supportive services but some, such as Hauora Waikato, provide specialist inpatient services as well as forensic and acute services.

Two broad workforce strategies have been used to increase levels of participation. First, efforts to recruit more Māori into the health professions have included affirmative action programmes. Initiated at the University of Otago in 1900 when two positions were created for Māori students at medical school, the policy has since been extended to the Auckland medical school and other tertiary educational institutions. There are now over 200 Māori medical practitioners across a range of specialties. In addition there are increasing numbers of specialist Māori mental health nurses, clinical psychologists, social workers and psychiatrists.

The second workforce strategy has been to engage cultural workers or Māori community health workers to work alongside health professionals, bringing first-hand knowledge of community and a capacity to engage diffident patients. Often the combination has been highly effective though there has also been concern that the two streams of workers – cultural and clinical – have created potential for professional and cultural interventions to diverge.

Three national Māori mental health workforce development programmes, Te Rau Puawai (1999), Te Rau Matatini (2002) and the Henry Rongomau Bennett Memorial Scholarships (2002), have all demonstrated how both capacity and capability can be expanded. Te Rau Puawai, funded by the Ministry of Health since 1999, is a scholarship scheme for Māori enrolled at Massey University in a mental health-related degree or diploma in the social sciences (for example health sciences, social work, psychology, rehabilitation studies).[14] Most of the bursars are new to tertiary education and are already employed in mental health services, often in supportive roles. However, some bursars are also involved in postgraduate, including doctoral, studies. In the first five years 103 students graduated and a similar number is expected to have gained undergraduate and postgraduate degrees by 2009.

A further health workforce scheme, Te Rau Matatini, is also specific to Māori mental health workforce development. Funded by the

Ministry of Health since 2002, and governed by a multidisciplinary board of Māori who have an active interest in the sector, it provides a national focus for Māori mental health workforce development. The contributions of Te Rau Matatini are at strategic and service levels.[15] Apart from advising the Ministry of Health and district health boards, it also provides advice to Māori provider organisations and to tribal authorities that are developing a Māori health capability. Te Rau Matatini has a strong interest in training and has initiated specialised university-based programmes for consumer advocates and for elders who provide cultural and spiritual advice in mental health services.

The Henry Rongomau Bennett Memorial Scholarships Committee was established in 2002, initially to provide bursaries for psychiatric registrars. However, the initial focus on psychiatrists-in-training was not intended to exclude other professional groupings nor to narrow the aims of the scholarships to the provision of psychiatric services, and in 2003 a decision was made to make scholarships available to emerging leaders in other mental health disciplines such as clinical psychology, nursing, and addiction treatment. The programme is managed by a committee with sector-wide representation and makes an annual scholarship allocation of some $600,000.

While all schemes have an element of overlap, each is unique. Collectively, however, they focus on the development of high calibre Māori leadership within clinical, organisational, cultural, policy, research and public health arenas of mental health.

Catalysts for transformation

Although the transformations over the past twenty-five years have been influenced by a wide range of national and international factors, it is possible to identify three themes that have accelerated action and contributed to positive outcomes.

Leadership

First, transformational Māori leadership has emerged. As the twentieth century closed, a Māori leadership network formed around the common goals of increased autonomy, self-sufficiency, tribal redevelopment, and cultural affirmation. The goals were about transforming society so that systems and institutions would be accessible, relevant to Māori, and able to lead to the best possible outcomes.

Transformational leadership demands a type of leadership that is essentially outward looking; integrative more than exclusive; ready to cross institutional boundaries and institutions; and strategic rather than bound by a set of operational conventions. Transformational leaders promote sustainable leadership. Stand-alone charismatic leaders have less to offer changing environments than leaders who can weld together other leaders – from political, tribal, community and professional arenas – and encourage a deliberate strategy of succession planning. Sustainable leadership develops leadership capacity and leadership networks where innovation, rather than standardisation, can flourish.[16]

Interventions at the interface

A second theme is a capacity to straddle an interface. Connecting with indigenous people means being able to live in two worlds, simultaneously. Language, cultural values, cultural protocols and indigenous associations at community, tribal and even national levels will be important vehicles for communicating and assisting indigenous clients. But equally, interventions to promote good health need to take account of findings from science and technology, medical advancement and clinical expertise. Working between two bodies of knowledge – science and indigenous knowledge – recognises that neither indigenous knowledge nor science alone provides a universal answer. Health care is firmly premised on science and the medical model depends on evidence derived from scientific inquiry. In contrast, indigenous knowledge is not fixated on science; instead it largely depends on a set of values and observations that link people into the wider natural environment. The challenge is not to dismiss either knowledge base, nor to explain one according to the tenets of the other, but to embrace both in order to reach fresh insights that might enrich the lives of those who are touched by both systems.[17]

In contemporary health care the interface can take many forms: the interface between health and other sectors; between physical health and mental health; primary care and secondary care; wellness and disease; professional leadership and consumer perspectives; technology and human compassion; and clinical skills and cultural paradigms.

Investments in innovation

A third theme concerns investments in innovation. Typically investments in Māori health innovation have been derived from three main sources: government, health agencies, and Māori tribes and communities. In the economic restructuring that commenced in 1984, the Ministries of Health and Māori Development invested in tribal and community organisations, and after the 1993 health reforms there were substantial investments by health funding agencies in the Māori health provider organisations. Research funders have meanwhile provided major investments in innovation, and the Health Research Council's innovative efforts to build Māori health research capacity, as well as research at the interface between science and indigenous knowledge, have been critical to strengthening Māori health capability.

Investments in health innovation present a degree of risk to investors since the outcomes are not always clear or certain. During the period 1983–2008 a number of Māori health programmes did not survive or were criticised for not realising greater returns. While risk can be minimised by the provision of clear guidelines and specified indicators, an element of risk is part of the innovation reality. But leaving no room for innovation can also present risks, especially where there is clear evidence that current practice does not meet actual need.

Although Māori health is a government priority, it is not always clear how the priority is rationalised. Sometimes it appears to be because of lower standards of health, at other times because of a Treaty of Waitangi obligation, and sometimes because of cultural difference. Insofar as there are a number of ethnic groups who have equally low standards of health, and many more for whom cultural perspectives are important to health outcomes, the argument for Māori priority is not robust. But if the case hinges on the Treaty of Waitangi, and Māori as the indigenous population of New Zealand, then the argument shifts from a focus on inequity and culture to a focus on indigeneity. There has been considerable inconsistency in the way successive governments have (or have not) valued indigeneity, but to be effective longer term planning requires a higher level of certainty.

The impacts

Four major impacts can reasonably be expected from the 1983–2008 transformations. First, health outcomes for Māori might be reasonably expected to have improved. Definitive large scale studies have yet to be completed, partly because Māori perspectives have been rapidly absorbed into practice, making it difficult to compare services where there is Māori content with services where there is none. But in addition there has been some concern about the best type of outcome measure. While conventional measures such as HONAS, SF 12 and SF 36 have been applied, a Māori-centred outcome measure, Hua Oranga, has also been trialled in a number of services. It is based on an assumption that a good outcome is one where an intervention can demonstrate gains in spiritual health (for example strengthened cultural identity), mental health (for example a positive mood), physical health (for example increased levels of fitness), and social health (for example positive family relationships).[18]

Second, while outcomes are important, the experience of treatment and care is also important. Not only should outcome indicators be relevant to indigenous and ethnic populations, but clinical process indicators that measure the quality of care should also be culturally responsive.[19] The impact of Māori approaches to mental health care and treatment has been shown to lead to improved engagement, endorsement of cultural identity and enhanced human dignity so that the therapeutic process is affirming rather than demeaning, with greater prospects of enlightenment rather than confusion. The process becomes normalised according to Māori conventions for social relationships and empowerment.

Third, arising from both experience and research, there is an expanded body of knowledge about approaches to Māori mental health, service delivery, health determinants, and epidemiological patterns. Publications from Māori researchers over the past two decades have added to the body of knowledge and justified the introduction of Māori-specific methods. Finally, as already noted, the Māori workforce capability has been significantly increased. A relatively large cohort of well qualified workers are now regularly employed in the sector and in related sectors. Their expertise represents an important contribution to the overall Māori workforce.

Indigenising the sector

The combined influences of systemic change in the mental health sector, clinical advancement, effective leadership and cultural relevance, provide some background for understanding the significant contributions Māori have made to sector transformations over more than two decades. In addition, the impact of a wider global indigenous movement towards cultural revitalisation, increased autonomy, and positive social and economic development has provided a platform for Māori interaction with all sectors including the mental health.

The Decade of Positive Māori Development, launched at the 1984 Hui Taumata, set Māori on a course that celebrated culture, aspired to tino rangatiratanga (autonomy), sought equity and aimed for 'by Māori for Māori' service provision. A second Hui Taumata in 2005 reiterated the positive message but placed additional emphasis on achieving potential, a theme which had also become built into government policy for Māori. The 'potential approach' encompasses wellbeing, knowledge, influence and resources and the desired outcome is one where 'Māori succeed as Māori'. The focus is away from deficit and failure towards success and achievement.[20]

The themes of positive Māori development and the realisation of potential, coupled with sector transformations, have been especially evident in mental health, to the extent that there is now a discernable and sustainable indigenisation of the sector.

SECTION 4

The 'Paerangi Lectures'

CHAPTER 23

Pae Matatū: Sustaining the Māori Estate

'Pae Matatū', the first of the three 'Paerangi Lectures', was delivered at
Massey University, Palmerston North, 24 June 2009.

The Paerangi Lectures

'Pae Matatū: Sustaining the Māori Estate' is the first of three 'Paerangi
Lectures' and is concerned with the assets that will become available
to future generations of Māori. Like the other two lectures it is
positioned in the future – 2020 and beyond – and considers the effects
of demographic change, tribal development, national priorities, global
transformations, and technological innovation on Māori. Because
these lectures are occurring at a time of rapid change, both nationally
and internationally, it is unlikely that the quality or the quantum of
the Māori estate can be predicted with any certainty. The consequences
of a global economic recession for example, have implications for
all indigenous peoples. Meanwhile the outcome of ongoing debates
about rights to the foreshore and seabed or the use of ancient Māori
place names instead of colonial versions, also highlights the ways in
which the Māori estate is shaped by forces beyond te ao Māori. Not
only will the size of the estate be subject to political, economic, and
technological determinants, but the make-up of the estate will also
change as well as the ways in which it is managed and transferred from
one generation to another. 'Sustaining the Māori Estate' raises questions
about impact of economic fluctuations, access to customary resources,
and the significance of new forms of heritage that have been fashioned
by Māori in modern times. But from another perspective, there will
also be questions about entitlement and the responsibilities placed on

those who inherit. Does inheritance create an obligation to add value to the estate before passing it on to others, or has the obligation been met simply by passing it on more or less intact?

In any event the Māori estate is not fixed or finite. It is bounded neither by time nor by quantum. Nor does it comprise elements that have been solely determined by pre-colonial concepts and conventions. Further, while the configuration of the estate is always in a state of fluctuation, identifying the rightful recipients of the estate cannot necessarily be guided by past practices and processes. Not all Māori will be equally entitled nor will the same principles of inheritance be applicable to all types of assets transferred from one generation to another. Principles underlying succession to land, for example, may not be appropriate for the transfer of fishing quota or the receipt of new and old cultural knowledge. Moreover, it is contentious whether the Māori estate includes all Māori assets, no matter how derived, or whether it applies only to those assets where a sense of collective interest exists.

In effect the Māori estate can no longer be linked solely to so-called traditional times. Indigeneity is always evolving and the idea that it can be defined entirely by the past ignores the reality of modern times and the prospect of living in a future world. By 2020 the indigenous estate will comprise both customary assets and assets that have been generated in the twentieth and early twenty-first centuries.

A futures scenario: Ahuwhenua Ltd

Although predictions about the future lack scientific precision, a number of tools have been developed to at least sketch some possibilities. Scenario building, for example, creates a picture of the future based on a set of possible (if not probable) trends and events. Ahuwhenua Ltd is a scenario about Māori land holdings, land utilisation, and the governance of land.

> Ahuwhenua Ltd began to take shape after deteriorating global food shortages were brought to public attention during the economic recession between 2008 and 2011. While the west was concerned about interest rates, the value of the dollar, and the plummeting real estate market, the plight of many African states and the scale of malnutrition and consequential disease

could no longer be hidden from world view. Eventually, in 2015, the World Health Organisation made an impassioned plea for international action declaring that the Millennium I goals formulated in 2000 were no longer achievable. Those goals had included the eradication of extreme poverty and hunger, achieving universal primary education, promoting gender equality and empowering women, reducing child mortality, improving maternal health, combating HIV/AIDS, malaria and other diseases, ensuring environmental sustainability, and establishing partnerships for development.

These goals had been undermined by inaction from the wealthy OECD countries. A lack of global solidarity at a time when it was most needed, coupled with serial droughts and unpredictable wind patterns had plunged one-third of the world's population into abject poverty and starvation. In contrast to the Millennium I goals, which depended on goodwill and benevolent actions, the Millennium II goals matched charitable action with substantial rewards.

New Zealand, conscious of its relative wealth and sensing an opportunity for altruism coupled with guaranteed markets abroad, was one of the first countries to respond. By 2017 the New Zealand government had developed a programme of land consolidation that would earn the country the title of 'the food bowl of the world.' All lands suitable for food crops were identified and zoned 'arable'. In 2017 the Māori Land Court commissioned a study of Māori land utilisation with a view to determining the feasibility of widespread cropping. The subsequent passage of the Māori Land Aggregation Act, 2020 required owners of suitable land to lease their properties to Ahuwhenua Ltd, a company established under the Act which quickly became the largest arable land-holding company in New Zealand. Māori land owners were shareholders in the company and those who were on the register received substantial dividends. But in return they had been required to forfeit using the land for their own purposes. That condition was unacceptable to many owners but the thousands living overseas were less perturbed and despite the three hīkoi of protest, the majority had consented.

Notwithstanding the dissent, by 2030, Ahuwhenua Ltd was not only playing a significant role in addressing world food shortages, it was well positioned to become the most successful food producer in New Zealand. Its board of directors comprised representatives from the eight Māori land court regions and in every year since 2025 the board had won the prestigious UN Global Village award. Although by then it was not at all clear who the shareholders were, Ahuwhenua Ltd was enjoying its position as New Zealand's number one producer of organic food.

Trends and forecasts

Ahuwhenua Ltd is not beyond the bounds of probability but the main point for introducing the scenario is not to argue for or against it but to demonstrate the range of factors that could influence the Māori estate. Māori will not be immune to global impacts: world food shortages, global forms of governance, and climate change. Nor will the estate be divorced from national policies or government legislation. But the Ahuwhenua Ltd scenario also suggests that the Māori estate could be a major economic force in New Zealand if a fair system of governance and management were instituted. Economies of scale could realise higher levels of return than is possible with many small largely independent operations.

Demographic change

Apart from scenario development, the characteristics of the Māori estate can also be gauged from the forward projection of patterns that are already observable. Two particular trends underpin the sustainability of the Māori estate. First, demographic changes point towards an expanding Māori population that will significantly increase the number of people who are potentially entitled to succeed. Second, current trends suggest that the Māori estate is not only expanding in size but is also becoming more diverse.

In contrast to scenario development which is accompanied by an element of doubt, Māori demographic trends carry a greater level of certainty based on patterns of population transitions over several census counts. Most obviously, the Māori population will continue to increase at a relatively fast rate for another four to five decades. The combination of a youthful population, increasing life expectancy, and birth rates that exceed the national average will lead to a greater proportion of New Zealand's total population having Māori descent. By 2051 for example, in contrast to accounting for some 15 percent of the total New Zealand population in 2006, the Māori ethnic population will almost double in size to close to a million, or 22 percent of the total New Zealand population. Even more significant, by 2051, 33 percent of all children in the country will be Māori. By then Māori in the working age group, fifteen to sixty-four years, will have increased by 85 percent. Yet although the younger age groups will continue to grow, the population will also begin to age, the proportion of men and women over the age of sixty-five years increasing from 3 percent in 1996 to 13 percent in 2051.

Demographic change will be accompanied by greater numbers of people able to claim rights to succession. Moreover, by 2020 much of the Māori population will have never lived in tribal territories nor will they have had any direct involvement with tribal affairs. They will be increasingly mobile, worldwide travellers, overseas residents, inhabitants of cities and metropolitan centres in New Zealand, and may be quite unfamiliar with tikanga Māori. Yet predictably they will value being Māori and will expect to be able to access the Māori estate, if not in its totality, then certainly in part.

The tribal asset base

Along with an expanding population, the Māori asset base will also increase. Trends already show a more than 300 percent increase in the assets of some iwi since concluding settlements. Both Tainui and Ngai Tahu have each grown settlements valued at 170 million dollars to almost half a billion dollars. As more settlements are concluded and investments mature, estates can be expected to grow in size for some decades. Land holdings, some held in trust by whānau and others represented by large scale incorporations, have been supplemented by additional lands negotiated as part of Treaty settlements. But the new land holdings are not necessarily large and the increase in assets has come from a mix of cash, real estate, and access to enterprises such as tourism.

In the past, customary assets have comprised the bulk of the Māori estate and continue to be the most definable elements of the estate. Lands inherited from earlier generations, for example, constitute a customary asset core. Māori land is distinctive, not only because it is under the jurisdiction of the Māori Land Court and subject to the provisions of specific legislation, the Ture Whenua Maori Act 1993, but more importantly because it has always been in Māori possession. Accounting for some 4 percent of New Zealand's total land mass, successive generations of Māori have succeeded to land interests through entitlements based on bloodline descent. However, because of policies promoting the individualisation of interests, rather than collective ownership, multiple titles have resulted and larger land holdings have been subdivided to accommodate individual ambitions. Much of the Māori Land Court's work is about determining entitlement to succeed and the allocation of interests between family members. The Ture Whenua Maori Act recognises the origins of Māori land and an objective of the Act is to ensure that the land remains in Māori ownership indefinitely. Under the Act it is difficult to alienate land, and owners who wish to sell an interest must first offer it to other owners who have the same tribal affiliations.

Land, however, is only one customary asset. Assets such as waterways, fisheries and forests have assumed greater significance following several Waitangi Tribunal reports that have declared past alienations to be unjust. Probably the most significant addition to the customary asset base in recent times has been the allocation of nearly one-third of all fishing quota to Māori. After the government had declared an ownership interest in fishing stock, and then on-leased quota to commercial fishermen, Māori rights to fisheries under the Treaty of Waitangi were revisited and a fair allocation was eventually negotiated. Unlike land interests, interests from fisheries have not been individualised and are held in trust by iwi or by the Treaty of Waitangi Fisheries Commission. Additional customary holdings, including the foreshore and seabed, have also been claimed by Māori. But when the foreshore claim was raised in the Māori Land Court in 1997 and uncertainty arose around whether there had been a previous legal declaration of alienation, the government passed a law enabling

Crown assumption of ownership. Māori dissatisfaction was highly palpable and after the 2008 election of a National Government, a taskforce was convened to review the situation, largely on the insistence of the Māori Party who were by then a coalition partner in the new government. At meetings throughout the country there was an overwhelming call for the Act to be repealed so that Māori customary rights could be enforced, rather than subsumed by the Crown.

Further customary interests have also been affirmed. Tribal rights to fishing reserves, river bed rights and waahi tapu (sacred sites) have been recognised in legislation mainly on the basis of customary usage but with some acknowledgement of developmental rights associated with the resource. Māori participation in aquaculture, for example, recognises a Māori interest in fish and other seafood and extends that right to entry into a relatively new venture with promising commercial possibilities. The Aquaculture Reform Act 2004 allocated 20 percent of marine farming space to Māori, though it required the Crown to be able to find willing sellers so that the resource could be reassigned to Māori. But elements of the plan were unworkable and in 2009 a new approach was agreed under which South Island and Hauraki iwi would receive a 97 million dollar payment for aquaculture space in nearly all current aquaculture development areas including the Marlborough Sounds, Tasman Bay, the Hauraki Gulf and the rest of the South Island. Alongside deep sea fishing, aquaculture is likely to become a significant industry based on a customary right to certain seabed sites and the use of modern technologies that will add economic value to those sites.

However, although customary assets are increasing in size, as measured, for example, by land holdings, fishing quota, and contemporary forests, they may not be the most significant components of the Māori estate into the future. Unlike Māori land, which is an asset earmarked for future generations, new tradable assets constitute an increasingly large proportion of tribal estates. Cash investments in property, shares, and technology have the potential to return greater dividends than many customary lands and can be used more flexibly to meet new situations, gain entry into the digital world, and take advantage of market opportunities.

Participation in the knowledge economy, for example, was recognised by the allocation of radio frequencies to Māori. The Māori estate now includes access to the 2 GHz frequencies. While radio frequencies were not used by Māori in former times as they are now, they nonetheless existed. In that sense they were a resource waiting to be further developed and Māori interests ought not to have been discounted when ownership was assumed by the Crown. In addition, third generation radio frequencies will be important vehicles for the transmission and development of Māori language. According to the Waitangi Tribunal the assumption by the Crown of an exclusive right to manage and on-lease the resource was inconsistent with the Treaty of Waitangi. The Tribunal's recommendations in the *Radio Spectrum Management and Development Final Report (Wai 776)* in 1999 were to lead to the establishment of the Māori Spectrum Charitable Trust He Huaraki Tikā and its commercial arm, Hautaki Ltd, to 'provide an investment stake in the telecommunications sector'. The assets of the trust are an integral part of the Māori estate and are further evidence of the estate's diversity.

Moreover, unlike land, where succession is defined by a legal process administered by the Māori Land Court, and ultimately made known by the names appearing on a title, the entitlements of future generations to dividends from various tradable assets is unclear. Three questions are of particular importance. First, which assets, if any, are better retained by a collective Māori body (such as an iwi or hapū); second, which assets are better assigned to individuals; and third, which assets belong to all Māori?

Another set of questions is concerned with the manner in which succession occurs. The long-lasting impact of individualisation through the Māori Land Court and its predecessor the Native Land Court has been the alienation of large tracts of Māori land. There is some fear that other assets could be similarly eroded if the same mechanisms for succession were pursued. Individual ownership may threaten sustainability. On the other hand, if Māori individuals do not experience any personal gain from an estate that rightfully belongs to them, will they ever be able to value it as part of a rich heritage?

To some extent the question has already been addressed by tribal authorities who have had to decide how best to apply benefits from Treaty of Waitangi settlements. Although the individuals entitled to a share in settlement proceeds have been identifiable, individual monetary payments or assignment of a portion of an actual resource have not been the preferred method of distribution. More often, group benefits derived from interest on investments have been provided, such as health insurance policies for older members, subsidies to marae, contributions to programmes for cultural advancement, and educational grants for young people. But the capital has been retained by the tribe as a whole rather than being distributed to family members. At a national level the same debate occurred in respect of the distribution of fishing quota. While the terms of the Treaty of Waitangi Fisheries Settlement had expected distribution to iwi, the problems associated with deciding on a formula for distribution, together with the advantages of scale, led to a strong move to maintain the quota as an aggregated resource. Only after ten years did most iwi receive quota for tribal use and management. Though indirect benefits to individuals followed, no iwi embarked on a process of transferring the resource (quota) directly to individual tribal members.

A futures scenario: the Asia Pacific Cultural–Carbon Agreements

In contrast to the earlier scenario, Ahuwhenua Ltd, a second scenario introduces the possibility that the Māori estate might be undermined by international agreements relating both to cultural properties and carbon credits.

In the Asia Pacific Cultural–Carbon Agreement scenario, by 2015 New Zealand had entered into two agreements with Australia, Korea, Japan, China and Singapore. The Cultural Agreement encouraged cultural exchanges between the countries while the Carbon Trading Agreement provided for buying and selling goods and services in exchange for carbon credits. The Asia Pacific Carbon Trading Agreement recognised that New Zealand had more carbon credits than other neighbouring nations and could use them to purchase education and access to commercial ventures. However, in 2017 the Mahutonga Festival, a national celebration of kāpa hakā held annually on February 6 at Waitangi, was abruptly cancelled when it was revealed that items from three groups had been pirated using sophisticated secret audio-visual recording technology. The original sounds and faces were disguised by automated voice-overs and substituted profiles, but the compositions were nonetheless recognisable. The pirated versions were on sale in Sydney and Tokyo a week before the Mahutonga Festival was to take place. Outraged by the piracy, festival leaders lobbied the government to pass sweeping intellectual property laws that would protect Māori cultural performances and be recognised by other nations who were also signatories to the Asia Pacific Cultural–Carbon Agreements. Although a Treaty settlement between the Ngāti Toa tribe and the Crown, signed in 2009, had recognised tribal rights to a popular haka, the government's argument in 2017 had backed away from indigenous rights to culture. Instead the Crown argued that 'any cultural item performed or about to be performed in a public place could not be claimed as private property even if it had historic significance'. According to the Crown there was no way of preventing widespread distribution. Probably, however, the real reason for the decision was linked to sensitive parallel government negotiations around the implementation of the 'Students for Carbon Credits Trading Scheme'. Under the scheme New Zealand students could have access to top Asian universities in exchange for surplus New Zealand carbon credits.

Nonetheless, for whatever reason, any exclusive claims to cultural compositions had been dismissed in 2017. By 2020, Australian, Japanese and Korean versions of 'Ka Mate', 'Uiui Noa' and 'Taku Rakāu' were available in audio, video, and dramatised form. By 2023 they had been registered as authentic cultural compositions in those countries and under the Asia Pacific Cultural–Carbon Agreements Māori performers were required to purchase back rights to use them. By 2025 the Mahutonga Festival had been permanently discontinued.

The cultural estate

The 'Cultural–Carbon Agreements' scenario is possible though not highly probable. It does, however, highlight two concerns about the Māori estate. In addition to physical resources and tradable assets, cultural resources constitute an important part of the expanding asset base. But existing attitudes to cultural value will predictably change. In 2009 Ngāti Toa were at pains to emphasise that their claim to the haka 'Ka Mate' was not driven by any desire for financial gain, but by pride in the exploits of an ancestor whose efforts played a major role in defining tribal history. However, that rationale is not likely to be maintained for ever. The progressive commodification of intellectual and cultural creations will require further consideration of intellectual resources as assets that have both cultural and commercial significance.

The value-adding function of culture has already become evident in the tourism industry, the marketing and branding of products such as Tohu wines, the design of clothing as demonstrated by the Kia Kāha line, in the broadcasting sector and in the curriculum vitae of Māori job seekers. On the other hand, while commercial gain is likely to be an increasingly significant aspect of cultural heritage, it is not the sole or the main reason for valuing culture as part of the Māori estate. The claim of Ngāti Toa, that their hakā has a tribal significance independent of financial gain, remains a widely held view. Similarly, efforts to revitalise te reo Māori have not been based on economic considerations but on a conviction that future generations should not be alienated from their culture. At the same time, it is clear that fluency in te reo Māori does bring career opportunities (in broadcasting, teaching, health and social services) that will translate into financial gain. In effect, physical, intellectual, and cultural resources will be cherished because they have, or will have, intangible value as well as tangible economic value.

Probably the most enduring material cultural asset has been the marae. Despite an extensive urbanisation process that occurred in the latter half of the twentieth century and the prospect that marae would become deserted memorials to a former era, the reverse has occurred. Marae flourish in traditional tribal areas but have also been developed in urban and metropolitan centres associated with schools, universities, hospitals, defence bases, and Māori urban communities. Marae have been constructed in overseas countries where significant Māori communities now reside and as global travel increases, it is likely that overseas marae will be part of a worldwide network of marae, some based around hapū, others around communities of interest, and others still around global travellers who seek to retain a cultural anchor in an otherwise assimilating environment.

A framework for sustaining the Māori estate

So far this paper has canvassed the Māori estate from four perspectives: the nature of the estate, the factors that will determine the sustainability of the estate, the principles governing entitlement, and the characteristics of those who will inherit the estate. In brief, by 2020 the Māori estate will be made up of customary resources such as land, forests, fisheries and waterways; tradable assets such as real estate, carbon credits, investments in commercial enterprises and communication technology; and cultural heritage including language, knowledge, visual and performing arts, and marae.

Growing the estate will be a function of many variables acting singly and together. Some variables will be outside direct Māori influence. Global warming, global overpopulation, and global catastrophes, for example, will impact on the Māori estate in ways that are largely beyond local control. The effects of climate change on oceans, coastlines and land production will have inevitable implications for the Māori estate. Further, the recent USA economic downturn, coupled with export subsidies and trade protectionism by superpowers, has shown how a crisis in one part of the world can have serious ripple effects in other parts. At the same time new global markets will greatly increase options for investment and trading while the global indigenous network will provide Māori with many more alternatives for international business. Technological advances will predictably outstrip the advances already seen in the past decade rendering current technologies obsolete and benefitting those who can access the latest versions quickly. New technologies will open fresh avenues for Māori, and increase the opportunities for adding value to customary resources and cultural heritage.

Closer to home, and also apparent in the debate about the Auckland Super City, the Māori estate will continue to be subject to political ideologies, narrow interpretations of the Treaty of Waitangi and indigenous rights, and shallow understandings that equate simple majoritarianism with 'a fair and just society'. As customary resources increase in value, so pressure to have them removed from the Māori estate will mount. Yet the past two decades have not only shown how Māori negotiators can act to counter assimilatory drives but also how agreements between Māori and the Crown can be reached in good faith and with mutual benefits. Much will depend on Māori leadership and the ways in which the Māori estate will be governed and managed. Short term gains will need to be balanced against long term benefits. Opportunities that hold the prospect of lucrative returns will need to be tempered by the reasonable entitlement of future generations for an estate that is growing rather than diminishing in size. No matter how attractive the proposition, investments that use customary land as security run the risk of alienating future generations from an already depleted land resource.

Two other determinants of sustainability warrant reiteration: economies of scale and collective succession. Since 1984 there has been a resurgence of both tribal governance and Māori community ownership of services and programmes. Competition for limited government resources, coupled with an ethic of winners and losers has led to a large number of relatively independent entities each with a separate infrastructure, a shortage of skilled advisors, and a determination to maintain a state of illusory autonomy. Some have performed well and are in strong economic positions that will advantage future generations. Others struggle in a climate where internal competition dominates. None have yet realised full potential. The saving grace of the Ahuwhenua Ltd scenario was not the number of Māori entities involved in arable farming but the aggregated resource which enabled Māori to provide a more comprehensive business than any other farming cluster. Economies of scale will be increasingly important to Māori as New Zealand expands its global ties, especially with Asia. Aggregating a resource does not necessarily mean abandoning title to it or forfeiting returns but it could mean increased security for the resource, shared technologies, greater dividends, and a leadership role in New Zealand's export business.

Decisions around entitlement to the Māori estate vary according to the type of resource but some common dilemmas underpin the options. An important question is whether entitlements should favour individuals or Māori collectives such as whānau or hapū. Because entitlements have generally been more readily alienated when awarded to individuals, group retention holds promise as a more sustainable option. A related entitlement decision hinges on whether the entitlement constitutes ownership or trusteeship. The Ture Whenua Maori Act places constraints on individuals who wish to alienate their land interests, even though those individuals are the legal owners. Under the Act other members of the whānau or hapū have first right of refusal if an owner wishes to sell. The longer term aim is that future generations should succeed and in that respect today's owners are acting more as trustees.

Yet another entitlement dilemma concerns 'absenteeism'. If a prospective successor has maintained an ongoing presence, either personally or through family members, ahi kā is said to exist and the case to succeed is stronger. In practice, however, the ahi kā principle is difficult to apply, especially in the face of legal entitlement: the law outweighs ahi kā. But, as more and more Māori take up residence overseas and the links through ahi kā are attenuated, absentee claims to ownership could threaten sustainability because of a likelihood of diminished attachment. Will entitlement in the future require some evidence of ahi kā, not necessarily based on place of residence but by attendance, online if necessary, at meetings and decision making arenas? Or perhaps by the payment of an archival fee?

In addition to changing the configuration of the Māori estate the profiles of future generations, the successors to the estate, will also change. First, as already noted the trends are for a steady increase in the Māori population for some decades to come. Second, although the proportion of younger people will still be relatively high (compared to the non-Māori population), many more older people will also be around to moderate young energies. Third, the population will be more mobile; many will spend lengthy periods of time abroad and many more will be aligned to other cultures and ethnicities. They will still be Māori but influenced as much by those other cultures that will be part of their heritage. Fourth, relatively few will have lived within the territories of their ancestors and although a sense of tribal affiliation may exist, it will be no guarantee of a commitment to tribal priorities or to tribal estates. In any case, most will have multiple tribal affiliations and choosing one over the other will be problematic. Fifth, by 2020 more Māori individuals will be well educated, employed in meaningful occupations, healthy and in strong positions to support themselves and their families. Few will be

FIGURE **23.1** A sustainability framework for the Māori estate

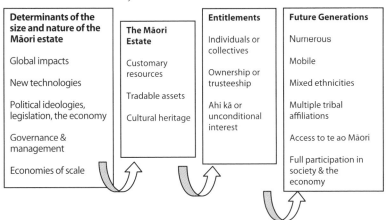

Determinants of the size and nature of the Māori estate	The Māori Estate	Entitlements	Future Generations
Global impacts	Customary resources	Individuals or collectives	Numerous
New technologies	Tradable assets	Ownership or trusteeship	Mobile
Political ideologies, legislation, the economy	Cultural heritage	Ahi kā or unconditional interest	Mixed ethnicities
Governance & management			Multiple tribal affiliations
Economies of scale			Access to te ao Māori
			Full participation in society & the economy

dependent on the Māori estate for day-to-day wellbeing. At the same time, any benefits coming to them from the estate will add value to their lives as Māori and enable them to be part of a vibrant Māori society with secure access to te ao Māori, ready opportunities to engage in Māori enterprise and at the same time an ability to participate fully in wider society.

Drawing on perspectives about the nature of the estate, factors that will determine the sustainability of the estate, the principles governing entitlement, and the characteristics of those who will inherit the estate, a sustainability framework can be constructed (Figure 23.1). It is shown diagrammatically as an interaction between the Māori estate, the determinants that shape the estate, the rationale for deciding entitlements, and the successors to the estate.

Future proofing the Māori estate

Marae trustees, trustees for Māori land incorporations, directors of companies concerned with Māori resources such as fishing quota and 2 GHz frequencies, and board members who have responsibilities for educational and other resources belonging to Māori are in positions to build the estate and guide its passage to future generations. They will exercise kaitiakitanga – trusteeship – on behalf of present and

TABLE **23.1** A future proofing matrix

	The Māori Estate		
	Customary resources	Tradable assets	Cultural heritage
Kaitiakitanga **Wise governance & management:** • scanning the future • securing the estate • developing the estate • maintaining faith with current generations • cooperating for economies of scale • clarifying entitlements • managing intergenerational transmission.			
Rangatiratanga **A Māori leaders' futures forum:** • future focused • engagement with the private sector • political influence • facilitation of economies of scale • champions for future generations.			

future generations. Importantly, those charged with the governance and management of the Māori estate must ensure that the estate is future proofed for successive generations. There is no template that can guarantee future proofing nor is it a task that can be undertaken with the certain knowledge that the future will unfold in a predetermined way. But it is possible to identify key considerations that might guide the process of future proofing (Table 23.1).

First, scanning the future will be increasingly important. Technological change, demographic trends, potential trade opportunities in New Zealand and abroad, and Māori aspirations for the future will all be important aspects of forward thinking governance.

Second, securing the estate is a necessary precondition. Security means making certain that the entity under which the estate is to be managed will be the most appropriate for the situation and will place the resource out of risk of alienation or diminishment. An estate that is well secured has a better chance of reaching future generations in a healthy state.

A third consideration is about developing the estate. An increase in the size of the Māori population and the number of people who might benefit means that the estate must expand in parallel to the expanding beneficiary roll, otherwise it will have lost per capita value. It is no longer sufficient to simply pass on the estate in the same condition as it was when inherited regardless of whether it is a marae, a land block, or a fishing company. Wise governance will lead to a resource that expands in size and value so that it becomes more relevant to the next generation.

Maintaining faith with current beneficiaries is a fourth consideration. They are the current successors to the estate; their efforts, aspirations, and plans are immediate and cannot be ignored. But balancing long term development against the wishes of current beneficiaries will always be challenging since it may require postponing instant gains in favour of benefits for future generations. In this respect the Māori estate differs significantly from conventional shareholding companies where investors might expect the best possible dividends in the shortest period of time. A conundrum for trustees is how to exercise their roles as trustees for future generations as well as trustees for current owners.

A fifth consideration for governors and managers is about aggregating resources. Economies of scale will assume increasing importance; sustainability is reduced when estates are too small to guarantee survival. While one generation may be prepared to make sacrifices and subsidise a collective venture, their successors, possibly living in Australia, are unlikely to feel a similar level of commitment. On the other hand, larger estates, even if they are made up of several distinct entities, are more likely to survive and to bring both economic and cultural benefits.

Sixth, identifying those entitled to succeed will be an important function. Decisions need to be made about the rationale for entitlement and how communication will be maintained with beneficiaries so that they can have an active role in decision-making.

A related seventh task will be ensuring that transmission of the estate between generations can be sufficiently explicit to avoid confusion and to provide the best possible option for sustainability. The relative advantages of collective inheritance or individual rights to succession will need to be weighed against transaction costs, the utility of the resource, as well as its endurance.

Wise governance and management hold the key to sustainability. But the wider environments within which decisions about the Māori estate are made, require another level of leadership – rangatiratanga – that can actively contemplate the future and the likely impacts on the total Māori estate. There are already examples that offer some guidance for a futures forum. The Federation of Māori Authorities, for example, provides a collective voice for a large number of Māori trusts and incorporations; the Hui Taumata group is a collective voice for Māori economic development; and the Pukawa Hui have potential as an iwi collective that might focus on resources such as water that will be compromised in the future. In any event, collective Māori leadership for estate sustainability is imperative. Energies spent on dealing with past grievances and responding to current crises have left relatively little time for ensuring that the Māori estate can survive and prosper for generations to come. There is a strong case for a Māori leadership network that has the capacity to support the guardians of Māori estates with a measure of certainty as they plan for the next twenty or thirty years. Establishing a high level 'futures leadership forum' must be a priority. The utility of the forum will rest on its deliberate focus on the future, an ability to engage with the private sector as well as with government, a constant monitoring of the legislative and regulatory environments, a readiness to mediate joint ventures that will bring economies of scale, and most importantly, a commitment to being champions for future generations.

'Pae Matatū: Sustaining the Māori Estate' has provided an opportunity to examine some of the parameters that will impact on Māori futures. Predictably the Māori estate will grow. It will expand in volume and diversity enabling Māori to remain grounded in Aotearoa but with new freedoms to explore other domains. The Māori estate will be a composite of lands, waterways, fisheries, forests, marae, whakāiro, waiata and haka; and it will grow to include greater shares in third and fourth generation radio frequency networks, a range of commercial enterprises, and access to technologies that will add value to customary resources and cultural heritage.

Over time the concept of indigeneity will also change. Indigeneity will be about embracing the lives that indigenous peoples live in modern times; it will rest on a reconfigured collective indigenous estate; and it will celebrate the ways in which indigenous peoples build on past experiences in order to face the future. In that respect the Māori estate in 2020 will not confine Māori ambitions to a bygone era. The nineteenth and twentieth century emphasis on territory and property will be both enriched and balanced if wise governance can add value to customary resources, attract additional assets to unlock global opportunities, and keep alive those cultural ideals that have enduring worth for future generations.

By 2035 a new generation of Māori parents will be confronted with a competitive economy, uncertain national and international political goals, a planet still reeling under the impact of a global population explosion, a changed landscape at home, many more Māori, and technologies that can unleash untold potential while also threatening immeasurable harm. Their children and grandchildren will live in different worlds. Survival as Māori will depend not only on their own initiatives and the efforts of their parents, but on the arrangements made twenty-five or more years previously when an earlier generation took steps to secure their entitlements to the expanding Māori estate.

CHAPTER 24

Pae Ora: Māori Health Horizons

'Pae Ora: Māori Health Horizons', the second of the three 'Paerangi Lectures', was delivered at Massey University, Albany, 7 July, 2009.

The Paerangi Lectures

'Pae Ora: Māori Health Horizons' is the second of three 'Paerangi Lectures'. It will consider the broad approaches to Māori health over the past two decades and the gains that have resulted. But like the other two lectures, 'Pae Ora' is primarily positioned in the future and contemplates the consequences of global, local, environmental, and family determinants on Māori health.

In the first lecture, 'Pae Matatū: Sustaining the Māori Estate', the rapid growth of the Māori asset base was seen as a positive development but one that would demand expert governance and management to ensure that future generations could enjoy the full benefits of their entitlements. Concerns relating to the transfer of assets from one generation to another were raised and the importance of 'future proofing' as a way of protecting the interests of future generations was explored. The major conclusion, however, was that the Māori estate will grow in both size and diversity; it will include customary resources such as land, tradable assets including real estate and shares in international companies, as well as cultural heritage typified by marae and te reo Māori.

The third lecture, 'Pae Mana: Waitangi and the Evolving State' will focus on the relationship between Māori and the Crown in a post-settlement environment. It will raise questions about the constitutional position of Māori beyond 2020, the relevance of the Treaty of Waitangi as a platform for forward development rather than as a vehicle for redress, and the ways in which indigeneity will, or will not, be valued in the future. The implications for Māori if New Zealand were to become a republic will be discussed in the context of Aotearoa as an evolving democracy in the South Pacific with longstanding links to Pasifika and strong trade and diplomatic relationships with Asian economies.

Meanwhile 'Pae Ora' explores the parameters surrounding Māori health and wellbeing in the future. Having emerged from a twenty-five-year period of Māori health transformation, the next quarter century will lead into a future environment where technological innovation, demographic transitions, and unexpected catastrophes and epidemics will interact with indigenous aspirations and strengthened Māori capability. Outcomes will be difficult to predict. Yet despite the uncertainties ahead and the rapidly changing nature of New Zealand society, a number of directional shifts will be necessary so that the gains made in recent decades can be extended into the future. Environmental sustainability, quality social relationships, balanced lifestyles, wise leadership, and access to knowledge and technology will be important drivers of health and wellbeing; and, as agents for the promotion of health, whānau could make the most significant difference to Māori wellbeing.

Foundations

The establishment of foundations for change over the past twenty-five years has already resulted in major transformations. Large scale societal transformations do not occur often and when they do they are often quickly absorbed by societal institutions so that later generations perceive them as longstanding norms. Signs of a new approach to Māori health had emerged in the 1970s[1] but the signals were especially strong in 1983. In its first major report, the Waitangi Tribunal released findings on the Motunui River claim.[2] Fears that a new petrochemical plant would increase pollution of the river and fishing reefs led to a case against the Crown, as the architect of 'Think Big' industrial development projects. A Māori environmental ethic, hitherto largely unknown to most New Zealanders, formed the basis for a recommendation that land-based disposal of waste should be pursued ahead of water disposal. The Tribunal had drawn attention to the link between industrial development and environmental sustainability at a time when a New Zealand green conscience had yet to form. Further, embedded in the Motunui report was also a finding that cultural values were integral to both environmental and human wellbeing.

In the same year legislation was passed to establish the New Zealand Board of Health. Although disestablished within a decade, the Board's Māori Standing Committee had meanwhile proposed that iwi could be effective champions for Māori health. The prospect that tribal leaders might involve themselves in health seemed unlikely then but the board supported the proposal and forwarded it to the government as a strong recommendation.[3] Meanwhile at a Young People's Hui held at the Raukawa Marae in Otaki, in 1983 also, a four part Māori perspective of health, later known as Whare Tapa Wha, was introduced and endorsed as an approach that was relevant to Māori and to rangatahi.[4] Another sign of change also emerged in 1983 when Whaiora was established. Located within the large Tokanui psychiatric hospital, Whaiora introduced Māori approaches to treatment and care adding a cultural dimension that had been totally lacking in the formal health services and arguing that health outcomes would be improved if the cultural context for service delivery were relevant to consumers.[5]

But the clearest indications of change became evident the following year in 1984. First, the Hui Whakaoranga was held at the Hoani Waititi Marae in West Auckland. Organised by a fledgling Māori health unit within the Department of Health, and led by Dr Paratene Ngata, the event was the first national Māori health hui in modern times.[6] In addition to departmental representatives, health specialists, hospital board members, and Māori health professionals, the participation of tribal elders and Māori community leaders injected a fresh dimension to the discussions. By the end of the three day conference, three directions had been endorsed: the incorporation of Māori health perspectives into the delivery of health programmes, increasing the professional Māori health workforce, and developing Māori health provider organisations.

The second significant event in 1984 was the Hui Taumata; a Māori Economic Summit held shortly after the election of the fourth Labour Government. Again, Māori leaders urged the government to adopt a positive approach to Māori development by fostering Māori economic capability, tribal delivery systems, and the revitalisation of culture, especially te reo Māori. Both the Hui Whakaoranga and the Hui Taumata had moved in the same direction, away from a total reliance on the state and towards self-management and self-determination, aspirations that were to be increasingly captured by the concept of tino rangatiratanga.

Potential for change

As a result of the initiatives introduced and consolidated over the past twenty-five years, strong platforms have been built for development into the future. There are now clear signs that Māori potential for high standards of health and wellbeing has never been greater. Not only is there the distinct possibility of substantial health gains in the years ahead but a broader level of Māori wellbeing is within reach.

In the face of the current health statistics those conclusions could be dismissed as rhetoric; they seem at odds with the evidence about disparities between Māori and non-Māori. Any suggestion of a transformation in Māori health over the past quarter century, for example, might be challenged by the known widespread prevalence of type 2 diabetes or the high levels of drug abuse among young people, or excessive mortality rates for cancer. Disparities in standards of health between Māori and non-Māori indicate that for almost all diagnostic categories, including mental disorders, injuries, and disabilities, the Māori rate exceeds that of non-Māori by two or three times.[7] But measuring Māori health and wellbeing simply as a ratio of non-Māori disease and injury fails to capture Māori advancement and masks those indicators that suggest potential rather than deficit. Benchmarking Māori health gains solely against non-Māori standards of health assumes that Māori health is best understood by reference to a national statistical norm.

The comparative approach needs to be balanced by a temporal approach that views Māori health through a Māori lens, relying neither entirely on non-Māori prevalence rates nor diagnostic categories. Other more useful measures of progress including Māori-referenced life expectancy, youthful vitality, Māori agendas for health, strengthened cultural identity, the dissemination of health knowledge, Māori participation in the health sector, and Māori health leadership.

Measures of progress

Life expectancy and mortality rates

The total Māori population has increased dramatically over the past century. By 1894 it was estimated to have fallen from around 200,000 in 1800 to 42,000. A reversal in a steady depopulation trend occurred around 1900 so that by the 2006 Census the population had reached more than 565,000. Even allowing for differences in measuring Māori ethnicity the rate of growth has been exceptionally high, a combination of high fertility rates prior to the 1960s and increased life expectancy. Importantly over the past twenty-five years there has been a further significant increase in Māori life expectancy. In 1985 Māori men could expect to live for sixty-eight years and Māori women for seventy-two years.[8] But by 2007 Māori life expectancy had increased to 70.4 years for males and 75.1 years for females,[9] increases of 2.4 years and 3.1 years respectively. Moreover, whereas the difference between Māori and non-Māori life expectancies was increasing during the 1980s and 1990s[10], by 2002 there were signs that the gap was narrowing.[11] Increased life expectancy will continue so that there will be larger cohorts of older Māori, many over the age of eighty years. Though still a youthful population with a relatively low median age (twenty-six years by 2021), the relative increase in older Māori will bring both balance and continuity, increasing the standing of iwi and Māori communities.

As life expectancy has increased, Māori mortality rates have declined. The reduction has been especially apparent for Māori men. In the early 1980s the death rate for men aged between twenty-five and fifty-nine years was around 550 per 100,000. But by the late 1990s it had dropped to around 460 per 100,000. For women over the same time period the reduction was less, but still significant – from 350 to 270 per 100,000.

Youthful vitality

Along with a growing population there will be further increases in the younger age groups; by 2051, for example, one-third of all schoolchildren in New Zealand will be Māori. There is already evidence that Māori youth have high potential in a number of areas important for future worlds. There is rapidly increasing participation in higher education, including at doctoral levels, together with brilliance in sport, digital technologies, the media, music, entrepreneurship, and business. The trends point towards increasingly high peaks of performance and achievement and levels of vitality that far outweigh the sum total of youthful misfortune or disadvantage.

A Māori health agenda

Measuring the health status of Māori individuals is one measure of health but given the lag between laying foundations and realising the full benefits, other indicators are also useful. An important indicator, for example, is health awareness and the inclusion of health as an item on the Māori agenda. Prior to 1984, fewer than three iwi included health as part of tribal business. For the most part health had been regarded as a function of health professionals, hospital boards, and the government. In contrast, all iwi now regard health as a high tribal priority and most have developed health programmes delivered by their own people. Iwi health interests are evident in environmental initiatives, marae health policies, and programmes such as marae smoke free, sport and exercise programmes, health governance, and the provision of health services. Within urban Māori communities the delivery of health services has assumed an even higher priority; early intervention for child health, mental health services, cancer care navigation and support, and walk-in clinic services are offered as part of a wider package of care for whānau.[12]

Strengthened cultural identity

A fourth indicator of progress especially evident over the past twenty-five years has been a strengthening of cultural identity. The connections between culture and health are well documented and the strong reassertion of a Māori identity has been a powerful influence in the promotion of health. Outward markers of a revitalised sense of identity have been the emergence of new generations of fluent Māori speakers, a reconnection with marae and tūrangawaewae, and high levels of participation in haka, waiata, and poi. While urbanisation carried a risk of assimilation into a monocultural New Zealand, the reverse happened: Māori asserted themselves as Māori and have demonstrated that a Māori identity is not only possible in urban situations but is associated with positive attitudes, high self-esteem, and a sense of purpose – attributes that are fundamental to good health. Earlier generations often had to contend with societal prejudices against the expression of Māori values, language and culture and as a result were often forced into apologetic positions or had to suffer a negative connotation about being Māori. That is no longer the case. Although pockets of prejudice remain, for the most part a Māori affiliation affords a sense of pride and satisfaction.

Māori health knowledge

A fifth measure of progress is the extent to which Māori knowledge is incorporated into accounts of health generally. Building on the Māori perspectives introduced in 1983/4, knowledge based on Māori understandings and Māori world views has become integral to treatment protocols, assessment procedures, measures of outcome, and frameworks for analysis. Not only has Māori knowledge become incorporated into practice but it has also become part of the health curriculum in universities, polytechnics, and wānanga. Moreover, the establishment of six Māori health research centres since 1993, all employing Māori methods alongside conventional approaches, has demonstrated the relevance of Māori knowledge to understanding contemporary health problems. By the same token, a Māori nursing programme instituted in 2009 aims to train nurses to work effectively with Māori using a mix of Māori and universal methods and theories.

Māori participation in health services and programmes

The most obvious measure of progress, however, has been growth in the Māori health workforce and the parallel growth in the number of Māori health providers. In 1984 there was one Māori health non-government organisation (NGO); by 2009 there were more than 270 delivering a wide range of programmes in mental health, child health, health promotion, disability support, midwifery, and public health. The number of Māori health professionals has similarly shown a spectacular increase. Between 1984 and 2009 the number of medical practitioners has increased from around fifty (0.5 percent) to over 250 (3 percent); from four dentists in 1984 there were some sixty in 2009; and from almost none twenty-five years ago there were more than 300 Māori addiction workers (20 percent) in 2009. The phenomenal increase in the number of Māori health support workers, community health workers, health professionals and cultural advisors has created a total workforce that has already revolutionised New Zealand's health sector and seems set to expand further over the next two to three decades.

Māori participation in health policy, health governance and health management has also increased over the past quarter century. Māori representation on district health boards (DHBs) has largely been achieved through ministerial appointments as part of a policy that recognises Māori health as a government priority. At both national and local levels, Māori participation in health policy formulation and policy implementation has been evident at senior management levels. In contrast to 1984 when no hospital boards employed Māori health managers, in 2009 Māori health management is strong in both DHBs and NGOs.

Māori health leadership

A seventh measure of progress, related to Māori provider development, can be seen in the network of Māori health leadership. Māori participation at governance and management levels has increased to the point that all major health providers and funders have senior Māori managers and Māori members of boards and trusts. Large numbers of older Māori men and women have also entered the health sector ready to play vital roles as advocates, conduits for tribes and communities, supporters for staff, and advisors on matters of tikanga and human ethics. Not only do Māori health providers now employ kaumātua as key members of the team, but DHBs, community programmes and government departments have similarly engaged kaumātua to effect better links with Māori communities and to provide advice on the implementation of Māori health policies and programmes. In addition the establishment of Māori professional organisations such as Te ORA (Māori Medical Practitioners' Association), Te Kaunihera (National Council of Māori Nurses), and Nga Maia (the Māori Midwives' Collective) has provided practitioners with coordinating and advocacy functions at a national level.

The twenty-five years ahead

Reviewing the past twenty-five years may seem peripheral to a discussion about the future. But there are two reasons for looking back in time. First, the gains made since 1984 have established the foundations upon which the next set of transformations will unfold. Although the directions will predictably shift to meet changing circumstances, it is unlikely that future policies or programmes will be revolutionary. Instead a process of progressive change will build on past successes to take Māori on a journey towards 2035. Second, among those who attended the Hui Whakaoranga in 1984, few if any would have been able to predict the transformations that have occurred. In that respect, forecasting the twenty-five years ahead, and the implications for Māori health and wellbeing will defy accurate prediction.

Yet, despite the difficulty in anticipating Māori health over the next twenty-five years, the future can be explored using a set of tools that include the analysis of past trends, statistical modelling, life course epidemiology, horizon scanning and scenario development.[13] Demographic projections, for example, have a reasonably high level of certainty; the Māori population will increase at a relatively fast rate – there will be some 800,000 by 2051 as well as 200,000 or more living overseas. Not only, as mentioned, will about one-third of all New Zealand children be Māori by 2051 but the percentage of men and women over the age of sixty-five years will have increased from 4 percent in 2006 to 13 percent.

Life course epidemiology predicts the future health status of populations by estimating the long term consequences of disease and injury. Otitis media in infancy, for example, increases risk for hearing and learning disability throughout life; and conduct disorders in childhood increase risk of serious offending in adolescence and early adulthood. The longer term effects of smoking in adolescence are well known and include cancer, heart disease, and hypertension. Obesity in childhood will often result in diabetes later in life and diabetes in the third and fourth decades will increase the risk of heart disease and renal disorders in the fifth and sixth decades. Given current standards of Māori health, life course epidemiology could suggest that the burden of disease will be heavy and that the larger older Māori population will have high health needs. Much will depend, however, on the effectiveness of intervening action. Progression along a downhill pathway is by no means inevitable; while early interventions will have the greatest prospect of lengthening life and avoiding disability, interventions later in life can still reverse progressive incapacity.

Scenario construction, a further tool for exploring the future, provides another vehicle for steering a course into the future.[14] Typically, scenarios navigate between emerging trends and patterns as well as allowing for the intrusion of the unexpected. They take into account global trends and impacts, environmental patterns like climate change, national and international economies, new technologies, the aspirations and socio-economic conditions of individuals and collectives, societal values and norms, and human capabilities such as levels of education and the acquisitions of skill sets.

Three scenarios illustrate the ways in which future situations can be portrayed according to different sets of circumstances; all three are centred on Māori health but respond to different triggers and lead to different conclusions.

Scenario 1: Whānau Ora

In the first scenario, by 2035 whānau have become beneficiaries of Treaty of Waitangi settlements. The Treaty of Waitangi (Whānau Vesting) Act 2014 had required that trustees who were managing settlement funds, make specific provisions for whānau. By 2035 young people, rangatahi, are performing above average at school, they are engaged in postgraduate tertiary education studies and are ready to compete in global markets. Whānau adults are employed in meaningful occupations, are wealthy compared to other New Zealanders, and are as active in civic and national endeavours as they are in marae and community organisations. Close family connections are maintained using state-of-the-art technology to communicate within New Zealand and across the globe.

Whānau health and wellbeing in 2035 reflect healthy lifestyles and whānau capability. By age two years immunisation uptake rates exceed 90 percent and there is a 90 percent uptake of the fourth generation vaccines for cancer of the breast, cervix and prostate. Whānau are guided as much by tikanga as by the latest findings posted on electronic health research bulletins, and as collectives they categorically reject alcohol and drug abuse. Over 80 percent of whānau households have personalised online health management programmes and maintain full responsibility for their own health records. As shareholders in Hauora@globe they have access to up-to-date health information together with cultural approaches to dealing with health risks; they supplement online information by calling on a range of health providers for advice and annual computerised health checks. An increase in the Māori population to account for more than 20 percent of the total population can be partly attributed to an increase in life expectancy of eighty years for men and more than eighty-five years for women.

Scenario 2: Whānau Rawakore

In contrast to Scenario 1 where whānau have prospered, scenario 2 describes a situation where whānau have become impoverished.

By 2035 it was clear that the 2008 economic recession was not to be short-lived. In 2035 whānau have borne more than their fair share of the brunt and have increasingly narrowed their activities to focus on survival. Home ownership has fallen to less than 20 percent and most whānau are renting substandard houses in greater Auckland and Bay of Plenty cities. Their lack of voice in city affairs has left them powerless to have their plight recognised and addressed. They live in high risk neighbourhoods, have unemployment rates over 20 percent, try to survive on government subsistence allowances, and are forced to endure trapped lifestyles. Most young people have had negative experiences at school with low achievement, fewer than 40 percent passing the Global Tertiary Entry Examination, instituted in 2016. Aggravating their situation has been the disastrous collapse of the Māori economy when the Oceanic Fish Epidemic (the OFE) of 2021 grossly depleted fishing stock, forcing the newly established Iwi Fisheries Co-op into receivership. Moreover, the expanding world population has led to a mass migration from underdeveloped countries, where food shortages have been severe and chronic, to developed countries such as New Zealand. In the process competition within society for jobs, education, and housing has become fierce.

Whānau health and wellbeing have been correspondingly affected. Nutrition is poor, recourse to alcohol, tobacco, and drugs is high, health care occurs on a crisis-by-crisis basis, and a failure to immunise led to an epidemic of diphtheria in 2030. Moreover, new versions of old diseases have emerged; the prevalence of 'tuberculosis strain 26' is thought to be exceptionally high. Strain 26 has now been linked to climate change and has so far been resistant to all therapeutic agents. By 2035 Māori life expectancy has actually fallen to sixty-eight years for men and seventy-three years for women, the same that it was in 1985.

Scenario 3: Whānau Hangarau

Scenario 3 takes account of inevitable technological advances for restoring health and functioning.

By 2035 global technologies are available to transform human suffering and disease. Research and innovation have resulted in genetic realignment procedures so that prospective parents can have desirable attributes added to a developing embryo and undesirable traits removed. Cloning has given way to genetic reconstruction and organ transplants have been largely replaced by auto-augmentation, a process depending on stimulated growth of new tissues and organs from within – one part of the body can be persuaded to act as a donor to another part. In the developed countries, including New Zealand, there are expectations that access to the new technologies is a basic right and there is considerable debate about national affordability and who might receive priority treatment.

However, the ethical debates, which had sparked the Human Genome Application Act 2024, have subsided as more and more people welcome stem cell research and its importance to wellbeing. Māori attitudes to assisted reproductive technologies have also changed, largely in response to an increasing fear that sterility could threaten the continuity of whakapapa placing whānau survival at risk. And transgenic technologies that involve transplanting animal tissues into human subjects are now more readily accepted because the preventative approaches to diabetes type 2 and cancer had been progressively underfunded from around 2009 and prevalence rates had soared. Mortality from diabetes and cancer threatened Māori life span and vitality. The principle of human sanctity has been forced to give way to the principle of survival.

Whānau health and wellbeing 2020 and beyond

Although all three scenarios are possible, none is highly probable. However, it is fairly certain that along with opportunities for gains in health the future will bring serious threats to health. Climate change for example will have major health consequences for Māori. Global warming has the potential to destabilise the entire planet. Natural catastrophes caused by floods, cyclones, tsunamis, droughts, and rising sea levels, will have both direct and indirect effects on health. Direct effects will occur in the wake of disasters: injury, drowning, homelessness, and food shortages; indirect effects will occur as more virulent forms of old diseases appear and new diseases emerge to challenge medical knowledge.[15] In addition limitations on food production could require a change of diet; away from dairy products and meat which lead to high carbon emissions, and towards fruit and vegetables, grown locally (fewer 'food miles') and more environmentally friendly.[16]

Similarly, whether or not genetic engineering will offer the panacea described in scenario 3, there is little doubt that technology will continue to reform health care.[17] Technology already has the power to examine every minute detail of the human body and to shrink the vast expanse of the world to a few nano-seconds. Health information will be readily available in homes and on cell phones and consultation with world experts will be within the grasp of ordinary citizens. A lack of health information will give way to an information avalanche. Technological advancement will not necessarily contribute to global goals; assisted reproductive technologies, for example, are thought to account for some thousands of births each year at a time when the world's overpopulation is considered to be a threat to the planet's capacity. Nor will nano-technologies be necessarily consistent with Māori world views.[18] But technology will also reduce the costs of procedures and resources that may be currently unaffordable to many people.

Scenario 2 was also a reminder that health and economics go hand in hand. Financial hardship leads to marginalisation, trapped lifestyles and lower standards of health and wellbeing. Resistance to disease is lowered and vulnerability to noxious agents is heightened.

The main purposes of introducing the scenarios were: first, to highlight how global, political, economic and technological change can impact on health and wellbeing; and second, to demonstrate that the future cannot be easily predicted. Because cultural, social and economic functions are interrelated, policies and programmes that appear to be whānau neutral can have implications for whānau health many years later.

Future takers and future makers

Even if Māori fortunes in 2035 cannot be clearly envisaged, it does not follow that the future cannot be actively shaped. In that respect it is possible to distinguish between 'future takers' and 'future makers'.

'Future takers' accept that the future will bring what it will bring; the determinants of change are considered to be so far removed from local control that iwi and Māori communities are powerless to change what will be. They might be ready to respond to change but not to direct change. 'Future makers', on the other hand, actively engage with the future; they look for signs of change and then create future spaces where hopes and opportunities can flourish. Rather than responding to change, 'future makers' will lead change. 'Future makers' identify what could be possible and work to make it happen.

In order to achieve the best possible standards of health and wellbeing for Māori it is necessary to identify the desirable outcomes that will be relevant and attainable in the future. The task then is to plot a course that will lead towards those outcomes. Clearly scenario 1 points towards an outcome that would be supported by most Māori but moving in that direction will require a number of conceptual leaps. In addition to pursuing the goals that have been emphasised over the past two decades, there will be a need to move beyond increased health awareness to demonstrable action for health. Ultimately the aim should be to empower whānau so they can champion their own health and to support that aim, directional shifts in government policy, iwi programmes, and Māori health leadership will be needed.

Government policy frameworks

Macro-economic policies will inevitably impact on Māori health and wellbeing. Moreover, government commitment to reductions in carbon emissions, environmental protection, eco-friendly consumerism, and disaster readiness could represent the most significant contributions to Māori health gains in the future. In addition a revision of Treaty of Waitangi policy to acknowledge the future more than the past and to approach Treaty negotiations as opportunities for mutual benefits, rather than settling past injustices or avoiding risk, will have greater chances of addressing Māori health from a positive perspective. So too will policies that recognise the holistic nature of health and wellbeing where education, employment, economics, sport and recreation, social services, and regional development are part of the same formula. Sectoral interventions frequently unbalance whānau priorities and hierarchies by focusing on one aspect of life that may be relatively unimportant to the whānau even if it is of great interest to a health worker. Whānau do not live their lives in sectoral silos; in real life health is not separated from learning, or from goods and services, or from language, culture and social obligations. Moreover, inefficiencies invariably result from interventions that are uncoordinated, address only one aspect of a situation with no regard for the whole, or fail to recognise wider whānau dynamics so that whānau strengths can be endorsed.

Iwi action

While government has an important role in determining macro-policy frameworks, iwi are well placed to facilitate whānau wellbeing through an integrated approach to social, economic, environmental and cultural development. Over the past twenty-five years iwi have gained considerable experience in health governance, management and service delivery. In the future, however, investing time and energy in the delivery of personal health services may not be the best option for iwi. Managing disease may be less useful than implementing holistic programmes that link whānau to knowledge and information relevant to human wellbeing and ensuring that whānau have access to the full range of iwi resources. Overall a stronger move towards primary prevention will represent more distinctive use of iwi energies and resources.

Whānau as agents for change

A focus on whānau functioning as key to Māori health and wellbeing assumes that whānau will be influential agents in shaping Māori potential, brokering entry into education and the economy, and promoting high standards of health. The fact that some families may be dysfunctional today does not negate the prospects of whānau being tomorrow's agents for wellbeing. Nor does the changing nature of whānau necessarily disqualify them from key roles in the future. Trends indicate that by 2035 whānau will be more mobile, more blended, more complex, older, and more dispersed. But they will also be ready to employ new technologies that can diminish the distance between brothers and sisters, cousins, uncles and aunts, parents and grandparents and lend greater accuracy to the transfer of information, including health records. Diversity, mobility, and dispersal will be offset by enhanced communication, reduced alienation, and a wider operating base.

Similarly the current negative indicators of wellbeing such as poor health, substandard housing and educational underachievement should not be regarded as evidence of whānau failure or a permanent underclass. The present does not justify or even predict the future. If current patterns continue, by 2035 Māori achievement will be exceptional in many areas where earlier generations faltered. Increases in Māori medical and dental graduates, Māori health workers, Māori inclusion in early childhood education, Māori participation in broadcasting, sport, and music, Māori enterprise, as well as the high enthusiasm for Māori performing arts, are sign of high levels of whānau accomplishment.

Building on Māori leadership for health

Shifting the focus is a task that will impact at many levels. Not only will it involve political leaders, the government, territorial authorities, iwi rūnanga, urban Māori authorities, the not-for-profit sector and community elders but there are also implications for local bodies and the wider Māori leadership. There are particular challenges for Māori leaders whose work links them directly to whānau. Māori health leadership is in a position to contribute to positive whānau development not only by reinforcing services and programmes that will benefit Māori individuals, as they do at present, but also by identifying the whānau collective as a force for health and wellbeing. A whānau focus will shift attention from disease management to the attainment of wellness. It will complement the advancement of the health of individuals with the development of whānau capability to promote health in the widest sense; and it will endorse every intervention as an opportunity for reinvigorating whānau resolve to act as effective change agents for future generations.

Health leaders today can be future makers for tomorrow. But future making will require rising above the demands and problems of the moment and securing space, energy, and expertise for planning ahead, beyond three to five year cycles, and towards more distant horizons. As managers, governors, clinicians, and community representatives today's leaders can take the initiative to empower whānau. Empowerment will mean whānau are confident enough to resolve a crisis without misrepresenting tikanga Māori, or without fear of loss of control or responsibility. Empowerment will also mean whānau ownership of online health records that can be used for consultations with health providers as well as for e-consultations with health experts in other centres or in other countries. Health leaders today have the opportunity to build online health sites, accessible to whānau and able to achieve similar levels of Māori uptake as Facebook, Bebo, YouTube and other social networks.

A whānau-at-the-centre policy also requires a radical rethink of the sectorisation of whānau life. Bridging the divide between health, social welfare, education, housing, sport and recreation, and labour, is a major challenge but an essential prerequisite for consolidating whānau health and wellbeing. To that end, health leaders have a significant part to play in redesigning the ways services are provided and the best means of ensuring that the specific expertise of each sector can be accessed so that they empower rather than fragment whānau. Simply adding a whānau dimension to services that are primarily designed for individuals will not provide the level of skill to address whānau capacity for the future. In this respect there is a serious lack of educational and professional training programmes that prepare practitioners to support whānau in, for example, the development of whānau kawa. While the application of kawa to marae encounters is well accepted, the use of kawa to guide day-to-day living for whanau has yet to be widely practised. Kawa has the potential to add a cultural dimension to family life and to provide a template for the transfer of knowledge and values between generations.

In brief, the challenges for the Māori health leaders and leaders in other social policy areas are to shift from disease and problem-based orientations to a focus on wellness, to develop programmes that will enable whānau to take ownership of their health and wellbeing, to bridge the divide between economic and social policies, and between primary and secondary health care, and to transform the delivery of services to whānau into empowerment of whānau so they can exercise their roles as carriers of culture and values, models for lifestyle, gateways to communities, guardians of the environment, and generators of wealth.

Māori health in the future will be shaped by multiple complex factors. Epidemics emanating from distant shores, global crises affecting the world's economy, and climate change that will threaten the survival of the planet will also threaten whānau wellbeing. Other forces will arise closer to home, from national policies, from the ways health and social services are delivered, from the vision of Māori leadership, and from the capacity of whānau to create an environment where health can prevail.

The next transformation

Transformations in Māori health over the past twenty-five years have been largely associated with workforce development, increased opportunities for Māori providers, iwi delivery systems, Māori models of practice, and increased capability in governance and management. Health, social services, corrections, services for youth, and educational programmes have been significantly reformed so that Māori are included within each sector. The results, as already noted, have more than justified the approach. Over the next twenty-five years, however, the current emphases should be balanced by approaches that lead more directly to the empowerment of whānau – a whānau-centred approach.

A strong and well qualified Māori health workforce is not in itself an endpoint, rather it is a means to an end. Māori provider development should be increasingly complemented by programmes that strengthen whānau capability. Whānau access to information, tools, and skills will be crucial for the intergenerational transmission of culture and values. Empowered whānau will manage and monitor their own health records and will expect health and social workers to provide electronic summaries of all interventions as well as adding useful comment about the significance of health bulletins posted on the web.

Over time the utilisation of Māori models of practice in health and social services will be mirrored by models of kawa that enhance the ways in which whānau promote and sustain the health of their people. While Māori perspectives have been valuable for service practitioners, models of whānau interaction, based on tikanga Māori, also need to be developed. Modelling healthy lifestyles so that health risks are minimised, can only be achieved if the whānau leadership is motivated, well informed and sufficiently aware of tikanga Māori to know how and when to implement a whānau kawa. A whānau kawa constructed to protect against risks to health and wellbeing, including risks that arise outside the whānau as well as risks that emerge from within, will be an important tool for maintaining healthy lifestyles.

Increasingly New Zealand society will become complex and highly competitive. Māori leaders will need to be comfortable in three spheres – the Māori world, New Zealand society, and global networks – and to know where future opportunities will lie in all of them. Whānau will depend on their leaders to ensure access to the economy, to sport and recreation, to political voice, to te reo Māori and Māori knowledge, and to the delivery of information that will empower them as champions for health.

On the basis of threats to health and wellbeing that will come from a range of sources, and building on the gains made over the past twenty-five years, goals for 2020 can be formulated. The Matariki 2020 goals for health expect that Māori will live in a healthy environment, participate fully in te ao Māori, enjoy balanced lifestyles, benefit from quality education, the wise use of technology and expert opinion, and belong to empowered whānau who are champions for health and wellbeing. While government, iwi, agencies and Māori leaders will contribute to the attainment of those goals, whānau will be the most sustainable and effective agents for change.

As guardians of the landscape, kaitiaki, whānau will face the considerable challenges of global warming. They will be expected to practice wise stewardship and to empower future generations with a Māori environmental ethic that recognises the interdependence of people, the land, sea, rivers and air. Whānau will be the conduit for the intergenerational transmission of culture, knowledge, values, and healthy lifestyles. They will also be the major entry points to communities as well as serving as gateways to te ao Māori. And they will have the potential to build enough social, cultural and economic capital to enable self-sufficiency and freedoms that might not otherwise be possible.

A priority will be to ensure that whānau are visible at the centre of government, iwi and community policies for Māori health, education, environmental management, social development and economic growth.

In brief, the best prospects for Māori health and wellbeing in the future will lie with whānau.

CHAPTER 25

Pae Mana: Waitangi and the Evolving State

'Pae Mana: Waitangi and the Evolving State', the third of the three 'Paerangi Lectures', was delivered at Massey University, Wellington, 14 July, 2009.

The Paerangi Lectures

'Pae Mana: Waitangi and the Evolving State' is the third and last of the 'Paerangi Lectures'. It considers the position of Māori beyond 2020 and has a particular emphasis on the relevance and applicability of the Treaty of Waitangi to the future. Although economic, political and global uncertainties make it difficult to predict the years ahead, it is highly probable that Māori will be a proportionately stronger force within New Zealand, and at the same time will be exposed to greater internal competitiveness as well as competition from neighbouring states and economies. The status of the Treaty, and perhaps of greater relevance, the status of Māori, will become part of a wide public debate, linked to New Zealand's own status as a democracy in the South Pacific with strong trade and diplomatic relationships with Asian economies.

In the first lecture, 'Pae Matatū: Sustaining the Māori Estate', the rapid growth of the Māori asset base was seen as a positive development but one that would demand expert governance and management to ensure that future generations could enjoy the full benefits of their entitlements. Concerns about the transfer of assets from one generation to another were raised and the importance of 'future proofing' as a way of protecting the interests of future generations was explored. The major conclusion, however, was that the Māori estate will grow in both size and diversity; it will include customary resources such as land; tradable assets including real estate and shares in international companies; as well as cultural heritage typified by marae and te reo Māori.

The second lecture 'Pae Ora: Māori Health Horizons', considered the broad approaches to Māori health over the past two decades and the resulting gains. But it was primarily positioned in the future and contemplated the consequences of global, local, environmental, and family determinants on Māori health. The impacts of technological innovation, demographic transitions, unexpected catastrophes and epidemics, indigenous aspirations and strengthened Māori capability were canvassed and a number of directional shifts were proposed so that the gains made in recent decades could be extended into the future. It posited that environmental sustainability, quality social relationships, balanced lifestyles, wise leadership, and access to knowledge and technology would be important drivers of health and wellbeing and, as agents for the promotion of health, whānau could make the most significant difference to Māori health and wellbeing.

Meanwhile the third lecture explores consequences for Māori of a nation that will be more populous, more diverse and more globally connected. 'Pae Mana' will address questions about the significance of the Treaty of Waitangi as a platform for forward development rather than as a vehicle for redress, and it will scope the implications for Māori if New Zealand were to become a republic.

The lecture has three main conclusions. First, the constitutional position of Māori in the future will depend as much on global forces as domestic agreements in Aotearoa. Second, the promise of the Treaty will not be realised by a schedule of property rights or legislative amendments, but by the ways in which Māori and the Crown can jointly advance New Zealand's economy and standards of living. Third, as New Zealand's ties with the northern hemisphere weaken while its interests in Asia and the Pacific expand, notions of sovereignty will take on new meanings. The relationship of Māori with the Crown may not be the most important articulation of the constitutional position of Māori; instead alliances with other parties in New Zealand and beyond New Zealand may confer a significant level of dominion that does not depend solely on the Crown for validation.

1840 and future opportunities

The stated intention of the British Crown was to use the Treaty of Waitangi to pave the way for annexation, the institution of British laws, and large-scale immigration from Britain without causing undue harm to Māori. Tribes were to benefit as much as the Crown. In that respect the Treaty was an international agreement that offered the prospect of fresh opportunities for both parties. Lord Normanby's 'Instructions'[1] had made it clear that colonisation in the past had wreaked havoc on indigenous peoples. Here was a chance to act with new honour by ensuring that indigenous rights would be respected, especially property rights, and individual Māori would profit from British understandings of citizenship.

The principled approach inherent in the Treaty of Waitangi marked a shift in the Crown's earlier colonisation policies which had scant regard for native populations. However, the noble sentiment may also have been prompted by the earlier recognition of Māori sovereignty when the Declaration of Independence was endorsed by the British Parliament. Having acknowledged tribal leaders as the rightful sovereigns of Aotearoa in 1835, by 1840 Britain was faced with the challenge of acquiring sovereignty. The Treaty provided the necessary instrument of annexation. Regardless, it seemed that the Treaty would provide Māori and the Crown with joint resolve to embark on a journey that would take both into new territory.

It is unlikely that either iwi or the settlers had any clear idea how their futures might be about to change. The settlers drew on their experiences in Britain, though soon discovered that neither agriculture nor commerce could be conducted in exactly the same way as they had practised at home. In order to flourish, adaptation to a different environment was necessary. Iwi also found that while the shift to a cash economy would substantially disrupt their ways of life, engagement with settlers would bring new technologies, education, and opportunities for trade on a larger scale than would have been possible in earlier years.

A sense of urgency must have been keenly felt by Māori leaders as wave after wave of settlers arrived to take up land interests. Their concerns about the way the future was unfolding were soon galvanised into collective action. In 1856, at Pūkawa on Lake Taupō, tribal leaders agreed on a two-part plan to curtail increasing encroachment and land alienation. The first part of the plan was to anoint a king as a symbol of collective Māori authority. The second part was to promote tribal accord. A united front would offer more effective opposition to land sales and avoid the 'divide and rule' tactics used by land purchasing agents. The Pūkawa resolution was to set aside long standing Māori political divisions in favour of greater collective bargaining power with the colonial government and within the framework of the Treaty of Waitangi.

New Zealand was on the verge of a double transformation: a Māori nation within a nation was about to be born while pastoral farming was about to manifestly change the landscape. In the event, for reasons which are too complex for discussion in this paper, neither transformation panned out as well as expected. The important point, however, is not that that Māori ambitions were aborted or that bargaining power was to prove less effective than the rule of might, but that iwi had recognised both opportunity and threat in the new environment. They had embarked on a process of futures planning to strengthen their position and establish a secure foothold for future generations. If the Treaty of Waitangi had been an instrument of annexation, then it was also to be a pathway to the future.

Beyond settlements

However, after a promising start, the Treaty was soon to become a marker of the past rather than a signpost to the future. Not only was the parchment itself allowed to fall into tatters, but the promise of a joint Māori–Crown approach to transformation gave way to a one-sided declaration of colonial rule. The establishment of a Māori electorate and four Māori seats in Parliament in 1867 was overshadowed a decade later by Justice Prendergast in a Supreme Court decision that declared the Treaty to be 'a simple nullity'; it could be virtually disregarded.[2] By the mid-1950s the Treaty of Waitangi was being recognised as a significant but essentially historic document largely irrelevant to modern times.

Māori, however, saw it differently. As land holdings dwindled and Māori decision making became marginalised, there was growing disquiet and a groundswell of indignation. Recourse to the courts had failed to reverse the Prendergast decision and by the 1970s a new generation was ready to take to the streets to protest land loss, loss of language, and loss of authority. The 1975 Māori Land March startled most non-Māori New Zealanders who had little idea how deeply embedded the sense of injustice was. In the same year, and largely due to the efforts of Matiu Rata, the Waitangi Tribunal was established.

In the Tribunal's first major publication, the 1983 *Motunui Report,* the relevance of the Treaty to contemporary New Zealand was articulated in terms that made sense to Māori, to jurists, and to local communities. Well before the emergence of a green philosophy, or warnings about global climate change, the Tribunal had highlighted the impact of industrial development on the environment, in particular on the Waitara River and the Taranaki reefs. A charge of a Treaty of Waitangi breach was levelled at the government and, importantly, echoed by a wide section of the community. The Tribunal's findings could not be ignored with the same indifference that Prendergast had used to dismiss the Treaty itself. Claims against the Crown for historic breaches of the principles of the Treaty dating back to 1840 followed, slowly at first and then by the score. Māori energies were now spent delving into government policies and practices in the nineteenth century.

While the claims process was eventually to bring a sense of closure if not justice for many iwi, it was also to locate the Treaty debate in the past. A focus on the settlement of claims has tended to mask the fact that the whole purpose of the Treaty was to plan ahead. Instead, for many New Zealanders, the Treaty has become synonymous with past grievances and the corollary is that once settlements are concluded then the Treaty will have exhausted itself. But while an investigation into historic breaches drew on the principles of the Treaty, the claims process has been more closely attuned to the delivery of justice rather than the ratification of the Treaty.

Although many settlements have yet to be concluded, most of the major historic claims have been resolved, including the Central North Island 'Tree Lords' claim lodged by eight iwi. A new age is dawning: it is a post-settlement era where Māori relationships with the Crown and with each other will not be premised on past injustices but on future development. The question now is whether Treaty experiences over the past two or more decades will provide a basis for a new type of relationship between Māori and the Crown. Working together to construct an agenda for New Zealand's future will be a major Treaty task that will require new approaches both from iwi and the Crown. Adversarial bargaining, a hallmark of direct negotiations for Treaty claims, will not be a productive way of deciding how best to reduce carbon emissions, or address worldwide food shortages, or develop a strategy for offshore investments, or ensure that all children have the best possible educational outcomes or whether New Zealand should become a republic or not. Adversarial bargaining perpetuates a colonial relationship, winners and losers, and discussions based on rights and wrongs. Nor will a reliance on party-political coalitions provide a consistent Treaty-based mechanism for ensuring Māori inclusion in strategic decision making. Though useful mechanisms for dealing with today, political timeframes – three years or so – are too short for grounding longer term plans. Moreover they rely heavily on deals made to satisfy other agendas. And having discussions only when a crisis occurs will do nothing to establish a clear plan for the future. They will inevitably lead to solutions that are short-lived and pragmatic rather than sustainable and strategic. Other relationship models should be entertained, including some aspects of the model constructed at Pūkawa in 1856 when iwi met to consider how best to face an uncertain future. Missing from Pūkawa, however, was an avenue for dialogue with the Crown. A post-settlement model might well contain elements of Pūkawa, especially the prospect of a collective Māori voice, as well as aspects of direct negotiation with opportunity for ongoing Māori–Crown dialogue, no longer about past injustices but about future possibilities.

This new type of relationship presupposes a shift away from claimant groups – their concerns will already have been resolved – towards groups that reflect wider Māori interests, sometimes iwi, sometimes sectoral. The question then will be how best Māori should be represented in future oriented discussions with the Crown. The vision of Kotahitanga, unity, first articulated at Pūkawa, has yet to be implemented in a sustainable way.

The bigger question, however, might not actually be about the nature of the relationship between Māori and the Crown in a post-settlement environment, but whether a relationship with the Crown will be the most relevant one for Māori.

New Zealand in a spinning globe

Considerations of future Māori standing in Aotearoa cannot ignore a fast changing world and the dynamic interactions that will impact on New Zealand and on Māori. Although technological and scientific change and the growing complexities of global living create a climate of unpredictability, some forecasts can nonetheless be made with a degree of certainty. New Zealand's future, for example, will be significantly shaped by a changing demography. The whole population will age; by 2026 the median age will be forty-one years compared to thirty-six years in 2006. In addition within the total population there will be significant differences in age structures between ethnic groups. The median age of the European population in 2006 was oldest at thirty-nine years while for Māori it was significantly younger, at twenty-three years. By 2021, the European median age will have increased to forty-four years, but Māori will still be a relatively youthful population with a median age of twenty-six years. The lag for Māori reflects higher fertility rates, a younger population base, and lower life expectancy.

Apart from an ageing population the other significant demographic transition will be an increase in New Zealand's ethnic diversity. English, Scottish, Welsh, Irish, and Dutch backgrounds will be joined by larger numbers of Chinese, Indian, Korean, Malay, Philippine, Samoan, Tongan, Fijian, Rarotongan, Kiribati, and Niue Islander settlers, as well as comings and goings from Australia. The diversity will not only add to the country's skill mix but will bring new understandings of society, democracy, commerce and sovereignty. Importantly, New Zealand's colonial attachment to Europe and the northern hemisphere will give way to a southern hemisphere identity and greater pride in being part of the Asian Pacific region. Just as early settlers from Europe in the nineteenth century showed little regard for Māori systems of governance, new settlers in the twenty-first century will not necessarily carry a sense of loyalty to the monarchy or even to the Westminster system.

Global challenges

New Zealand's future, however, will also reflect worldwide trends. The USA economic recession, for example, has had sufficient impact in the southern hemisphere to seriously pressure New Zealand industries, generate new levels of unemployment, and freeze real estate prices. Moreover, the consequences of the recession will not necessarily be short term; the immediate crisis may pass in the short term but the consequences may linger for a decade or more.

Even more lasting, however, will be the perpetuation of inequalities between rich nations and poor nations. Already over 130 million people live in extreme poverty and as a result many children will never reach adulthood. A rapidly growing world population predicted to increase from 6.4 billion now to nine billion by 2050, coupled with a worldwide food shortage will greatly exacerbate the extent of their plight. Though distant from the major continents of the world, New Zealand is no longer in a position to ignore the consequences of global inequalities. Coping with the health effects of too much food, a major health challenge in developed countries, is in sharp contrast to the greater harm that will come to children who grow up with insufficient food to sustain life and healthy development. It is a global crisis, impacting directly on near neighbours in the Pacific; and it is a problem that will of necessity involve New Zealand.

In addition to global inequalities and widespread malnutrition, a further challenge will come from the effects of global warming and climate change. Already there is clear evidence that without worldwide agreements to reduce carbon emissions and re-vegetate denuded landscapes the planet will be seriously compromised and so will humanity. Not only will previously controlled diseases such as malaria and tuberculosis reappear but global changes in climate will result in cataclysmic events including drought, cyclones, gales and floods leading to serious loss of life and property. The age of oil will come to an end and other forms of energy will need to be harnessed. Natural resources such as fresh water will become scarce commodities and their ownership will be a source of tension between iwi, farmers, commercial interests, local authorities and government, all vying for control. As a developed nation, New Zealand contributes disproportionately to global warming, but even greater impacts will come from those parts of the world where population densities are high. In any event, unless there is collective agreement on strategies to reduce carbon emissions and attain carbon neutrality, the welfare, if not the existence of generations yet to come will be threatened and much of the planet will be destroyed in the process.

A fourth challenge has a double edge. Global colonisation, a process already in train, brings with it entry to worldwide markets, international educational prospects, access to unprecedented volumes of knowledge and information, and exposure to the world's music, art and literature. The opportunities for Māori at home and abroad will be unlimited, though not without compromise. Increased globalisation may mean that te ao Māori is submerged by other customs and in the process a distinctive way of life may be transformed into a bland adaptation of a global norm. There is a risk that tikanga, kawa, te reo Māori and those other markers that characterise Māori in modern times will be lost to whatever global fashion holds dominance in the world at any particular time.

Māori in a reconfigured world

It may not be immediately obvious how the impact of population changes within New Zealand and the more threatening global transitions will affect Māori standing in Aotearoa New Zealand or alter the promise of the Treaty of Waitangi. But it would be short-sighted to assume that New Zealand will be sufficiently isolated from the rest of the world to have immunity from those wider transitions.

The potential impact of national and international events on Māori can be illustrated through a set of three scenarios. Scenario development is a way of exploring the future. Scenarios can be constructed on the basis of already known existing trends such as demographic trends, previous patterns of development such as nineteenth century colonisation, horizon scanning to detect, for example, the emergence of new technologies, and vigorous imagining.

Scenario 1: The Republic of New Zealand (RNZ)

The first scenario is about New Zealand's constitutional future. By 2029 New Zealand was ready to declare itself a republic, still part of the Commonwealth but with a new head of state. The possibility had been canvassed at a national conference in 2000 but no firm conclusions had been reached and because it all seemed too hard, the possibility was shelved. But in the wake of developments in the European Union and the consequent impositions placed on royalty in Scandinavia as well as Great Britain, constitutional monarchies had become increasingly out of favour. In addition the large number of New Zealanders of Asian and South American descent had little or no interest in perpetuating a constitutional framework that emanated from the northern hemisphere.

In the event, transitioning towards a republic had been surprisingly uneventful except for three questions. First, should the president of the new republic be appointed or elected? Second, should there be a written constitution or simply a continuation of the nation's reliance on a series of conventions, supported by pragmatic innovation as required? Third, with a final exodus from a colonial past, what would be the status of the Treaty of Waitangi?

Of the three questions the third proved to be the least problematic. Despite a rearguard concern that the Treaty was an instrument of division and should be ignored, most Kiwis, including Pacific and Asian communities, thought that the rights of indigenous peoples should be maintained and the Treaty seemed to be the least difficult way of doing that. Moreover, the Treasury had long since reached the conclusion that New Zealand's distinctiveness was a function of a vibrant Māori economy and retaining the Treaty not only affirmed indigenous interests but also affirmed the brand necessary for New Zealand to be competitive in a global economy.

Once agreement had been reached that the benefits of a written constitution far outweighed the dangers of having no constitution at all, the Treaty of Waitangi was integrated into the constitution as an overriding statement about New Zealand's indigenous peoples and their resources. For the first time the Treaty now had explicit recognition as an entrenched constitutional element rather than existing solely as a part of a fuzzy national conscience. By 2035 the Republic of New Zealand had become a champion for social cohesion and indigenous participation as indigenous people.

Scenario 2: The Confederation of the States of Australasia (CSA)

In the second scenario, by 2035 New Zealand has become integrated into Australia and is part of the Confederation of the States of Australasia. Two factors had contributed to the formation of the Confederation. First, concerns about global warming and the high expenditure of carbon credits on long distance flying meant that northern hemisphere markets, including tourists, were less lucrative. Second, strong Asian economies were competing with both Australia and New Zealand and effectively playing one off against the other. Largely in response to the new economic circumstances evident by 2025, New Zealand, Australia and some small Pacific nations agreed to explore the possibility of a new set of alliances with a single currency, a single passport and a single government (but with some devolved authority for the previous nation states).

New Zealand was generally enthusiastic about the proposition but a stumbling block had been Crown commitments to the Treaty of Waitangi. Australia was reluctant to see any reference to indigenous peoples incorporated into the new arrangements for fear that it would unsettle the now 'settled' Aboriginal population. Despite having agreed to the 2006 Declaration of the Rights of Indigenous Peoples, Australian states had effectively 'bought out' aboriginal demands through a system of compensatory payments that expired in 2020. Any obligations had been met. New Zealand eventually complied with the majority view and reluctantly accepted that the Treaty status would be confined to cultural matters and would not impose obligations on the federal government. A constitutional encumbrance had been removed and in the process the Treaty had been consigned to history. By 2035 the State of New Zealand had taken its place as one of ten states making up the Confederation.

Scenario 3: Māori Integrated Economies Inc (MIE)

In contrast to scenario 2, scenario 3 expects that Māori will be leaders in worldwide indigenous networks. One network, Global Indigenous Systems (GIS) was established in 2025 largely as an initiative of the Indigenous People's Forum at the United Nations. The global economic recession which started in 2008 and continued through to 2011 had unfortunate longer lasting repercussions for indigenous peoples in many countries. Further, although many nations had signed up to the Declaration on the Rights of Indigenous Peoples in 2006, few had encouraged indigenous economic development. The GIS goal was to advance indigenous economies through worldwide indigenous collaboration.

Meanwhile by 2020 it had become clear in New Zealand that Māori investments following Treaty settlements had led to new wealth, experience in economic development, and expertise in financial governance and management. The impact of the economic recession had not been as severe as it had been for First Nations, Australian Aborigines, Saami people, Native Americans or Native Hawaiians. Nonetheless Māori were keen to maximise economic returns and build economies of scale. As a result Māori Integrated Economies Inc was established in 2022. It represented an amalgam of Sealords, Treelords, Māori Providers Ltd, and the Ahuwhenua Trust – a consortium of Māori Land incorporations. MIE had provided a model for integrating economic and social capital and by bringing together a mix of resources had become a major player in the New Zealand economy and a leader in indigenous economic development. When GIS was established in 2025, MIE was invited to provide overall leadership and to extend their model across the GIS networks. By then, Māori had become world leaders in integrated solutions and MIE was the dominant economic force in New Zealand.

Tino rangatiratanga

The three scenarios are all possible though clearly not all would be equally popular. Scenario 2 (the Confederation of the States of Australasia) would probably have least appeal to Māori while both scenario 1 (the Republic of New Zealand) and scenario 3 (Māori Integrated Economies Inc) would be more attractive options. However, the intention for sharing these scenarios was not to enter into a debate about which of the three would be more probable or even more desirable but to illustrate how the position of Māori in Aotearoa in the future cannot be contemplated without considering the global context and the inevitability of significant economic and political change.

Importantly, it cannot be assumed that current Māori perceptions of constitutional rights will necessarily apply in the future. Take, for example, the Treaty of Waitangi. While the Treaty has been both an enabling and a disabling instrument, it may also have inadvertently narrowed Māori horizons. The Treaty of Waitangi was essentially an understanding about the relationship of Māori and the Crown. Under the Treaty, sovereignty, or at least the right to govern, was exchanged for guarantees about property and citizenship. The Treaty gave some protections but also positioned Māori alongside the Crown. In a sense Māori had been captured by the state at the expense of other potentially more profitable relationships. There is no good reason why the Treaty should be the single most important defining statement about the position of Māori in history, in Aotearoa, or, for that matter, in the world.

Debates about the relationship between Māori and the Crown, which have occupied great legal and academic minds – both Māori and Pākehā – have tended to argue Māori political legitimacy against the criterion of sovereignty, a concept that is culturally constrained, and likely to be increasingly modified. Not only will notions of sovereignty be subject to the permeation of global philosophies and global greed, as evidenced by multinational companies, but the sovereign boundaries between states will become blurred as digital technologies shrink distance, and the mix between public and private interests become increasingly intertwined.

For more than two decades, in an attempt to draw a distinction between the sovereign powers of the state on the one hand, and Māori autonomy on the other, tino rangatiratanga has been used as an articulation of Māori authority. However, it is unlikely that the New Zealand state as it currently exists will remain unchanged over the next three to five decades or that the concept of sovereignty inherent in the Treaty when it was signed in 1840 will remain fixed in time. In that respect it could be unwise for Māori to measure tino rangatiratanga solely against the parameters of the Crown's sovereignty, whatever meaning sovereignty might have in the future.

In addition, in a post-settlement environment, it is likely that Māori engagement with the Crown will alter in both purpose and intensity. That does not mean there will be no relationship with government but a two-directional change in the nature of the relationship can be expected. First, Māori involvement with the Crown will be increasingly focused on New Zealand's agenda for the future, rather than on compensation for the past. Recent discussions between the Crown and the Iwi Leadership Forum in relationship to water management provide an example of a new type of relationship. Second, Māori will predictably choose to spend more time and energy exploring relationships with the private sector and seeking investment opportunities with overseas companies, and less time engaging with the Crown. In the future, tino rangatiratanga may not be best measured by concessions won from the government but on the strength of the Māori economy and the number of influential partners outside government.

A global role for Māori can also be identified, even in 2009. Two aspects of scenario 3 are not improbable. Already Māori are highly regarded among other indigenous peoples for their leadership in language revitalisation, innovative health care, reformed education at preschool and tertiary levels, and iwi enterprise. Extending the leadership to embrace economic growth investment strategies, and wise use of resources is within reach. There are already early indications that more realistic economies of scale will be achievable between Māori providers and between iwi. If all Māori fishing interests, forestry interests, land interests, and provider interests were linked to the same company or incorporation, without losing individual identity, Māori would be in an unassailable economic position, both in New Zealand and in wider indigenous networks.

The point is that the practice of measuring tino rangatiratanga against the single yardstick of sovereignty may soon be outdated. Instead two other measures have the potential to be much more defining in the future: the extent to which Māori have economic influence within New Zealand, and the degree to which Māori play leadership roles in indigenous networks across the globe. These measures place less emphasis on jurisprudential arguments, the differences between law and lore, and the assumption that Māori as indigenous New Zealanders can be defined by somewhat outdated legal constructs. Rather than authenticating the Māori position in law, Māori authority is a product of economic might and acknowledgement by peers. Ironically, that position may not in fact be too far removed from the situation in 1840 when Britain became aware of Māori economic strength and the wealth of New Zealand, and recognised Māori as rightful proprietors of the country. Indeed they were the very reasons for the Treaty of Waitangi.

The Paerangi Lectures

The three 'Paerangi Lectures' have all attempted to project Māori interests into the future, beyond 2020 and towards 2035. They have explored the impacts of various scenarios on Māori and have identified a range of pathways that could be relevant in the decades ahead. Building on gains made over the past twenty-five years, retaining a Māori world view, being ready to shift direction, and taking on the role of future maker rather than future taker have been seen as important ways of positioning Māori to take advantage of the future rather than being overwhelmed by its complexities.

There are three major conclusions. First, arising from the first lecture, it is clear that the Māori estate will grow. It will expand in volume and diversity enabling Māori to remain grounded in Aotearoa but with new freedoms to explore other domains. The Māori estate will be a composite of lands, waterways, fisheries, forests, marae, whakāiro, waiata and hakā; and it will grow to include greater shares in third and fourth generation radio frequency networks, a range of commercial enterprises, and access to technologies that will add value to customary resources and cultural heritage. The challenge will be to future proof the estate so that future generations can benefit and add their own contributions.

The second lecture explored the impacts of future demographic, technological, economic and global transformations on Māori health and wellbeing. Five outcome goals (the Matariki 2020 goals) were identified: to live in a healthy environment, participate fully in te ao Māori, enjoy balanced lifestyles, benefit from quality education, the wise use of technology and expert opinion, and belong to empowered whānau who are champions for health and wellbeing. While government, iwi, agencies and Māori leaders will contribute to the attainment of those goals, the conclusion was that whānau will be the most sustainable and effective agents for change.

This lecture, 'Pae Mana: Waitangi and the Evolving State', has been about the constitutional and economic position of Māori in the future. It has considered the Treaty of Waitangi, its significance to the past and to the future, and has concluded that the full impact of the Treaty relationship between Māori and the Crown will be the way in which both parties can work together to shape an agenda for the future.

Four goals about Māori standing in New Zealand and in the world can be distilled. The first goal is to establish a working relationship with the Crown in order to pursue an agenda that will benefit future generations of New Zealanders. The second is to establish closer working relationships between iwi, between Māori sectoral interests, and between Māori commercial entities in order to consolidate Māori interests, achieve economies of scale, exercise economic strength within New Zealand, and contribute to the wellbeing of Māori and wider society. The third goal will be to engage with the private sector in New Zealand, building on the gains already made and forging new pathways that will add to the Māori economy and to the national wealth. A fourth goal will be to play a significantly expanded role within global indigenous networks especially in the Pacific so that expertise can be shared, joint ventures established and inequalities overcome. To meet those goals it may be opportune to enter into a new set of treaties geared to the twenty-first rather than the nineteenth century.

Finally, the standing of Māori in Aotearoa New Zealand will not be defined solely or even mainly by notions of legal sovereignty but by the range, strength and impact of national, global and iwi alliances. Partnerships with the Crown, with the private sector, between iwi, with overseas commercial interests, and with indigenous peoples across the globe will be the hallmarks of Māori in the future.

Endnotes

Introduction

1 'Just as a myriad of stars grace the heavens, so the people of Rangitāne inhabit the land'. A Rangitāne proverb.
2 The Southern Cross.
3 Mason Durie, *Ngā Kāhui Pou: Launching Māori Futures*. Wellington: Huia Publishers, 2003.
4 Pacific Rim Indigenous Doctors' Congress.

Chapter 1 – Mental Health Promotion in a Global Village

1 Fifth World Conference on the Promotion of Mental Health and the Prevention of Mental and Behavioral Disorders, The Melbourne Declaration. Melbourne: World Federation for Mental Health, Clifford Beers Foundation, The Carter Centre, Victoria Health, 2008.
2 Richard Skolnik, *Essentials of Global Health*. Washington DC: The George Washington University, 2008.
3 Minister of Health, *Te Tāhuhu – Improving Mental Health 2005–2015: The Second New Zealand Mental Health and Addiction Plan*. Wellington: Ministry of Health, 2005.
4 Wikipedia, *2010 Pakistan Floods*. http://en.wikipedia.org/wiki/2010_Pakistan_floods, accessed 28 February 2011.
5 United Nations, *Human Development Report 2007/2008. Fighting climate change: Human solidarity in a divided world*. New York: United Nations Development Programme, 2007. http://hdr.undp.org/en/media/HDR_20072008_EN_Complete.pdf., retrieved 9 February 2011.
6 World Health Organisation, *Protecting Health from Climate Change. World Health Day 2008*. Geneva: World Health Organisation, 2008. http://www.who.int/world-health-day/toolkit/report_web.pdf., accessed 9 February 2011.
7 Jeffrey Sachs, *Common Wealth: Economics for a Crowded Planet*. Australia: Penguin Group, 2008, pp. 166-74.
8 Statistics New Zealand, *Subnational Population Projections: 2006 (base) – 2031*. Wellington: Department of Statistics, 2007.

9 J. Reading, *The Crisis of Chronic Disease among Aboriginal Peoples: A Challenge for Public Health, Population Health and Social Policy*. British Columbia: Centre for Aboriginal Health Research, University of Victoria, 2009, pp. 75-6.

10 International Food Policy Research Institute, *2010 Global Hunger Index, The Challenge of Hunger: Focus on the Crisis of Child Undernutrition*. Bonn, Washington DC, Dublin: International Food Policy Research Institute, Concern Worldwide and Welthungerhilfe, 2010. http://bit.ly/9vdYv2., retrieved 9 February 2011.

11 Permanent Forum on Indigenous Issues: 'Territories, Land, and Natural Resources', New York: United Nations Economic and Social Council HR/4918, 2007. Information on meeting on www.un.org/News/Press/docs/2007/hr4918. doc.htm., retrieved 9 February 2011.

12 Globalization Knowledge Network, *Towards Health-Equitable Globalisation: Rights, Regulation and Redistribution. Final Report to the Commission on Social Determinants of Health*. Ottawa: Institute of Population Health, University of Ottawa, 2007, p. 9.

13 Clive Nettleton, Dora A. Napolitano, Carolyn Stephens, *An Overview of Current Knowledge of the Social Determinants of Indigenous Health, a Working Paper*. Geneva: Commission on Social Determinants of Health, World Health Organisation, 2007, p. 114.

14 S. Prakash, 'Nurturing traditional knowledge systems for development', *IK Notes No. 61*. Washington DC: The World Bank, 2003, pp. 1-4.

15 For example the collaboration between CISCO and NASA on the 'planetary skin' project (see www.theenergyroadmap.com/futureblogger/show/1699-cisco-partners-with-nasa-on-planetary-skin-project-previews-massive-web-collaboration-platform, retrieved 9 February 2009).

16 Secondary Futures, *The Place of Technology*. Wellington: Secondary Futures, 2008.

17 The World Bank, Expanding Opportunities and Building Competencies for Young People A New Agenda for Secondary Education. Washington DC: The World Bank, 2005, pp. 50-62.

18 Leona Okakok, 'Serving the Purpose of Education', in M. Villegas, S. R. Neugebauer, K. R. Venegas (eds.), *Indigenous Knowledge and Education Sites of Struggle, Strength, and Survivance*. Cambridge: Harvard Educational Review, 2008, pp. 268-86.

19 Y. Neria, S. Galea, F. H. Norris (eds.), *Mental Health and Disasters*. Cambridge: Cambridge University Press, 2009.

20 Commission on Social Determinants of Health, *Closing the gap in a generation: Health equity through action on the social determinants of health*. Geneva: World Health Organisation, 2008, p. 2.

21 ibid., pp. 16-21.

22 Ministry of Health, *Te Rau Hinengaro: The New Zealand Mental Health Survey*. Wellington: Ministry of Health, 2008.

23 M. Durie, 'A Māori Perspective of Health', in *Social Science and Medicine*, 1985, 20: 5, 483-6.

24 Maui Solomon, 'The Wai 262 Claim: A Claim by Māori to Indigenous Flora and Fauna: Me ō rātou taonga katoa', in Michael Belgrave, Merata Kawharu, David

Williams (eds.), *Waitangi Revisited Perspectives on the Treaty of Waitangi*, Melbourne: Oxford University Press, 2005, pp. 217-21.

25   E. Duran, B. Duran, *Native American Postcolonial Psychology*, Albany, NY: State University of New York Press, 1995, pp. 14-5.

26   V. Deloria, *God is Red*, Colorado: Fulcrum Publishing 1994, pp. 172-3.

27   Ban Ki-moon, 'Protect, Promote Endangered Languages', Message for International Day of World's Indigenous People. New York: United Nations, Department of Public Information, 2008.

28   R. R. De Marco, 'The epidemiology of major depression: implications of occurrence, recurrence, and stress in a Canadian community sample', *Canadian Journal of Psychiatry*, 2000, 45(1), 67-74.

29   S. L. Syme, 'Social Determinants of Health: the Community as an Empowered Partner', *Preventing Chronic Disease – Public Health Research, Practice, and Policy*, 2004, 1(1), 1-5.

30   Reading, *The Crisis of Chronic Disease*, p. 147.

31   G. Hall, H. A. Patrinos, *Indigenous Peoples, Poverty and Human Development in Latin America*, New York: Palgrave MacMillan, 2006, pp. 240-241.

32   T. Alfred, 'Warrior Scholarship', in Mihesuah, D. A., & Wilson, A. C. (eds), *Indigenizing the Academy Transforming Scholarship and Empowering Communities*, Lincoln: University of Nebraska Press, 2004, pp. 88-99.

33   See chapter five.

34   M. Durie, R. Cooper, D. Grennell, S. Snively, N. Tuaine, *Whānau Ora: Report of the Taskforce on Whānau Centred Initiatives to Hon. Tariana Turia Minister for the Community and Voluntary Sector*. Wellington: Ministry of Social Development, 2010.

35   Te Puni Kōkiri, *Whānau Ora Providers*. Wellington: Ministry of Māori Development, 2010.

36   Te Puni Kōkiri, *Whānau Ora Fact Sheet*. Wellington: Ministry of Māori Development, 2010.

Chapter 2 – Indigenous Resilience: From Disease and Disadvantage to the Realisation of Potential

1   John Gorst, *The Maori King*. Hamilton, Auckland, London: Pauls Book Arcade & Oxford University Press, (1959 Reprint), 1864, pp. 54-5.

2   Ranginui Walker, 'Māori Sovereignty, Colonial and Post-colonial Discourses', in Paul Havemann (ed.) *Indigenous Peoples' Rights in Australia, Canada and New Zealand*. Auckland: Oxford University Press, 1999, pp. 113-6.

3   Pei te Hurunui, *King Potatau*. Auckland: Polynesian Society, 1959, pp. 190-6.

4   Ian Ring, Ngaire Brown, 'The health status of indigenous peoples and others', *British Medical Journal*. 2003, no. 7412: pp. 404-5.

5   Richard Horton, 'Indigenous peoples: time to act now for equity and health', *The Lancet*, 2006, 367:9524: pp. 1705-7.

6   Statistics New Zealand Te Tari Tatau, *New Zealand Census of Population and Dwellings 2001 Maori;* Wellington: Department of Statistics, 2002.

7   ibid., pp. 17-8.

8   Australian Bureau of Statistics, Canberra, 2001.

9   Ministry of Education, *Education Statistics of New Zealand for 2001*. Wellington: Ministry of Education, 2002.

10   Ministry of Education, *Education Statistics of New Zealand for 2002*. Wellington: Ministry of Education, 2004.

11   Health Workforce Advisory Committee, *The New Zealand Health Workforce A stocktake of issues and capacity*. Wellington: Health Workforce Advisory Committee, 2001, pp. 52-4.

12   Health Workforce Advisory Committee, *Fit for Purpose and for Practice. A Review of the Medical Workforce in New Zealand*. Health Workforce Advisory Committee, Wellington, 2005, pp. 127-31.

13   Australian Government, *National Report to Parliament on Indigenous Education and Training*. Canberra: 2005.

14   Deanne Minniecon, Kelvin Kong, *Healthy Futures Defining best practice in the recruitment and retention of indigenous medical students*. Australian Indigenous Doctors' Association, 2005.

15   Mason Durie, 'Indigeneity: Challenges for Indigenous Doctors', in Mason Durie *Ngā Kāhui Pou Launching Māori Futures*. Wellington: Huia Publishers, 2003, pp. 269-288.

16   ibid.

17   Steven Kuatei, 'Environmental Sacredness and Health in Palau', *Pacific Health Dialogue*, 2005, 12:1:92-5.

18   Mary F. Oneha, Sheila Beckham, 'Re-examining Community Based Research Protocols', *Pacific Health Dialogue*. 2004, 11:1:102-6.

19   Sitaleki Finau, 'Traditional Medicine in Tonga: a preamble to a Pacific model', *Traditional Healing and Pacificans*, Tongan Health Society, 2004, Vol 1, pp. 27-36.

20   A Māori economic summit convened by Hon. Koro Wetere.

21   New Zealand Institute of Economic Research, *Māori Economic Development Te Ōhanga Whanaketanga Māori*. Wellington: NZIER, Te Puni Kokiri, 2003.

22   Sunia Foliaki, Neil Pearce, 'Changing patterns of ill health for indigenous peoples', *British Medical Journal*. 2003, no. 7412; p. 406.

23   Anthony McMichael, Rosalie Woodruff, Simon Hales, 'Climate change and human health: present and future risks', *Lancet*, 2006, 367: 9513, 859-69.

24   Mark Oakley Browne, Elisabeth Wells, Kate Scott (eds.), *Te Rau Hinengaro: The New Zealand Mental Health Survey*. Wellington: Ministry of Health, 2006.

25   *New Zealand Herald*. 17 August 1874.

26   Te Puni Kōkiri, *Mana Tangata: Draft Declaration on the Rights of Indigenous Peoples 1993*. Wellington: Ministry of Māori Development, 1994.

27   K. S. Coates, P. G McHugh, *Living Relationships Kokiri Ngatahi The Treaty of Waitangi in the New Millenium*. Wellington: Victoria University Press, 1998, pp. 22-26.

28   New Zealand eventually signed the Declaration in 2010.

29   Te Ahukaramu Charles Royal, 'Indigenous Worldviews A Comparative Study, A report of research in progress', Ōtaki: Te Wānanga o Raukawa, 2002.

Chapter 3 – Indigenous Transformations in Contemporary Aotearoa

1   The New Zealand Institute became the Royal Society of New Zealand in 1933.

2   P. Walsh, 'The passing of the Maori: an inquiry into the principal causes of the decay of the race', *Transactions and Proceedings of the New Zealand Institute*. 1907, 40, 154-175.

3   Statistics New Zealand *QuickStats About Māori*. Wellington: Department of Statistics, 2007.

4   Statistics New Zealand, *New Zealand Now Māori*. Wellington: Department of Statistics, 2002, pp. 17-8.

5   M. Durie 'A Framework for Considering Māori Educational Advancement', *Ngā Kāhui Pou, Launching Māori Futures*. Wellington: Huia Publishers, 2003, pp. 197-211.

6   Waitangi Tribunal, *Report of the Waitangi Tribunal on the Te Reo Māori Claim (Wai 11)*. Wellington: Department of Justice, 1986.

7   Ministry of Education, *Ngā Haeata Mātauranga Annual Report on Māori Education & Direction for 2002/2003*. Wellington: Ministry of Education, 2004, pp. 17-9.

8   Ministry of Education, *Ngā Haeata Mātauranga Annual Report on Māori Education 2005*. Wellington: Ministry of Education, 2006.

9   New Zealand Qualifications Authority, *He Rautaki Māori me te Mahere Whakatinana The Māori Strategic and Implementation Plan for the New Zealand Qualifications Authority 2007–2012*. Wellington: New Zealand Qualifications Authority, 2007, p. 7.

10 Ministry of Social Development, *The Social Report Te Pūrongo Oranga Tangata 2007*. Wellington: Ministry of Social Development, 2007, pp. 38-9.

11 Ministry of Education, 2004, pp. 6-7.

12 Te Puni Kōkiri, *Māori Economic Development Te Ōhanga Whanaketanga Māori (Summary)*. Wellington: Ministry of Māori Development, 2003.

13 Te Puni Kōkiri, 2003.

14 New Zealand Institute of Economic Research, *Māori business and economic performance: A summary report*. Wellington: New Zealand Institute of Economic Research, 2005.

15 ibid.

16 Ministry of Social Development, 2007, pp. 80-1.

17 New Zealand Institute of Economic Research, 2005.

18 A. Hargreaves, D. Fink, 'The Seven Principles of Sustainable Leadership'. *Educational Leadership*, 2003, 61(7), 9-13.

19 http://www.iwgia.org/sw248.asp, accessed 28 February 2011.

20 New Zealand eventually signed the Declaration in 2010.

21 Ministry of Social Development, *The Social Report Te Purongo Oranga Tangata 2006*. Wellington: Ministry of Social Development, 2006, pp 24-5.

22 T. Blakely, M. Tobias, J. Atkinson, L-C Yeh, K. Huang, *Tracking Disparity: Trends in ethnic and socio-economic inequalities in mortality, 1981–2004*. Wellington: Ministry of Health, 2007.

23   Mason Durie, E. Fitzgerald, Te K. Kingi, S. McKinley, B. Stevenson, *Māori Specific Outcomes and Indicators, A Report Prepared For Te Puni Kōkiri The Ministry of Māori Development*. Palmerston North: School of Māori Studies, Massey University, 2002.

24   Hui Taumata, *Hui Taumata 2005 Summary Report*. Wellington, 2005.

25   C. James (ed.), *Building the Constitution*. Wellington: Institute of Policy Studies, Victoria University of Wellington, 2000.

26   Ken S. Coates, P. G. McHugh, *Living Relationships Kōkiri Ngātahi The Treaty of Waitangi in the New Millennium*. Wellington: Victoria University Press, 1998, pp. 170-9.

27   I. Anderson, S. Crengle, M. L. Kamaka, T. Chen, N. Palafox, L. Jackson-Pulver, 'Indigenous Health in Australia, New Zealand and the Pacific', *Lancet*, 2005, 367:9524, 1775-85.

28   Ministry of Social Development, 2007.

Chapter 4 – Global Transitions: Implications for a Regional Social Work Agenda

1   United Nations, 'Implementing Declaration on Indigenous Rights Will Bring "Historical Justice"', General Assembly, GA/SHC/3954, New York: Department of Public Information, News and Media Division, 2009.

Chapter 5 – Towards Social Cohesion: The Indigenisation of Higher Education in New Zealand

1   Ministry of Education, *Māori in Tertiary Education: a picture of the trends, a report prepared for the Hui Taumata 2005*. Wellington: Ministry of Education, 2005.

2   Fulbright New Century Scholars, 'Working Group Three: Higher Education and Social Cohesion – A Global Challenge', *Symposium on Higher Education, Statements and Recommendations*. Paris: UNESCO, 2006.

3   D. A. Mihesuah, 'Academic Gatekeepers', in Mihesuah, D. A., & Wilson, A. C. (eds), *Indigenizing the Academy: Transforming Scholarship and Empowering Communities*. Lincoln: University of Nebraska Press, 2004, pp. 31-47.

4   T. Alfred, 'Warrior Scholarship', in Mihesuah, D. A., & Wilson, A. C. (eds), *Indigenizing the Academy: Transforming Scholarship and Empowering Communities*. Lincoln: University of Nebraska Press, 2004, pp. 88-99.

5   Te Wānanga o Raukawa, *Profile 2008–2010 (Investment Plan)*. Ōtaki: Te Wānanga o Raukawa, 2008.

6   S. Ussher, *Participation in Tertiary Education A Birth Cohort Approach*. Wellington: Ministry of Education, 2007.

7   Ministry of Education, *Ngā Haeata Mātauranga Annual Report on Māori Education & Direction for 2002/2003*. Wellington: Ministry of Education, 2004 (a), pp. 40-1.

8   ibid., pp. 6-7.

9   Ministry of Education, *Ngā Haeata Mātauranga Annual Report on Māori Education*. Wellington: Ministry of Education, 2005(b), pp. 77-8.

10   Massey University, *KIA MAIA Key Initiatives for a Māori Academic Investment Agenda*. Palmerston North: Massey University, 2007.

11   Tertiary Education Commission, *Baseline Monitoring Report: Massey University*, Wellington: Tertiary Education Commission, 2007, pp. 12-5.

12   Ministry of Education, *Ngā Haeata Mātauranga Annual Report on Māori Education*. Wellington: Ministry of Education, 2007, pp. 128-9.

13   ibid.

14   Ministry of Education, *Profiles and Trends 2007 New Zealand's Tertiary Education Sector*. Wellington: Ministry of Education, 2008 (b), pp. 167-8.

15   Pro Vice-Chancellor (Māori), *Te Amorangi National Māori Academic Excellence Awards 2008*. Hamilton: University of Waikato, 2009.

16   Ministry of Education, *Tertiary Education Strategy 2002-2007 Baseline Monitoring Report*. Wellington, Ministry of Education, 2004 (b), pp. 63-4.

17   Ministry of Education, *Review of the Implementation and Effectiveness of Special Supplementary Grants for Māori and Pasifika Students at Tertiary Education Institutions from 2001–2002: Māori Report*. Wellington: Ministry of Education, 2003.

18   M. Durie, 'The Development of Māori Studies in New Zealand Universities', *He Pukenga Kōrero A Journal of Māori Studies*, 1996, Volume 1, no. 2, 21-32.

19   Ngā Pae o te Māramatanga, *Annual Report 2008*. Auckland: Ngā Pae o te Māramatanga, 2009.

20   University of Waikato, *Calendar*. Hamilton: University of Waikato. 2009.

21   R. Walker, *He Tipua The Life and Times of Sir Apirana Ngata*. Auckland: Viking, 2001, pp. 66-7; M. P. K. Sorrenson, 'Ngata, Apirana Turupa – Biography', from the Dictionary of New Zealand Biography. Te Ara – the Encyclopedia of New Zealand, updated 1-Sep-10, URL: http://www.TeAra.govt.nz/en/biographies/3n5/1, accessed 7 March 2011.

22   J. F. Cody, *Man of Two Worlds: a Biography of Sir Maui Pomare*. Wellington: A.H. & A.W. Reed, 1953.

23   J. B. Condliffe, *Te Rangi Hiroa The Life of Sir Peter Buck*. Christchurch: Whitcombe and Tombs, 1971, pp. 75-7; M. P. K. Sorrenson. 'Buck, Peter Henry – Biography', from the Dictionary of New Zealand Biography. Te Ara – the Encyclopedia of New Zealand, updated 1-Sep-10, URL: http://www.teara.govt.nz/en/biographies/3b54/1, accessed 7 March 2011.

24   I. Pool, *Te Iwi Maori: A New Zealand Population Past, Present, and Projected*. Auckland: Oxford University Press, 1991.

25   Statistics New Zealand, *New Zealand Now Māori*. Wellington: Department of Statistics, 2002.

26   M. Durie, *Te Mana, Te Kāwanatanga The Politics of Māori Self Determination*. Auckland: Oxford University Press, 1998, pp. 6-7.

27   'Māori political muscle at last', *Mana: the Māori News Magazine for all New Zealanders*, Summer 1996/97, no. 14, pp. 38-9.

28   Royal Commission on Social Policy, *The April Report: Future Directions*, Wellington: Royal Commission on Social Policy, 1988, Vol. 2, pp. 26-151.

29   Office of the Minister for Social Development and Employment, *Opportunity for All New Zealanders*. Wellington: Parliament, 2004, p. 15.

30   Office of the Associate Minister of Education (Tertiary Education,), *Tertiary Education Strategy 2002/07*. Wellington: Ministry of Education, 2002, p. 30.

31   Minister of Tertiary Education, *Tertiary Education Strategy 2007–12*. Wellington: Parliament, 2006.

32   Ministry of Education, *Ngā Haeata Mātauranga Annual Report on Māori Education*, Wellington: Ministry of Education, 2007.

33   L. Kame'eleihiwa, *Native Land and Foreign Desires Pehea Lā E Pono Ai?* Honolulu: Bishop Museum Press, 1992, pp. 23-5.

34   M. Durie, 'Indigenous Knowledge within a Global Knowledge System', *Higher Education Policy*, 2005, 18, 301-12.

35   Auckland University of Technology, *University Investment Plan 2008–2010*. Auckland: Auckland University of Technology, 2007.

36   University of Otago, *Strategic Direction to 2012*. Dunedin: University of Otago, 2007.

37   Massey University, *KIA MAIA Key Initiatives for a Māori Academic Investment Agenda*. Palmerston North: Massey University, 2007.

38   T. Duster, 'They're Taking Over! And other Myths About Race on Campus', in Berube, M., Nelson, C. (eds.), *Higher Education Under Fire*. New York: Routledge, 1995, pp. 276-83.

39   W. G. Bowen, D. Bok, *The Shape of the River: Long term consequences of considering race in college and university admissions*. New Jersey: Princeton University Press, 1988, pp. 275-90.

40   K. James, 'Corrupt State University: The Organizational Psychology of Native Experience of Higher Education', in Mihesuah, D. A., & Wilson, A. C. (eds), *Indigenizing the Academy: Transforming Scholarship and Empowering Communities*. Lincoln: University of Nebraska Press, 2004.

41   V. Deloria, 'Marginal and Submarginal', in Mihesuah, D. A., & Wilson, A. C. (eds), *Indigenizing the Academy: Transforming Scholarship and Empowering Communities*. Lincoln: University of Nebraska Press, 2004, pp. 16-30.

42   G. Boulton, *GLOBAL: What are universities for?* University World News, http://www.universityworldnews.com/article.php?story=20090326200944986, 2009, accessed 30 March 2009.

Chapter 6 – Indigenous Partnerships: The Academy as a Site for Enduring Relationships and the Transmission of Old and New Knowledge

1   M. Durie, H. Milroy, E. Hunter, 'Mental Health and the Indigenous Peoples of Australia and New Zealand', in Kirmayer, LJ., Valaskakis GG. (eds.) *Healing Traditions: The Mental Health of Aboriginal Peoples in Canada*. Vancouver: University of Vancouver Press, 2009, pp. 36-55.

2   R. Howitt, J. Connell, P. Hirsch, (eds.), *Resources, Nations and Indigenous Peoples*. Melbourne: Oxford University Press, 1996, p. 10.

3   United Nations, 'Implementing Declaration on Indigenous Rights Will Bring "Historical Justice"', General Assembly, GA/SHC/3954, New York: Department of Public Information, News and Media Division, 2009. (http://www.un.org/News/Press/docs/2009/gashc3954.doc.htm, accessed 11 February 2011).

4   New Zealand signed in 2010.

5   United Nations, 2009.

6   A. Eruiti, 'The Recognition of Indigenous Peoples Rights to Traditional Lands: The Evaluation of States by International Treaty Bodies', in Charters C., Eruiti A. (eds.) *Māori Property Rights and the Foreshore and Seabed*. Wellington: Victoria University Press, 2007, pp. 183-7.

7   M. Solomon, 'The Wai 262 Claim: A Claim by Māori to Indigenous Flora and Fauna: Me ō rātou taonga katoa', in Belgrave, M., Kawharu, M., Williams, D. (eds.), *Waitangi Revisited: Perspectives on the Treaty of Waitangi*. Melbourne: Oxford University Press, 2005, pp. 213-323.

8   M. Stewart-Harawira, *The New Imperial Order: Indigenous Responses to Globalisation*. Wellington: Huia Publishers, 2005, pp. 250-2.

9   P. G. McHugh, 'Aboriginal Identity and Relations in North America and Australasia', in Coates, K.S., & McHugh, P.G. (eds.), *Living Relationships: The Treaty of Waitangi in the New Millennium*. Wellington: Victoria University Press, 1998, pp. 107-86.

10 Waitangi Tribunal, *Orakei Report (Wai 9)*. Wellington: Department of Justice, 1987.

11 Royal Commission on Social Policy, *The April Report, Volume II Future Directions*. Wellington: Royal Commission on Social Policy, 1988, Vol. II, pp. 27-80.

12 G. Hall, H.A. Patrinos, *Indigenous Peoples, Poverty and Human Development in Latin America*. New York: Palgrave McMillan, 2006, pp. 221-40.

13 I. Anderson, 'Towards a Koori Healing Practice', in McDonald, D. (ed.) *The Boyer Collection: Highlights of the Boyer Lectures 1959-2000*. Sydney: ABC Books, 2001, pp. 433-43.

14 R. Vaithianathan, 'Is Economics Always Good for Your Health', in Otim, M., Anderson, I., Scott, I. (eds.) *Economics and Indigenous Australian Health Policy*. Melbourne: VicHealth Koori Health Research and Community Development Unit, 2004, pp.31-3.

15 Te K. Kingi, 'Hua Oranga Best Outcomes for Māori', PhD thesis. Massey University, Palmerston North, 2002.

16 M. Durie, E. Fitzgerald, Te K. Kingi, S. McKinley, B. Stevenson, *Māori Specific Outcomes And Indicators, A Report Prepared For Te Puni Kōkiri The Ministry Of Māori Development*. Palmerston North: Massey University, School of Māori Studies, 2002.

17 M. Durie, 'Indigenous Knowledge Within a Global Knowledge System', *Higher Education Policy*. 2005, 18, 301-12.

18 R. Kirikiri, 'Ngā Mahi Rangahau a Manaaki Whenua', in Te Pūmanawa Hauora (ed.), *Proceedings of Te Oru Rangahau Māori Research and Development Conference*. Palmerston North: Massey University, School of Māori Studies, 1998, pp. 140-2.

19 W. Walsh-Tapiata, 'Research within Your Own Iwi: What are some of the issues?' in Te Pūmanawa Hauora (ed.), *Proceedings of Te Oru Rangahau Māori Research and Development Conference*. Palmerston North: School of Māori Studies, Massey University, 1998, pp. 250-8.

20 A. Durie, 'Me Tipu Ake te Pono: Māori Research, Ethicality and Development', in Te Pūmanawa Hauora (ed.), *Proceedings of Te Oru Rangahau Māori Research*

and Development Conference. Palmerston North: Massey University, School of Māori Studies, 1998, pp. 259-66.

21 L. Tuhiwai Smith, 'Towards the New Millennium: International Issues and Projects in Indigenous Research', in Te Pūmanawa Hauora (ed.), *Proceedings of Te Oru Rangahau Māori Research and Development Conference.* Palmerston North: Massey University, School of Māori Studies, 1998, pp. 12-31.

22 Te A. C. Royal, 'Te Ao Mārama – A Research Paradigm', in Te Pūmanawa Hauora (ed.), *Proceedings of Te Oru Rangahau Māori Research and Development Conference.* Palmerston North: Massey University, School of Māori Studies, 1998.

23 B. J. Caldwell, *A blueprint for leadership for the successful transformation of schools in the twenty-first century.* Nottingham: National College for School Leadership, 2003.

24 T. Alfred, 'Warrior Scholarship', in Mihesuah, A., Wilson AC. (eds.), *Indigenizing the Academy Transforming Scholarship and Empowering Communities.* Lincoln: University of Nebraska Press, 2004, pp. 88-99.

25 K. T. Lomawaima, 'Tribal Sovereigns: Reframing Research in American Indian Education', in Villegas, M., Neugebauer, SR., Venegas, KR. (eds.), *Indigenous Knowledge and Education.* Cambridge: Harvard Educational Review, 2008, pp. 183-203.

26 J. P. Gone, 'Encountering Professional Psychology: Re-envisioning Mental Health Services for Native North America', in Kirmayer, LJ., Valaskakis GG. (eds.) *Healing Traditions: The Mental Health of Aboriginal Peoples in Canada.* Vancouver: University of Vancouver Press, 2009, pp. 419-39.

27 J. K. Mihesuah, 'Graduating Indigenous Students by Confronting the Academic Environment', in Mihesuah, A., Wilson AC. (eds.), *Indigenizing the Academy Transforming Scholarship and Empowering Communities.* Lincoln: University of Nebraska Press, 2004, pp. 191-9.

28 J. Altman, 'The Establishment of a Corpus of Indigenous Economic Policy Research', in Otim, M., Anderson, I., Scott, I. (eds.) *Economics and Indigenous Australian Health Policy.* Melbourne: VicHealth Koori Health Research and Community Development Unit, 2004, pp. 174-86.

29 United Nations, 2009.

Chapter 7 – Race and Ethnicity in Public Policy: Does it Work?

1 Morag McDowell, Duncan Webb, *The New Zealand Legal System* (2nd ed). Wellington: Butterworths, 1998, p. 105.

2 Cristina Torres Parodi, 'Working to Achieve Health Equity with an Ethnic Perspective: What has been Done and Best Practices', paper presented at the Intergovernmental Working Group on the Implementation of the Declaration and Program of Action of Durban, Third Session. Geneva: 2004, 11-12 October.

3 P. Reid, B. Robson, C. Jones, 'Disparities in health: common myths and uncommon truths', *Pacific Health Dialogue.* 2000, 7: 38-48.

4 Ministry of Health, *Reducing Inequalities in Health.* Wellington, Ministry of Health, 2002, pp. 18-22.

5 Trauer T, Eagar K, Gaines P and Bower A *New Zealand Mental Health Consumers and their Outcomes.* Auckland: Health Research Council, 2004, pp. 83-6.

6   R. Bishop, M. Berryman, *The Experiences of Indigenous Māori Students in New Zealand Classrooms*. Hamilton: University of Waikato, 2002.

7   J. Cummins, 'HER Classic – Empowering minority students: A Framework for Intervention', *Harvard Educational Review*. 2001, 71(4) 649-75.

8   Arohia Durie, 'Te Rerenga o te Rā Autonomy and Identity: Māori Educational Aspirations', PhD Thesis. Palmerston North: Massey University, 2002.

9   Fred Biddullph. Jeanne Biddulph, Chris Biddulph, *Best Evidence Synthesis: The Complexity of Community and Family Influences on Children's Achievement in New Zealand*, a report prepared for the Ministry of Education. Wellington: Ministry of Education, 2003, pp. 62-3.

10   Veronica Jacobsen, Nicholas Mays, Ron Crawford, Barbara Annesley, Paul Christoffel, Grant Johnston, Sid Burbin, *Investing in Well-being: an Analytical Framework*. Working paper 02/23. Wellington: The Treasury, 2002, pp. 11-2.

11   Tertiary Education Commission, *Review of the Implementation and Effectiveness of Special Supplementary Grants for Māori and Pasifika Students at Tertiary Education Institutions From 2001-2002: Māori Report*. Wellington: Tertiary Education Commission, 2003.

12   University of Otago, *Charter*. Dunedin: University of Otago, 2003.

13   Tertiary Education Commission, *Priorities Statement of Tertiary Education Priorities 2005/07 Discussion Document*. Wellington: Tertiary Education Commission, 2004.

14   William G. Bowen, Derek Bok, *The Shape of the River: Long term consequences of considering race in college and university admissions*. New Jersey: Princeton University Press, 1998, pp. 275-90.

Chapter 9 – Te Tai Tini: Transformations 2025

1   Statistics New Zealand, *New Zealand Census of Population and Dwellings 2001: Māori*. Wellington: Department of Statistics, 2002.

2   J. Miller, *Early Victorian New Zealand*. London: Oxford University Press, 1958, p. 104.

3   Ian Pool, *The Maori Population of New Zealand 1769-1971*. Auckland: Auckland University Press and Oxford University 1977.

4   Mason Durie, *Whaiora Māori Health Development* (second ed). Auckland: Oxford University Press, 1998, pp. 26-37.

5   Ranginui Walker, *He Tipua, The Life and Times of Sir Apirana Ngata*. Auckland: Viking, 2001, pp. 106-11.

6   I. L. G. Sutherland, 'Leader of Genius', *The Journal of the Polynesian Society*, Memorial Number to Sir Apirana Nohopari Turupa Ngata. 1950, Volume 59, Number 4, pp. 293-4.

7   Hon. K. T. Wetere, *Te Urupare Rangapū: Partnership Response*. Wellington: Office of the Minister of Māori Affairs, Parliament, 1988.

8   A. Fleras, J. Elliot, *The Nations Within: Aboriginal-State Relations in Canada, the United States, and New Zealand*. Toronto: Oxford University Press, 1992, pp. 203-18.

9   M. Durie, *Te Mana, Te Kāwanatanga The Politics of Māori Self Determination*. Auckland: Oxford University Press, 1998, pp. 10-3.

10   Waitangi Tribunal, *Report of the Waitangi Tribunal on Te Reo Māori Claim (Wai 11)*, Wellington: Department of Justice, 1986.

11   Ministry of Education, Data Management and Analysis Unit, Wellington: 2002.

12   Ministry of Education, *Ngā Haeata Mātauranga Annual Report on Māori Education & Direction for 2002/2003*. Wellington: Ministry of Education, 2004, pp. 17-9.

13   Ministry of Education, 2004, pp. 6-7.

14   M. Durie, 'A Framework for Considering Māori Educational Advancement', *Ngā Kāhui Pou, Launching Māori Futures*. Wellington: Huia Publishers, 2003, pp. 197-211.

15   Maori Fisheries Act 2004 (part 1, 3 – Purposes).

16   Te K. Kingi, 'Hua Oranga Best Outcomes for Māori', PhD Thesis. Palmerston North: Massey University, 2002.

17   M. Durie, E. Fitzgerald, Te K. Kingi, S. McKinley, B. Stevenson, *Māori Specific Outcomes and Indicators, A Report Prepared for Te Puni Kōkiri*. Palmerston North: Massey University, School of Māori Studies, 2002.

18   Te Rūnanga o Ngāi Tahu, *Ngāi Tahu 2025*, Christchurch, 2003.

Chapter 10 – Indigenous Higher Education: Māori Experience in New Zealand

1   John A. Williams, 'The Foundations of Apirana Ngata's Career 1891-1909', in J. G. A. Pocock (ed.), *The Maori and New Zealand Politics*. Auckland: Blackwood and Janet Paul, 1965, pp. 55-60.

2   J. B. Condliffe, *Te Rangi Hiroa The Life of Sir Peter Buck*. Christchurch: Whitcombe and Tombs, Christchurch, 1971, pp. 67-8.

3   J. F. Cody, *Man of Two Worlds A Biography of Sir Maui Pomare*. Wellington: A. H. and A. W. Reed, 1953, pp. 25-9.

4   Ministry of Education, (*Ngā Haeata Mātauranga Annual Report on Māori Education & Direction for 2002/2003*. Wellington: Ministry of Education, 2004, pp. 17-9.

5   Ministry of Education, *Education Statistics of New Zealand for 2001*, Wellington, Ministry of Education, 2002.

6   Ministry of Education, 2004, pp. 6-7.

7   Ministry of Education, *Ngā Haeata Mātauranga Annual Report on Māori Education*. Wellington: Ministry of Education, 2005, pp. 92-3.

8   Royal Commission on Social Policy, *The April Report*. Wellington: RCSP, 1988, Vol. 2.

9   Working Group on Indigenous Populations, *Draft Declaration on the Rights of Indigenous Peoples: Report of the Eleventh Session of the United Nations Working Group on Indigenous Populations*, Geneva: United Nations, 1993.

10   New Zealand Qualifications Authority, *National Certificates & Diplomas Te Waharoa & Te Ngutu Awa and other field Māori qualifications on the National Qualifications Framework*. Wellington: NZQA, 2003.

11   Tertiary Education Commission, *Tertiary Education Strategy*. Wellington: 2003.

12   Tertiary Education Commission, *Review of the Implementation and Effectiveness of Special Supplementary Grants for Māori and Pasifika Students at Tertiary Education Institutions From 2001-2002: Māori Report*. Wellington: 2003.

13   University of Otago, *Charter*, Dunedin: University of Otago, 2003.

14 See chapter seven of this volume.

15 William G. Bowen, Derek Bok, *The Shape of the River Long term consequences of considering race in college and university admissions*. New Jersey: Princeton University Press, 1998, pp. 275-90.

16 Danica Waiti, *Hei Tautoko i ngā Wawata Māori: ētahi tauira nā ngā Kura Wānanga. Supporting Māori Achievement: a collection of tertiary provider initiatives*. Wellington: Ministry of Education, 2001.

17 S. Hatcher, S. Mouly, D. Rasquinha, W. Miles, J. Burdett, H. Hamer, G. Robinson, *Improving Recruitment to the Mental Health Workforce in New Zealand*. Auckland: Health Research Council of New Zealand, 2005, p. 60.

18 Māori Tertiary Reference Group, *Māori Tertiary Education Framework*. Wellington: Ministry of Education, 2003.

19 Pakariki Harrison, *Te Kete Uruuru Matua*. Auckland: Manukau Institute of Technology, 1999.

20 AUQA Good Practice Database, (2004), http://auqa.edu.au/gp/ (Key word: Māori).

21 Māori Tertiary Reference Group, 2003, pp. 23-4.

Chapter 11 – Whānau, Education and Māori Potential

1 John Gorst, *The Maori King*. Auckland: Pauls Book Arcade & Oxford University Press, (Reprint), 1959, pp. 54-5.

2 Pei te Hurunui, *King Potatau*. Auckland: Polynesian Society, 1959, pp. 190-6.

3 Ranginui Walker, 'Māori Sovereignty, Colonial and Post-colonial Discourses', in Paul Havemann (ed.) *Indigenous Peoples Rights in Australia, Canada and New Zealand*. Auckland: Oxford University Press, 1999, pp. 113-6.

4 Evelyn Stokes, *Wiremu Tamihana Rangatira*. Wellington: Huia Publishers, 2002, pp. 134-41.

5 Robyn Seth-Purdie, Andrew Cameron, Francis Luketina, *What makes your family tick*? Research Report 1/06, Wellington: Families Commission, 2006.

6 Ann Weatherall, Annabel Ramsay, (2006), *New Communication Technologies and Family Life*, Blue Skies Report 5/06, Wellington: Families Commission, 2006.

7 Ministry of Social Development, *2006 The Social Report Te Pūrongo Oranga Tangata*, Wellington: Ministry of Social Development, 2006.

8 R. Bishop, M. Berryman, C. Richardson, S. Takiwa, *Te Kotahitanga: The Experiences of Year 9 and 10 Māori Students in Mainstream Classrooms*. Wellington: Ministry of Education, 2003.

9 Hui Taumata, *Hui Taumata 2005: Summary Report*. Wellington, 2005, pp. 6-7.

10 A. H. Frederick, G. Chittock, *Global entrepreneurship monitor Aotearoa New Zealand*. Auckland: Centre for Innovation & Entrepreneurship, Unitech, 2005.

11 C. Hawkins, M. Durie, M. Barcham, T. Black, C. Cunningham, A. Durie, T. Kingi, Te K. Kingi, F. Palmer, W. Simon, *Te Hihiri Umanga Whānau Successful Whānau Participation in Small and Medium-sized Enterprises, a Report Prepared for Te Puni Kōkiri*. Palmerston North: Massey University, Palmerston North, 2006.

12 Ministry of Education, *Ngā Haeata Mātauranga Annual Report on Māori Education 2004*. Wellington: Ministry of Education, 2005, pp. 15-6.

13   Ministry of Education, *Ngā Haeata Mātauranga Annual Report on Māori Education 2004.* Wellington: Ministry of Education, 2005, pp. 91-2.

14   Ministry of Education, *Ngā Haeata Mātauranga – Annual Report on Māori Education 2005.* Wellington: Ministry of Education, 2006, pp. 32-3.

15   Ministry of Education, *Ngā Haeata Mātauranga – Annual Report on Māori Education 2005.* Wellington: Ministry of Education, 2006.

16   Guardians Group, *Students First – Implications, Consequences and Outcomes.* Paper presented at the 'Marking a Future Path' Symposium. Wellington: Secondary Futures, 2006.

17   K. Sparrow, H. Sparrow, P. Swan, 'Student Centred Learning: Is it Possible?', in A. Herman and M. M, Kulski (eds), *Flexible Futures in Tertiary Teaching.* Proceedings of the 9ᵗʰ Annual Teaching Learning Forum, 2-4 February 2000. Perth: Curtain University of Technology. 2000.

18   Guardians Group, 2006.

19   Ministry of Education, *Individual Education Plan Guidelines.* Wellington: Ministry of Education, http://www.minedu.govt.nz/NZEducation/EducationPolicies/SpecialEducation/FormsAndGuidelines/IEPGuidelines.aspx, accessed 17 April 2011.

20   Secondary Futures. *Students First.* Wellington: Secondary Futures, pp. 8-9.

21   Secondary Futures, *The Conversation has Begun, Report 2004.* Wellington: Secondary Futures, 2004, p. 20.

22   Jacqui True, *Methodologies for analysing the impact of public policy on families.* Wellington: Families Commission, 2005.

23   Te Puni Kōkiri, *Māori Potential Framework a presentation.* Wellington: Ministry of Māori Development, 2005. See also Te Puni Kōkiri Statement of Intent 2006.

24   R. Fancourt, *Brainy Babies: Build and Develop Your Baby's Intelligence.* Auckland: Penguin Books, 2000.

25   Ministry of Education, *The System in Change Tertiary Education Strategy 2002/07 Monitoring Report 2005.* Wellington: Ministry of Education, 2006.

26   Ministry of Education, 2005, p. 80.

27   R. Curson, *Māori in Industry Training Recent Trends.* Wellington: Industry Training Federation, 2005.

28   Ministry of Social Development, 2006, pp. 26-31.

29   ibid., pp. 110-1.

30   Hui Taumata, *Hui Taumata 2005 Summary Report.* Wellington: 2005, p. 15.

Chapter 12 – From Indigenous Exclusion towards Full Participation: The Māori Experience

1   S. J. Kunitz, *Disease and Social Diversity: The European Impact on the Health of Non-Europeans.* New York: Oxford University Press, 1994.

2   Cited in Richard Howitt, John Connell, Philip Hirsch (eds.), *Resources, Nations and Indigenous Peoples.* Melbourne: Oxford University Press, 1996, p. 10.

3   Lilikala Kame'eleihiwa, *Native Land and Foreign Desires Pehea Lā E Pono Ai?* Honolulu: Bishop Museum Press, 1992, pp 23-5.

4   Te Ahukaramu Charles Royal, *Indigenous Worldviews: A Comparative Study*, A report of research in progress. Ōtaki: Te Wānanga o Raukawa, 2002.

5   Mason Durie, 'Indigenous Knowledge Within a Global Knowledge System', *Higher Education Policy*, 2005, 18, 301-12.

6   Mason Durie, *Whaiora Māori Health Development* (second ed). Auckland: Oxford University Press, 1998, pp. 26-37.

7   J. D. Waldram, A. Herring, T. K. Young, *Aboriginal Health in Canada Historical, Cultural, and Epidemiological Perspectives*. Toronto: University of Toronto Press, 1995, pp. 55-61.

8   R. Horton, 'Indigenous Peoples: time to act now for equity and health', Comment, *Lancet*, 2005, 367:9524: 1705-7.

9   Kunitz, 1994.

10 G. Hall, H. A. Patrinos, *Indigenous Peoples, Poverty and Human Development in Latin America*. New York: Palgrave MacMillan, 2006, pp. 241-57.

11 Statistics New Zealand, *New Zealand Now Māori* Wellington: Department of Statistics, 2002, pp. 13-5.

12 ibid., pp. 17-8.

13 ibid.

14 Te Puni Kōkiri, *Progress Towards Closing Social and Economic Gaps Between Māori and Non-Māori*. Wellington: Ministry of Māori Development, 1998, pp. 14-6.

15 I. Anderson, S. Crengle, M. L. Kamaka, T. Chen, N. Palafox, L. Jackson-Pulver, 'Indigenous Health in Australia, New Zealand and the Pacific', *Lancet*, 2005, 367:9524, 1775-85.

16 Ministry of Social Development, *The Social Report 2006 Te Pūrongo Oranga Tangata*. Wellington: Ministry of Social Development, 2006.

17 United Nations, *Draft Declaration of the Rights of Indigenous Peoples as Agreed upon by the Members of the Working Group at its Eleventh Session*, New York: 1993, UN Doc. E/CN.4/Sub.2/1994/2/Add. 1.

18 H. Frederick, P. Carswell, E. Henry, I. Chaston, J. Thompson, J. Campbell, A. S. Pivac, Māori Entrepreneurs, in *Bartercard New Zealand Global Entrepreneurship Monitor 2002*. Auckland: UNITEC New Zealand Centre for Innovation and Entrepreneurship, 2002, pp.23-5.

19 Ministry of Education, *Ngā Haeata Mātauranga Annual Report on Māori Education & Direction for 2002/2003*. Wellington: Ministry of Education, 2004, pp. 17-9.

20 Ministry of Education, *Ngā Haeata Mātauranga Annual Report on Māori Education 2005*. Wellington: Ministry of Education, 2006.

21 Ministry of Education, *Education Statistics of New Zealand for 2001*. Wellington: Ministry of Education, 2002.

22 Ministry of Education, 2004, pp. 6-7.

23 Ministry of Education, 2006, pp. 92-3.

24 Kōmiti Whakahaere, *Hui Whakaoranga Māori Health Planning Workshop*. Wellington: Department of Health, 1984.

25 Health Workforce Advisory Committee, *The New Zealand Health Workforce A stocktake of issues and capacity*. Wellington: Health Workforce Advisory Committee, 2001, pp. 52-4.

26   Health Workforce Advisory Committee, *Fit for Purpose and for Practice. A review of the Medical Workforce in New Zealand.* Wellington: Health Workforce Advisory Committee, 2005, pp. 127-31.

27   Ministry of Social Development, 2006, pp 24-5.

28   M. Durie, 'A Framework for Considering Māori Educational Advancement', *Ngā Kāhui Pou, Launching Māori Futures.* Wellington: Huia Publishers, 2003, pp. 197-211.

29   Te Puni Kōkiri, *Māori Potential Framework a presentation.* Wellington: Ministry of Māori Development, 2005. See also Te Puni Kōkiri *Statement of Intent,* 2006.

30   Hui Taumata Steering Committee, *Hui Taumata 2005: Summary Report.* Wellington: 2005.

31   Te K. Kingi, *Hua Oranga Best Outcomes for Māori,* PhD Thesis, Palmerston North: Massey University, 2002.

32   M. Durie, E. Fitzgerald, Te K. Kingi, S. McKinley, B. Stevenson, *Māori Specific Outcomes and Indicators, A Report Prepared for Te Puni Kōkiri.* Palmerston North: Massey University, School of Māori Studies, 2002.

Chapter 13 – The Treaty of Waitangi in New Zealand 2008

1   New Zealand was later to sign the Declaration of the Rights of Indigenous Peoples in 2010.

Chapter 14 – The Treaty of Waitangi: Domestic Relations, Global Impacts and a New Zealand Agenda

1   Claudia Orange, *The Treaty of Waitangi.* Wellington: Bridget Williams Books, 1987, pp. 145-6.

2   Anake Goodall, 'Aoraki Matatū – Being Steadfast in Ngāi Tahu Identity', in Continuing Legal Education (ed.), *Governing and Running Māori Entities Intensive.* Wellington: New Zealand Law Society, 2009, pp. 9-20.

Chapter 15 – Indigeneity, and the Promotion of Positive Mental Health

1   Whanganui River Māori Trust Board, *Whanganui River Charter.* Whanganui: Whanganui River Māori Trust Board, 1993.

2   V. Deloria, *God is Red.* Colorado: Fulcrum Publishing, 1994, pp. 172-3.

3   Working Group on Indigenous Populations, *Draft Declaration on the Rights of Indigenous Peoples: Report of the Eleventh Session of the United Nations Working Group on Indigenous Populations.* Geneva: United Nations, 1993.

4   Committee on Indigenous Health, *The Geneva Declaration on the Health and Survival of Indigenous Peoples.* New York: United Nations Permanent Forum on Indigenous Issues, 2002.

5   James Waldram, D. Ann Herring, T. Kue Young, *Aboriginal Health in Canada Historical, Cultural, and Epidemiological Perspectives.* Toronto: University of Toronto Press, 1995, pp. 55-61.

6   J. Cunningham, J. R. Condon, 'Premature mortality in aboriginal adults in the Northern Territory, 1979-1991', *Medical Journal of Australia,* 1996, 165(6): 309-12.

7   For further discussion see Kunitz, Stephen J., *Disease and Social Diversity The European Impact on the Health of Non-Europeans*. New York: Oxford University Press, 1994.

8   M. Durie, 'Providing Health Services to Indigenous Peoples', Editorial, *British Medical Journal*, 2003, 7412, 23 August 2003, pp. 408-9.

9   National Health Committee, *The Social, Cultural and Economic Determinants of Health in New Zealand: Action to Improve Health*. Wellington: National Health Committee, 1998.

10   P. Gaines, A. Bower, B. Buckingham. K. Eagar, P. Burgess. J. Green, G. Mellsop, *Mental Health Classification Outcomes Study: Brief Report*. Auckland: Health Research Council, 2004.

11   E. Duran, B. Duran, *Native American Post-colonial Psychology*. Albany NY: State University of New York, 1995, pp. 93-156.

12   A. Cohen, *The Mental Health of Indigenous Peoples: An International Overview*. Geneva: Nations for Mental Health, Department of Mental Health, World Health Organisation, 1999, pp. 7-10.

13   M. Durie, 'Te Pae Māhutonga: a model for Māori health promotion', *Health Promotion Forum of New Zealand Newsletter*, 1999, 49: pp. 2-5.

14   Vicki Hyde, *Night Skies Above New Zealand*. Auckland: New Holland Publishers, 2003, pp. 150-3.

15   Ministry of Health, *Building on Strengths A new approach to promoting mental health in New Zealand/Aotearoa*. Wellington: Ministry of Health, 2002, p. 44.

16   M. Durie, 'Te Pae Māhutonga: Mental Health Promotion for Young Māori', in M. Durie, *Ngā Kāhui Pou Launching Māori Futures*. Wellington: Huia Publishers, 2003, pp. 141-156.

17   W. W. Isajiw, 'Ethnic-identity Retention', in R. Breton, W. W. Isajiw, W. E. Kalbach, J. G. Reitz (eds), *Ethnic Identity and Equality*. Toronto: University of Toronto Press, 1990, pp. 34-91.

18   Te Puni Kōkiri, *Progress Towards Closing Social and Economic Gaps Between Māori and Non-Māori*. Wellington: Ministry of Māori Development, 2000.

19   M. Durie, 'Indigeneity: Challenges for Indigenous Doctors', in M. Durie, *Ngā Kāhui Pou Launching Māori Futures*. Wellington: Huia Publishers, 2003, pp. 269-88.

Chapter 16 – Impacts of an Ageing Population on New Zealand Society

1   Ministry of Social Development, *The Social Report 2006 Te Pūrongo Oranga Tangata*. Wellington: Ministry of Social Development, 2006, pp 24-5.

2   Statistics New Zealand, *National Population Projections: 2006 (base) – 2061*. Wellington: Department of Statistics, 2007.

3   William Shakespeare, *As You Like It*. Act II, Scene VII, lines 139-66.

4   E. Erikson, *Childhood and Society* (2nd ed). New York: Norton & Co, 1963.

5   H. M. Mead, N. Grove, *Ngā Pēpeha a ngā Tīpuna, The Sayings of the Ancestors*. Wellington: Victoria University Press, 2001.

6   Monty Soutar, Lloyd Ashton, 'Was the cost too high?', *Mana*, 1998, 27: 22-7.

7   Mason Durie, 'Kaumātuatanga reciprocity: Māori elderly and whānau', in Susan Gee (ed.), *Experience of a Lifetime: Older New Zealanders as Volunteers*. Wellington: Victoria University of Wellington, 2001, pp. 31-7.

8   Ministry of Social Development, *The Social Report 2007 Te Pūrongo Oranga Tangata*. Wellington: Ministry of Social Development, 2007, pp. 80-1.

9   V. Wilton, J. A. Davey, *Grandfathers – Their Changing Family Roles and Contributions*. Wellington: Families Commission, 2006.

10   M. Durie, G. R.Allan, C. W. Cunningham, W. Edwards, M. E. Forster, A. Gillies, Te K. Kingi, M. M. Ratima, J. A. Waldon, *Oranga Kaumātua The Health and Wellbeing of Older Māori People*. Wellington: Ministry of Māori Development, 1997.

11   Ministry of Health, *Tobacco Trends 2006: Monitoring tobacco use in New Zealand*, Wellington: Ministry of Health, 2006.

12   Ministry of Health, *A Portrait of Health: Key results of the 2002/03 New Zealand Health Survey*. Wellington: Ministry of Health, 2004.

13   Ministry of Social Development 2007, pp. 52, 86, 87.

14   M.A Browne, J. E. Wells, K. M. Scott (eds.), *Te Rau Hinengaro: The New Zealand Mental Health Survey*. Wellington: Ministry of Health, 2006, pp. 39-41.

15   Elizabeth Murchie, *Rapuora. Health and Māori Women*. Wellington: Māori Women's Welfare League, 1984.

16   Michael King, *Whina: a biography of Whina Cooper*. Auckland: Penguin Books, 1983, pp. 212-22.

17   Waitangi Tribunal, *Report on the Findings and Recommendations of the Waitangi Tribunal on an application by Aila Taylor for and on behalf of Te Atiawa Tribe in relation to fishing grounds in the Waitara District*. Wellington: Department of Justice, 1983.

Chapter 17 – Bioethics in Research: The Ethics of Indigeneity

1   G. Hall, H. A. Patrinos, *Indigenous Peoples, Poverty and Human Development in Latin America*. New York: Palgrave MacMillan, 2006, pp. 221-40.

2   Lilikalä Kame'eleihiwa, *Native Land and Foreign Desires Pehea Lā E Pono Ai?* Honolulu: Bishop Museum Press, 1992, pp. 23-5.

3   E. Duran, B. Duran, *Native American Postcolonial Psychology*. Albany NY: State University of New York, 1995, pp. 14-5.

4   Ranginui Walker, *Ka Whawhai Tonu Mātou Struggle Without End*. Auckland: Penguin Books, 1990, pp. 11-5.

5   Vine Deloria, *God is Red*. Colorado: Fulcrum Publishing, 1994, pp. 172-3.

6   Statistics New Zealand, *Quickstats about Māori: Census 2006*. Wellington: Department of Statistics, 2007.

7   Te Ahukaramu Charles Royal, *Indigenous Worldviews A Comparative Study, A report of research in progress*, Ōtaki: Te Wānanga o Raukawa, 2002.

8   I. H.Kawharu, *Maori Land Tenure Studies of a changing institution*. Oxford: Oxford University Press, 1977, pp. 60-2.

9   Anne Salmond, 'Te Ao Tawhito: A Semantic Approach to the Traditional Māori Cosmos'. *Journal of the Polynesian Society*, 1978, 87, 1, 166-7.

10   Mason Durie, 'Marae and implications for a Modern Māori Psychology', Elsdon Best Memorial Medal Address, *The Journal of the Polynesian Society*, 1999, 108, 4, 351-66.

11   I. H. Kawharu, 'Urban Immigrants and Tangata Whenua', in Eric Schwimmer (ed.), *The Maori People in the Nineteen-sixties*. Auckland: Blackwood and Janet Paul, 1968, pp. 180-1.

12   Mason Durie, 'Marae and Implications for a Modern Māori Psychology', *Journal of the Polynesian Society*, 1999, 108, 4, 351-66.

13   G. Harmsworth, 'The Role of Biodiversity in Māori Advancement: a Research Framework', *He Pukenga Kōrero*, 2004, Volume 8, No. 1, 9-16.

14   J. Hutchings, 'Claiming our space – Mana Wahine conceptual framework for discussing genetic modification', *He Pukenga Kōrero*, 2004, Volume 8, No. 1, 17-25.

15   Ngā Kaihautū Tikanga Taiao, *Report to the Environmental Risk Management Authority* (GMF98009), Wellington: EMR, 1999.

16   M.Glover, A. McCree, L. Dyall, *Māori attitudes to assisted human reproduction: an exploratory study, Summary report*. Auckland: University of Auckland, 2007.

17   R. Selby, P. Moore, 'Māori research in Māori communities: No longer a new phenomenon', *Alternative An International Journal of Indigenous Scholarship*, Special Supplement, 2007, volume 3, No. 2, pp. 96-107.

18   V. Blair, I. Martin, D. Shaw, I. Winship, D. Kerr, J. Arnold, P. Harawira, M. McLeod, S. Parry, A. Charlton, M. Findlay, B. Cox, B.Humar, H.More, P. Guilford, (2006), 'Hereditary diffuse gastric cancer: diagnosis and management', *Clin Gastroenterol Hepatol*, 4(3): pp. 262-75.

19   H. Gifford, A. Boulton, 'Conducting excellent research within indigenous communities', *Alternative An International Journal of Indigenous Scholarship*. Special Supplement, 2007, volume 3, No. 2, pp. 24-45.

20   L. Smith, 'Towards the New Millennium: International Issues and Projects in Indigenous Research'. *He Pukenga Kōrero*, 1998, volume 4, No. 1, pp. 43-61.

21   W. Parnell, R. Scragg, N. Wilson, D. Schaaf, E. Fitzgerald, *NZ Food NZ Children Key results of the 2002 National Children's Nutrition Survey*. Wellington: Ministry of Health, 2003.

22   Mark Oakley Browne, Elisabeth Wells, Kate Scott (eds.), *Te Rau Hinengaro: The New Zealand Mental Health Survey*. Wellington: Ministry of Health, 2006.

23   A. Sporle, J. Koia, 'Māori responsiveness in health and medical research: clarifying the roles of the researcher and the institution', *New Zealand Medical Journal*, 2004, vol. 117, no. 1190, 998-1000.

24   Canadian Institutes of Health Research–Institute of Aboriginal Peoples' Health, *Commemorative Report 2000 to 2008*, Ottawa: CIHR-IAPH, 2008.

25   Health Research Council, *Guidelines for Researchers on Health Research Involving Māori*. Auckland: Health Research Council of New Zealand, 2008.

26   The Bioethics Council, *The Cultural, Ethical and Spiritual Aspects of Animal-to Human Transplantation, a report on xenotransplantation*. Wellington: Toi te Taiao: the Bioethics Council, 2005.

27   See http://www.waitangi-tribunal.govt.nz/inquiries/genericinquiries2/florafauna/ accessed 28 February 2011.

28   M. Hudson, 'He Matatika Māori: Māori and ethical review in health research', Master of Health Science Thesis. Auckland: Auckland University of Technology, 2004.

Chapter 18 – Quality Health Care for Indigenous Peoples: The Māori Experience

1   Lilikalā Kame'eleihiwa, *Native Land and Foreign Desires Pehea Lā E Pono Aī?* Honolulu: Bishop Museum Press, 1992, pp. 23-5.

2   Kekuni Blaisdell, Noreen Mokuau, 'Kānaka Maoli, Indigenous Hawaiians', in Hasager U., Friedman J., (eds.), *Hawai'i Return to Nationhood*. Copenhagen: IWGIA – Document 75, 1994, pp. 49-67.

3   Ranginui Walker, *Ka Whawhai Tonu Mātou Struggle Without End*, Auckland: Penguin Books, 1990, pp. 11-5.

4   Whanganui River Māori Trust Board, *Whanganui River Charter*, Whanganui: Whanganui River Māori Trust Board, 1993.

5   Committee on Indigenous Health, *The Geneva Declaration on the Health and Survival of Indigenous Peoples*. New York: United Nations Permanent Forum on Indigenous Issues, 2002.

6   Statistics New Zealand, *New Zealand Now Māori*. Wellington: Department of Statistics, 1998, pp. 13-5.

7   ibid., pp. 17-8.

8   Paul McHugh, *The Māori Magna Carta: New Zealand Law and the Treaty of Waitangi*. Oxford: Oxford University Press, 1991, pp. 113-7.

9   The Terms of Reference for the Royal Commission on Social Policy described the principles of the Treaty as one of the 'foundations of our society and economy.'

10 Geoffrey Palmer, *New Zealand's Constitution in Crisis Reforming our Political System*. Dunedin: John McIndoe, 1992, pp. 71-102.

11 S. Ajwani, T. Blakely, B. Robson, M. Tobias, M. Bonne, *Decades of Disparity: Ethnic mortality trends in New Zealand 1980-1999*. Wellington: Ministry of Health & University of Otago, 2003, pp. 21-6.

12 ibid., pp. 50-1.

13 E. Murchie, (1984), *Rapuora Health and Māori Women*. Wellington: Māori Womens Welfare League, 1984.

14 Health Workforce Advisory Committee, *The New Zealand Health Workforce A stocktake of issues and capacity*, Wellington: Health Workforce Advisory Committee, 2001, pp. 52-4.

15 C. Cunningham, *He Taura Tieke: Measuring Effective Health Services for Māori*. Wellington: Ministry of Health, 1996.

16 Te K. Kingi, 'Hua Oranga A Māori Mental Health Outcome Measure', PhD Thesis. Palmerston North, Massey University, 2002.

17 New Zealand Board of Health, *Annual Report of the New Zealand Board of Health 1986-87*. Wellington: New Zealand Board of Health, 1987.

18 Standing Committee on Māori Health, *Tribal Authorities as Advocates for Health*. Wellington: New Zealand Board of Health, 1987.

Chapter 19 – Māori Health Impact Assessment

1   Donna Durie-Hall, Joan Metge, 'Kua Tutū Te Puehu Kia Mau, Māori Aspirations and Family Law', in M. Henaghan, B. Atkin (eds.), *Family Law Policy in New Zealand*. Auckland: Oxford University Press, 1992, pp. 70-3.

2   John Cody, 'Devolution, Disengagement and Control in the Statutory Social Services', in Peter McKinley (ed.), *Redistribution of Power? Devolution in New Zealand*. Wellington: Victoria University Press, 1990, pp. 167-9.

3   Waitangi Tribunal, *Report Findings and Recommendations of the Waitangi Tribunal on an Application by Aila Taylor for and on behalf of Te Atiawa Tribe in Relation to Fishing Grounds in the Waitara District (Wai 6)*. Wellington: Waitangi Tribunal, Department of Justice, 1983.

4   New Zealand Government, *Crown Proposals for the Settlement of Treaty of Waitangi Claims, Detailed Proposals*. Wellington: Office of Treaty Settlements, 1994.

5   Ministry of Education, *Education Statistics of New Zealand for 2001*. Wellington: Ministry of Education, 2002.

6   Mason Durie, *Te Mana, Te Kāwanatanga*. Auckland: Oxford University Press, 1998, pp. 43-4.

7   Mason Durie, 'Providing Health Services to Indigenous Peoples', Editorial, *British Medical Journal*, 2003, 7412, 23 August 2003, pp. 408-9.

8   National Health Committee, *The Social, Cultural and Economic Determinants of Health in New Zealand: Action to Improve Health*. Wellington: National Health Committee, 1998.

9   E. Duran, B. Duran, *Native American Post-colonial Psychology*. Albany NY: State University of New York, 1995, pp. 93-156.

10 A. Cohen, *The Mental Health of Indigenous Peoples: An International Overview*. Geneva: Nations for Mental Health, Department of Mental Health, World Health Organisation, 1999, pp. 7-10.

11 Te Rangi Hiroa (Peter Buck), *The Coming of the Maori*. *Wellington:* Maori Purposes Fund Board and Whitcombe andTombs, 1949, pp. 404-6.

12 M. Durie, E. Fitzgerald, Te K. Kingi, S. McKinley, B. Stevenson, *Māori Specific Outcomes And Indicators, A Report Prepared for Te Puni Kōkiri the Ministry of Māori Development*. Palmerston North: Massey University, School of Māori Studies, 2002.

Chapter 20 – Indigenous Health: Catalysts for Innovation

1   See chapter two of this volume.

2   Archdeacon Walsh, 'The Passing of the Maori', *Transactions of the New Zealand Institute*. Wellington: Government Printer, 1907, pp. 154-74.

3   *New Zealand Herald* 17 August 1874.

4   John A. Williams, (1965), 'The Foundations of Apirana Ngata's Career 1891-1909', in J. G. A. Pocock (ed.), *The Maori and New Zealand Politics*. Auckland: Blackwood and Janet Paul, 1965, pp. 55-60.

5   J. B. Condliffe, *Te Rangi Hiroa The Life of Sir Peter Buck*. Christchurch: Whitcombe and Tombs, 1971, pp. 67-8.

6   Statistics New Zealand, *Quick Stats. About Māori*. Wellington: Department of Statistics, 2007.

7   Statistics New Zealand, *New Zealand Now Māori*, Wellington: Department of Statistics, 2002, pp. 17-8.

8   E. Murchie, *Rapuora Health and Māori Women*. Wellington: Māori Womens Welfare League, 1984.

9   Te Puni Kōkiri, *Progress Towards Closing Social and Economic Gaps Between Māori and Non-Māori.* Ministry of Māori Development, Wellington, 1998, pp. 14-6.

10   Ministry of Education, *Ngā Haeata Mātauranga Annual Report on Māori Education & Direction for 2002/2003.* Wellington: Ministry of Education, 2004, pp. 17-9.

11   Ministry of Education, *Ngā Haeata Mātauranga Annual Report on Māori Education 2005.* Wellington: Ministry of Education, 2006.

12   Ministry of Education, *Education Statistics of New Zealand for 2001.* Wellington: Ministry of Education, 2002.

13   Ministry of Education, 2004, pp. 6-7.

14   Health Workforce Advisory Committee, *Fit for Purpose and for Practice. A review of the Medical Workforce in New Zealand.* Wellington: Health Workforce Advisory Committee, 2005, pp. 127-31.

15   Ministry of Social Development, *The Social Report 2006 Te Pūrongo Oranga Tangata.* Wellington: Ministry of Social Development, 2006, pp 24-5.

16   T. Blakely, M. Tobias, J. Atkinson, L-C Yeh, K. Huang, *Tracking Disparity: Trends in ethnic and socio-economic inequalities in mortality, 1981-2004.* Wellington: Ministry of Health, 2007.

17   A. Hargreaves, D. Fink, 'The Seven Principles of Sustainable Leadership'. *Educational Leadership.* 2003, 61(7), 9-13.

Chapter 21 – Indigenous Responses to Health and Disease: Principles, Goals, and Pathways

1   A. Zumila, Z. Mullan, 'Turning the tide against tuberculosis', *Lancet,* 2006, 367: 9514; pp. 877-8.

2   P. Webster, *Rua and the Maori Millennium.* Wellington: Victoria University Press, 1979, pp. 221-4.

3   J. F. Cody, *Man of Two Worlds: A Biography of Sir Maui Pomare.* Wellington: AH & AW Reed, 1953.

4   J. M. Mason, *Report of Dr Mason.* Chief Medical Officer, Parliamentary Report, Wellington: Parliament, 1901.

5   M. Pomare, *Annual Report of Dr Pomare* Health Officer to the Maoris, Parliamentary Report. Wellington: Parliament, 1902.

6   M. Pomare, *Annual Report of Dr Pomare,* Health Officer to the Maoris, Parliamentary Report. Wellington: Parliament, 1903.

7   M. Durie, *Whaiora Māori Health Development* (2nd ed.). Auckland: Oxford University Press, 1998.

8   Statistics New Zealand, *Selected Summary Characteristics for the Māori Ethnic Group.* Wellington: Department of Statistics, 2007.

9   J. Cunningham, J. R. Condon, 'Premature mortality in aboriginal adults in the Northern Territory, 1979-1991'. *Medical Journal of Australia,* 1996; 165, 6: 309-12.

10   M. Oakley Browne, E. Wells, K. Scott (eds.), *Te Rau Hinengaro: The New Zealand Mental Health Survey.* Wellington: Ministry of Health, 2006.

11   S. Ajwani, T. Blakely, B. Robson, M. Tobias, M. Bonne, *Decades of Disparity: Ethnic mortality trends in New Zealand 1980-1999.* Wellington: Ministry of Health & University of Otago, 2003, pp. 21-6.

12   Ministry of Social Development, *The Social Report 2004 Te Pūrongo Oranga Tangata*. Wellington: Ministry of Social Development, 2004, pp. 26-7.

13   Ministry of Health, *Tatau Kahukura Māori Health Chart Book*. Wellington: Ministry of Health, 2006, p. 22.

14   I. Anderson, S. Crengle, M. L. Kamaka, T. Chen, N. Palafox, L. Jackson-Pulver, 'Indigenous Health in Australia, New Zealand and the Pacific'. *Lancet*, 2005, 367:9524, 1775-85.

15   Ajwani et. al. 2003, pp. 50-1.

16   A. Cohen, *The Mental Health of Indigenous Peoples: An International Overview*. Geneva: Nations for Mental Health, Department of Mental Health, World Health Organisation, 1999, pp. 7-10.

17   New Zealand was to sign the Declaration in 2010.

18   E. Murchie, *Rapuora Health and Māori Women*. Wellington: Māori Women's Welfare League, 1984.

19   P. Swan, B. Raphael, "*Ways forward*": *national consultancy report on Aboriginal and Torres Strait Islander mental health*. Canberra ACT: A.G.P.S., 1995, p. 2 v.

20   New Zealand Board of Health, *Annual Report of the New Zealand Board of Health 1986-87*. Wellington: New Zealand Board of Health, 1987.

21   Standing Committee on Māori Health, *Tribal Authorities as Advocates for Health*. Wellington: New Zealand Board of Health, 1987.

22   Health Workforce Advisory Committee, *The New Zealand Health Workforce A stocktake of issues and capacity*. Wellington: Health Workforce Advisory Committee, 2001, pp. 52-4.

23   Te K. Kingi, 'Hua Oranga A Māori Mental Health Outcome Measure', PhD Thesis, Palmerston North: Massey University, 2002.

24   Kōmiti Whakahaere, *Hui Whakaoranga Māori Health Planning Workshop*. Wellington: Department of Health, 1984.

25   C. Smith, H. Burke, G. Ward, 'Globalisation and Indigenous Peoples: Threat or Empowerment?', in Claire Smith, Graeme Ward (eds.), *Indigenous Cultures in an Interconnected World*,. Australia: Allen and Unwin, 2000, pp. 1-24.

Chapter 22 – Indigenous Participation in Mental Health: Māori Experience

1   M. Sheldon, (1997), 'Psychiatric Assessment in Remote Aboriginal Communities of Central Australia', Dissertation for Fellowship of the Royal Australian and New Zealand College of Psychiatrists. New South Wales: Child and Adolescent Mental Health State-wide Network, 1997.

2   Statistics New Zealand, *Quickstats about Māori: Census 2006*. Wellington: Department of Statistics, 2007.

3   S. Ajwani, T. Blakely, B. Robson, M. Tobias, M. Bonne, *Decades of Disparity: Ethnic mortality trends in New Zealand 1980-1999*. Wellington: Ministry of Health & University of Otago, 2003, pp. 50-1.

4   M. Durie, 'A Māori Perspective of Health', *Journal of Social Sciences and Medicine*. 1985, vol. 20, no. 5, pp. 483–6.

5   T. Trauer, K. Eagar, P. Gaines, A. Bower, *New Zealand Mental Health Consumers and their Outcomes*, Mental Health Research and Development Strategy. Auckland: Health Research Council, 2004.

6   J. Baxter, J Kokaua, E. Wells, J.E. McGee, M.A. Oakley Browne, 'Ethnic comparisons of the 12 month prevalence of mental disorders and treatment contact in Te Rau Hinengaro: The New Zealand Mental Health Survey'. *Australian and New Zealand Journal of Psychiatry*, 2006, 40:905-13.

7   P. Reid, B. Robson, C. Jones, 'Disparities in health: common myths and uncommon truths', *Pacific Health Dialogue*. 2000, 7: 38-48.

8   J. F. A. Rankin, 'Whaiora A Māori Cultural Therapy Unit', *Community Mental Health New Zealand*. 1986, vol. 3, no. 2, pp. 38-47.

9   T. Williams, 'Traditional Healers', in B. Ferguson, D. Barnes, D (eds.), *Perspectives on Transcultural Mental Health*. Parramatta: Transcultural Mental Health Centre, 1997.

10   Ministry of Health, *Te Tāhuhu – Improving Mental Health 2005-2015: The Second New Zealand Mental Health and Addiction Plan*. Wellington: Ministry of Health, 2005.

11   L. Pere, 'Oho Mauri,' PhD thesis. Palmerston North: Massey University, 2006.

12   Mental Health Commission, *Te Haerenga mō te Whakaoranga 1996-2006 The Journey of Recovery for the New Zealand Mental Health Sector*. Wellington: Mental Health Commission, 2007, pp. 108-9.

13   Te Rau Matatini, *Kia Puāwai Te Ararau National Māori Mental Health Workforce Development Strategic Plan 2006-2010*. Palmerston North: Te Rau Matatini, 2006, pp. 11-2.

14   S. Hatcher, S. Mouly, D. Rasquinha, W. Miles, J. Burdett, H. Hamer, G. Robinson, *Improving Recruitment to the Mental Health Workforce in New Zealand*. Auckland: Health Research Council of New Zealand, 2005, p. 60.

15   Te Rau Matatini, 2006, pp. 11-2.

16   A. Hargreaves, D. Fink, 'The Seven Principles of Sustainable Leadership'. *Educational Leadership*, 2003, 61(7), 9-13.

17   M. Durie, 'Māori Science and Māori Development', *People & Performance*, 1997, vol. 4, no. 3, 20-6.

18   Te Kani Kingi, 'Hua Oranga, Best Health Outcomes for Māori', PhD Thesis. Palmerston North: Massey University, 2002.

19   A. P. O'Brien, J. M. Boddy, D. J. Hardy, 'Culturally specific process measures to improve mental health clinical practice: indigenous focus', *Australian and New Zealand Journal of Psychiatry*, 2007, 41:667-74.

20   Te Puni Kōkiri, *Māori Potential Framework, a presentation*. Wellington: Ministry of Māori Development, 2005.

Chapter 24 – Pae Ora: Māori Health Horizons

1   M. Durie, 'Māori Attidudes to Sickness, Doctors and Hospitals', *New Zealand Medical Journal*, 1977, 86: 483-5.

2   Waitangi Tribunal, *Report Findings and Recommendations of the Waitangi Tribunal on an Application by Aila Taylor for and on Behalf of Te Atiawa Tribe in Relation to*

Fishing Grounds in the Waitara District (Wai 6). Wellington: Waitangi Tribunal, Department of Justice.

3   Standing Committee on Māori Health, *Tribal Authorities as Advocates for Māori Health.* Wellington: New Zealand Board of Health, 1987.

4   W. Winiata, 'The Raukawa Tribal Planning Experience and Health', in *Hui Whakaoranga: Māori Health Planning Workshop.* Wellington: Department of Health, 1984.

5   J. F. A. Rankin, 'Whaiora A Māori Health Cultural Therapy Unit', in *The Future of Mental Health Services in New Zealand – Proceedings of the Mental Health Foundation of New Zealand Conference.* Wellington: Mental Health Foundation, 1986.

6   Komiti Whakahaere (eds.), *Hui Whakaoranga: Māori Health Planning Workshop.* Wellington: Department of Health, 1984.

7   B. Robson, R. Harris (eds.) *Hauora Māori Standards of Health a study of the years 2000-2005.* Wellington: Te Rōpū Rangahau Hauora a Eru Pomare, University of Otago, 2007.

8   I. Pool, *Te Iwi Maori A New Zealand Population Past, Present and Projected.* Auckland: Auckland University Press, 1990, pp. 190-3.

9   Statistics New Zealand, *Births and Deaths: March 2009 Quarter.* Wellington: Department of Statistics, 2009.

10   S. Ajwani, T. Blakely, B. Robson, M. Tobias, M. Bonne, *Decades of Disparities: ethnic mortality trends in New Zealand 1980-1999.* Wellington: Ministry of Health & University of Otago, 2003.

11   Ministry of Social Development, *The Social Report 2006 Te Purongo Oranga Tangata.* Wellington: Ministry of Social Development, 2006, pp 24-5.

12   Te Whānau o Waipareira Trust, *Annual Report 2007/2008.* Auckland: Te Whānau o Waipareira Trust, 2008.

13   Future Makers, *Review of futures resources in the New Zealand Government sector.* Wellington: Institute of Policy Studies, Victoria University, 2005.

14   W. McGuinness, D. Henley, L. Foster, J. Perquin, *Four Possible Futures for New Zealand in 2058.* Wellington: Sustainable Futures Limited, 2008.

15   L. Garrett, *The Coming Plague: Newly Emerging Diseases in a World Out of Balance.* New York: Penguin Books, 1995.

16   B. Vale, R. Vale, 'Carbon Neutral Living in the Typical New Zealand House', in Harre N., Atkinson Q. D. (eds), *Carbon Neutral by 2020.* Nelson: Craig Potton Publishing, 2007, pp. 78-96.

17   Ministry of Science Research and Technology, 'Trend Summary – New Gene Sequencing Technologies', in *Future Watch.* Wellington, Ministry of Research Science and Technology, 2009.

18   J. Hutchings, 'A Transformative Māori Approach to Bioethics' in Te Mata o te Tau, *Matariki.* Wellington: Massey University, 2009, vol 1, no. 3, pp. 173-94.

Chapter 25 – Pae Mana: Waitangi and the Evolving State

1   Claudia Orange, *The Treaty of Waitangi.* Wellington: Bridget Williams Books, 1987, pp. 49-51.

2   Paul McHugh, *The Māori Magna Carta: New Zealand Law and the Treaty of Waitangi.* Oxford: Oxford University Press, 1991, pp. 113-7.

Selected Bibliography

Ajwani, S., Blakely, T., Robson, B., Tobias, M., Bonne, M. *Decades of Disparity: Ethnic mortality trends in New Zealand 1980-1999*. Wellington: Ministry of Health & University of Otago, 2003.

Alfred, T. 'Warrior Scholarship', in Mihesuah, A., Wilson A.C. (eds.), *Indigenizing the Academy Transforming Scholarship and Empowering Communities*. Lincoln: University of Nebraska Press, 2004.

Altman, J. 'The Establishment of a Corpus of Indigenous Economic Policy Research', in Otim, M., Anderson, I., Scott, I. (eds.) *Economics and Indigenous Australian Health Policy*. Melbourne: VicHealth Koori Health Research and Community Development Unit, 2004.

Anderson, I., et al. 'Indigenous Health in Australia, New Zealand and the Pacific', *Lancet*, 2005, 367:9524, 1775-1785.

Anderson, I. 'Towards a Koori Healing Practice', in McDonald, D. (ed.) *The Boyer Collection Highlights of the Boyer Lectures 1959-2000*. Sydney, ABC Books, 2001.

Auckland University of Technology, *University Investment Plan 2008-2010*, Auckland: Auckland University of Technology, 2007.

AUQA Good Practice Database, (2004), http://auqa.edu.au/gp/ (Key word: Māori).

Australian Government, *National Report to Parliament on Indigenous Education and Training*. Canberra: 2005.

Ban Ki-moon, *Protect, Promote Endangered Languages, Message for International Day of World's Indigenous People*. New York: United Nations, Department of Public Information, 2008.

Baxter, J., Kokaua, J., Wells, E., McGee, J. E., Oakley Browne, M. A. 'Ethnic comparisons of the 12 month prevalence of mental disorders and treatment contact in Te Rau Hinengaro: The New Zealand Mental Health Survey'. *Australian and New Zealand Journal of Psychiatry*, 2006, 40:905-913.

Biddullph, F., Biddulph, J., Biddulph, C. *Best Evidence Synthesis: The Complexity of Community and Family Influences on Children's Achievement in New Zealand, a report prepared for the Ministry of Education*. Wellington: Ministry of Education, 2003.

Bishop, R., Berryman, M. *The Experiences of Indigenous Māori Students in New Zealand Classrooms*. Hamilton: University of Waikato, 2002.

Bishop, R., Berryman, M., Richardson, C., Takiwa, S. *Te Kotahitanga: The Experiences of Year 9 and 10 Māori Students in Mainstream Classrooms*, Wellington: Ministry of Education, 2003.

Blair, V., et al. 'Hereditary diffuse gastric cancer: diagnosis and management', *Clin Gastroenterol Hepatol*, 2006, 4(3): pp. 262-75.

Blaisdell, K., Mokuau, N. 'Kānaka Maoli, Indigenous Hawaiians', in Hasager U., Friedman J. (eds.), *Hawai'i Return to Nationhood*. Copenhagen: IWGIA – Document 75, 1994.

Blakely, T., Tobias, M., Atkinson, J., Yeh, L. C., Huang, K. *Tracking Disparity: Trends in ethnic and socio-economic inequalities in mortality, 1981-2004*. Wellington: Ministry of Health, 2007.

Boulton, G. *GLOBAL: What are universities for?* University World News, http://www.universityworldnews.com/articlephp?story=20090326200944986, 2009, accessed 30 March 2009.

Bowen, W. G., Bok, D. *The Shape of the River: Long-Term Consequences of Considering Race in College and University Admissions*. New Jersey: Princeton University Press, 1988.

Browne, M. A., Wells, J. E., Scott, K. M., (eds.), *Te Rau Hinengaro: The New Zealand Mental Health Survey*. Wellington: Ministry of Health, 2006.

Caldwell, B. J. *A blueprint for leadership for the successful transformation of schools in the twenty-first century*. Nottingham: National College for School Leadership, 2003.

Canadian Institutes of Health Research–Institute of Aboriginal Peoples' Health, *Commemorative Report 2000 to 2008*, Ottawa: CIHR-IAPH, 2008.

Coates, K. S., McHugh, P. G. *Living Relationships Kōkiri Ngātahi The Treaty of Waitangi in the New Millennium*. Wellington: Victoria University Press, 1998.

Cody, J. 'Devolution, Disengagement and Control in the Statutory Social Services', in Peter McKinley (ed.), *Redistribution of Power? Devolution in New Zealand*. Wellington: Victoria University Press, 1990.

Cody, J. F. *Man of Two Worlds: a Biography of Sir Maui Pomare*. Wellington: A.H. & A.W. Reed, 1953.

Cohen, A. *The Mental Health of Indigenous Peoples: An International Overview*. Geneva: Nations for Mental Health, Department of Mental Health, World Health Organisation, 1999.

Commission on Social Determinants of Health. *Closing the gap in a generation: Health equity through action on the social determinants of health*. Geneva: World Health Organisation, 2008.

Committee on Indigenous Health. *The Geneva Declaration on the Health and Survival of Indigenous Peoples*. New York: United Nations Permanent Forum on Indigenous Issues, 2002.

Condliffe, J. B. *Te Rangi Hiroa The Life of Sir Peter Buck*. Christchurch: Whitcombe and Tombs, 1971.

Cummins, J. 'HER Classic – Empowering minority students: A Framework for Intervention'. *Harvard Educational Review*, 2001, 71(4) 649-675.

Cunningham, C. *He Taura Tieke: Measuring Effective Health Services for Māori* Wellington: Ministry of Health, 1996.

Cunningham, J., Condon, J. R. 'Premature mortality in aboriginal adults in the Northern Territory, 1979-19991'. *Medical Journal of Australia*, 1996, 165(6): 309-12.

Curson, R. *Māori in Industry Training Recent Trends.* Wellington: Industry Training Federation, 2005.

De Marco, R.R. 'The epidemiology of major depression: implications of occurrence, recurrence, and stress in a Canadian community sample.' *Canadian Journal of Psychiatry*, 2000, 45(1), 67-74.

Deloria, V. 'Marginal and Submarginal', in Mihesuah, D. A., & Wilson, A. C. (eds), *Indigenizing the Academy Transforming Scholarship and Empowering Communities.* Lincoln: University of Nebraska Press, 2004.

Deloria, V. *God is Red.* Colorado: Fulcrum Publishing, 1994.

Duran, E., Duran, B. *Native American Postcolonial Psychology.* Albany NY: State University of New York Press, 1995.

Durie, A. 'Me Tipu Ake te Pono: Māori Research, Ethicality and Development', in Te Pumanawa Hauora (ed.), *Proceedings of Te Oru Rangahau Māori Research and Development Conference.* Palmerston North: Massey University, School of Māori Studies, 1998.

Durie, A. 'Te Rerenga o te Rā Autonomy and Identity: Māori Educational Aspirations', PhD Thesis. Palmerston North: Massey University, 2002.

Durie, M. 'A Framework for Considering Māori Educational Advancement', *Ngā Kāhui Pou, Launching Māori Futures.* Wellington: Huia Publishers, 2003.

Durie, M. 'A Māori Perspective of Health', *Journal of Social Science and Medicine.* 1985, vol. 20, no. 5, pp. 483–486.

Durie, M. 'Indigeneity: Challenges for Indigenous Doctors', in Durie, M. *Ngā Kāhui Pou Launching Māori Futures.* Wellington: Huia Publishers, 2003.

Durie, M. 'Indigenous Knowledge within a Global Knowledge System', *Higher Education Policy*, 2005, 18, 301-12.

Durie, M. 'Kaumātuatanga reciprocity: Māori elderly and whānau', in Gee, S. (ed.), *Experience of a Lifetime: Older New Zealanders as Volunteers.* Wellington: Victoria University of Wellington, 2001.

Durie, M. 'Māori Attitudes to Sickness, Doctors and Hospitals', *New Zealand Medical Journal,* 1977, 86: 483-5.

Durie, M. 'Māori Science and Māori Development', *People & Performance*, 1997, vol. 4, no.3, 20-6.

Durie, M. 'Marae and implications for a Modern Māori Psychology, Elsdon Best Memorial Medal Address', *The Journal of the Polynesian Society*, 1999, 108, 4, 351-366.

Durie, M. 'Providing Health Services to Indigenous Peoples', Editorial, *British Medical Journal*, 2003, 7412, 23 August 2003, pp. 408-409.

Durie, M. 'Te Pae Māhutonga: a model for Māori health promotion.' *Health Promotion Forum of New Zealand Newsletter*, 1999, 49: pp. 2-5.

Durie, M. 'Te Pae Māhutonga: Mental Health Promotion for Young Māori', in Durie, M., *Ngā Kāhui Pou Launching Māori Futures*. Wellington: Huia Publishers, 2003.

Durie, M. *Ngā Kāhui Pou, Launching Māori Futures*. Wellington: Huia Publishers, 2003.

Durie, M. *Te Mana, Te Kāwanatanga The Politics of Māori Self Determination*. Auckland: Oxford University Press, 1998.

Durie, M. 'The Development of Māori Studies in New Zealand Universities', *He Pukenga Kōrero A Journal of Māori Studies*, 1996, Volume 1, no. 2, 21-32.

Durie, M. *Whaiora Māori Health Development*, second edition. Auckland: Oxford University Press, 1998.

Durie, M. et al. *Māori Specific Outcomes and Indicators, A Report Prepared for Te Puni Kōkiri the Ministry of Māori Development*. Palmerston North: Massey University, School of Māori Studies, 2002.

Durie, M. et al. *Oranga Kaumātua The Health and Wellbeing of Older Māori People*. Wellington: Ministry of Māori Development, 1997.

Durie, M. et al. *Whānau Ora: Report of the Taskforce on Whānau Centred Initiatives to Hon. Tariana Turia Minister for the Community and Voluntary Sector*. Wellington: Ministry of Social Development, 2010.

Durie, M., Milroy, H., Hunter, E. 'Mental Health and the Indigenous Peoples of Australia and New Zealand', in Kirmayer, LJ., Valaskakis GG. (eds.) *Healing Traditions The Mental Health of Aboriginal Peoples in Canada*. Vancouver: University of Vancouver Press, 2009.

Durie-Hall, D., Metge, J. 'Kua Tutū te Puehu Kia Mau, Māori Aspirations and Family Law', in Henaghan, M., Atkin B. (eds.), *Family Law Policy in New Zealand*. Auckland: Oxford University Press, 1992.

Duster, T. 'They're Taking Over! And other Myths About Race on Campus' in Berube, M., Nelson C. (eds.), *Higher Education Under Fire*. New York: Routledge, 1995.

Erikson, E. *Childhood and Society*, (2nd ed.). New York: Norton & Co., 1963.

Eruiti, A. 'The Recognition of Indigenous Peoples Rights to Traditional Lands: The Evaluation of States by International Treaty Bodies', in Charters C., Eruiti A. (eds.) *Māori Property Rights and the Foreshore and Seabed*. Wellington: Victoria University Press, 2007.

Fancourt, R. *Brainy Babies: Build and Develop Your Baby's Intelligence*. Auckland: Penguin Books, 2000.

Fifth World Conference on the Promotion of Mental Health and the Prevention of Mental and Behavioural Disorders, The Melbourne Declaration. Melbourne: World Federation for Mental Health, Clifford Beers Foundation, The Carter Centre, Victoria Health, 2008.

Finau, S. 'Traditional Medicine in Tonga: a preamble to a Pacific model', *Traditional Healing and Pacificans*, Tongan Health Society, 2004, Vol 1, pp. 27-36.

Fleras, A., Elliot, J. *The Nations Within: Aboriginal–State Relations in Canada, the United States, and New Zealand*. Toronto: Oxford University Press, 1992.

Foliaki, S., Pearce, N. 'Changing patterns of ill health for indigenous peoples', *British Medical Journal*. 2003, no. 7412; p. 406.

Frederick, A. H., Chittock, G. *Global entrepreneurship monitor Aotearoa New Zealand*, Auckland: Centre for Innovation & Entrepreneurship, Unitech, 2005.

Frederick, H., et al. 'Māori Entrepreneurs', in *Bartercard New Zealand Global Entrepreneurship Monitor 2002*. Auckland: UNITEC New Zealand Centre for Innovation and Entrepreneurship, 2002.

Fulbright New Century Scholars, 'Working Group Three: Higher Education and Social Cohesion – A Global Challenge', *Symposium on Higher Education, Statements and Recommendations,* Paris: UNESCO, 2006.

Future Makers, *Review of futures resources in the New Zealand Government sector.* Wellington: Institute of Policy Studies, Victoria University, 2008.

Gaines, P., et al. *Mental Health Classification Outcomes Study: Brief Report.* Auckland: Health Research Council, 2004.

Garrett, L. *The Coming Plague: Newly Emerging Diseases in a World Out of Balance.* New York: Penguin Books, 1995.

Gifford, H., Boulton, A. 'Conducting excellent research within indigenous communities', *Alternative An International Journal of Indigenous Scholarship.* Special Supplement, 2007, volume 3, No. 2, pp. 24-45.

Globalization Knowledge Network, *Towards Health-Equitable Globalisation: Rights, Regulation and Redistribution, Final Report to the Commission on Social Determinants of Health.* Ottawa: Institute of Population Health, University of Ottawa, 2007.

Glover, M., McCree, A., Dyall, L. *Māori attitudes to assisted human reproduction: an exploratory study, Summary report.* Auckland: University of Auckland, 2007.

Gone, J. P. 'Encountering Professional Psychology: Re-envisioning Mental Health Services for Native North America', in Kirmayer, L. J., Valaskakis G. G. (eds.) *Healing Traditions The Mental Health of Aboriginal Peoples in Canada.* Vancouver: University of Vancouver Press, 2009.

Gorst, J. *The Maori King.* Auckland: Pauls Book Arcade & Oxford University Press, (1959 Reprint), 1959.

Guardians Group, *Students First – Implications, Consequences and Outcomes*, paper presented at the 'Marking a Future Path' Symposium. Wellington: Secondary Futures, 2006.

Hall, G., Patrinos, H. A. *Indigenous Peoples, Poverty and Human Development in Latin America.* New York: Palgrave MacMillan, 2006.

Hargreaves, A., Fink, D. 'The Seven Principles of Sustainable Leadership'. *Educational Leadership*, 2003, 61(7), 9-13.

Harmsworth, G. 'The Role of Biodiversity in Māori Advancement: a Research Framework.' *He Pukenga Korero*, 2004, Volume 8, No. 1, 9-16.

Harrison, P. *Te Kete Uruuru Matua.* Auckland: Manukau Institute of Technology, 1999.

Hatcher, S., et al. *Improving Recruitment to the Mental Health Workforce in New Zealand.* Auckland: Health Research Council of New Zealand, 2005.

Hawkins, C., et al. *Te Hihiri Umanga Whānau Successful Whānau Participation in Small and Medium-sized Enterprises: a Report Prepared for Te Puni Kōkiri.* Palmerston North: Te Mata o te Tau, Massey University, 2006.

Health Research Council, *Guidelines for Researchers on Health Research Involving Māori.* Auckland: Health Research Council of New Zealand, 2008.

Health Workforce Advisory Committee, *Fit for Purpose and for Practice. A review of the Medical Workforce in New Zealand*. Health Workforce Advisory Committee, Wellington, 2005.

Health Workforce Advisory Committee, *The New Zealand Health Workforce A stocktake of issues and capacity*. Wellington: Health Workforce Advisory Committee, 2001.

Horton, R. 'Indigenous peoples: time to act now for equity and health', *The Lancet*, 2006, 367:9524: pp. 1705-1707.

Howitt, R., Connell, J., Hirsch P. (eds.), *Resources, Nations and Indigenous Peoples*. Melbourne: Oxford University Press, 1996.

Hudson, M. 'He Matatika Māori: Māori and ethical review in health research', Master of Health Science Thesis. Auckland: Auckland University of Technology, 2004.

Hui Taumata, *Hui Taumata 2005 Summary Report*. Wellington, 2005.

Hurunui, Te P. (1959*), King Potatau*. Auckland: Polynesian Society, 1959.

Hutchings, J. 'A Transformative Māori Approach to Bioethics' in Te Mata o te Tau, *Matariki*. Wellington: Massey University, 2009, Volume 1, No. 3, 173-194.

Hutchings, J. 'Claiming our space – Mana Wahine conceptual framework for discussing genetic modification.' *He Pukenga Kōrero*, 2004, Volume 8, No. 1, 17-25.

Hyde, V. *Night Skies Above New Zealand*. Auckland: New Holland Publishers, 2003.

International Food Policy Research Institute, Concern Worldwide and Welthungerhilfe, *2010 Global Hunger Index, The Challenge of Hunger: Focus on the Crisis of Child Undernutrition*. Bonn, Washington DC, Dublin: International Food Policy Research Institute, Concern Worldwide and Welthungerhilfe, 2010. http://bit. ly/9vdYv2, accessed 9 February 2011.

Isajiw, W. W. 'Ethnic-identity Retention', in Breton, R., Isajiw, W. W., Kalbach, W. E., Reitz J. G. (eds), *Ethnic Identity and Equality*. Toronto: University of Toronto Press, 1990.

Jacobsen, V., et al. *Investing in Well-being: an Analytical Framework*, Working paper 02/23. Wellington: The Treasury, 2002.

James, C. (ed.), *Building the Constitution*. Wellington: Institute of Policy Studies, Victoria University of Wellington, 2000.

James, K. 'Corrupt State University: The Organizational Psychology of Native Experience of Higher Education,' in Mihesuah, D. A., & Wilson, A. C. (eds), *Indigenizing the Academy Transforming Scholarship and Empowering Communities*. Lincoln: University of Nebraska Press, 2004.

Kame'eleihiwa, L. *Native Land and Foreign Desires Pehea Lā E Pono Ai?* Honolulu: Bishop Museum Press, 1992.

Kawharu, I. H. *Maori Land Tenure Studies of a changing institution*. Oxford: Oxford University Press, 1977.

Kawharu, I. H., 'Urban Immigrants and Tangata Whenua', in Schwimmer, E. (ed.), *The Maori People in the Nineteen-sixties*. Auckland: Blackwood and Janet Paul, 1968.

King, M. *Whina: a biography of Whina Cooper*. Auckland: Penguin Books, 1983.

Kingi, Te K. 'Hua Oranga Best Outcomes for Māori', PhD Thesis. Palmerston North: Massey University, 2002.

Kirikiri, R. 'Ngā Mahi Rangahau a Manāki Whenua', in Te Pumanawa Hauora (ed.), *Proceedings of Te Oru Rangahau Māori Research and Development Conference*. Palmerston North: Massey University, School of Māori Studies, 1998.

Komiti Whakahaere (eds.), *Hui Whakaoranga: Māori Health Planning Workshop*. Wellington: Department of Health, 1984.

Kuatei, S. 'Environmental Sacredness and Health in Palau'. *Pacific Health Dialogue*, 2005, 12:1:92-95.

Kunitz, S. J. (1994), *Disease and Social Diversity: The European Impact on the Health of Non-Europeans*. New York: Oxford University Press, 1994.

Lomawaima, K. T. 'Tribal Sovereigns: Reframing Research in American Indian Education, in Villegas', M., Neugebauer, SR., Venegas, KR. (eds.), *Indigenous Knowledge and Education*. Cambridge: Harvard Educational Review, 2008.

Māori Tertiary Reference Group, *Māori Tertiary Education Framework*. Wellington: Ministry of Education, 2003.

Mason, J. M. *Report of Dr Mason, Chief Medical Officer, Parliamentary Report*, Wellington: Parliament, 1901.

Massey University, *KIA MAIA Key Initiatives for a Māori Academic Investment Agenda*. Palmerston North: Massey University, 2007.

McDowell, M., Webb, W. *The New Zealand Legal System*, 2nd edition, Wellington: Butterworths, 1998.

McGuinness, W., Henley, D., Foster, L., Perquin, J. *Four Possible Futures for New Zealand in 2058*. Wellington: Sustainable Futures Limited, 2008.

McHugh, P. G. 'Aboriginal Identity and Relations in North America and Australasia', in Coates, KS, & McHugh, PG. (eds.), *Living Relationships The Treaty of Waitangi in the New Millennium*. Wellington: Victoria University Press, 1998.

McHugh, P. *The Māori Magna Carta: New Zealand Law and the Treaty of Waitangi*. Oxford: Oxford University Press, 1991.

McMichael, A., Woodruff, R., Hales, S. 'Climate change and human health: present and future risks', *Lancet*, 2006, 367: 9513, 859-869.

Mead, H. M., Grove, N. *Ngā Pēpeha a ngā Tīpuna, The Sayings of the Ancestors*. Wellington: Victoria University Press, 2001.

Mental Health Commission, *Te Haerenga mō te Whakaoranga 1996-2006 The Journey of Recovery for the New Zealand Mental Health Sector*. Wellington: Mental Health Commission, 2007.

Mihesuah, D. A. 'Academic Gatekeepers', in Mihesuah, D. A., & Wilson, A. C. (eds), *Indigenizing the Academy Transforming Scholarship and Empowering Communities*. Lincoln: University of Nebraska Press, 2004.

Mihesuah, J. K. 'Graduating Indigenous Students by Confronting the Academic Environment', in Mihesuah, A., Wilson AC. (eds.), *Indigenizing the Academy Transforming Scholarship and Empowering Communities*. Lincoln: University of Nebraska Press, 2004.

Miller, J. *Early Victorian New Zealand*. London: Oxford University Press, 1958.

Minister of Health, *Te Tāhuhu – Improving Mental Health 2005-2015: the second New Zealand Mental Health and Addiction Plan*. Wellington: Ministry of Health, 2005.

Minister of Tertiary Education, *Tertiary Education Strategy 2007-12*, Wellington: Parliament, 2006.

Ministry of Education, *Ka Hikitia - Managing for Success: The Māori Education Strategy 2008–2012*, Wellington: Ministry of Education, 2008.

Ministry of Education, *Education Statistics of New Zealand for 2001*. Wellington: Ministry of Education, 2002.

Ministry of Education, *Education Statistics of New Zealand for 2002*. Wellington: Ministry of Education, 2004.

Ministry of Education, *Individual Education Plan Guidelines*. Wellington: Ministry of Education, http://www.minedu.govt.nz/NZEducation/EducationPolicies/SpecialEducation/FormsAndGuidelines/IEPGuidelines.aspx, accessed 17 April 2011.

Ministry of Education, *Māori in Tertiary Education: a picture of the trends, a report prepared for the Hui Taumata 2005*. Wellington: Ministry of Education, 2005.

Ministry of Education, *Ngā Haeata Mātauranga Annual Report on Māori Education 2004*. Wellington: Ministry of Education, 2005.

Ministry of Education, *Ngā Haeata Mātauranga Annual Report on Māori Education 2005*. Wellington: Ministry of Education, 2006.

Ministry of Education, *Ngā Haeata Mātauranga Annual Report on Māori Education 2006*. Wellington: Ministry of Education, 2007.

Ministry of Education, *Ngā Haeata Mātauranga Annual Report on Māori Education & Direction for 2002/2003*. Wellington: Ministry of Education, 2004.

Ministry of Education, *Profiles and Trends 2007 New Zealand's Tertiary Education Sector*. Wellington: Ministry of Education, 2008.

Ministry of Education, *Review of the Implementation and Effectiveness of Special Supplementary Grants for Māori and Pasifika Students at Tertiary Education Institutions From 2001-2002: Māori Report*, Wellington: Ministry of Education, 2003.

Ministry of Education, *Tertiary Education Strategy 2002-2007 Baseline Monitoring Report*, Wellington, Ministry of Education, 2004.

Ministry of Education, *The System in Change: Tertiary Education Strategy 2002/07 Monitoring Report 2005*. Wellington: Ministry of Education, 2006.

Ministry of Health, *A Portrait of Health: Key results of the 2002/03 New Zealand Health Survey* Wellington: Ministry of Health, 2004.

Ministry of Health, *Building on Strengths A new approach to promoting mental health in New Zealand/Aotearoa*. Wellington: Ministry of Health, 2002.

Ministry of Health, *Reducing Inequalities in Health*. Wellington, Ministry of Health, 2002.

Ministry of Health, *Te Rau Hinengaro: The New Zealand Mental Health Survey*. Wellington: Ministry of Health, 2008.

Ministry of Health, *Te Tāhuhu – Improving Mental Health 2005–2015: The Second New Zealand Mental Health and Addiction Plan*. Wellington: Ministry of Health, 2005.

Ministry of Health, *Tobacco Trends 2006: Monitoring tobacco use in New Zealand*, Wellington: Ministry of Health, 2006.

Ministry of Science Research and Technology, 'Trend Summary – New Gene Sequencing Technologies', in *Future Watch*. Wellington: Ministry of Research Science and Technology, 2009.

Ministry of Social Development, *The Social Report 2004 Te Purongo Oranga Tangata 2004*. Wellington: Ministry of Social Development, 2004.

Ministry of Social Development, *The Social Report 2006 Te Purongo Oranga Tangata.* Wellington: Ministry of Social Development, 2006.

Ministry of Social Development, *The Social Report 2007 Te Purongo Oranga Tangata.* Wellington: Ministry of Social Development, 2007.

Minniecon, D., Kong, K. *Healthy Futures Defining best practice in the recruitment and retention of indigenous medical students.* Australian Indigenous Doctors Association, 2005.

Murchie, E. *Rapuora: Health and Māori Women.* Wellington: Māori Women's Welfare League, 1984.

National Health Committee, *The Social, Cultural and Economic Determinants of Health in New Zealand: Action to Improve Health.* Wellington: National Health Committee, 1998.

Neria, Y., Galea, S., Norris F. H. (eds.), *Mental Health and Disasters.* Cambridge: Cambridge University Press, 2009.

Nettleton, C., Napolitano, D., Stephens, C. *An Overview of Current Knowledge of the Social Determinants of Indigenous Health, a Working Paper.* Geneva: Commission on Social Determinants of Health, World Health Organisation, 2007.

New Zealand Board of Health, *Annual Report of the New Zealand Board of Health 1986-87,* Wellington: New Zealand Board of Health, 1987.

New Zealand Government, *Crown Proposals for the Settlement of Treaty of Waitangi Claims, Detailed Proposals.* Wellington: Office of Treaty Settlements, 1994.

New Zealand Institute of Economic Research, *Māori business and economic performance: A summary report.* Wellington: New Zealand Institute of Economic Research, 2005.

New Zealand Institute of Economic Research, *Māori Economic Development Te Ōhanga Whanaketanga Māori.* Wellington: NZIER, Te Puni Kōkiri, 2003.

New Zealand Qualifications Authority, *He Rautaki Māori me te Mahere Whakatinana The Māori Strategic and Implementation Plan for the New Zealand Qualifications Authority 2007-2012,* Wellington: New Zealand Qualifications Authority, 2007.

New Zealand Qualifications Authority, *National Certificates & Diplomas Te Waharoa & Te Ngutu Awa and other field Māori qualifications on the National Qualifications Framework.* Wellington: NZQA, 2003.

Ngā Kaihautū Tikanga Taiao, *Report to the Environmental Risk Management Authority (GMF98009),* Wellington: EMR, 1999.

Ngā Pae o te Māramatanga, *Annual Report 2008.* Auckland: Ngā Pae o te Māramatanga, 2009.

O'Brien, A. P., Boddy, J. M., Hardy, J. 'Culturally specific process measures to improve mental health clinical practice: indigenous focus'. *Australian and New Zealand Journal of Psychiatry,* 2007, 41:667-674.

Oakley Browne, M., Wells, E., Scott, K. (eds.), *Te Rau Hinengaro: The New Zealand Mental Health Survey.* Wellington: Ministry of Health, 2006.

Office of the Associate Minister of Education (Tertiary Education), *Tertiary Education Strategy 2002/07.* Wellington: Ministry of Education, 2002.

Office of the Minister for Social Development and Employment, *Opportunity for All New Zealanders.* Wellington: Parliament, 2004.

Okakok, L. 'Serving the Purpose of Education', in M. Villegas, S. R. Neugebauer, K. R. Venegas (eds.), *Indigenous Knowledge and Education Sites of Struggle, Strength, and Survivance*. Cambridge: Harvard Educational Review, 2008.

Oneha, M. F., Beckham, S. 'Re-examining Community Based Research Protocols', *Pacific Health Dialogue*. 2004, 11:1:102-106.

Palmer, G. *New Zealand's Constitution in Crisis Reforming our Political System*. Dunedin: John McIndoe, 1992.

Parnell, W., Scragg, R., Wilson, N., Schaaf, D., Fitzgerald, E. *NZ Food NZ Children Key results of the 2002 National Children's Nutrition Survey*. Wellington: Ministry of Health, 2003.

Parodi, C. T. *Working to Achieve Health Equity with an Ethnic Perspective: What has been Done and Best Practices*, paper presented at the Intergovernmental Working Group on the Implementation of the Declaration and Program of Action of Durban, Third Session. Geneva: 2004, 11-12 October.

Pere, L. 'Oho Mauri', PhD thesis. Palmerston North: Massey University, 2006.

Permanent Forum on Indigenous Issues, *Territories, Land, and Natural Resources Forum*, New York: United Nations Economic and Social Council HR/4918, 2007. Information on meeting on www.un.org/News/Press/docs/2007/hr4918.doc.htm, accessed 9 February 2011

Pomare, M. *Annual Report of Dr. Pomare, Health Officer to the Maoris, Parliamentary Report*. Wellington: Parliament, 1902.

Pomare, M. *Annual Report of Dr. Pomare, Health Officer to the Maoris, Parliamentary Report*. Wellington: Parliament, 1903.

Pool, I. *Te Iwi Maori: A New Zealand Population Past, Present and Projected*. Auckland: Auckland University Press, 1991.

Pool, I. *The Maori Population of New Zealand 1769-1971*. Auckland: Auckland University Press and Oxford University 1977.

Prakash, S. 'Nurturing traditional knowledge systems for development', *IK Notes No. 61. Washington DC:* The World Bank, 2003.

Pro Vice-Chancellor (Māori), *Te Amorangi National Māori Academic Excellence Awards 2008*. Hamilton: University of Waikato, 2009.

Rankin, J. F. A. 'Whaiora A Māori Cultural Therapy Unit', *Community Mental Health New Zealand*. 1986, vol. 3, no. 2.

Rankin, J. F. A. 'Whaiora A Māori Health Cultural Therapy Unit', in *The Future of Mental Health Services in New Zealand – Proceedings of the Mental Health Foundation of New Zealand Conference*. Wellington: Mental Health Foundation, 1986.

Reading, J. *The Crisis of Chronic Disease among Aboriginal Peoples: A Challenge for Public Health, Population Health and Social Policy*. British Columbia: Centre for Aboriginal Health Research, University of Victoria, 2009.

Reid, P., Robson, B., Jones, C. 'Disparities in health: common myths and uncommon truths', *Pacific Health Dialogue*, 2000, 7: 38-48.

Ring, I., Brown, N. 'The health status of indigenous peoples and others', *British Medical Journal*. 2003, no. 7412: pp. 404-405.

Robson, B., Harris, R. (eds.) *Hauora Māori Standards of Health a study of the years 2000-2005*. Wellington: Te Rōpū Rangahau Hauora a Eru Pomare, University of Otago, 2007.

Royal Commission on Social Policy, *The April Report: Future Directions*, Wellington: Royal Commission on Social Policy, 1988.

Royal, Te A, C. *Indigenous Worldviews A Comparative Study*, A report of research in progress. Ōtaki: Te Wānanga o Raukawa, 2002.

Royal, Te A. C. 'Te Ao Mārama – A Research Paradigm', in Te Pūmanawa Hauora (ed.), *Proceedings of Te Oru Rangahau Māori Research and Development Conference*. Palmerston North: Massey University, School of Māori Studies, 1998.

Sachs, J. *Common Wealth: Economics for a Crowded Planet*. Australia: Penguin Group, 2008.

Salmond, A. 'Te Ao Tawhito: A Semantic Approach to the Traditional Māori Cosmos'. *Journal of the Polynesian Society*, 1978, 87, 1, 166-167.

Secondary Futures. *The Conversation has Begun, Report 2004*, Wellington: Secondary Futures, 2004.

Secondary Futures. *The Place of Technology*. Wellington: Secondary Futures, 2008.

Selby, R., Moore, P. 'Māori research in Māori communities: No longer a new phenomenon.' *Alternative An International Journal of Indigenous Scholarship*, Special Supplement, 2007, volume 3, No. 2, pp. 96-107.

Seth-Purdie, R., Cameron, A., Luketina F. *What makes your family tick?* Research Report 1/06, Wellington: Families Commission, 2006.

Sheldon, M. (1997), 'Psychiatric Assessment in Remote Aboriginal Communities of Central Australia', Dissertation for Fellowship of the Royal Australian and New Zealand College of Psychiatrists. New South Wales: Child and Adolescent Mental Health State-wide Network, 1997.

Skolnik, R. *Essentials of Global Health*. Washington DC: The George Washington University, 2008.

Smith, C., Burke, H., Ward, G. 'Globalisation and Indigenous Peoples: Threat or Empowerment?' in Smith, C., Ward G. (eds.), *Indigenous Cultures in an Interconnected World*. Australia: Allen and Unwin, 2000.

Smith, L. 'Towards the New Millennium: International Issues and Projects in Indigenous Research'. *He Pukenga Kōrero*, 1998, volume 4, No. 1, pp. 43-61.

Solomon, M. 'The Wai 262 Claim: A Claim by Māori to Indigenous Flora and Fauna: Me ō rātou taonga katoa', in Belgrave, M., Kawharu, M., Williams, D. (eds.), *Waitangi Revisited Perspectives on the Treaty of Waitangi*. Melbourne: Oxford University Press, 2005.

Soutar, M., Ashton, L. 'Was the cost too high?', *Mana*, 1998, 27: 22-27.

Sparrow, K., Sparrow, H. & Swan, P. 'Student Centred Learning: Is it Possible?' In Herman A., Kulski, M. M. (Eds), *Flexible Futures in Tertiary Teaching*. Proceedings of the 9th Annual Teaching Learning Forum, 2-4 February 2000. Perth: Curtain University of Technology, 2000.

Sporle, A., Koia, J. 'Māori responsiveness in health and medical research: clarifying the roles of the researcher and the institution'. *New Zealand Medical Journal*, 2004, vol. 117, no. 1190, 998-1000.

Standing Committee on Māori Health, *Tribal Authorities as Advocates for Health*. Wellington: New Zealand Board of Health, 1987.

Statistics New Zealand, *Births and Deaths: March 2009 Quarter*. Wellington: Department of Statistics, 2009.

Statistics New Zealand, *National Population Projections: 2006 (base) – 2061*. Wellington: Department of Statistics, 2007.

Statistics New Zealand, *New Zealand Census of Population and Dwellings 2001: Māori*. Wellington: Department of Statistics, 2002.

Statistics New Zealand, *New Zealand Now Māori*. Wellington: Department of Statistics, 1998.

Statistics New Zealand, *New Zealand Now Māori*, Wellington: Department of Statistics, 2002.

Statistics New Zealand, *Quickstats about Māori: Census 2006*. Wellington: Department of Statistics, 2007.

Statistics New Zealand, *Selected Summary Characteristics for the Māori Ethnic Group*. Wellington: Department of Statistics, 2007.

Statistics New Zealand, *Subnational Population Projections: 2006 (base) – 2031*. Wellington: Department of Statistics, 2007.

Stewart-Harawira, M., *The New Imperial Order Indigenous Responses to Globalisation*. Wellington: Huia Publishers, 2005.

Stokes, E. *Wiremu Tamihana: Rangatira*. Wellington: Huia Publishers, 2002.

Sutherland, I. L. G. 'Leader of Genius', *The Journal of the Polynesian Society,* Memorial Number to Sir Apirana Nohopari Turupa Ngata. 1950, Volume 59, Number 4, pp. 293-4.

Swan, P., Raphael, B. *'Ways forward': national consultancy report on Aboriginal and Torres Strait Islander mental health*. Canberra ACT: A.G.P.S., 1995.

Syme, S. L. 'Social Determinants of Health: the Community as an Empowered Partner. In *Preventing Chronic Disease – Public Health Research, Practice, and Policy*, 2004, 1(1), 1-5.

Te Puni Kōkiri, *Māori economic development Te Ōhanga Whanaketanga Māori (Summary)*. Wellington: Ministry of Māori Development, 2003.

Te Puni Kōkiri, *Māori Potential Framework a presentation*. Wellington: Ministry of Māori Development, 2005.

Te Puni Kōkiri, *Progress Towards Closing Social and Economic Gaps Between Māori and Non-Māori*. Wellington: Ministry of Māori Development, 1998.

Te Puni Kōkiri, *Progress Towards Closing Social and Economic Gaps Between Māori and Non-Māori*. Wellington: Ministry of Māori Development, 2000.

Te Rangi Hiroa, Te R. (Peter Buck), *The Coming of the Maori. Wellington:* Maori Purposes Fund Board and Whitcombe and Tombs, 1949.

Te Rau Matatini, *Kia Puāwai Te Ararau National Māori Mental Health Workforce Development Strategic Plan 2006-2010*. Palmerston North: Te Rau Matatini, 2006.

Te Rūnanga o Ngāi Tahu, *Ngāi Tahu 2025*, Christchurch, 2003.

Te Wānanga o Raukawa, *Profile 2008-2010 (Investment Plan)*. Ōtaki: Te Wānanga o Raukawa, 2008.

Te Whānau o Waipareira Trust, *Annual Report 2007/2008*. Auckland: Te Whānau o Waipareira Trust, 2008.

Tertiary Education Commission, *Baseline Monitoring Report: Massey University*, Wellington: Tertiary Education Commission, 2007.

Tertiary Education Commission, *Priorities Statement of Tertiary Education Priorities 2005/07 Discussion Document*. Wellington: Tertiary Education Commission, 2004.

Tertiary Education Commission, *Review of the Implementation and Effectiveness of Special Supplementary Grants for Māori and Pasifika Students at Tertiary Education Institutions From 2001-2002: Māori Report*. Wellington: Tertiary Education Commission, 2003.

Tertiary Education Commission, *Tertiary Education Strategy*. Wellington: 2003.

The Bioethics Council, *The Cultural, Ethical and Spiritual Aspects of Animal-to Human Transplantation, a report on xenotransplantation*. Wellington: Toi te Taiao: the Bioethics Council, 2005.

Trauer, T., Eagar, K., Gaines, P., Bower, A. *New Zealand Mental Health Consumers and their Outcomes*, Mental Health Research & Development Strategy. Auckland: Health Research Council, 2004.

True J. *Methodologies for analysing the impact of public policy on families*. Wellington: Families Commission, 2005.

Tuhiwai Smith, L. 'Towards the New Millennium: International Issues and Projects in Indigenous Research', in Te Pūmanawa Hauora (ed.), *Proceedings of Te Oru Rangahau Māori Research and Development Conference*. Palmerston North: Massey University, School of Māori Studies, 1998.

United Nations, *Draft Declaration of the Rights of Indigenous Peoples as Agreed upon by the Members of the Working Group at its Eleventh Session*, New York: 1993, UN Doc. E/CN.4/Sub.2/1994/2/Add. 1.

United Nations, *Human Development Report 2007/2008 Fighting climate change: Human solidarity in a divided world*. New York: United Nations Development Programme, UNDP, 2007. http://hdr.undp.org/en/media/HDR_20072008_EN_Complete.pdf, accessed 9 February 2011.

United Nations, 'Implementing Declaration on Indigenous Rights Will Bring "Historical Justice" ', *General Assembly, GA/SHC/3954*, New York: Department of Public Information, News and Media Division, 2009.

University of Otago, *Charter*, Dunedin: University of Otago, 2003.

University of Otago, *Strategic Direction to 2012*. Dunedin: University of Otago, 2007.

University of Waikato, *Calendar*. Hamilton: University of Waikato. 2009.

Ussher, S. *Participation in Tertiary Education A birth cohort approach*. Wellington: Ministry of Education, 2007.

Vaithianathan, R. 'Is Economics Always Good for Your Health', in Otim, M., Anderson, I., Scott, I. (eds.) *Economics and Indigenous Australian Health Policy*. Melbourne: VicHealth Koori Health Research and Community Development Unit, 2004.

Vale, B., Vale, R. 'Carbon Neutral Living in the Typical New Zealand House', in Harre N., Atkinson Q. D. (eds), *Carbon Neutral by 2020*. Nelson: Craig Potton Publishing, 2007.

Waitangi Tribunal, *Ōrākei Report (Wai 9)*. Wellington: Department of Justice, 1987.

Waitangi Tribunal, *Report of the Waitangi Tribunal on te Reo Māori Claim (Wai 11)*, Wellington: Department of Justice, 1986.

Waitangi Tribunal, *Report on the Findings and Recommendations of the Waitangi Tribunal on an application by Aila Taylor for and on behalf of Te Atiawa Tribe in relation to fishing grounds in the Waitara District*. Wellington: Department of Justice, 1983.

Waiti, D. *Hei Tautoko i ngā Wawata Māori: ētahi tauira nā ngā Kura Wānanga. Supporting Māori Achievement: a collection of tertiary provider initiatives.* Wellington: Ministry of Education, 2001.

Waldram, J. D., Herring, A., Young, T. K. *Aboriginal Health in Canada Historical, Cultural, and Epidemiological Perspectives.* Toronto: University of Toronto Press, 1995.

Walker, R. *He Tipua The Life and Times of Sir Apirana Ngata.* Auckland: Viking, 2001.

Walker, R. *Ka Whawhai Tonu Mātou Struggle Without End*, Auckland: Penguin Books, 1990.

Walker, R. 'Māori Sovereignty, Colonial and Post-colonial Discourses', in Havemann, P. (ed.) *Indigenous Peoples Rights in Australia, Canada and New Zealand.* Auckland: Oxford University Press, 1999.

Walsh, P. 'The passing of the Maori: an inquiry into the principal causes of the decay of the race', *Transactions and Proceedings of the Royal Society of New Zealand.* 1907, 40, 154-75.

Walsh-Tapiata, W. 'Research within Your Own Iwi: What are some of the issues?' in Te Pūmanawa Hauora (ed.), *Proceedings of Te Oru Rangahau Māori Research and Development Conference.* Palmerston North: School of Māori Studies, Massey University, 1998.

Weatherall, A., Ramsay, A. *New Communication Technologies and Family Life*, Blue Skies Report 5/06. Wellington: Families Commission, 2006.

Webster, P. *Rua and the Maori Millennium.* Wellington: Victoria University Press, 1979.

Wetere, Hon. K. T. *Te Urupare Rangapū: Partnership Response*, Wellington: Office of the Minister of Māori Affairs, Parliament, 1988.

Whanganui River Māori Trust Board, *Whanganui River Charter*, Whanganui: Whanganui River Māori Trust Board, 1993.

Williams, J. A. (1965), 'The Foundations of Apirana Ngata's Career 1891-1909', in Pocock J. G. A. (ed.), *The Maori and New Zealand Politics.* Auckland: Blackwood and Janet Paul, 1965.

Williams, T. 'Traditional Healers,' in Ferguson, B., Barnes, D. (eds.), *Perspectives on Transcultural Mental Health.* Parramatta: Transcultural Mental Health Centre, 1997.

Wilton, V., Davey, J. A. *Grandfathers – Their Changing Family Roles and Contributions.* Wellington: Families Commission, 2006.

Winiata, W. 'The Raukawa Tribal Planning Experience and Health', in *Hui Whakaoranga: Māori Health Planning Workshop.* Wellington: Department of Health, 1984.

Working Group on Indigenous Populations, *Draft Declaration on the Rights of Indigenous Peoples: Report of the Eleventh Session of the United Nations Working Group on Indigenous Populations*, Geneva: United Nations, 1993.

World Bank, *Expanding Opportunities and Building Competencies for Young People A New Agenda for Secondary Education*. Washington DC: The World Bank, 2005.

World Health Organisation, *Protecting Health from Climate Change. World Health Day 2008*. Geneva: World Health Organisation, 2008. http://www.who.int/world-health-day/toolkit/report_web.pdf, accessed 9 February 2011.

Zumila., A., Mullan, Z. 'Turning the tide against tuberculosis'. *Lancet,* 2006, 367: 9514; pp. 877-8.

Index